ART & LOVE

My Life Illuminated in Egg Tempera

LORA ARBRADOR

with poetry by Ilse Lehnert

SYCAMORE PRESS
SAN FRANCISCO, CALIFORNIA

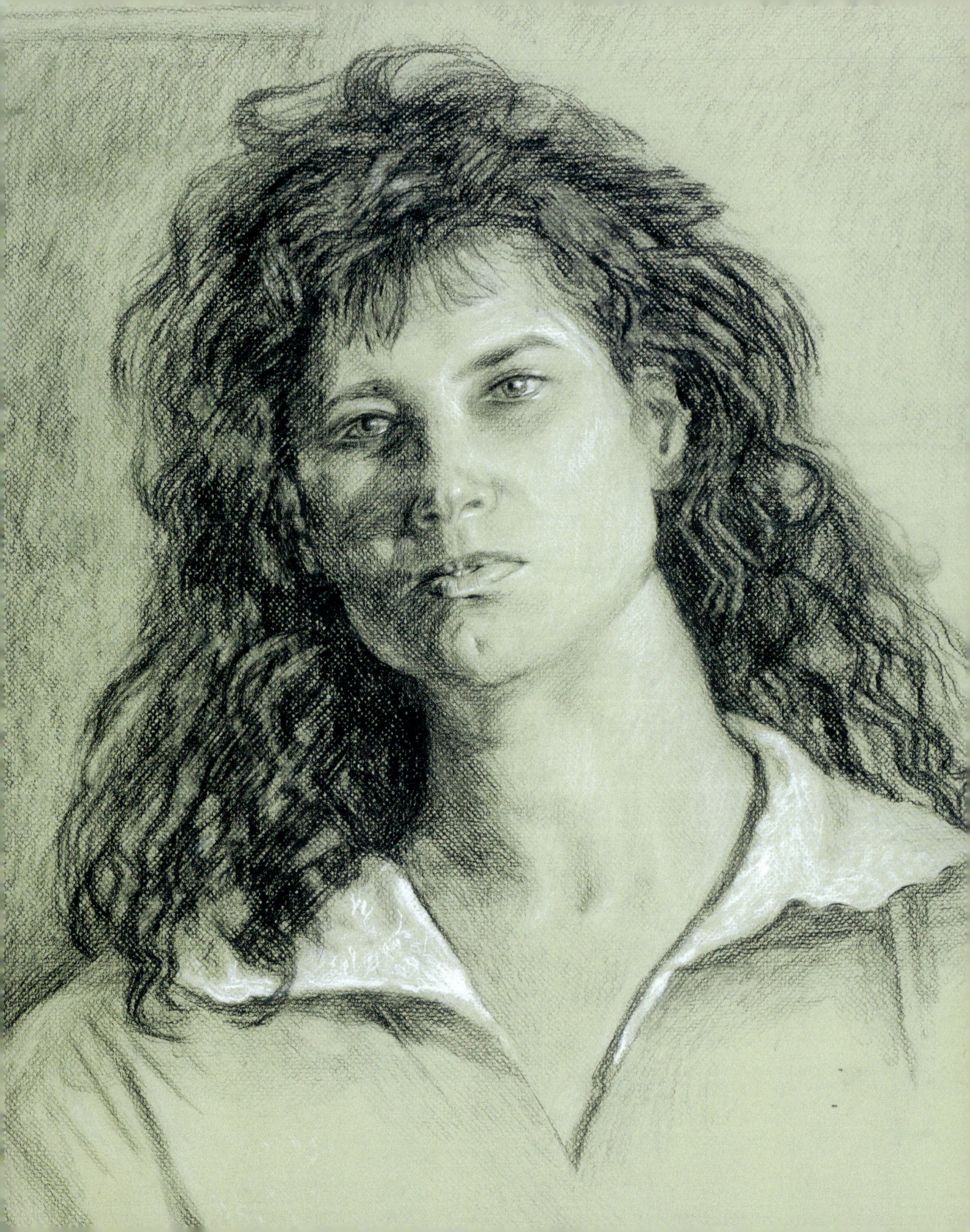

FOR MY ART MENTORS

Ruth Brody

David Hardy

Dianne Mitchell

Koo Schadler

Thank you for sharing your
deep knowledge, skill,
and love of painting.

You fortify the desire in me
to ascend to the lofty
places you inhabit.

First Edition
Sycamore Press
San Francisco, California, US
www.arbrador.com

Cover: Detail: *The Blossoming of Love,* c. 1995. Egg tempera on gesso panel, 12 × 19 in. (30.4 × 48.2 cm)
Frontispiece: *Self-Portrait,* 1989. Charcoal pencil on green-toned paper, 25 × 19½ in. (63.5 × 49.5 cm)
Back cover: author photo by The Artist Hines.

Book design and production by Domini Dragoone, Sage Folio Creative
Edited by Anne Rainbow

Paperback ISBN: 979-8-9909469-1-0
Library of Congress Control Number: 2025917183

Publisher's Cataloging-in-Publication data
Names: Arbrador, Lora, author. | Lehnert, Ilse, contributor.
Title: Art & love : my life illuminated in egg tempera / by Lora Arbrador; with poetry by Ilse Lehnert.
Description: Includes bibliographical references and index. | San Francisco, CA: Sycamore Press, 2025.
Identifiers: LCCN: 2025917183 | ISBN: 979-8-9909469-1-0
Subjects: LCSH Arbrador, Lora. | Artists—United States—Biography. | Nurses—United States—Biography. | United States—History—20th century—Biography. | BISAC BIOGRAPHY & AUTOBIOGRAPHY / Memoirs | BIOGRAPHY & AUTOBIOGRAPHY / Artists, Architects, Photographers | ART / Individual Artists / Monographs
Classification: LCC N6537.A73 2025 | DDC 759.13092—dc23

Hardcover ISBN: 979-8-9909469-0-3
Ebook ISBN: 979-8-9909469-2-7
Audiobook: ISBN: 979-8-9909469-3-4

Printed in the USA

AUTHOR'S NOTES

CONTENT WARNING

This memoir contains tasteful, but explicit text and images describing menstruation, lactation, and defecation, as well as aspects of sexuality (including concensual BDSM). No slang or curse words are included.

NOTE ON NAMES

This is a work of nonfiction based on the author's memories and experiences. Some names have been changed to protect the privacy of individuals. Pseudonyms are generally presented as first names only.

CONTENTS

Introduction 1

PART I

CHAPTER ONE
Not a Prodigy: My Early Years 5

CHAPTER TWO
Flower Child of the Sixties 11

CHAPTER THREE
The Ethereal Egg Tempera 21

CHAPTER FOUR
Adventures in Nursing School 35

CHAPTER FIVE
Tipi Time: Life in Rural Maine 43

CHAPTER SIX
The Blood Mysteries 53

CHAPTER SEVEN
Communes & California 59

CHAPTER EIGHT
Ways of Dying: A Chronicle of the AIDS Epidemic 65

CHAPTER NINE
Art & Love Come Together 87

CHAPTER TEN
Travels in Europe & Beyond 93

CHAPTER ELEVEN
Life in the Kaliflower Compound 107

CHAPTER TWELVE
The Concept of Free 121

CHAPTER THIRTEEN
Motherhood Calling . . . 129

CHAPTER FOURTEEN
Refuge for a Single Mother . . . 141

CHAPTER FIFTEEN
Classical Realism: More Real than Reality . . . 151

CHAPTER SIXTEEN
Five Thousand Years of Egg Tempera History . . . 157

CHAPTER SEVENTEEN
At Last! Three Egg Tempera Teachers . . . 161

CHAPTER EIGHTEEN
On the Edge: Finding My Sensual Self . . . 175

CHAPTER NINETEEN
Retreat to Celibacy & Meeting My Mate . . . 185

CHAPTER TWENTY
Surrender to Slow . . . 193

CHAPTER TWENTY-ONE
Art Paradise . . . 201

PART II

Which Came First? A Taste of Egg Tempera History . . . 208

Obituaries from the *Ways of Dying* series . . . 235

Endnotes . . . 236

Selected Bibliography . . . 246

Permissions & Credits . . . 249

Index . . . 256

Acknowledgments . . . 266

About the Author . . . 270

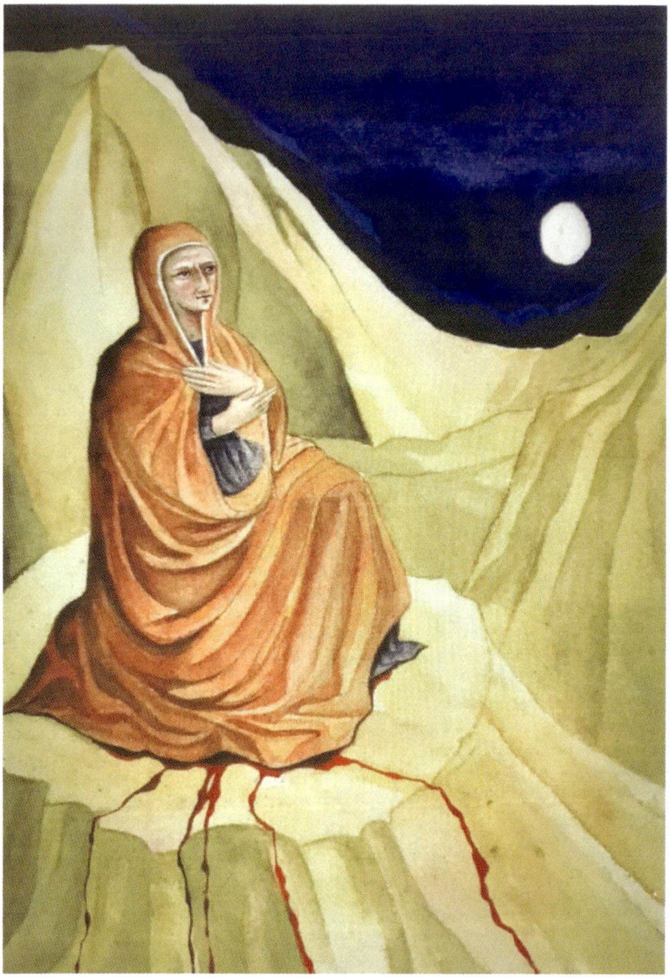
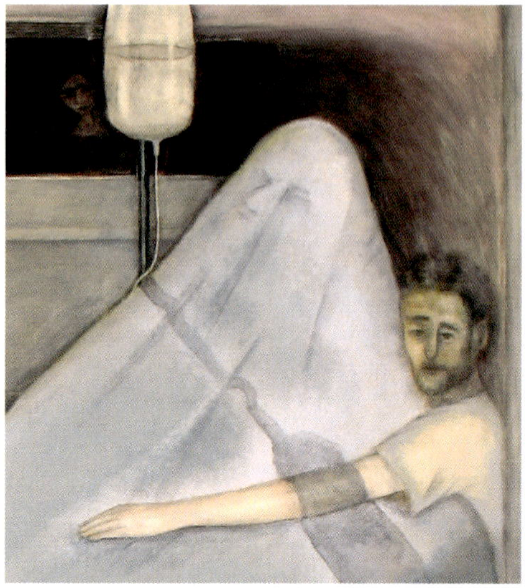
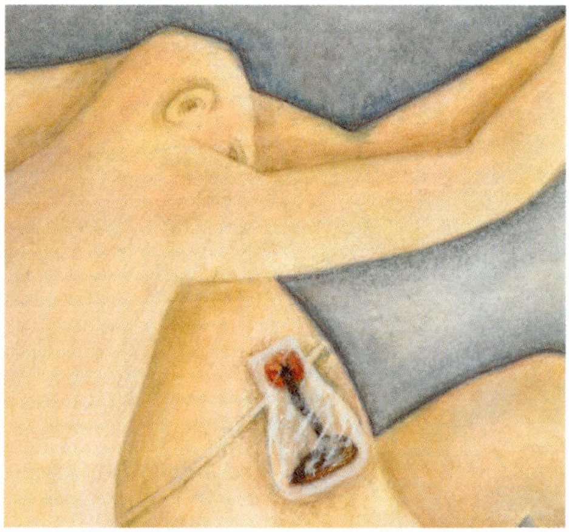
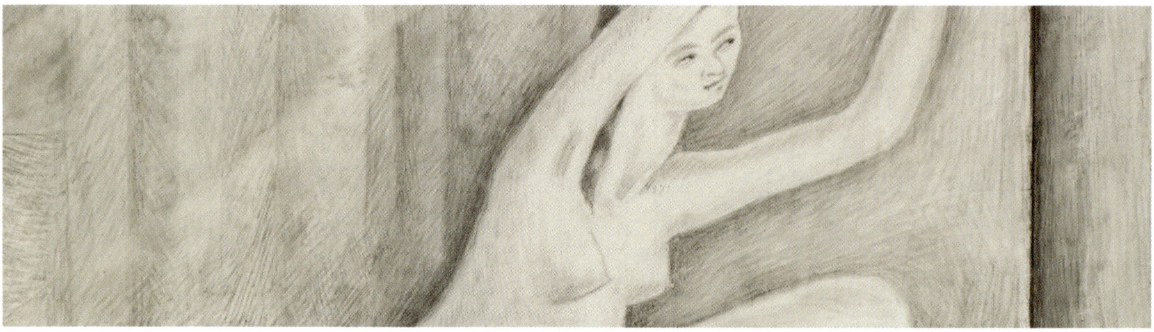

INTRODUCTION

Painting is just another way of keeping a diary.
—Pablo Picasso

"I like your pornography," my mother once said. However, an erotic art dealer deemed my art non-pornographic on the grounds that it wasn't arousing. My art has been called "challenging," but I don't seek out taboo subject matter. Rather, images visit my imagination and ask to become paintings: the mysteries of lactation and menstruation, surgery and death, love and sex—many inspired by my work as a registered nurse.

There is pain but there is hope.
—A viewer at an exhibition of my paintings

I fell in love with egg tempera when I was introduced to the medium in a college class. The professor handed out a one-page recipe, saying he had no knowledge of the technique but that everyone had to try it.

Combining colorful pigments with egg yolk and applying this homemade paint onto an ivory-like gesso ground set me off on a lifetime of fascination—along with frustration—in my attempts to learn this difficult technique without a mentor or teacher.

In addition, I was held back by a belief that I had no talent in art. The challenge of mastering egg tempera while confronting demons of self-doubt spilled over into my love life, where inhibition and love addiction put romantic stability out of reach.

This book was originally conceived as a showcase for my art, but as I wrote descriptions for each painting, the images seemed to tell my life story. My editor, Anne Rainbow, urged me to write more, and I unearthed long-buried stories revealing myself more than I had intended.

The themes of the art mirror periods in my life, traversing the suppressive McCarthy years of the 1950s, the Berkeley counterculture of the 1960s, the back-to-the-land and feminist health movements of the 1970s, and the AIDS epidemic and San Francisco sex underground of the 1980s.

I feel shy and a bit apprehensive about sharing this intimate self-portrait with you. Gathering my art and words in these pages has given me the opportunity to savor decades of image-making and living. Thank you for joining me on this path.

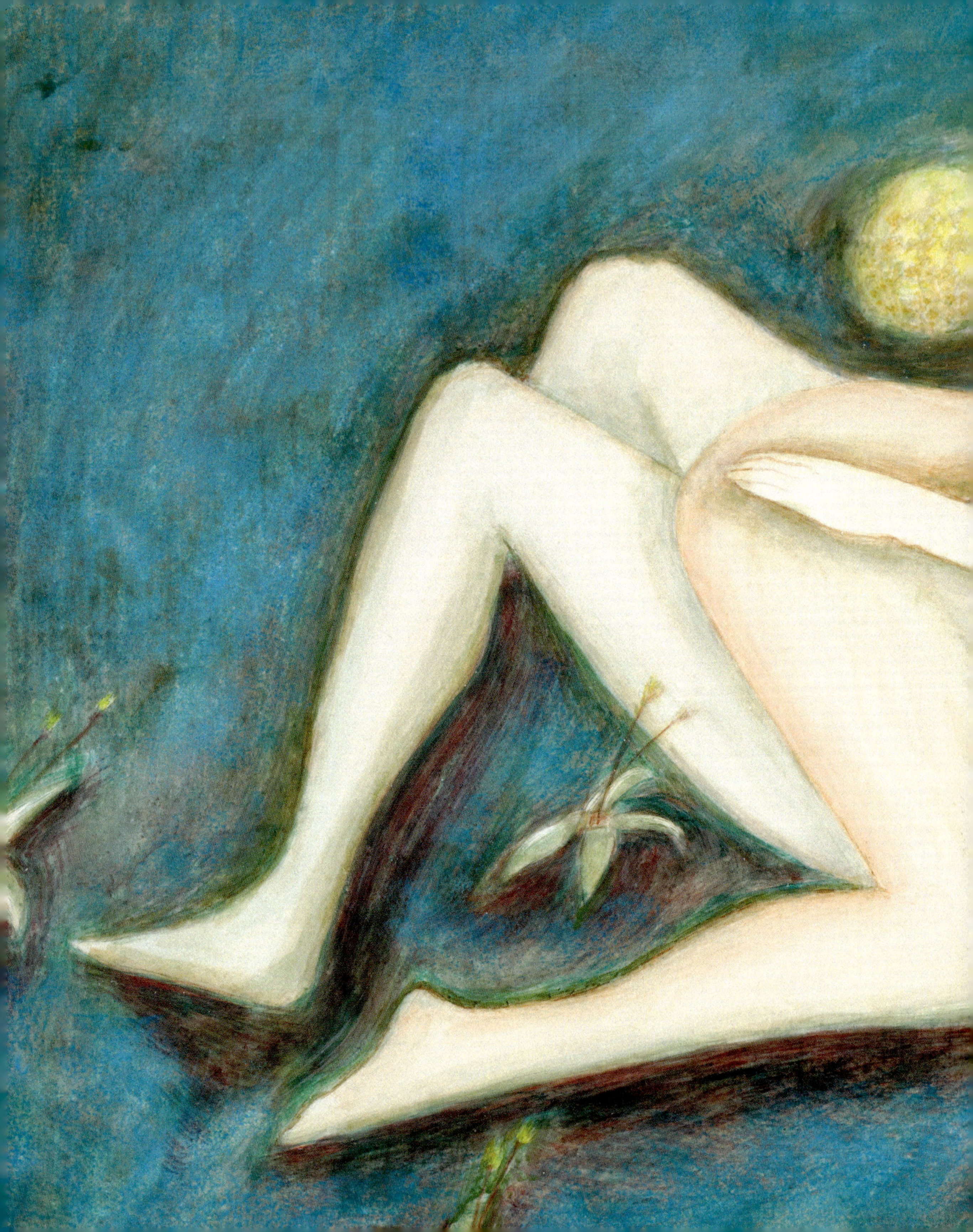

PART I

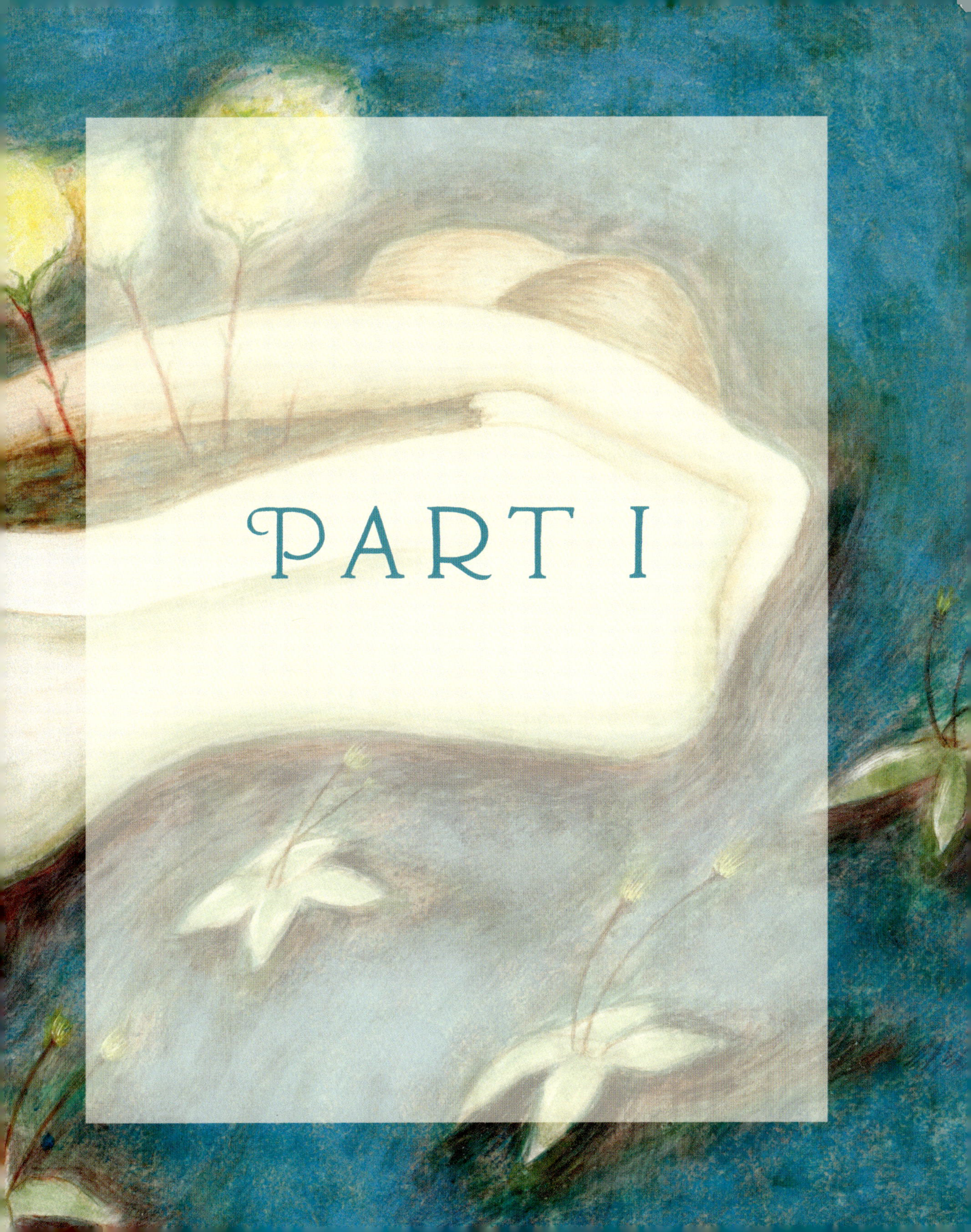

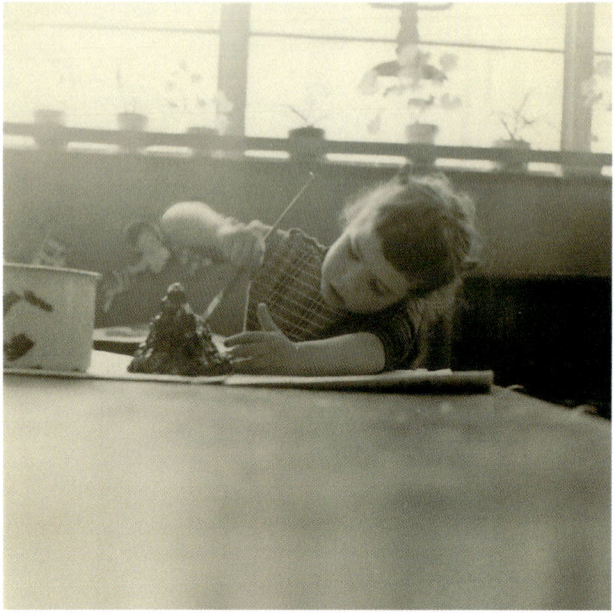

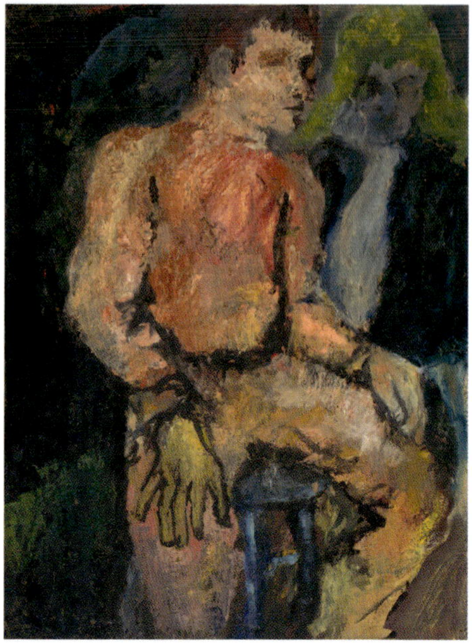

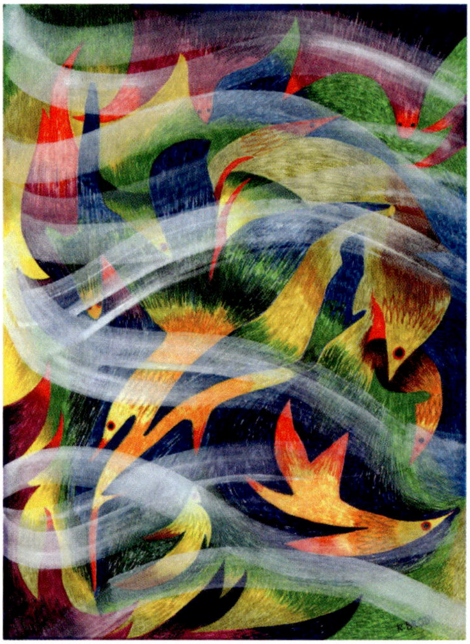

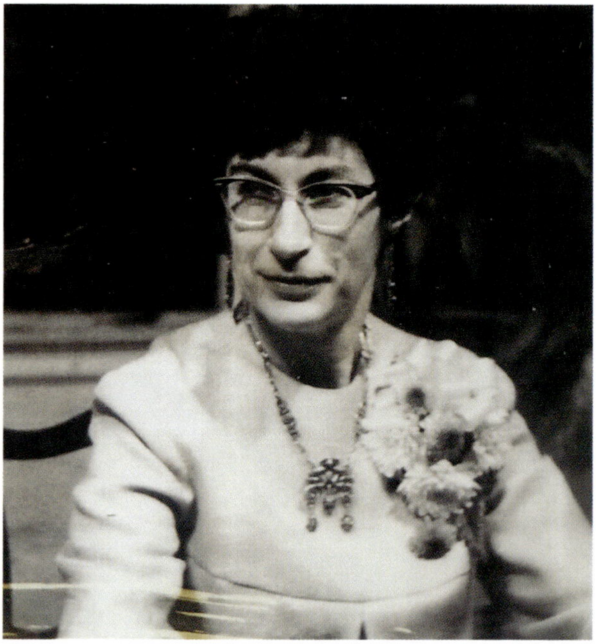

(ABOVE LEFT) Me in nursery school, c. age four

(ABOVE RIGHT) *Untitled,* c. 1965. Oil on canvas board, 26 × 18½ in. (66 × 46.9 cm)

(BELOW LEFT) Ruth Brody, *Frenzy,* c. 2005. Mixed media on paper, 16½ × 12 in. (41.9 × 30.4 cm.). In private collection.

(BELOW RIGHT) Ruth Brody, c. 1950. Photographer unknown.

CHAPTER ONE

NOT A PRODIGY: MY EARLY YEARS

The four-year-old me avidly painting her creation gives lie to my memory that as a child I had no interest in art. But the arts were important to my parents, so they sent me for lessons—modern dance, piano and, finally, at the age of twelve, art instruction with a family friend, Ruth Brody.

Brody, an accomplished watercolor artist, gave lessons to preteens in her basement studio. She had been a student of Raphael Soyer, a Russian-born American Social Realist who portrayed people in everyday settings and was dubbed the "East Side Degas."

Ruth treated me as an adult, which I had never experienced before. She did not heap on praise; it was more her discerning eye and how she challenged me to refine my work. Under her respectful tutelage, I discovered in myself a budding passion for art. Ruth helped her students prepare portfolios for admission to the High School of Music & Art, a public school in Manhattan. I believe my parents were happy I had found something I was interested in. But it was clear to them that I did not have natural talent, and they were not into giving false praise.

I went on to the High School of Music & Art, where I studied drawing, painting, and printmaking. My oil painting *Untitled* won honorable mention at the school's "Semi-Annual" exhibit in 1966.

My father seemed bewildered that the judges recognized this ugly-duckling painting with an award. He seemed to dismiss it as faulty judgement on the part of the awards committee. I never liked the painting either, but recently someone commented, "I really like this painting; it looks as if someone older painted it." So, years later, I appreciate some merit in the work, and I sense a missed opportunity to shore up my confidence.

My non-prodigy beginnings left me with insecurity that remains to this day. Still, I found myself turning to art as a means of expression.

My Parents

My father, Abraham Albert Goldbaum, known as "Al," and my mother, Etta Stock Goldbaum, were both high school teachers. Al taught physics and chemistry, and Etta business skills. My mother was born in the shtetl (village) of Brzeżany in the southwestern part of Poland (now Ukraine) and arrived in the US at age nine. My father was born in the US, but nine months before his birth, his parents had emigrated from Bilgoraj, a shtetl in the countryside of eastern Poland.

He was an accomplished nature and travel photographer, and she was a groundbreaking batik artist, jeweler, and wizard with her hands as well as with words. (She won two limerick contests!) Coming from immigrant families, they embraced education, the richness of the arts, and the radical politics of New York City. Art and music of all kinds were appreciated in our home.

My parents were traumatized by the McCarthy era, and my sister and I were warned never to discuss our family politics except with trusted friends. McCarthyism was a post-WWII practice in which many citizens were recklessly accused, without evidence, of disloyalty, subversion, or treason by Republican-led committees. Sometimes I think my fear of going public with my controversial art dates back to my childhood of secrecy as a "red diaper baby."

Even in this memoir, I feel fear about revealing my family's connection to communism. Now often a dirty word, in my family it stood for equality for all, an end to racism and poverty, and other lofty ideals. However, as I grew older, the specter of Stalinism and other unsavory policies entered my consciousness, and I challenged my parents with these troubling inconsistencies. I was very proud of my father when he denounced Stalin, quit the Communist Party, and joined the Committees of Correspondence, a reformist group now called the Committees of Correspondence for Democracy and Socialism. My mother always had "questions," so she never formally joined the CP but called herself a proud radical. But she was no "armchair radical"—she shared her love and creativity with her disadvantaged students at Walton High School in the Bronx for many years.

I remember being praised mainly for being sweet and pretty, not for any talent, but my dad did recognize my interest in science and nature. I credit him for telling me about Madame Curie, the legendary chemist and physicist. It was rare for a girl in the 1950s to be presented with a role model in the sciences. Dad would perform simple experiments with household items and also bring home chemicals from the lab where he taught. He challenged me to think using the Socratic method—asking questions rather than imparting information. This may have contributed to my later interest in medicine and the decision to study nursing.

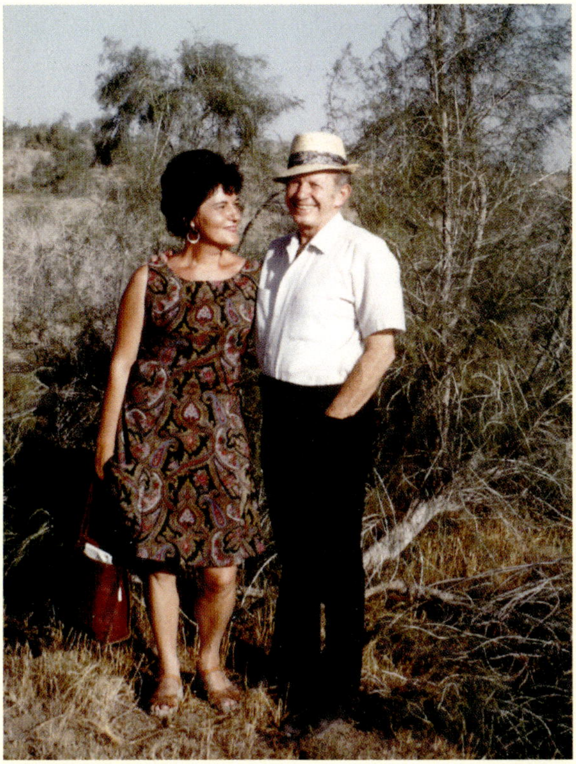

(LEFT) Etta and Al Goldbaum, c. 1975

(BELOW LEFT) *My Mother, Last Year of Life*, 2009. Charcoal pencil and chalk on gray-colored paper, 3 × 2 in. (7.6 × 5 cm)

(BELOW RIGHT) *My Father Sleeping at Age Eighty*, 1992. Charcoal pencil and chalk on gray-colored paper, 3 × 2 in. (7.6 × 5 cm)

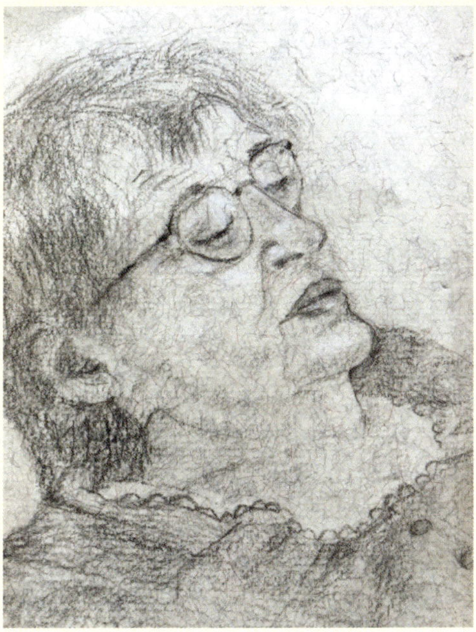

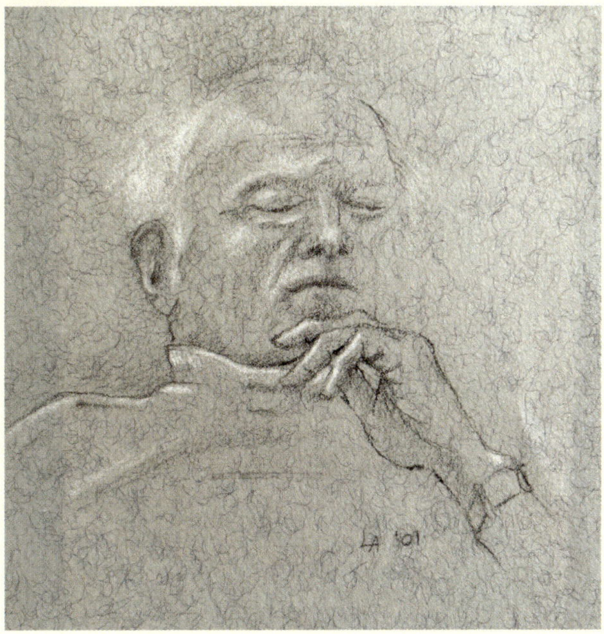

California Dreaming

"If you don't find a summer job, you'll have to come to California with us," my father warned. He had enrolled in a summer enrichment course for high school science teachers in Berkeley, and my mom had arranged ceramics classes for herself nearby.

My aversion to spending the summer with my parents was apparently not incentive enough to look for a job in New York, so the three of us boarded a California-bound plane. We held hands as the plane took off from JFK—none of us had ever flown before.

Although I was just sixteen, my father had thoughtfully arranged for me to take art classes at the University of California at Berkeley and to live in a dorm. I was excited to be living away from home for the first time, although their rented apartment was just a few blocks away.

I fell in love with Berkeley and vowed to return to attend college. I gave my parents an ultimatum: "If I can't go to Berkeley, I'm not going to college at all."

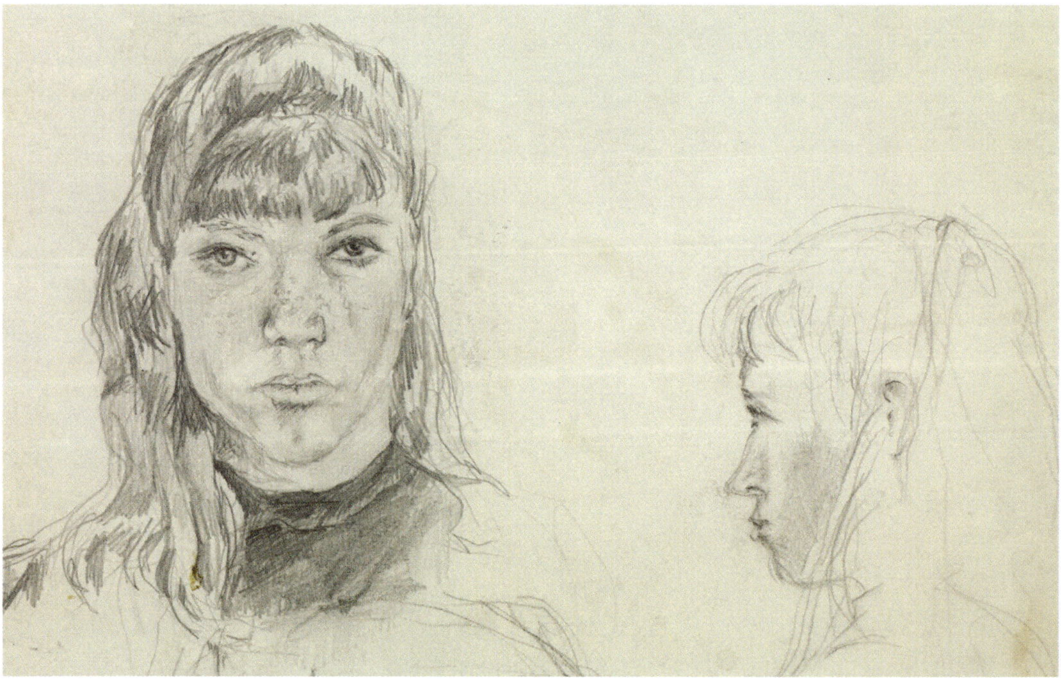

(ABOVE) *Self-Portrait, Age Fifteen*, c. 1964. Pencil on paper, 6¼ × 5½ in. (15.8 × 13.9 cm)

(OPPOSITE) *Self-Portrait*, c. 1965. Colored pencil on paper, 24 × 19 in. (60.9 × 48.2 cm)

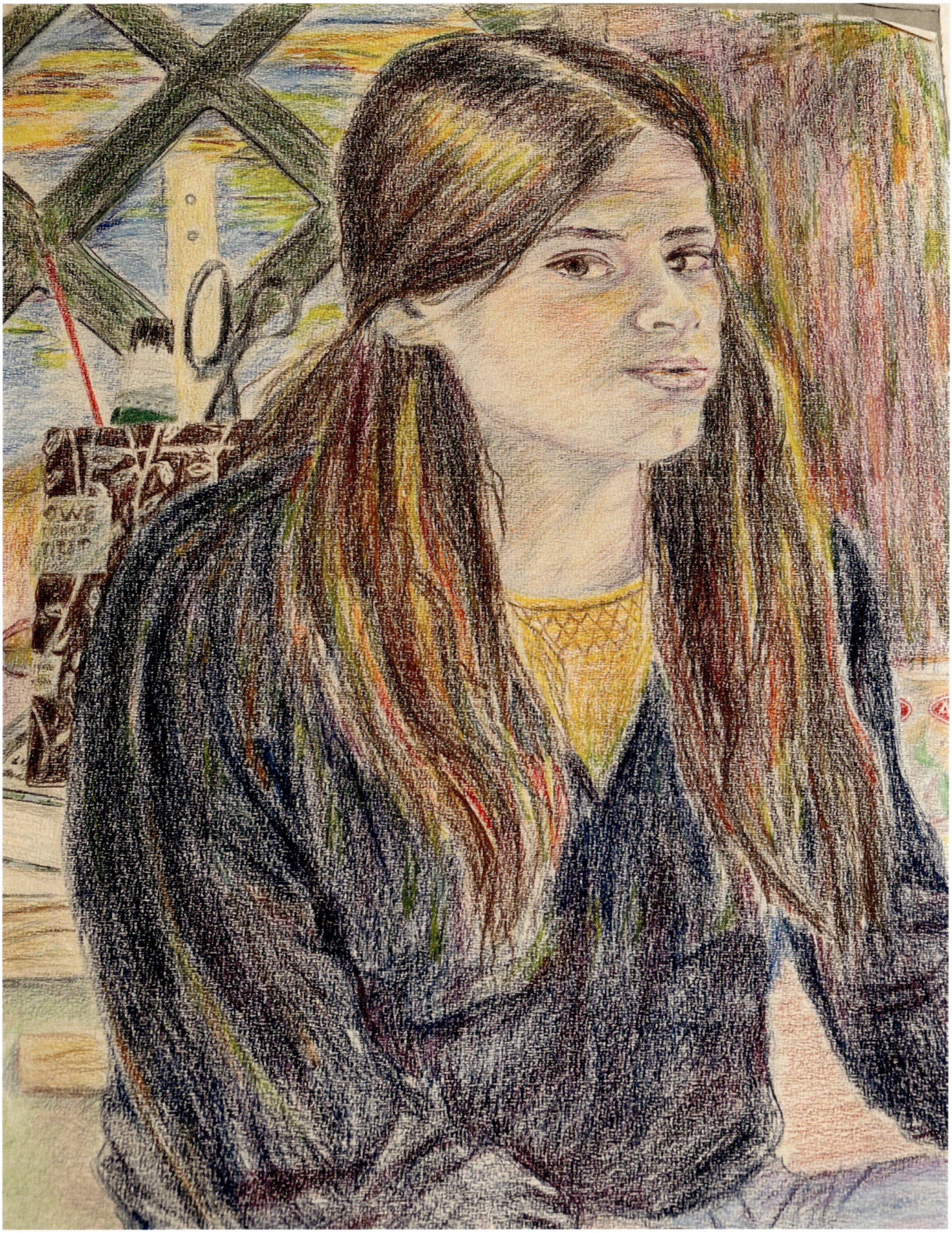

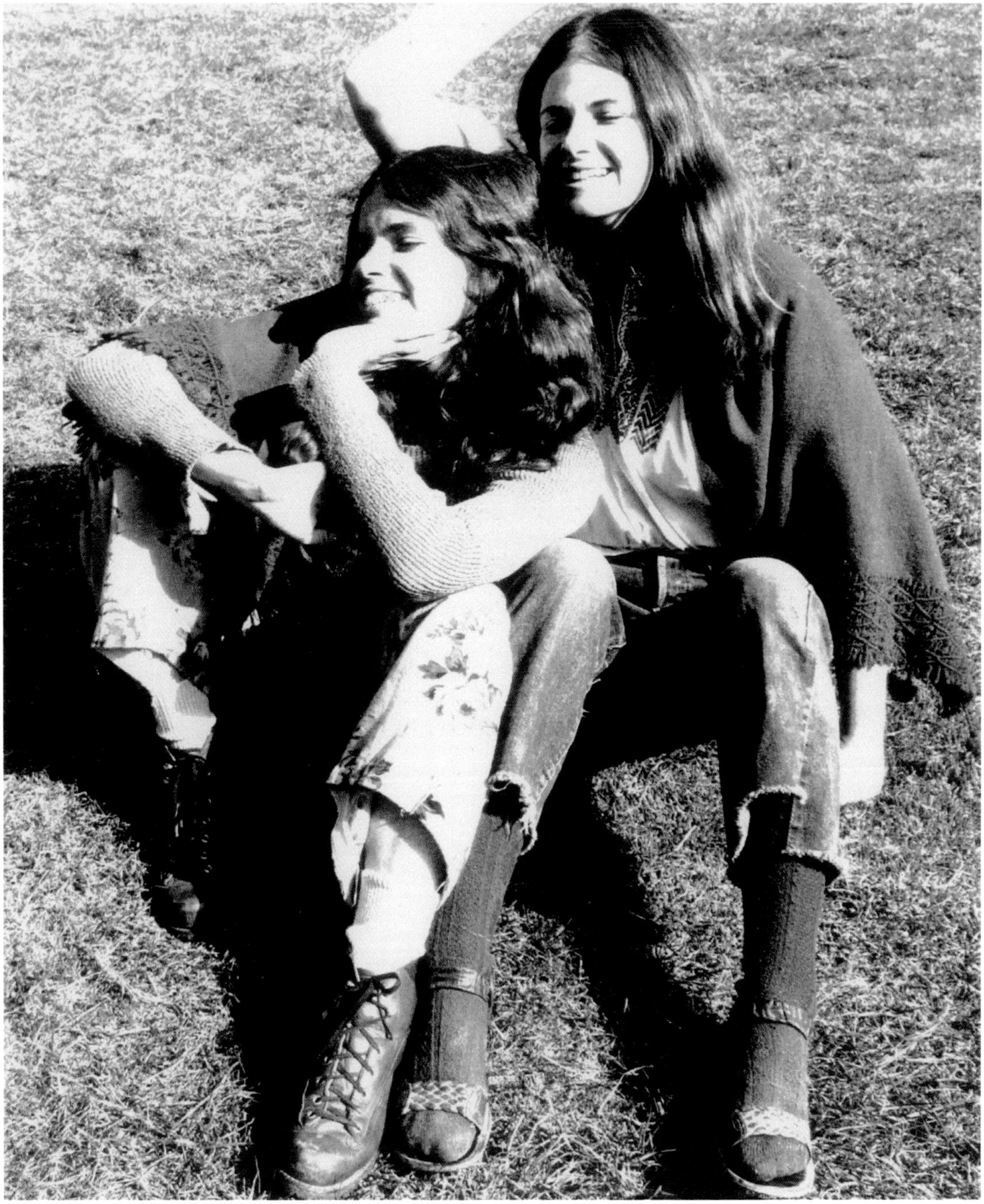

(ABOVE) Me (left) and my darling sister, Ruthie. This is the only photo I have of myself in the sixties.
(OPPOSITE) *The Ghost*, c. 1967. Pastel on paper, 11 × 8½ in. (27.9 × 21.5 cm)

CHAPTER TWO

FLOWER CHILD OF THE SIXTIES

I arrived in Berkeley a virginal seventeen-year-old in the fall of 1966. My parents admired the Free Speech Movement that had flourished on the Berkeley campus just a few years earlier. Who could forget the impassioned words of Mario Savio on the steps of Sproul Hall?

> *There's a time when the operation of the machine becomes so odious, makes you so sick at heart that you can't take part! You can't even passively take part! And you've got to put your bodies upon the gears and upon the wheels, upon the levers, upon all the apparatus—and you've got to make it stop! And you've got to indicate to the people who run it, to the people who own it—that unless you're free the machine will be prevented from working at all.*[1]

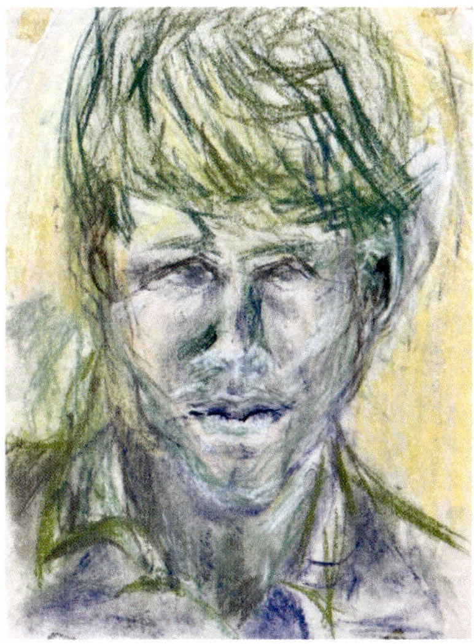

Thinking Berkeley a wholesome environment for their daughter, they gave their blessing—as much as atheists give blessings. But upon arrival, I became caught up in the counterculture tsunami. Soon I was wearing long flowing skirts, trying psychedelics, and gingerly embracing the sexual revolution.

My first Berkeley boyfriend was a tall, pale graduate student I nicknamed (only to myself) The Ghost.

It was with him that I lost my virginity, and it was he who casually took me to The Fillmore in San Francisco on weekends. Under psychedelic light shows, sparks flew off the stages of Jimi Hendrix, Janis Joplin, Jefferson Airplane, and others. Although I thought of

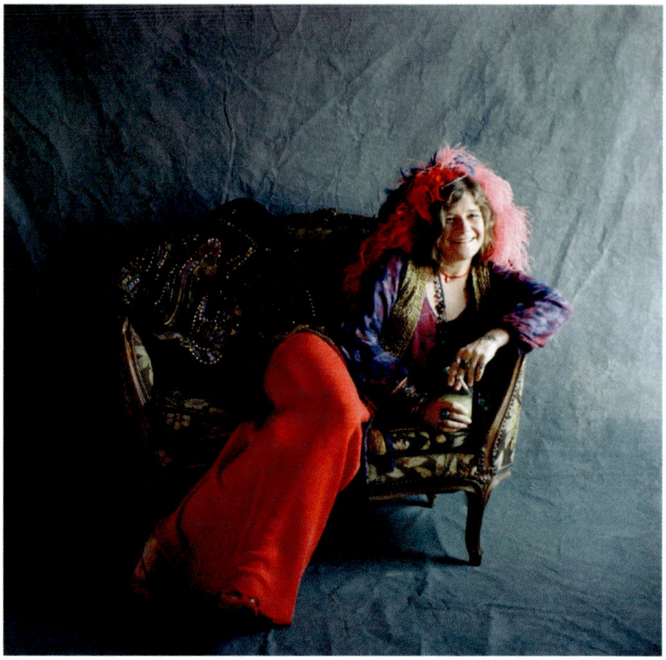

(ABOVE) Janis Joplin, 1970, Hollywood, California. The photograph was taken the day before her untimely death. Photo used with permission of Barry Feinstein Photography and Jampol Artist Management.

them as just our local bands, I felt something extraordinary and was swept away by the intensity and the mind-blowingly over-the-top performances.

One afternoon at the Fillmore, I stepped away from my Ghost boyfriend to find the bathroom. Moving through the dark, crowded, gargantuan ballroom, I found myself in the embrace of a boy, our mouths locked in a kiss, before breaking away. I continued to the bathroom and returned to my boyfriend without mentioning it. Such was life in the sixties.

At the Human Be-In in Golden Gate Park in 1967, I saw the Grateful Dead's legendary organist and singer, Ron "Pigpen" McKernan, perform. He would die in 1973 of liver cirrhosis due to alcoholism. Fast-forward to 2018, I'm riding with a young Lyft driver and see a skull and lightning-bolt decal in his car. We got to talking about the Grateful Dead. When I told him I was around when Pigpen was playing, he became reverential toward me for having been in the presence of such an icon.

My first and only acid trip was initiated by Ghost boyfriend. As I licked the blotter paper impregnated with LSD, he assured me that his friend Bruce was experienced with psychedelics and would act as my guru if needed. I introduced myself to Bruce, who replied, "I'm a very sleepy guru," and promptly went off to bed.

Not long after, the walls started dripping with the cliché kaleidoscope of color. When I peered out the window into the dark street, I hallucinated that the red taillights of every passing vehicle were menacing police cars with sirens blaring. My friend Gilda was tripping with me and was also having terrifying experiences. After several hours, somebody offered us Thorazine, a known antidote for a bad trip. Gilda took it, but I declined. Perhaps I was not as frightened as Gilda and was curious to see what would happen next.

The trip was supposed to last eight hours. Right on schedule, all the technicolor visuals disappeared. I was relieved but had an intense feeling of being dissociated from myself. I consulted the "guru," who advised, "Oh, that's the way it is, you're never the same after acid." That's when I really freaked out. But after another eight hours, I was relieved to return to my "normal" self. Later, I was told that my dose of LSD was probably spiked with speed.

Years later, sitting in the Grand Piano, a café on Haight Street, I recognized Gilda, barefoot and dirty, begging from table to table. I had a fleeting urge to help her but quickly suppressed it, instead feeling a wave of gratitude for my comparatively sane life path.

I never tried LSD again but did not want to miss out on the transformative experiences others were having on psychedelics, so I decided to try mescaline, known to provide a gentler trip. I took it twice, both times in natural settings with people I trusted. In one episode, I experienced myself as a deer, blissfully chomping huckleberries from a branch. The other time, walking down a wooded path, I heard drumbeats and was transported to an ancient Native American gathering.

Psychedelic imagery never showed up in my art, but perhaps a loosening of my brain fibers allowed for freer expression in future work.

College Dropout

UC Berkeley was an academic factory with giant lecture halls and little one-on-one attention. I tried attending professors' office hours but did not find these interactions satisfying. Along with the students, many professors were taking psychedelics and dropping out or just doing the minimum to get by.

My philosophy professor gave no exams and didn't assign papers or make other requirements. At the end of the quarter, we met in a room, and one by one each student was told to say something about philosophy. When it was my turn, I hastily crafted these three words: "I said nothing." He verbally awarded me an A for my profound statement. But other professors took their teaching seriously, and I did have some courses that stimulated me—for

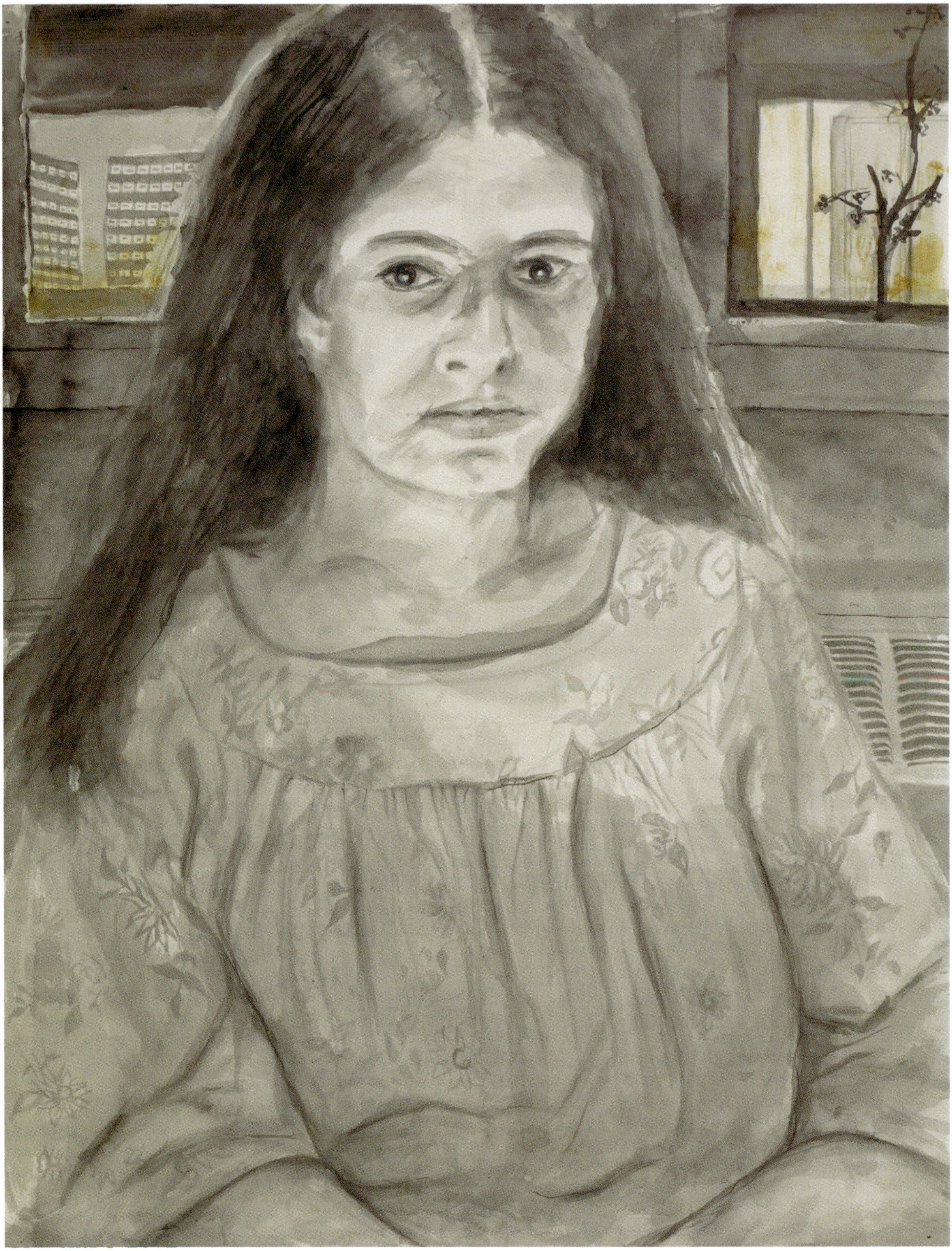

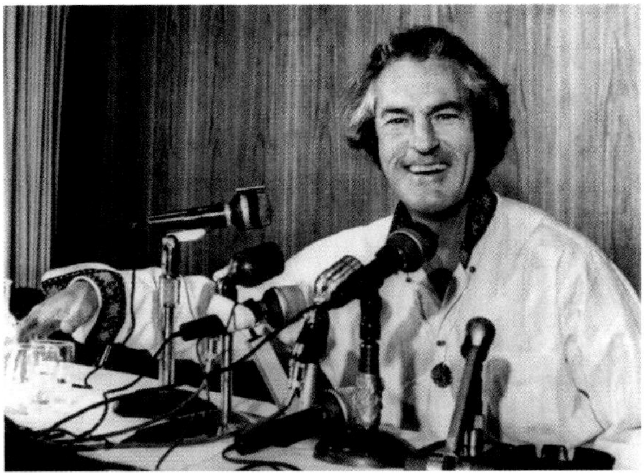 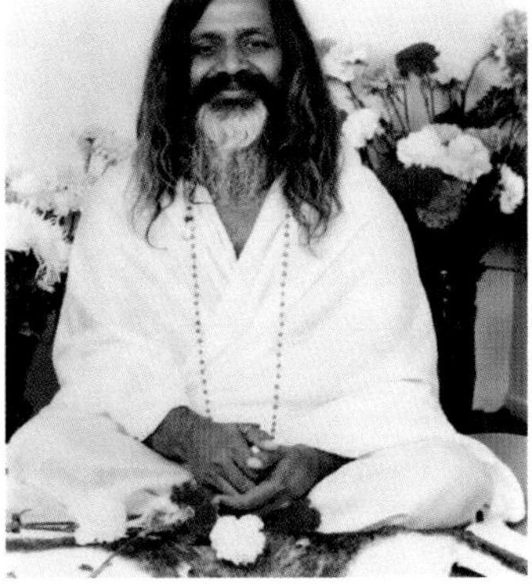

(OPPOSITE) *Self-Portrait*, c. 1968. Ink wash on paper, 22½ × 17½ in. (57 × 44.4 cm)

(LEFT) Timothy Leary at New Haven College, 1968. Colorado State University Archives. Photographer unknown.

(RIGHT) Maharishi Mahesh Yogi, guru of Transcendental Meditation, late 1970s. Photographer unknown.

example, botany and landscape architecture classes, including soil science and dendrology (the study of trees).

Guided by psychedelic guru Timothy Leary's dictum "Turn on, tune in, drop out," I left the university in the fall of 1967, as I was about to start my sophomore year.[2]

My life until then had been highly scheduled by school and summer camp. I had no plan or intention when I dropped out—I wanted to try "just being." I wandered the streets of Berkeley for hours when not working at my part-time job scooping ice cream at Swensen's.

I was initiated into Transcendental Meditation shortly after the Beatles adopted it, and I meditated faithfully twice a day for three years until I became disenchanted with the organization. Later, my negative instincts were affirmed by the Maharishi's bizarre promise of achieving "levitation" by practicing "yogic flying." However, I still meditate occasionally using the TM technique. TM mantras are costly when transmitted by the organization but are readily available on the internet.

In my parents' mind, meditation was worse than drugs, since they believed, as Karl Marx is frequently quoted as saying, "Religion is the opiate of the masses." The actual quote translates as "Religion is the sigh of the oppressed creature, the heart of a heartless world, and the soul of soulless conditions. It is the opium of the people."[3]

Although I was raised in a secular home, spared from the sometimes-narrow and abusive nature of organized religion, there was an impalpable void that transformed me into a seeker and even fair game for cult membership.

My mother and father had both rebelled against their Orthodox Jewish upbringings and were horrified to witness their daughter seemingly seduced by religion. My dropping out of college was the last straw for them, so they consulted the family doctor. Fearing drug addiction or worse, the doctor advised an emergency trip to Berkeley.

My mother arrived and insisted on an appointment with the school psychologist. By chance, my assigned psychologist was Dr. Alan Y. Cohen. Dr. Cohen was a former colleague of early Harvard researchers in psychedelics Timothy Leary and Richard Alpert. Alpert, later known as Ram Dass, was a spiritual teacher, psychologist, and author of the widely known 1971 book *Be Here Now.*

After speaking with us separately and then together, Dr. Cohen reassured my mother that her daughter was entirely normal. It was obvious he had his finger on the counterculture pulse and supported my bid for self-exploration. I will always be grateful to him for defusing this fraught situation. A naturally fun-loving person, my mother then relaxed, and we had a delightful visit.

When I dropped out of college, my parents cut off all financial support. I knew they were wise not to finance my free-spirited lifestyle, and I immediately set out to find part-time employment. For most of my life, I have worked part-time to leave space for art.

To save money, I bought a 1948 Ford panel truck for $125 that became my new home. I built shelves out of woven branches and stored my clothes and laundry in zippered satchels that doubled as decorative pillows.

Being a New Yorker, I didn't know how to drive, so my friends moved the van from place to place when needed. The seller warned me that the engine was on its last legs and should be kept topped off with crankcase oil.

One day, we traveled north to visit communes in Oregon. I had a mystical sense that only women should drive my truck. One time, I let a man drive, and sure enough the van threw a rod and became incapacitated. I recall the man pouring beer on the smoking engine block.

I left my truck with a farmer on a back road, promising to return one day to tow it home. Months later, I retrieved it with the help of a boyfriend. All my belongings were gone, but we towed it back to Berkeley. I painted the truck blue but soon after had it hauled to a junkyard.

For a short time in 1969, I was a chorus member in the mystically-inspired theater group Floating Lotus Magic Opera Company. Although we mainly performed in parks in Berkeley,

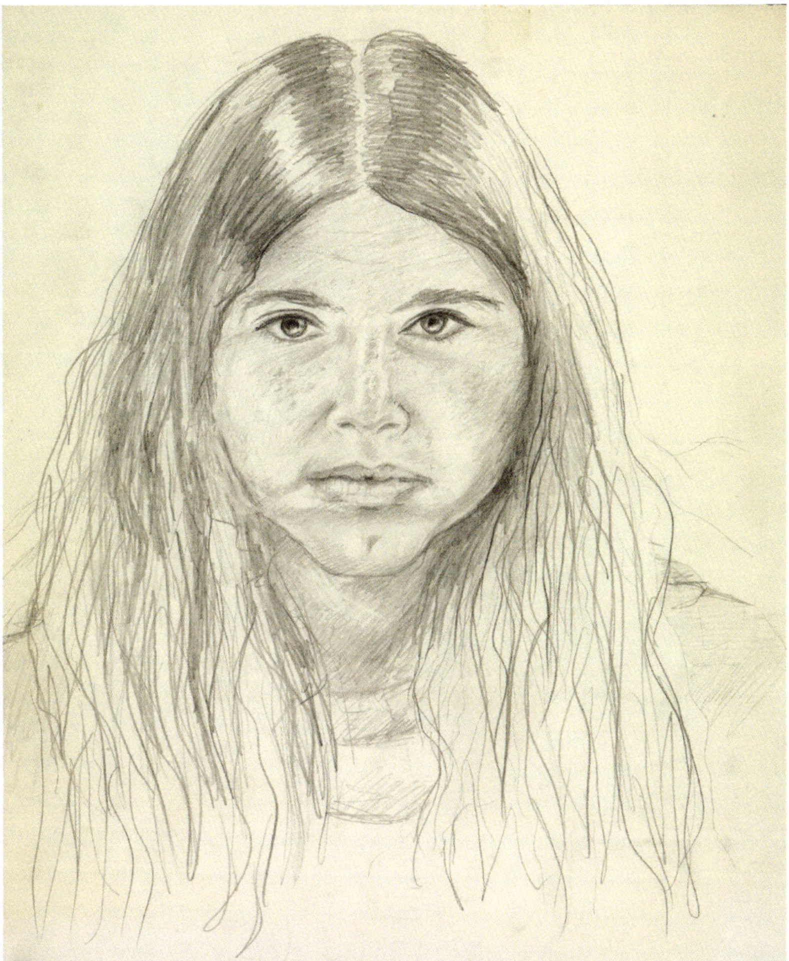

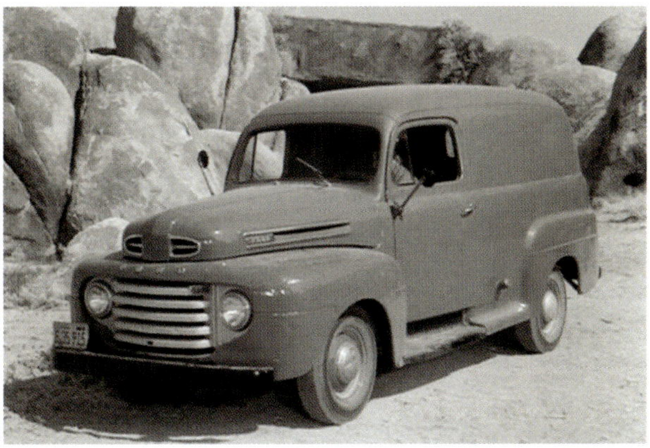

(ABOVE) Self-Portrait, c. 1969. Pencil on paper, 10 × 14 in. (25.4 × 35.5 cm)

(LEFT) 1948 Ford panel truck. This photo is not my actual truck but highly reminiscent of it—the exact model, year, and color. Date and photographer unknown.

my most vivid memory was at an indoor performance at The Family Dog, a since-demolished rock venue in Playland at Ocean Beach in San Francisco.

After a performance of *Bliss Apocalypse,* we spread out into the audience, climbing over chairs and on and off the laps of the astonished audience. This felt radical and intimate—perhaps an experience that set the stage for breaking barriers in my future artwork.

But the hippie movement was not just psychedelics and rock music. The Vietnam War was raging, and it seemed the band Country Joe and the Fish was everywhere singing their anthem, "Feel-Like-I'm-Fixin'-to-Die Rag":

And it's one, two, three, what are we fightin' for?
Don't ask me, I don't give a damn
Next stop is Vietnam
And it's five, six, seven, open up the pearly gates
Ain't no time to wonder why
Whoopee! We're all gonna die!

Even the saffron-robed devotees of Krishna consciousness were present at some demonstrations. While I'm not sure whether it was the devotees or the protesters, I heard their sacred Hare Krishna chant transform into:

Hare Krishna, Hare Rama
Stop the war in Vietnam-a

I experienced tear gas and a terrifying "flying wedge," a triangular formation of police used to break up large crowds. These were the infamous "Blue Meanies," Alameda County Sheriff officers. I'd never seen so many police in riot gear, but it was the noxious tear gas that sent me and others running. This occurred not at an anti-war demonstration but a People's Park protest.[4]

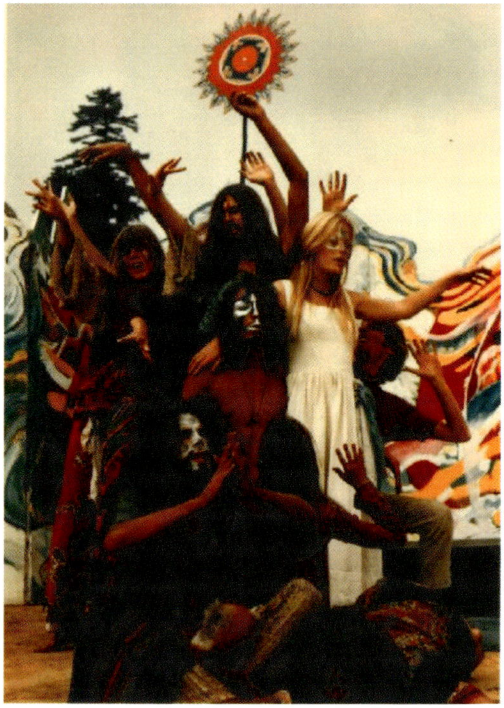

(ABOVE) *Bliss Apocalypse*, performed by The Floating Lotus Magic Opera Company, c 1969. Photographer unknown.

Although the sixties were a time of enchantment and discovery, as an insecure teenager, I had a shaky sense of self—an older woman referred to me as "a wounded bird." The hippie

Lost in the Easter Parade

While writing about scary police tactics at protests, I was reminded of a contrasting experience when, as a five-year-old, I became lost in the Easter Parade in New York City. As we strolled down Fifth Avenue, I recall leaping from manhole cover to manhole cover, then discovering that my parents were nowhere in sight. I was trained to "go up to a kind policeman" If I ever became lost.

I soon found a policeman who gave me a Life Saver from a roll of the colored candy. I was taken to a police station, where I was given a giant chocolate Easter bunny—a glorious treat for a little Jewish girl! Not long after, my parents arrived to fetch me.

I never felt traumatized by the episode. But because police may be suspicious, unhelpful, or blatantly racist, many parents must have "the talk" with their children of color to warn them of the danger of interacting with police. As tender as this memory is, it also reminds me of the gross unfairness of white privilege.

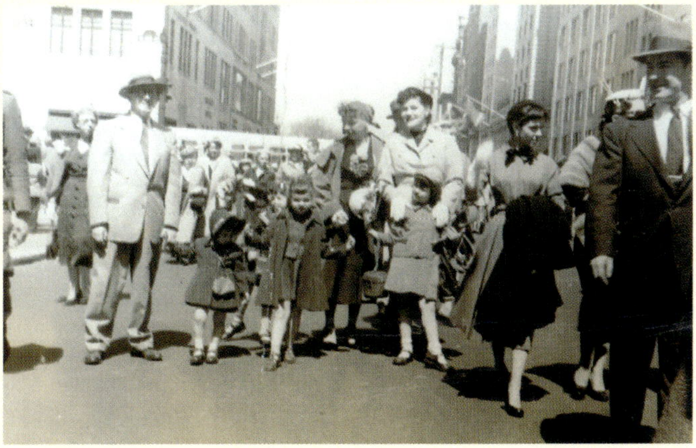

(ABOVE) Easter Parade, Fifth Avenue, New York City, c. 1954. Left to right: Al Goldbaum (my father), Sheila Kassoy, Merry Kassoy (barely visible, behind me), me (forward center), Honey Kassoy, Etta Goldbaum (my mother), and Ruthie Goldbaum (my sister). Photo by Bernard Kassoy.

culture was no paradise for women. I felt we were mostly valued for our looks and domestic skills—not much different from the 1950s values I grew up with.

After several months without the constraints of school, I found myself painting again. It occurred to me that I was better off returning to the university, taking art classes, and again receiving financial support from my parents. So, after a year away, I reenrolled at UC Berkeley.

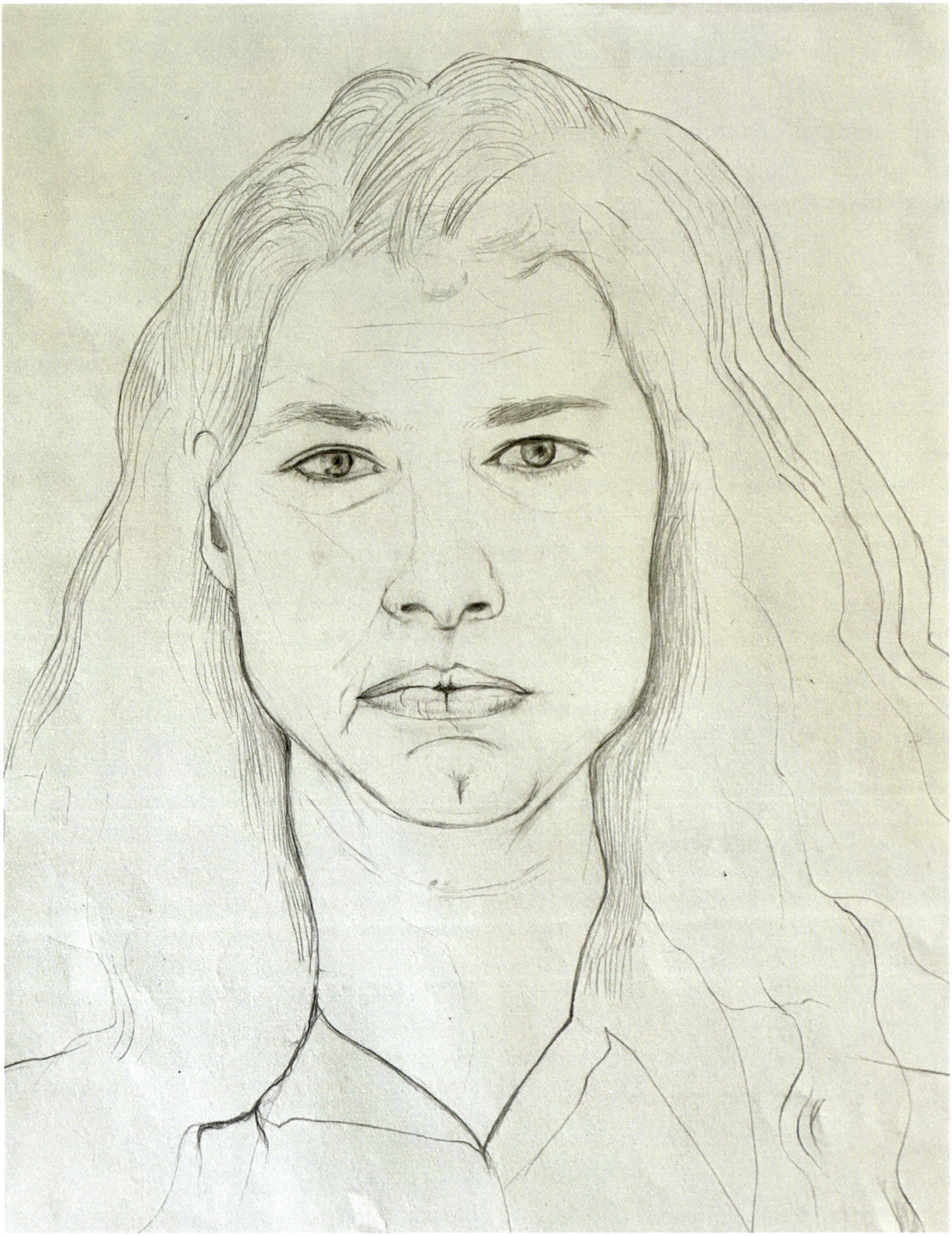

(ABOVE) *Self-Portrait* (unfinished), 1971. Pencil on paper, 14 × 10 in. (35.5 × 25.4 cm)

(OPPOSITE) *The Practice of Tempera Painting: Materials and Methods* by Daniel V. Thompson, Jr., first published in 1936

CHAPTER THREE

THE ETHEREAL EGG TEMPERA

One of the first courses I took when I returned to the university was Materials & Techniques, taught by Boyd Allen. One day, he handed us a paper with instructions for making egg tempera paint. He told us he had no knowledge of the technique but said that everybody had to try it.

I had never heard of egg tempera but obediently bought an assortment of pigments, a sheet of plywood, the materials to make gesso (to prime the surface), and, of course, eggs. I could not get the paint to work well but was captivated as each brushstroke was magically absorbed into the ivory-like gesso ground. This was the start of a lifelong passion for egg tempera painting.

I could not find a teacher for many years, so I followed instructions from the few books that I could find, notably *The Practice of Tempera Painting: Materials and Methods* by Daniel V. Thompson, Jr. (1936).

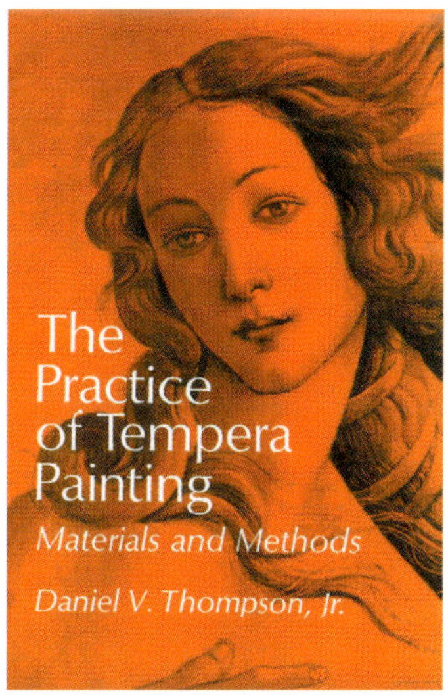

I'm often asked why I paint in egg tempera to the exclusion of other media. The word "luminous" is often used to describe tempera. But other media, such as oil or watercolor, may also feature luminosity. Tempera has an ethereal quality that keeps me enthralled with the technique. As layer after layer of paint is built up, unique optical effects appear as if by alchemy: a satiny, velvety, slightly waxy surface with a bit of light glowing through from the white gesso ground.

Watercolor can be a gorgeous technique, but I find it lacks body—it has, at times, a wishy-washy, unsubstantial look, bordering on wimpy. Many artists love the luscious,

Egg Tempera Definition

Egg tempera is simply the binding of colored material called "pigment" with egg in some form—yolk, whole egg, or sometimes egg combined with additives, such as oil. Some artists add a preservative—vinegar, vodka or other, but I don't. I keep my palette in the refrigerator after a day's work and start with a fresh egg every few days.

The Latin root of tempera is *temperare,* which mean to blend or mix. But it has multiple meanings: to exercise moderation, to restrain oneself, to moderate, to bring to a proper strength or consistency by mixing. There are temperas besides egg tempera, such as glue tempera (distemper), milk tempera (casein), and many others.

The word "temper" has also come to be used to describe emotion—for example, tempering criticism with kindness.

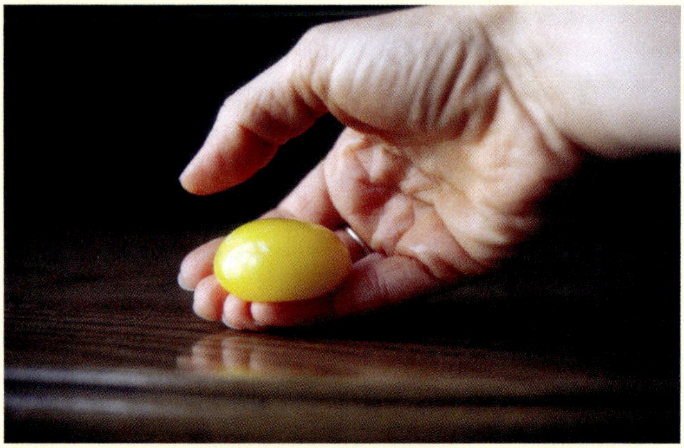

(ABOVE RIGHT) The egg yolk is separated from the white and then rolled around on a paper towel until all traces of the egg white are removed.

(BELOW RIGHT) The yolk is punctured with a toothpick or knife, allowing it to run into a jar, leaving the yolk sac behind to be eaten or composted. The yolk is then diluted with distilled water; the proportion of yolk to water varies amongst tempera artists.

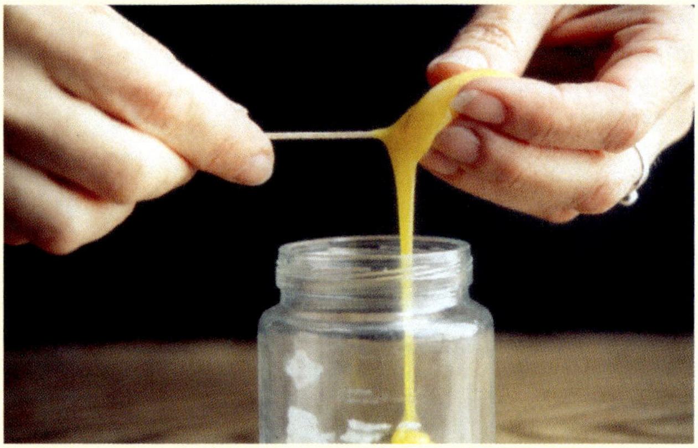

buttery texture of oil paint, yet I find it a bit greasy and somewhat gross to handle. Acrylic paint is versatile; it can appear similar to watercolor, oil paint, and even egg tempera. But I notice a chemical smell, and its plastic nature manifests in the handling of the paint and the appearance of the painted surface.

The Goldilocks principle explains it: For me, egg tempera is the "just right" painting medium. Egg yolk is an emulsion of oil suspended in water, so it has characteristics of both watercolor and oil paint yet has its own personality.

Please note that this book is not intended to be a "how to" manual. For detailed instructions, I wholeheartedly direct readers to *Egg Tempera Painting: A Comprehensive Guide* by Koo Schadler (2021).

Pigments

Most people have never heard of egg tempera or may know only that it entails an artist making their own paint. While it's true that I make the paint, nowadays it's a simple matter of dispersing the powdered pigment into diluted egg yolk, which serves as a binder. Most pigments come finely ground from the manufacturer—only rarely does a particularly gritty pigment need further grinding.

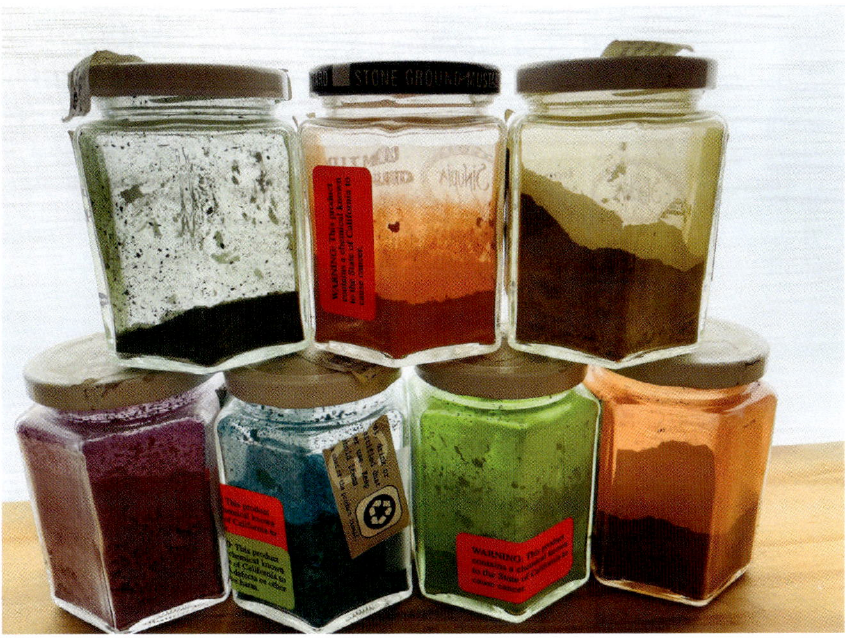

Pigments are the substances that give paint color. I try to use only pigments that are lightfast, which means they will not fade with time. Egg tempera is known as one of the most archival media, some paintings lasting hundreds of years with their colors still vibrant. But eventually the rigors of time, the environment, and politics will damage or destroy most artwork.

Egg tempera artists have an intimate relationship with their pigments. They are the precious jewels of the process—and sometimes they are literally jewels, or at least semiprecious stones (see Chapter 8). Pigments are like friends: each one has its own character and personality. Some characteristics are transparency, tinting strength, and particle size. Many of us egg tempera artists collect pigments from all over the world, and some artists make pigments from colored soil that they find.[5] I counted my pigments while writing this paragraph, and the current number is ninety-seven, plus I keep a wish list. I don't use them all on every painting; to create harmony, I limit my palette to a few colors but often add others for some sparkle or other needed boost.

(PREVIOUS) A few jars from my extensive collection of pigments

(RIGHT) My pigment shelves. The tiny containers you see are "pigment pastes"—pigment powder mixed only with water. When I am ready to paint, I combine equal amounts of pigment paste with diluted egg yolk. I also purchase some "pigment dispersions," which are pigments finely ground in water or water-based substances.

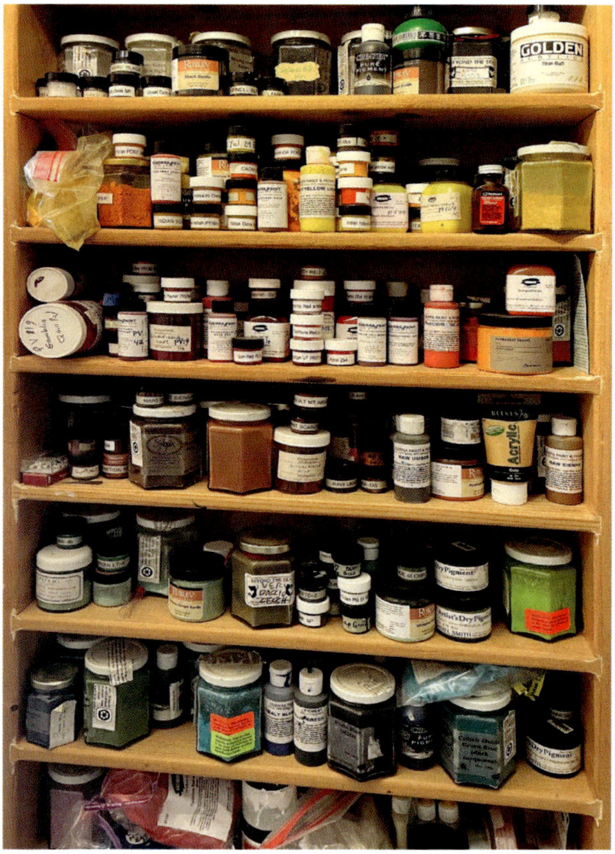

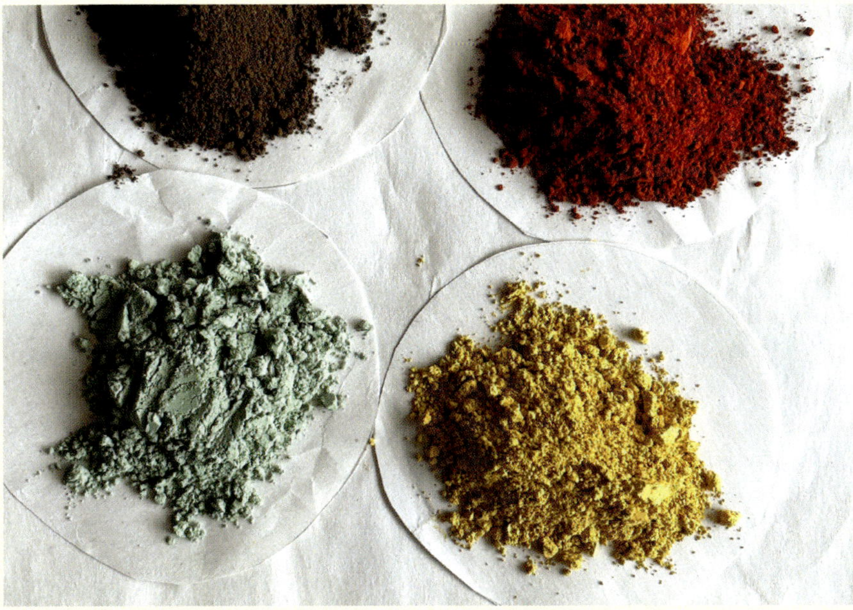

Egg Tempera: Nontoxic?

Some assume egg tempera is nontoxic because of the culinary association with eggs. This is somewhat true, if one uses only earth pigments or other nontoxic pigments.

Still, all powdered pigments are dangerous if inhaled. I wear a respirator mask when scooping powdered pigment from a jar. Once combined with egg yolk or water, the pigment is no longer dangerous to breathe. But no pigment should be ingested—for example, by licking a brush to form a sharp point. I'm also careful not to get pigment on my skin, especially toxic pigments, such as cadmiums, cobalts, and lead (which is rarely used nowadays). It's best to wear protective gloves while painting with toxic pigments. Although I am careful, I don't wear gloves, as I feel they interfere with my experience of painting.

(ABOVE) Earth pigments

(BELOW) My collection of green earth pigments, commonly called "terre verte" (from the French). I try to go by pigment number—terre verte is pigment green 23 (PG23)—but as you can see, colors with the same name and even the same number can look very different.

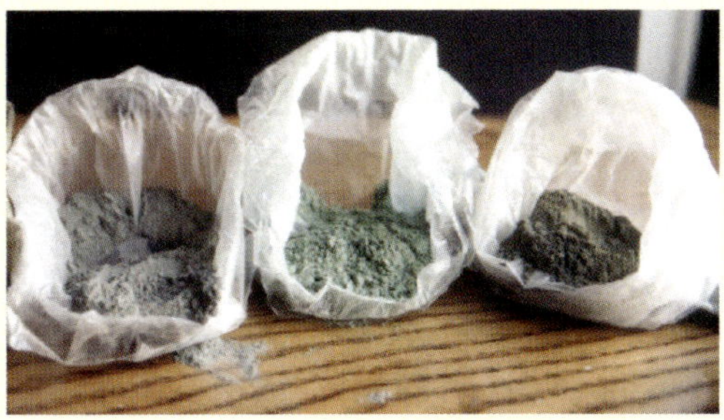

Types of Pigments

Pigments are grouped into four categories: inorganic natural, inorganic synthetic, organic synthetic, and organic natural. Organic pigments are carbon based, and inorganic pigments are mineral based.

Most organic natural pigments are not lightfast (with the exception of bone and lamp black) and so are mainly of historical interest. An example would be rose madder, from the madder root.[6] Many have been replaced by organic synthetic alternatives. Some manufacturers sell modern pigments using historical names because of the romantic appeal, but this tends to cause confusion.

Inorganic Natural

Inorganic natural pigments are the earth colors. They tend to be gentle and transparent; many are nontoxic (see sidebar on previous page). One of my favorites is burnt sienna. I own burnt sienna Mt. Amiata, which was mined from a historical quarry on Mount Amiata near Arcidosso, Italy. It is called "burnt" because the raw pigment must be roasted to achieve its glowing reddish-brown hue. Fissures in rock or soil contain "seams" or "veins" of pigment and are finite. The quarry at Mt. Amiata is now exhausted. Pigments that are labeled "Mt. Amiata" today come from an inventory from before the 1970s, or else the company is illegally using the name without disclosing that it is an imitation hue, or it was mined at a different quarry.

Inorganic Synthetic

Inorganic synthetic pigments are generally opaque and good for covering large areas. Cadmiums and cobalts are in this category. They are rated as toxic and require care if you use them, which I do. Cobalt blue turquoise light is one of my favorite pigments in this category.

Organic Synthetic

Organic synthetic pigments tend to be more vibrant and have a wide range of colors. A favorite is quinacridone magenta, which I call "quin mag"—we do give our pigments nicknames! This type of pigment was developed for industry. It is used for car coatings, among other uses.[7]

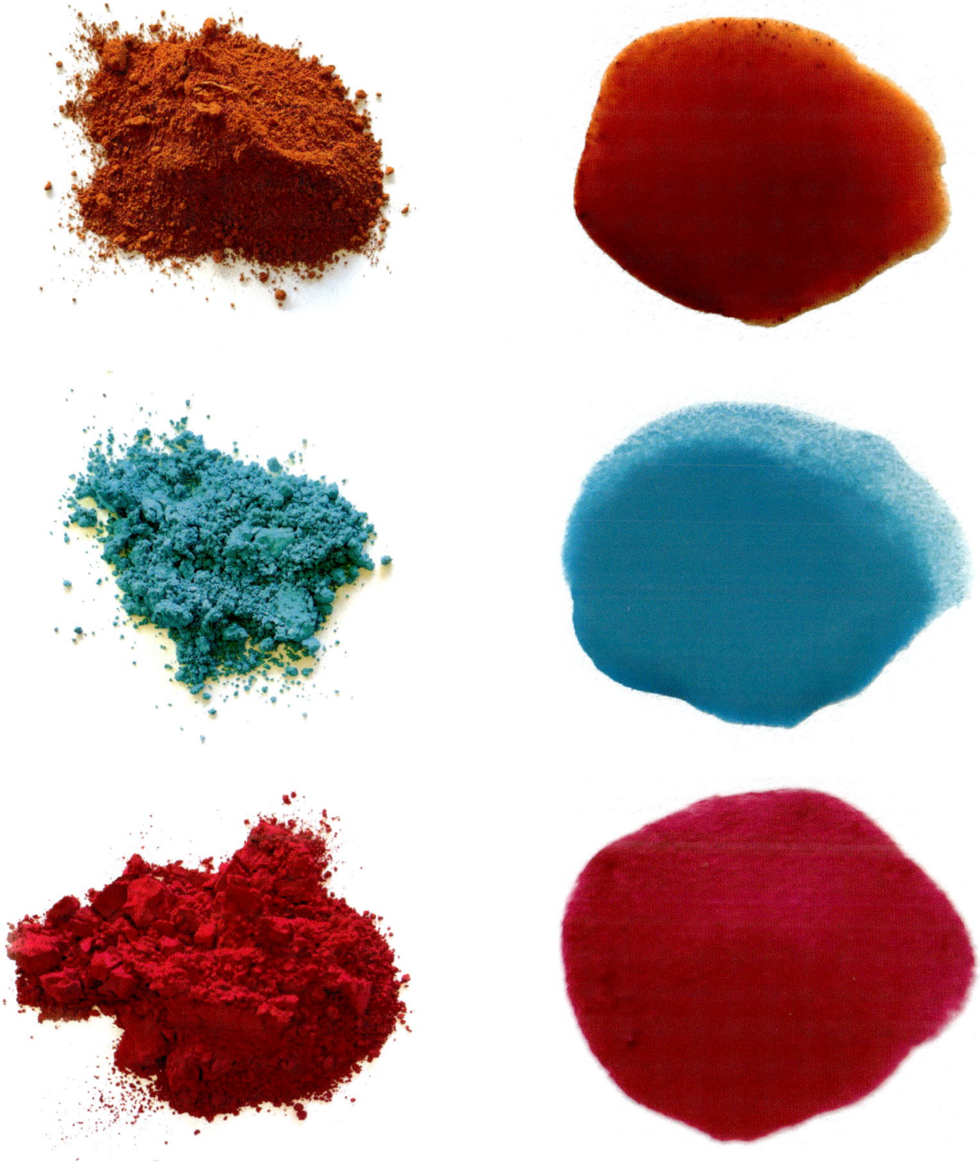

(ABOVE) Burnt sienna Mt. Amiata (Left: pigment powder; Right: egg tempera)
(MIDDLE) Cobalt blue turquoise light (Left: pigment powder; Right: egg tempera)
(BELOW) Quinacridone magenta (Left: pigment powder; Right: egg tempera)

Why Not Canvas?

I'm often asked, "Why don't you paint on canvas?" The reason is that both traditional gesso and the egg tempera paint film are brittle and could crack if applied to canvas that has been stretched over wooden bars.

It's okay to paint with egg tempera on canvas, museum board, or hot-pressed (smooth) watercolor paper as long as they are glued to a board or other rigid surface, such as aluminum. I use hardboard, a product manufactured from the waste generated from the milling of lumber. (It was formerly branded as Masonite.)

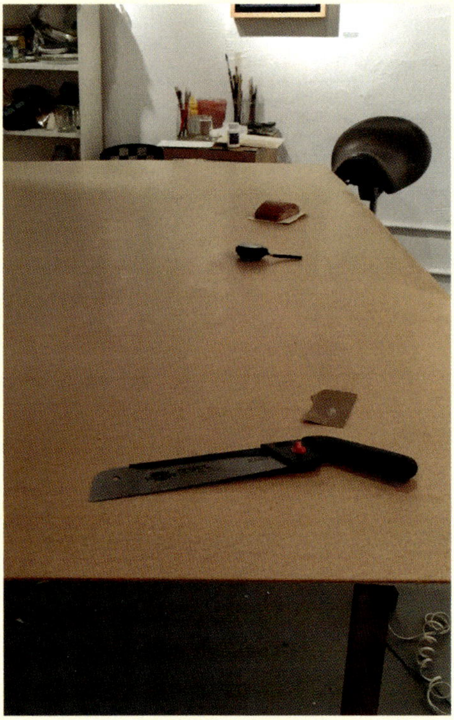

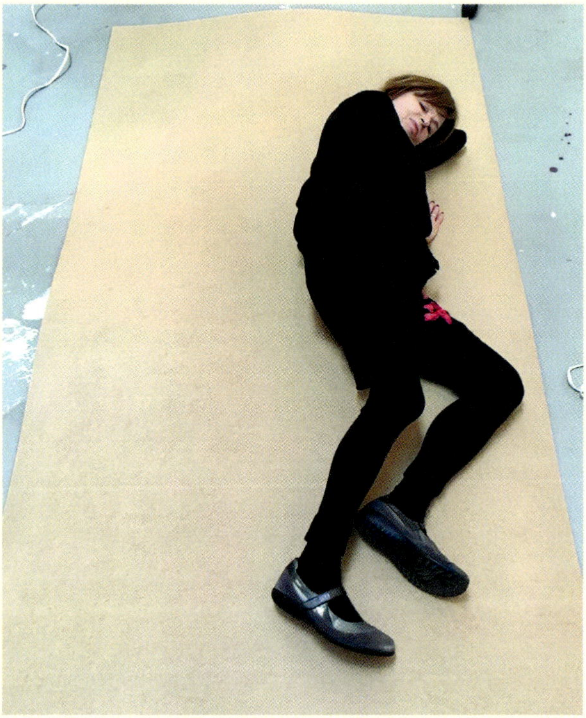

(ABOVE LEFT) A large sheet of hardboard, which will need strips of wood glued to the back to prevent warping. This is called "bracing" or "cradling."

(ABOVE RIGHT) Lying on a sheet of hardboard in my studio. Many tempera artists now prefer Aluminum Composite Material (ACM) panels which are less prone to warping and decay than wood products.

The Allure of Traditional Gesso

Egg yolk is only partially responsible for the luminous surface that keeps me captivated by the technique. I believe the egg yolk and gesso are of equal importance; it's the marriage of the two that creates the tempera magic. Although egg tempera can be painted on other surfaces, in my experience, the full glory of tempera appears only when it is applied to a traditional gesso ground. The Natural Pigments company makes a product called Tempera Ground. Although it is a polymer emulsion, it behaves similarly to traditional gesso but is not quite as absorbent.[8]

Painting on traditional gesso feels like painting on pure white ivory—except unlike ivory, gesso is highly absorbent. It slurps up the paint almost instantly, offering a dry surface upon which many layers can quickly be built up.

Traditional gesso is not the same as the acrylic gesso used by most oil and acrylic painters; the substance used to bind the white matter is very different. A polymer resin (a form of plastic) is used as a binder for acrylic gesso, and rabbit skin glue is used to bind traditional gesso.[9]

According to Koo Schadler, "The term 'Rabbit Skin Glue' (RSG) doesn't necessarily mean rabbits were involved in the production. RSG denotes a quality of glue: specifically, a pure collagen hide glue. Most rabbit skin glues are in fact derived from cow and pig sources."[10]

Water is added to the glue granules and allowed to soak for several hours or overnight. Then it is gently warmed over a double boiler so that the temperature is no higher than 135°F.

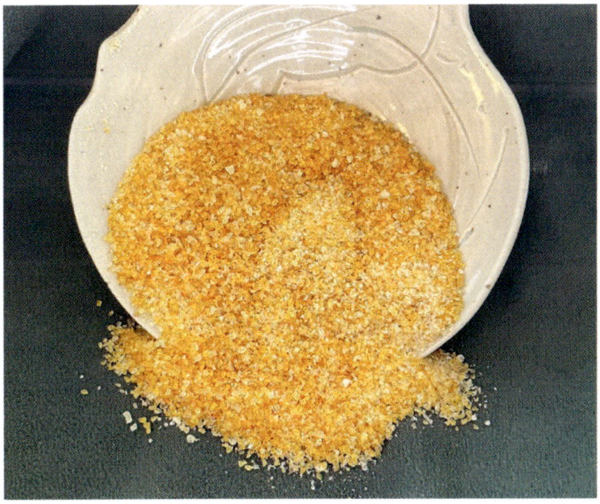

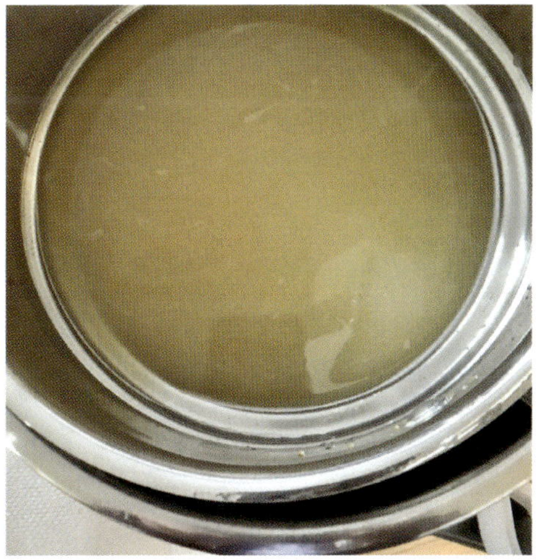

(ABOVE LEFT) Rabbit skin glue granules

(ABOVE RIGHT) Rabbit skin glue warming in a double boiler

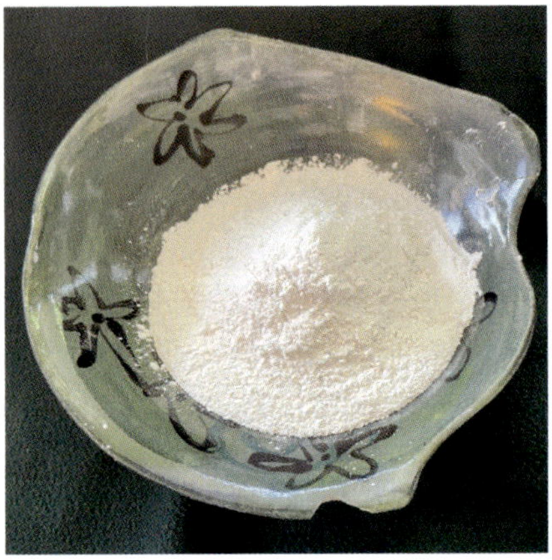

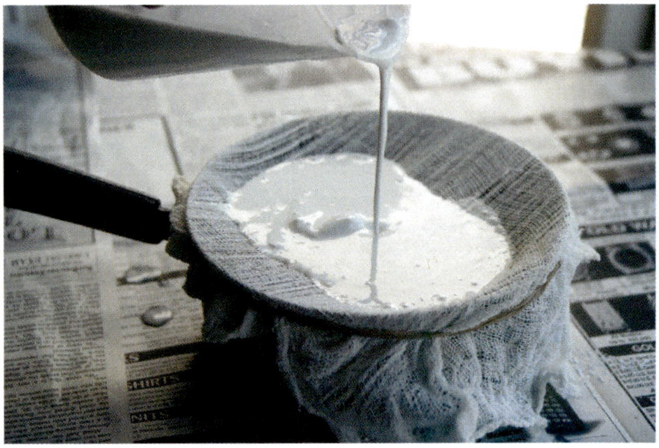

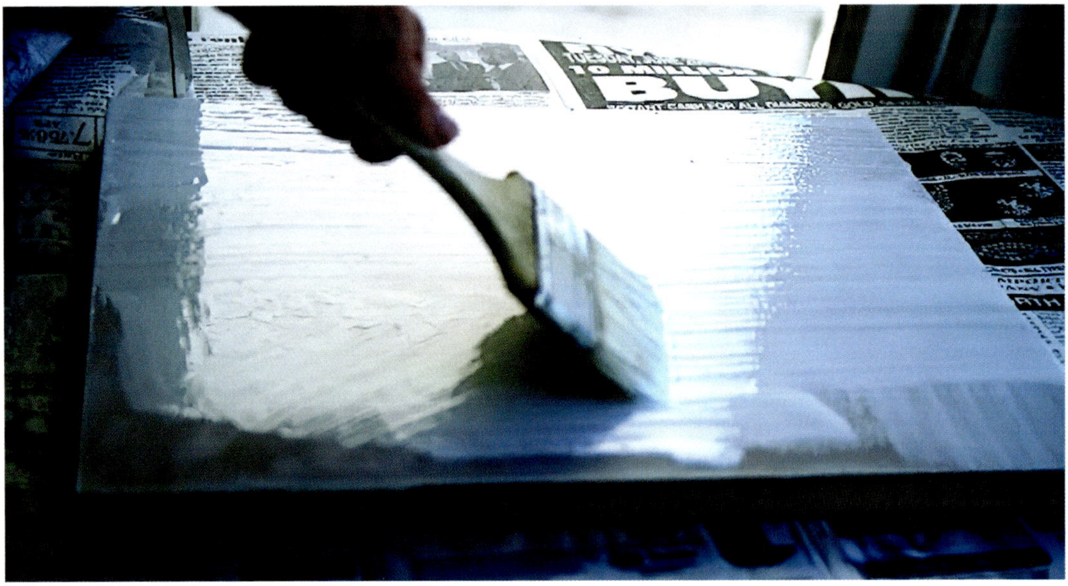

(ABOVE LEFT) Chalk (whiting)
(ABOVE RIGHT) Straining gesso
(ABOVE) Brushing on warm gesso
(RIGHT) Gesso panels drying

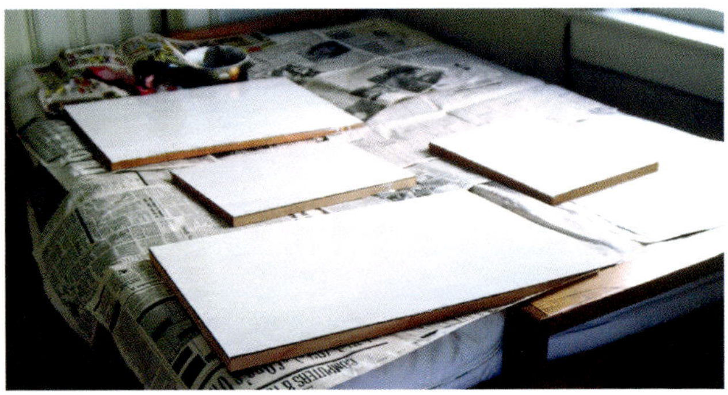

Next, the chalk or marble dust is sifted into the warm glue. Sometimes, a small amount of white pigment, such as titanium, is added to the white substance to make the finished gesso more opaque. The gesso needs to be strained before use—cheesecloth or a metal sieve are typically used.

About eight coats of gesso are applied with a brush, alternating layers between vertical and horizontal brushstrokes. When the gesso is no longer shiny, it's time for the next layer; all layers are applied over the course of a single day, which probably helps prevent separation of the layers. After a day or two, when the gesso is completely dry, I sand the panels using progressively finer sandpaper.

Transfer to the University of California, Santa Cruz

As I approached my senior year, I realized that UC Berkeley was too vast an environment for me. I had not made meaningful contact with professors, and my self-confidence was at a low ebb. I was accepted as a transfer student at the University of California at Santa Cruz (UCSC). UCSC is modeled after the University of Oxford and the University of Cambridge in England. In both institutions, smaller colleges make up the greater university. I enrolled in the arts college, now called Porter College, and for the first time, I encountered professors who recognized my artistic spark.

One professor who encouraged me was Jasper Rose. Prof. Rose passed away in 2019 after a long retirement in his native England, where he spent his days painting in watercolor. But I remember him as a flamboyant teacher of art history who sported professorial robes and a cane at every lecture. A graduate of King's College, Cambridge, he was a founding faculty member who helped establish the Oxford/Cambridge model at UCSC.

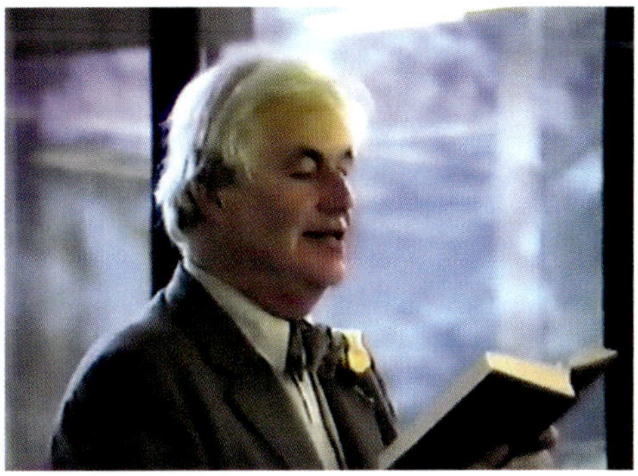

(ABOVE) Jasper Rose reading selections of his favorite poetry on the occasion of his retirement from UCSC, 1986. Photographer unknown

The course I took from Prof. Rose was about the Arts and Crafts (A&C) movement. The A&C movement was a trend in the decorative and fine arts which started in the British Isles about 1860 and spread to the rest of Europe and America between 1880 and 1920. It was a response to industrialization that hearkened back to traditional craftsmanship and advocated economic and social reform.

For our final project, we could choose between writing a paper or creating a project in the spirit of the A&C movement. I wrote a paper titled *A History of Roman Calligraphy.* Like a medieval scribe, I spent countless hours calligraphing the text into book format. I had previously studied calligraphy but had never undertaken such an ambitious project.

On our final day, Prof. Rose called out the names of students who had submitted outstanding projects. He recognized my accomplishment by giving me a page from an antique volume of spider illustrations! Sadly, I have since lost the page.

Hardy Hanson was the other professor who encouraged me at UCSC. A year after graduating, I visited Prof. Hanson in his home.[11] When I informed him that I planned to become a nurse, he exclaimed, "That's a tragedy!" I heard this as a forceful expression of confidence in my art and dismay that I would be veering off my true path. At times, his words reverberate when I feel my day job as a nurse interferes with my artistic aspirations.

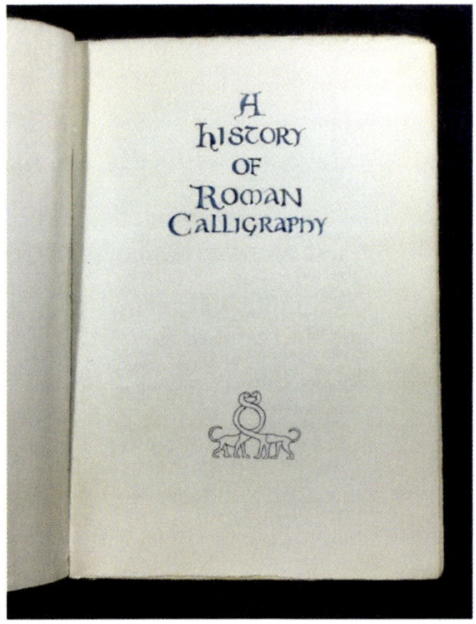

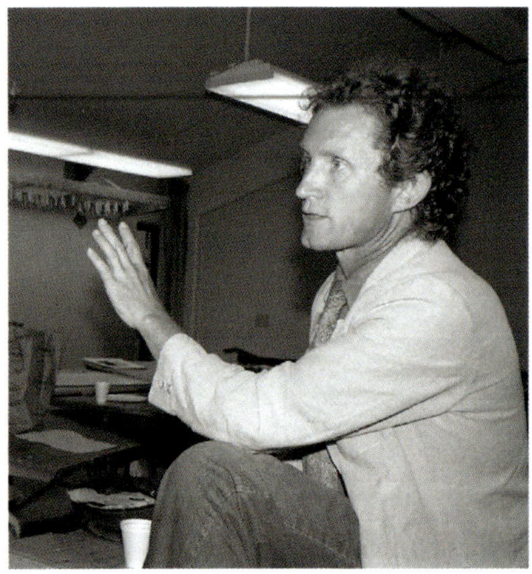

(ABOVE) *A History of Roman Calligraphy*, 1971. Marjorie G. and Carl W. Stern Book Arts & Special Collections Center, San Francisco Public Library

(BELOW) Hardy Hanson, professor of art at UC Santa Cruz, c. 1985. Prof. Hanson passed away in 2012. Photo by Andrew Neuhart.

(OPPOSITE) *Self-Portrait on Orange Paper*, c. 1970. India ink on toned paper, 12 × 9½ in. (30.4 × 24.1 cm). Painted in Hardy Hanson's class at UCSC

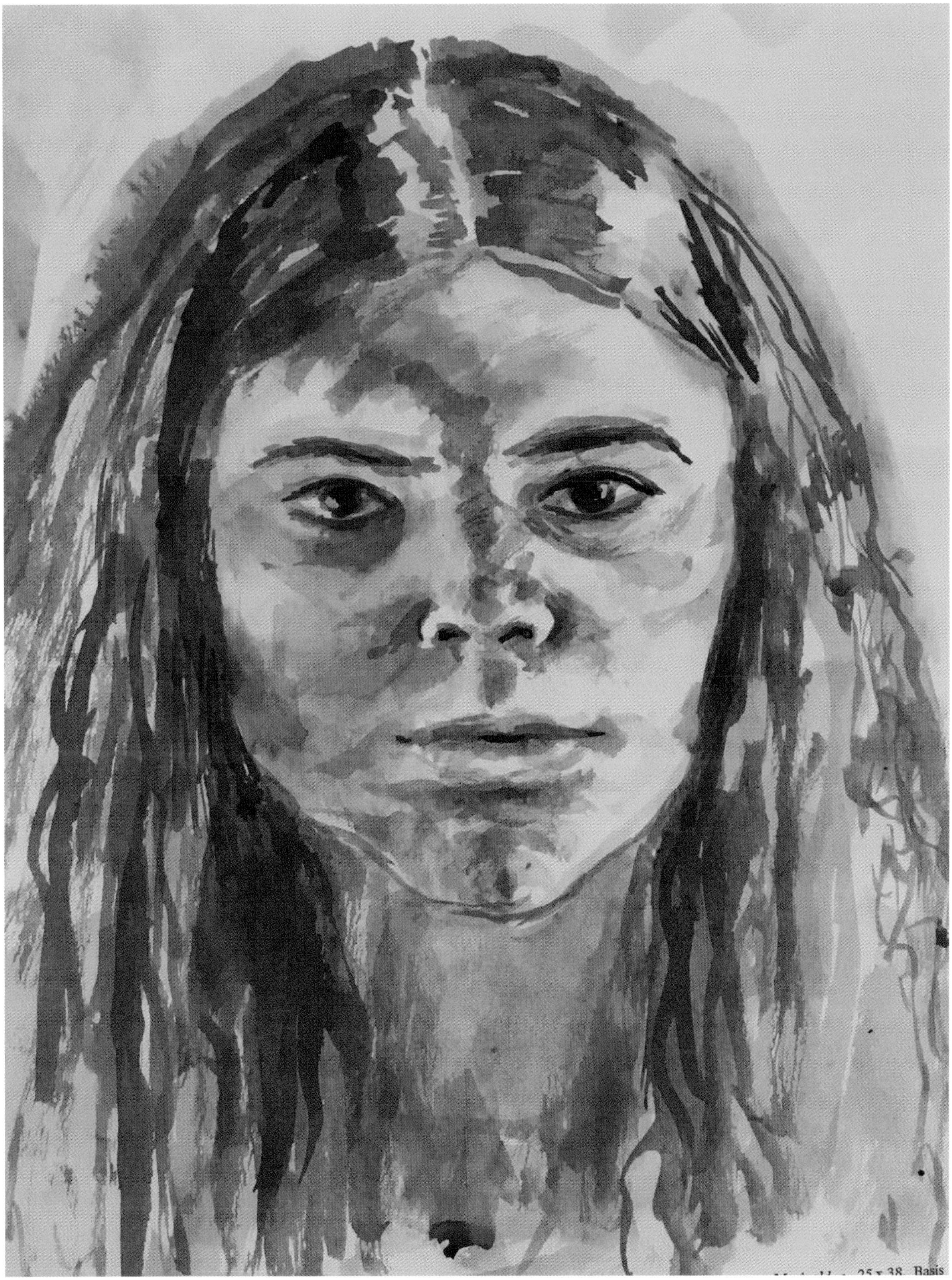

25 x 38. Basis

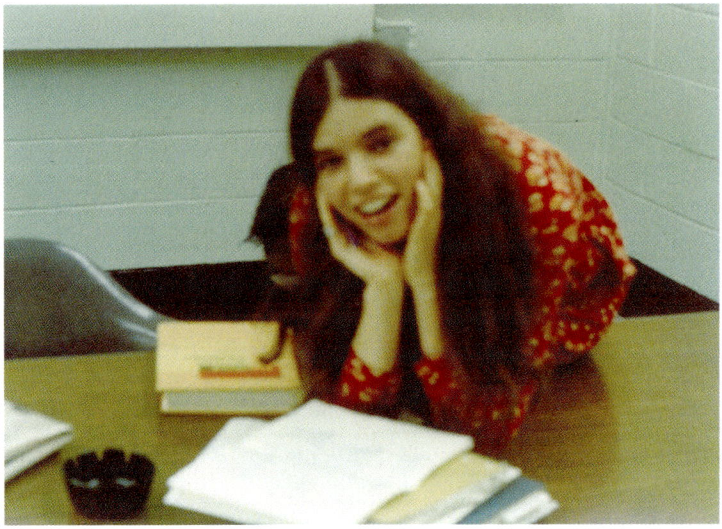

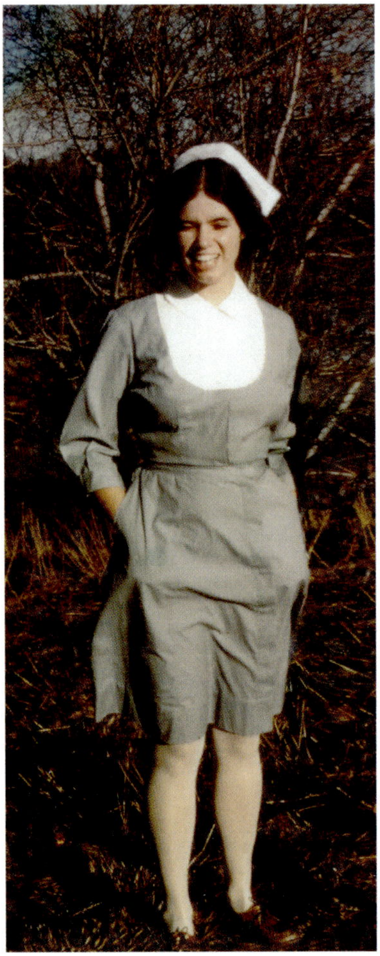

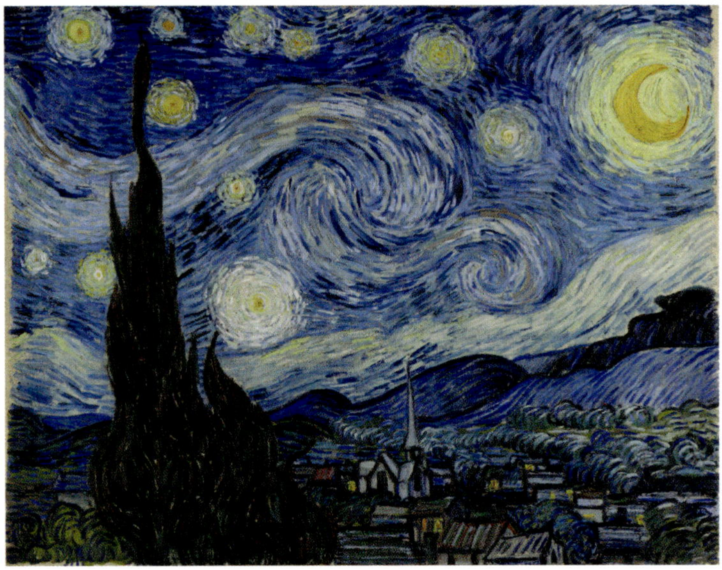

(ABOVE RIGHT) Hitting the books in nursing school, 1972

(LEFT) Nursing school graduation, 1974. Photo by Al Goldbaum.

(BELOW RIGHT) Vincent van Gogh, *The Starry Night*, 1889. Oil on canvas, 29 × 36¼ in. (73.6 × 92 cm). Museum of Modern Art, New York City

CHAPTER FOUR

ADVENTURES IN NURSING SCHOOL

After graduating from college in 1971, I became interested in how mental illness may enhance creativity.[12] Vincent van Gogh, for example, was a creative genius who suffered from mental illness. Hoping to find relief from the mental disorder that tortured him, in 1889, Van Gogh admitted himself to the Saint Paul de Mausole Asylum in Saint Rémy, in southern France. *Starry Night* was inspired by the view out his window, and he painted many versions of it.

I had a theory that art created by people with mental illness might dazzle if professional art supplies were available instead of the cheap student-grade materials normally stocked in institutional facilities.

I presented my idea to an administrator at Napa State Hospital, a large psychiatric facility. At that time, I had no professional credentials nor any connection to the hospital, so I was surprised that they permitted me to carry out my plan. I was ushered into a room and left alone with a few patients. I distributed professional art supplies and was enthused by the vibrant colors and designs in the drawings they created with oil pastels.

I did not return to Napa State Hospital, but weeks later, I spent a day volunteering at a community mental health center where a friend was doing his psychotherapy internship. I noticed several female staffers talking to the patients—they were not wearing uniforms—not even name tags. I thought, "I could see myself doing this." (It was becoming clear that my art was not going to pay the rent.)

I later found out that they were registered nurses. My negative stereotype of a nurse in a starched white uniform and cap was dashed, and I started to explore the idea of becoming a nurse. While living in Berkeley, I had studied native plants and enjoyed concocting herbal teas to care for friends who were ill, so the idea of nursing appealed to me.

My parents were not thrilled, as they associated nursing with menial tasks such as emptying bedpans—they much preferred that I follow their path into teaching. But the working-class cachet of nursing appealed to me. In later years, my parents let me know they were proud of me. My dad loved quoting the Gallup poll that ranked nursing as "the most trusted profession" for many years running.

I also explored art therapy and medical illustration as possible career paths, but I settled on nursing because of its versatility. Indeed, in my fifty years of nursing, I have worked in a variety of roles: research nurse, breast cancer patient advocate, telephone advice nurse, nurse practitioner, editorial director of a nursing magazine, nursing care manager, opioid safety nurse, and several others.

Back to New York City

During the intense, idealistic years of the sixties, I believed a worldwide transformation in consciousness was unfolding. But by 1971, it became clear to me that the dream had collapsed. I left Berkeley and moved back to New York City. And although I had almost no experience with illness or hospitals, I followed through on my plan to become a registered nurse.

I enrolled in a school that catered to students who had already completed non-nursing college degrees. This was one of the first ELMSN (Entry Level Master of Science in Nursing) programs. It was called the Graduate School of Nursing, now part of the Lienhard School of Nursing at Pace University.

Concerned whether I could handle the sight of blood and a patient in pain, I challenged myself to watch a painful procedure when my mother was in the hospital. My reaction was a reassuring disinterest and a stirring of empathy.

I had naively thought nurse training would be learning basic skills such as applying bandages, hanging IV bottles, and assisting doctors—I was not prepared for the intensity. Modern nursing education felt more like what I'd imagined the rigors of medical school to be. In the first grueling weeks, I was relieved to find myself fascinated by medical science and the art of nursing.

Florence Nightingale, "The Lady with the Lamp"

Before studying nursing, I was not aware of the rigorous evidence-based foundation of the profession that began with Florence Nightingale. Before Nightingale's work, nursing was viewed as menial work performed by untrained women. As an upper-class English woman, she had to go against her family and society to pursue nursing.

Nightingale is most known for her role during the Crimean War between Great Britain and Russia, where the troops were dying in great numbers from infectious diseases—much more than from battleground trauma. She introduced handwashing, sterilization of medical equipment, and a system for recording patient data, thus dramatically reducing the mortality rate. She also emphasized the importance of patient-centered care, including comforting and supporting patients psychologically. Nightingale was called "The Lady with the Lamp" based on her reputation for making rounds at all hours of the night.

When she returned to England, Nightingale founded the first nursing school, which became a model for nursing education worldwide. Her legacy continues to influence nursing education and practice to this day. At the medical center where I work, we joyously celebrate Nurses' Week around the occasion of Nightingale's birthday, May 12, 1820.

But in spite of the foundation laid by Nightingale, as recently as fifty years ago, there were far fewer university-based bachelor's or master's degree nursing programs in the US. Since the 1870s, most training had taken place in diploma nursing programs in which students were housed on the grounds of a hospital. Rigorous clinical training was easily integrated into the curriculum, but the absence of university-based education contributed to a lack of respect for the nursing profession.

Increasing academic requirements have advanced the profession—but have perhaps resulted in some decline in the skills of direct patient care.

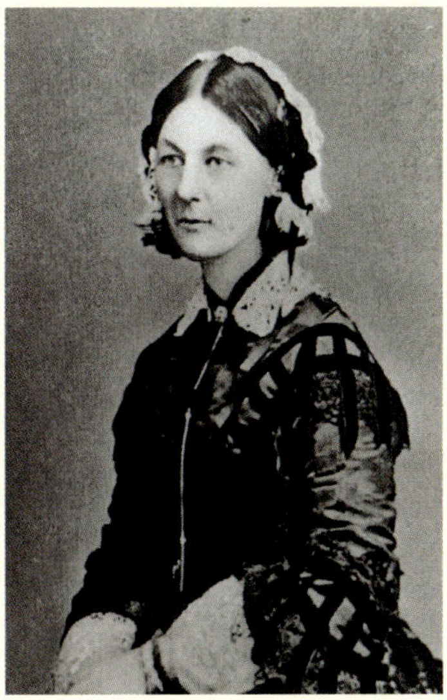

(RIGHT) Florence Nightingale. Date and photographer unknown.

Student Nurse

My first clinical rotation was at Bird S. Coler Hospital, a public facility on Welfare Island (renamed Roosevelt Island in 1973) that provided long-term care for people with chronic or disabling conditions.

I stayed with my aunt Clara at her apartment in Lower Manhattan so I could be on the floor, in uniform, at 7 a.m.

My first patient was an eighty-something woman named Miss Weigert. As I bent over to change her diaper, she produced a giant tarry black bowel movement right beneath my face. I later learned that the tar-like consistency was caused by the iron supplement she was taking. Later that week, while lunching in the cafeteria, a few of us student nurses found ourselves blithely discussing diarrhea. That's when I thought, "I feel like a real nurse now!"

Miss Elizabeth E. Plummer, our main instructor and mentor, delivered an intense message to us: "Put the patient first, be caring, and build on strong nursing ethics and skills."[13] While modern nursing theory espouses "professional distancing," her philosophy was rooted in love. She encouraged us to hug and kiss our patients, although today it would be against regulations, for good reason. She also preached, "Singing is good for the lungs."[14]

My most memorable patients were Bernie Leight and Despina "Peppie" Vafiadis. Bernie explained, "We used to be an item, but now we're just friends." Both were wheelchair users, Bernie with cerebral palsy, and Peppie with multiple sclerosis.

Bernie gave nursing students an orientation talk in his booming voice, concluding with "We don't want your sympathy—we want your empathy." Bernie had a spastic type of cerebral palsy that caused his arms to flail out uncontrollably unless tied down with fabric restraints. I had to wrestle his arms while giving him his morning bath. He took it in good humor, belting out instructions all the while. Peppie was almost entirely paralyzed, needing total care.

When Peppie told me of her Greek heritage, it bruised my soul to see her surviving on a diet of bland hospital food. Although the sixties were now in my past, the spirit of "question authority" stayed with me. I cooked up a plan to take Peppie to a Greek restaurant. My fellow

---

(TOP LEFT) Aerial photograph of Roosevelt Island, located in the East River off of Manhattan Island in New York City. Photo by Cameron Davidson.

(TOP RIGHT) Miss Elizabeth M. Plummer, MA, RN. Date and photographer unknown.

(BELOW) *Portrait of Aunt Clara Goren*, 1971. Ink wash on colored paper, 12 × 15 in. (30.4 × 38.1 cm)

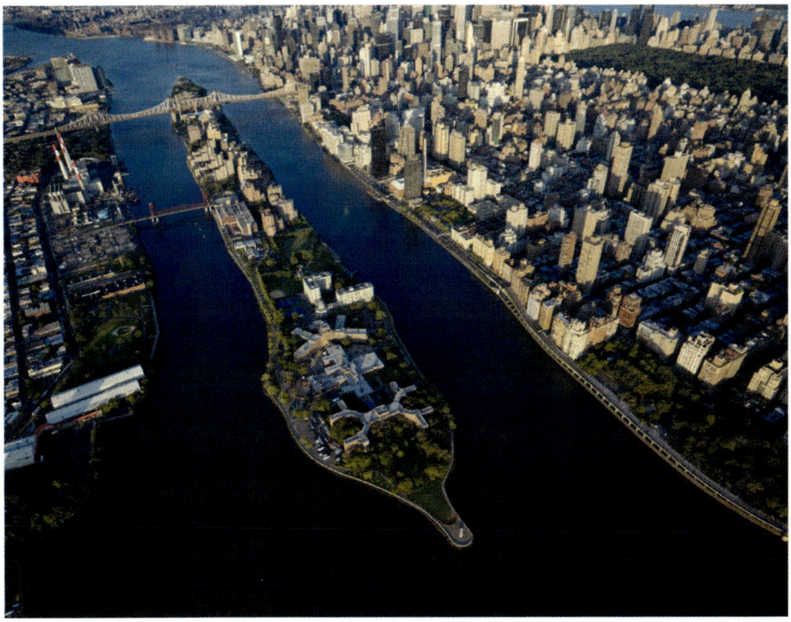

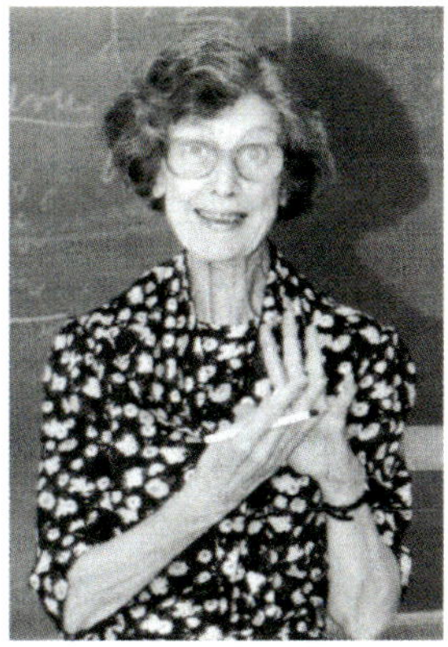

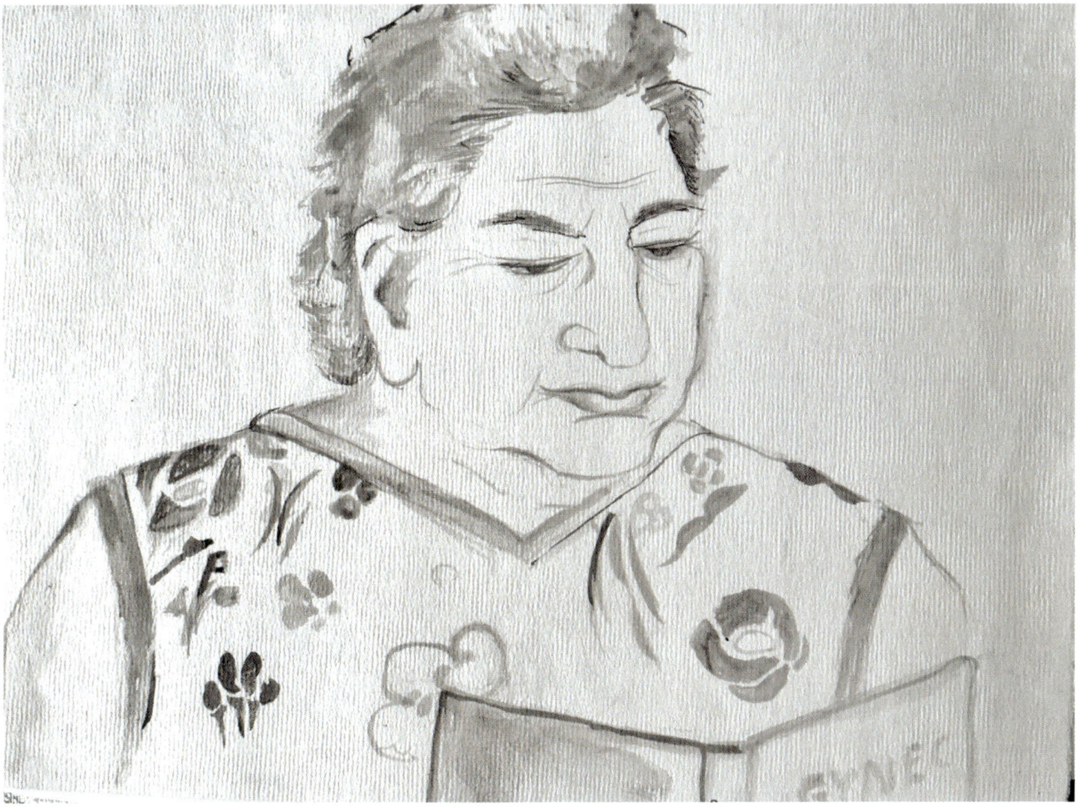
GYNEC

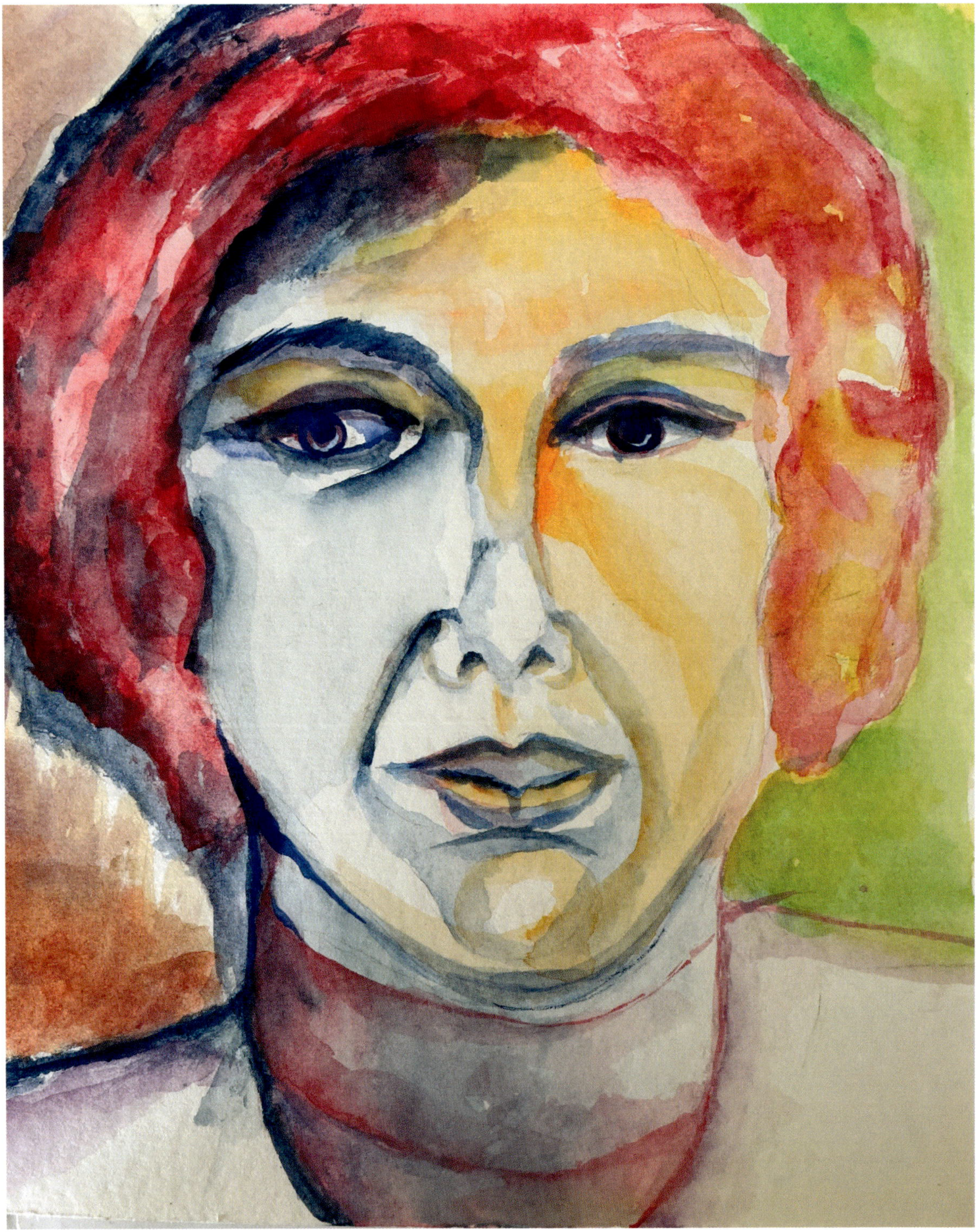

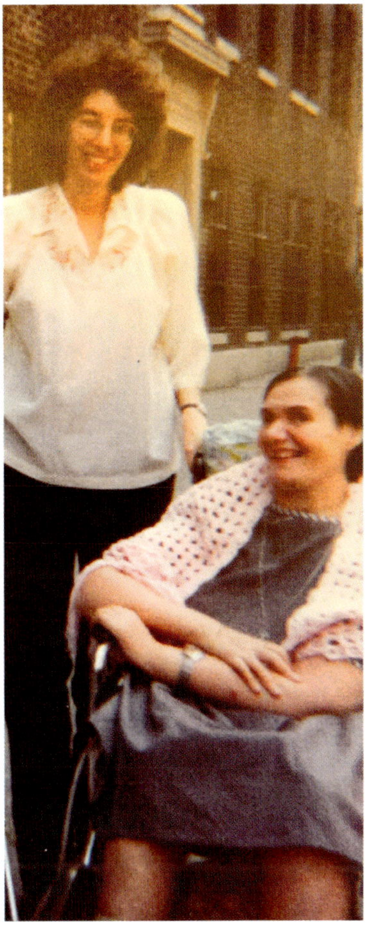

nursing student Carol Cruickshank was my enthusiastic co-conspirator, and we obtained permission to hire a van equipped to drive two adults with disabilities to the restaurant Symposium on the Upper West Side of Manhattan.

Arriving at our destination, our hearts sank when we saw a narrow staircase leading down to the restaurant. But a flock of Greek waiters suddenly appeared and carried Peppie and Bernie down the stairs in their wheelchairs. I don't recall the meal, perhaps because we were busy spoon-feeding Bernie and Peppie, but Carol remembers that they greatly enjoyed it.

This event planted a seed, and within the next few years, both Bernie and Peppie were able to leave the hospital and live independently with caregivers.[15]

Years later, I visited Peppie in her small, dark apartment in a marginal neighborhood in Brooklyn. I felt perhaps she would have been better off staying in the nursing facility. I asked her, and without any hesitation, she replied that she much preferred living independently with a caregiver.

Although I did not paint during those years of intense training, much of my future subject matter would be mined from my new profession.

(ABOVE) Despina "Peppie" Vafiadas with Carol Cruickshank, c. 1975. Photographer unknown.

(OPPOSITE) *Portrait of Carol Cruickshank*, c. 1978. Watercolor on paper, 12 × 10 in. (30.4 × 25.4 cm)

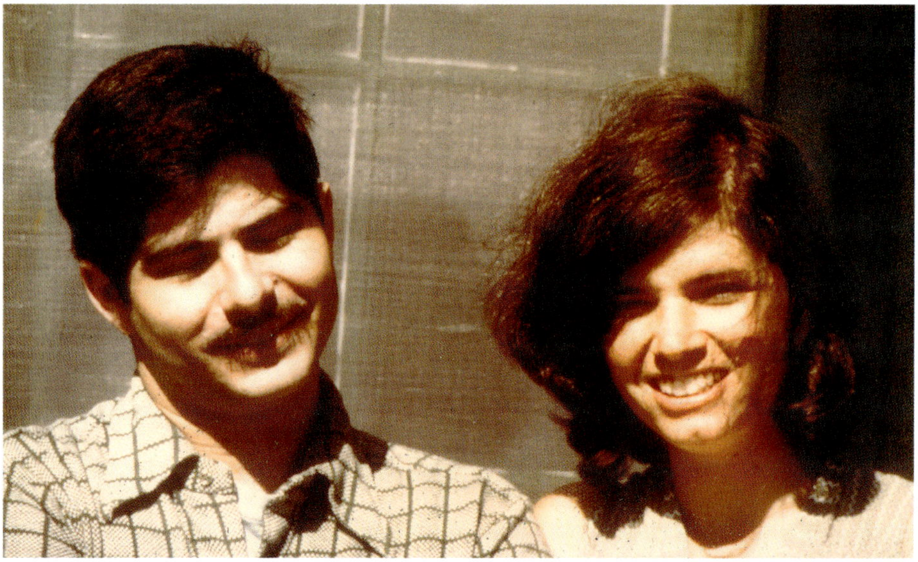

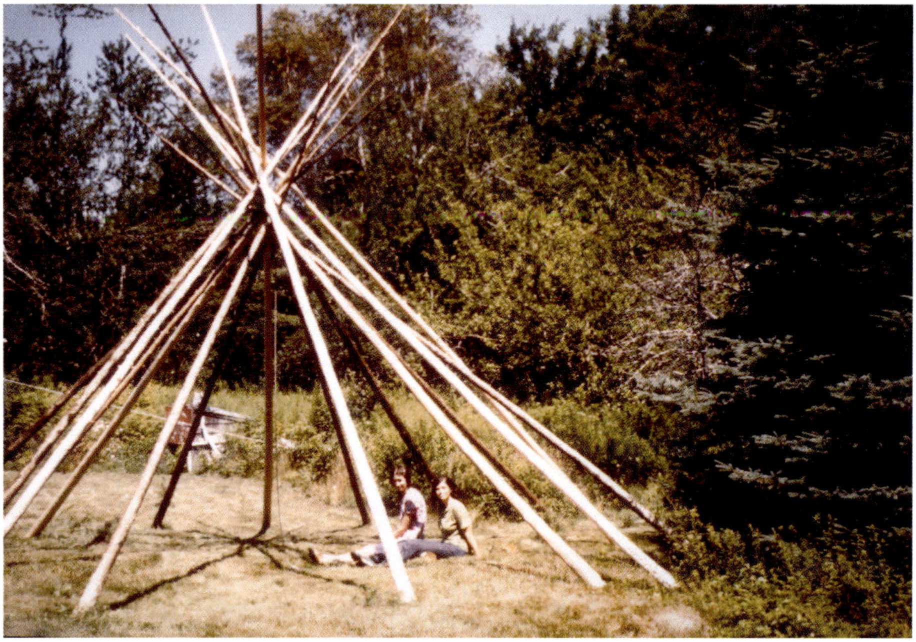

(ABOVE) Me and Peter Wharton, c. 1974

(BELOW) Cedar poles drying

(OPPOSITE LEFT) Sawing down cedar trees with Ginny Poland on her land

(OPPOSITE RIGHT) Cottage in Sandy Point, Maine

CHAPTER FIVE

TIPI TIME: LIFE IN RURAL MAINE

For some time, I had yearned to live in the country, and soon after graduation, I attended a seminar designed to attract health professionals to rural areas. The images of Maine were especially entrancing. At the conference, I met Peter Wharton, a recent graduate of a physician assistant program.[16] Peter and I fell in love and, weeks later, moved to a cottage on the banks of the Penobscot River, in the tiny village of Sandy Point, Maine.

But after about a year, my life in Maine felt more suburban than rural. I longed to live outdoors and be closer to nature. I admired Native American culture and decided to construct a tipi in the Sioux tradition. I borrowed an industrial sewing machine that Peter's father had used to repair sails for his boat and began sewing oceans of canvas. At this point, Peter and I broke up due to lifestyle differences—and, in retrospect, my emotional immaturity.

I sawed down and stripped the bark off of cedar poles harvested from a friend's land.

Another friend invited me to set up my tipi on his property. When hoisted up on the poles, the tipi stood eighteen feet where the poles crossed and eighteen feet in diameter at the base.

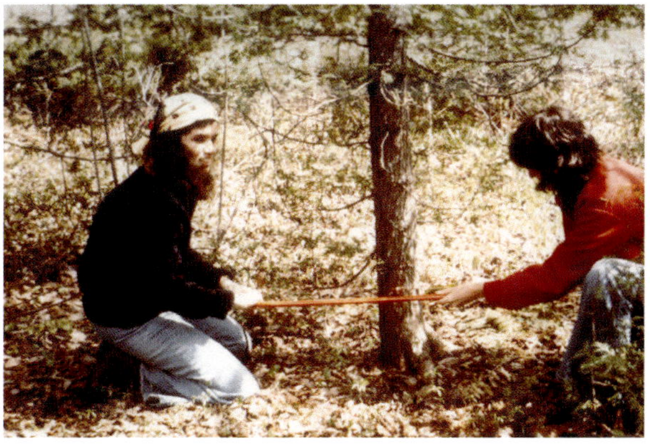

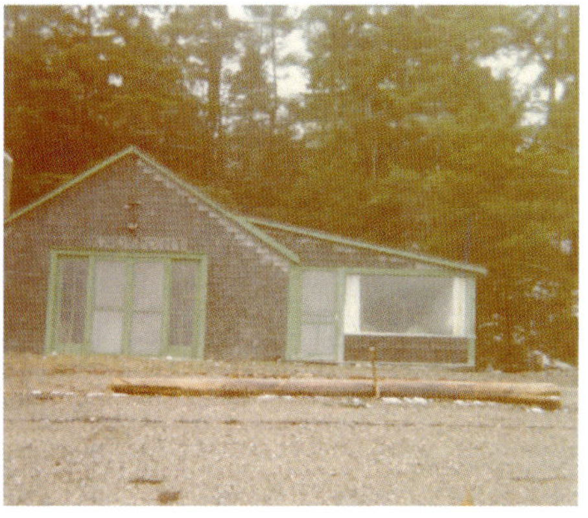

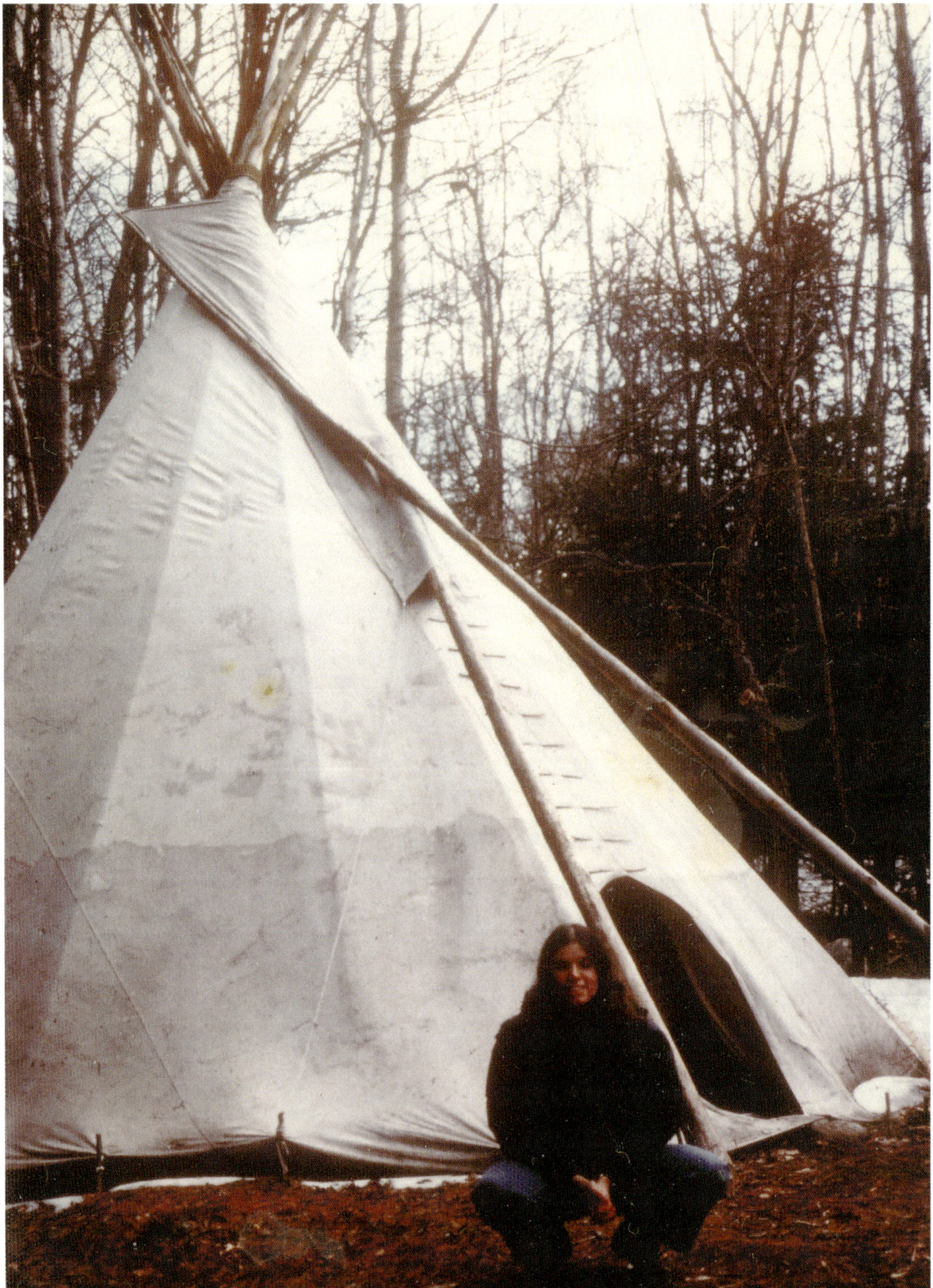

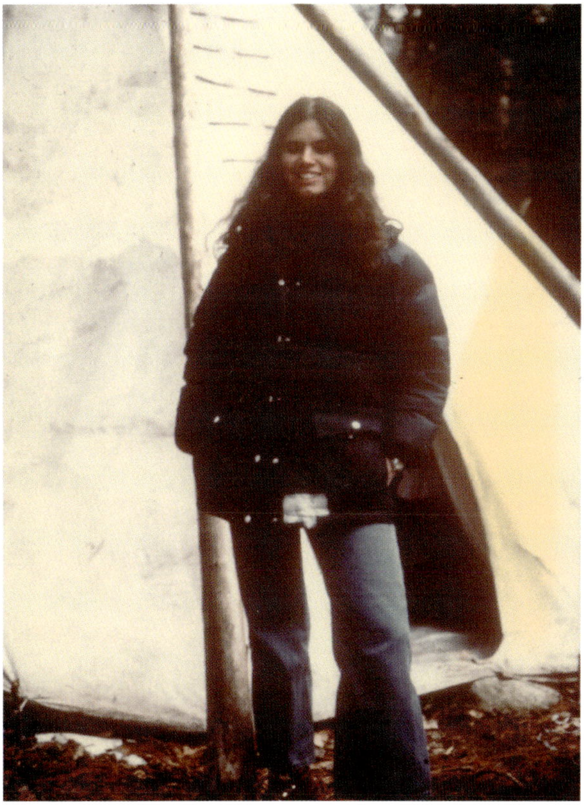 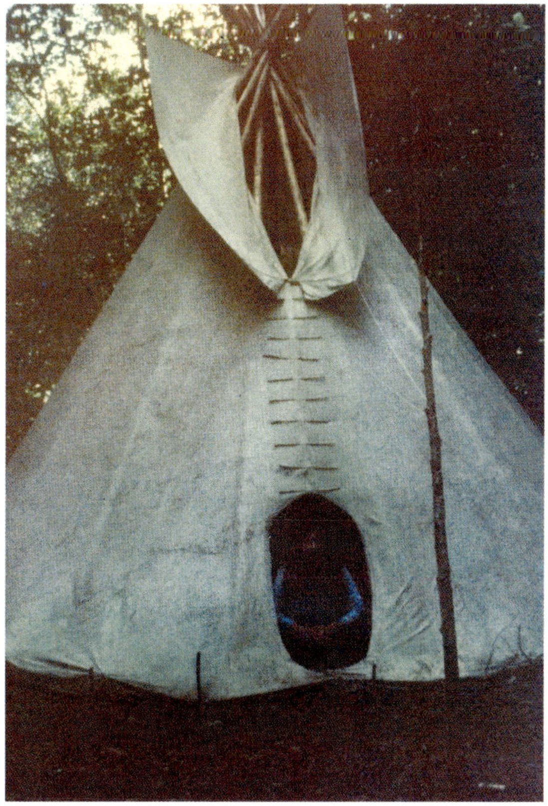

I lived in my tipi over two extended summers, retreating to a rented house for the intense winter months. I learned to cook in a fire pit, set the smoke flaps, bathe in a tin tub, and go to the "bathroom" in the great outdoors.

A joyful aspect of living close to nature was experiencing myself as just another woodland creature. The three images in the *Process of Elimination* series (FOLLOWING PAGES) reflect a lack of self-consciousness about bodily functions.

In *Nature's Call*, the cross design of the wooden planks was not meant as a reference to Christianity, as some viewers interpreted it, but perhaps presages a future theme in my work of sanctifying the seemingly profane.

(ABOVE LEFT) Standing with my tipi, c 1976. Photo by Al Goldbaum.

(ABOVE RIGHT) The tipi with smoke flaps open, me barely visible in doorway

(OPPOSITE) Checking on my tipi in the winter, smoke flaps closed, c. 1976. Photo by Al Goldbaum.

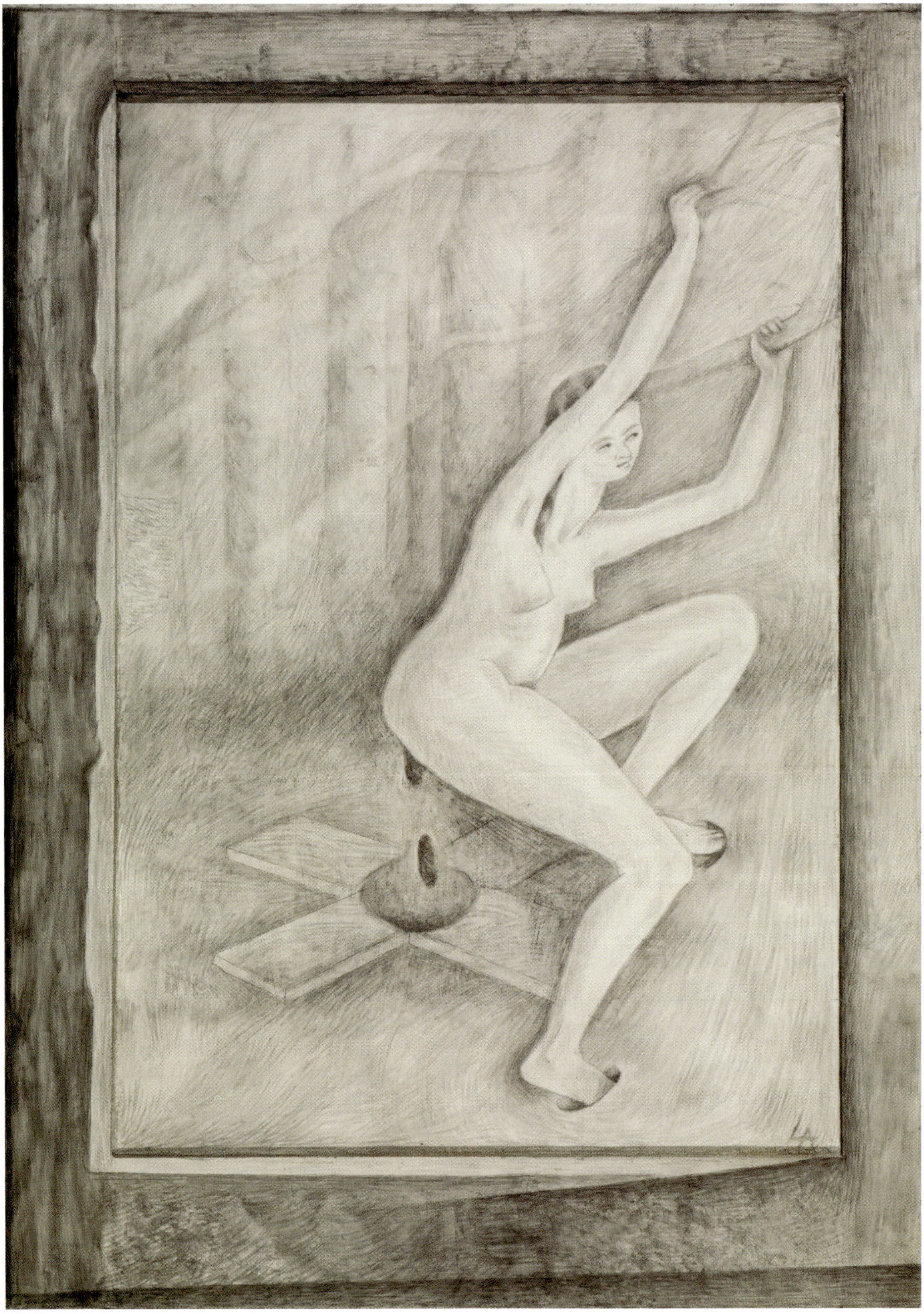

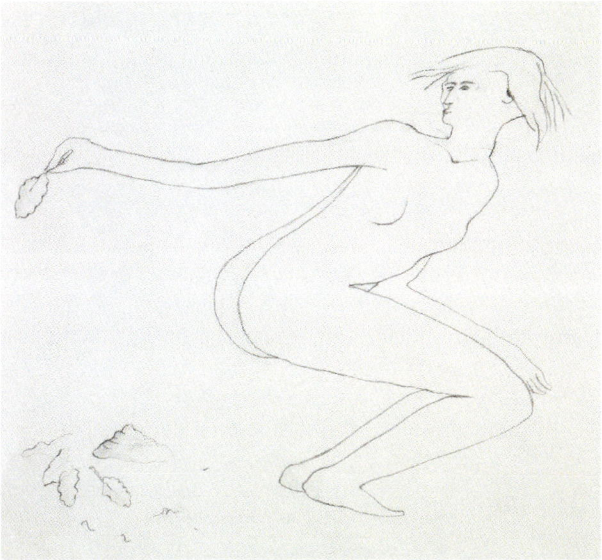

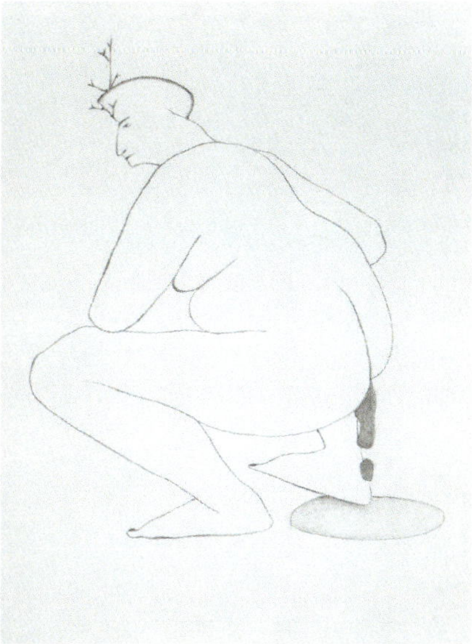

Nature's Call was intended to be an underpainting for a full-color rendering, but I became attached to the fine feathery markings and lacked the courage to complete it in egg tempera.

Wiping With a Leaf is a literal representation of what a camper might use as a toilet paper substitute, but the drawing captures the superior aesthetics of the leaf over toilet paper.

The figure in *Crown of Branches* came to me as a half-woman, half-woodland creature. It's a subtle reference to Christ's crown of thorns, but with a gentle pastoral feeling.

I'VE ALWAYS FELT close to nature, and living in my tipi intensified this feeling. In *Limb to Limb*, (FOLLOWING PAGES, LEFT) the limbs of a tree are intertwined with the limbs of a human, creating a cross-species romance.

In *Fertile Flesh* (FOLLOWING PAGES, RIGHT), the flower literally grows out of the flesh of the woman's belly, obliterating the separation between human and nature. Some women have told me that they placed reproductions of this image on their personal altars in preparation for childbirth.

(OPPOSITE) ***Nature's Call***, c. 1988. Chinese ink stick on gesso panel, 17 × 12 in. (14.3 × 30.4 cm)

(ABOVE LEFT) ***Wiping with a Leaf***, c. 1976. Pencil on paper, 8½ × 11 in. (21.5 × 27.9 cm)

(ABOVE RIGHT) ***Crown of Branches***, c. 1976. Pencil on paper, 11 × 8½ in. (27.9 × 21.5 cm)

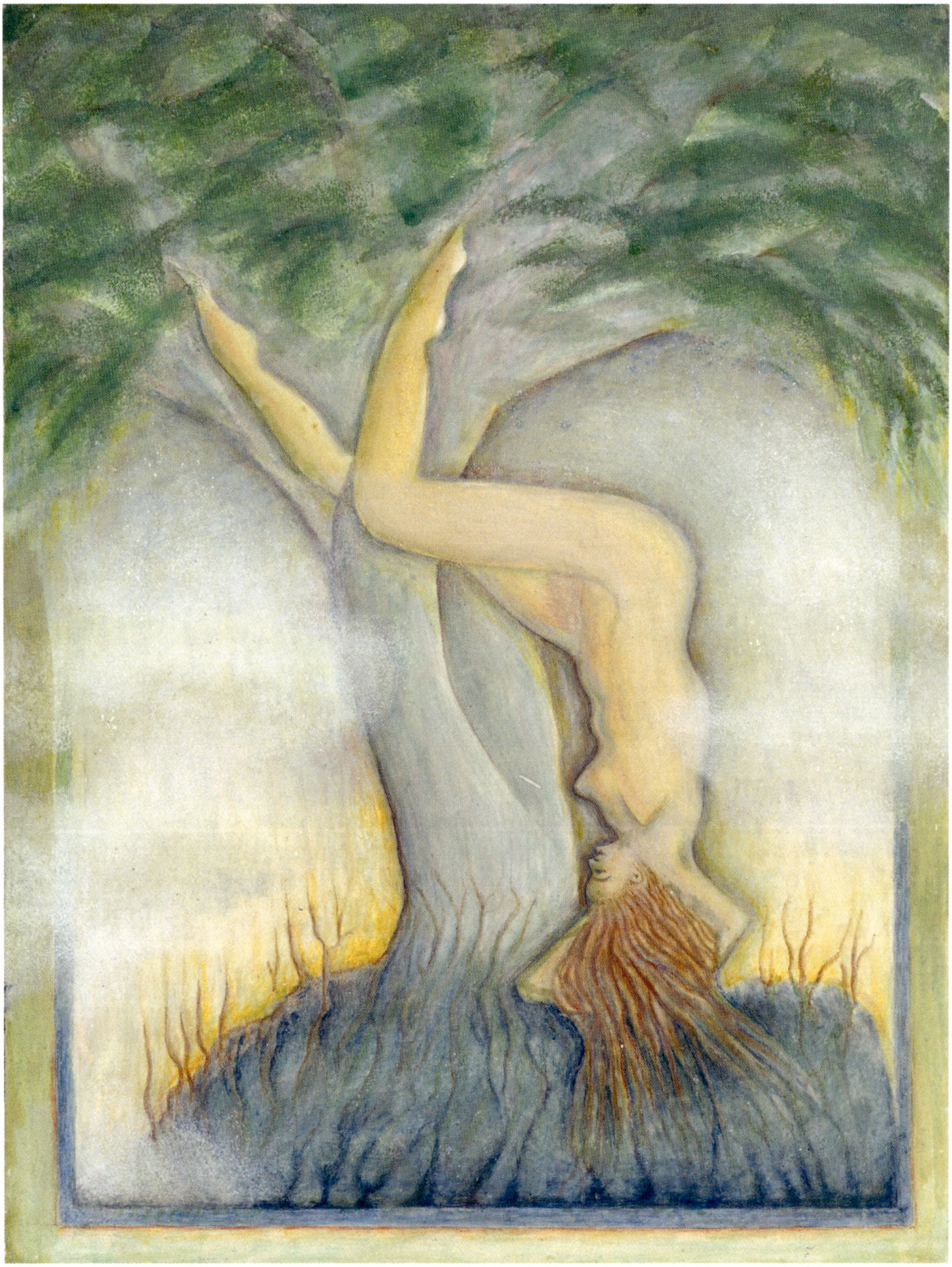

(ABOVE) ***Limb to Limb,*** c. 1989. Egg tempera on gesso panel, 15 × 11 in. (38.1 × 27.9 cm)

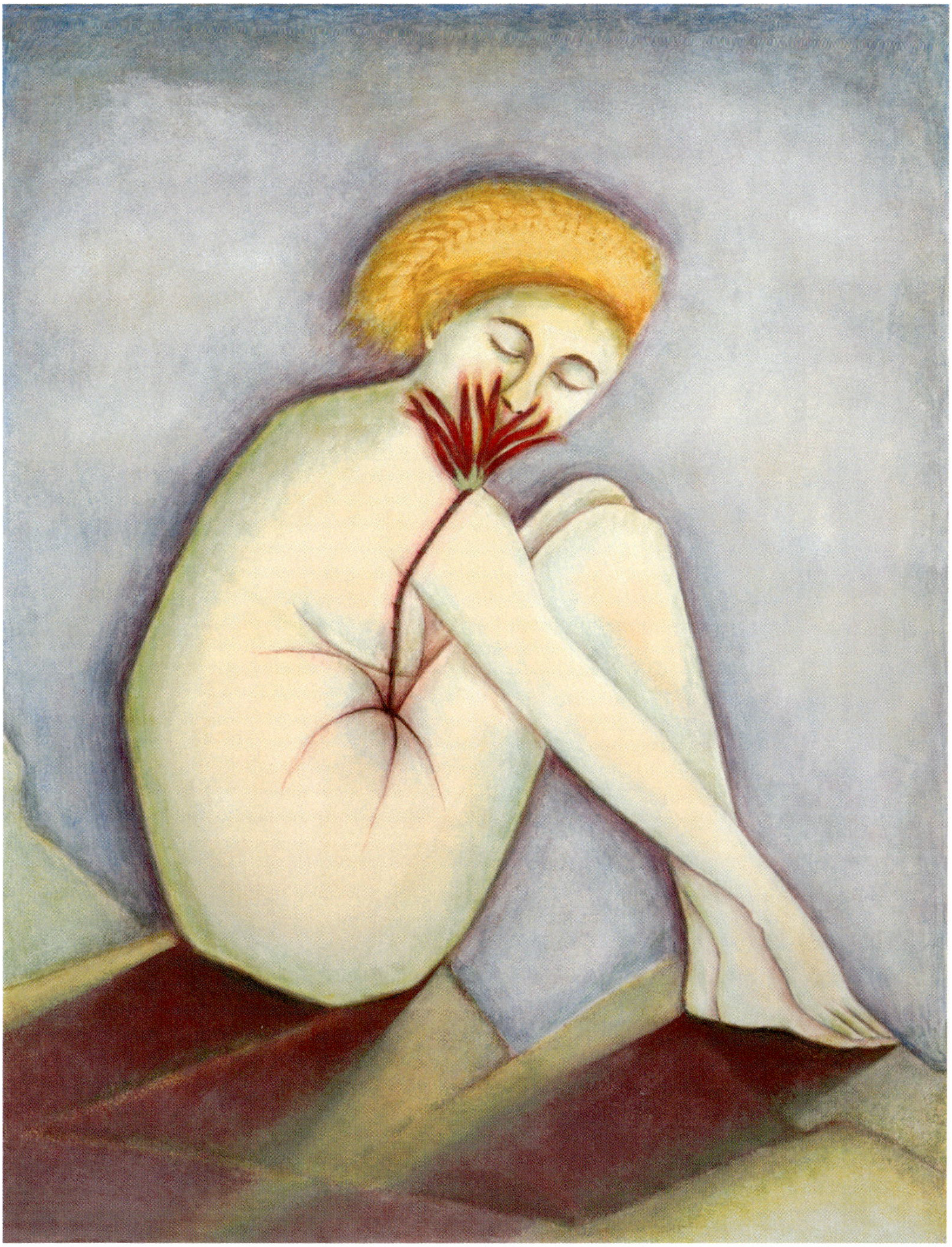

(ABOVE) *Fertile Flesh,* c. 1990. Egg tempera on gesso panel, 20 × 16 in. (50.8 × 40.6 cm)

About the poetry:
My dear friend Ilse Lehnert first wrote this and other poems included in this book to accompany my paintings at an exhibition at Studio For in 1998.[17]

LIMB TO LIMB

peaks and valleys
woman's depths
bowing to
demands of life
take root
bloom

—ILSE LEHNERT

While living in my tipi, I worked as a community health nurse visiting elderly Mainers in their homes. A memorable patient was Madeleine, who was terminally ill with cervical cancer. She shared a home with her sister-in-law Helen, who cared for her. The two widows had been married to brothers and were very close.

Madeleine's cancer had metastasized to her intestines, and she was given a colostomy. Unfortunately, the appliance did not adhere well to her emaciated body. Helen would drive to a spot near my tipi and shout into the woods: "Madeleine is leaking!"—there were no cell phones in those days. Years later, I painted *Lovers with Colostomy.*

The image portrays a couple in an intimate moment. The colostomy is downplayed to evoke normalcy, yet it draws the eye and becomes the center of interest. The man is bald, echoing the theme of sensuality in the midst of imperfection. Mini airplanes suggest flying or swimming sperm. A viewer at open studios noted the man's head is positioned over the woman's heart, signifying an emotional bond. Another visitor suggested, "The man is listening to the woman's heartbeat."

But the first time I exhibited the painting, a woman came up to me and said, "I hate your painting, and your painting is me." She told me she has a permanent colostomy, which she hates, and resented that I was romanticizing colostomies. But more often, the painting has been acknowledged for its message of positivity and tenderness. My hope is that viewers might come away with a more expansive view of life, beyond the constraints of perceived normality.

(OPPOSITE) *Lovers with Colostomy,* c. 1992. Egg tempera on gesso panel, 16 × 12 in. (40.6 × 30.4 cm)

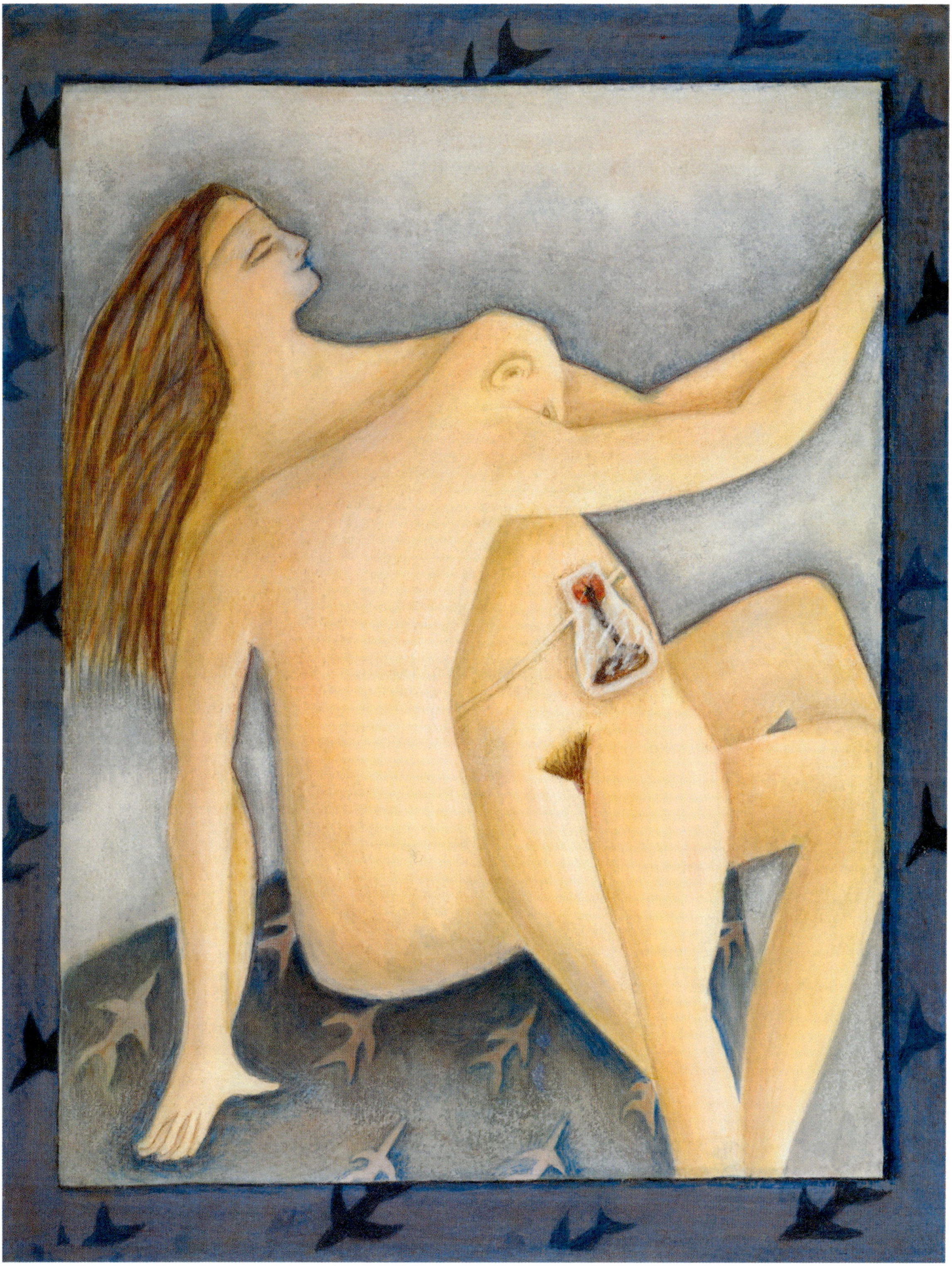

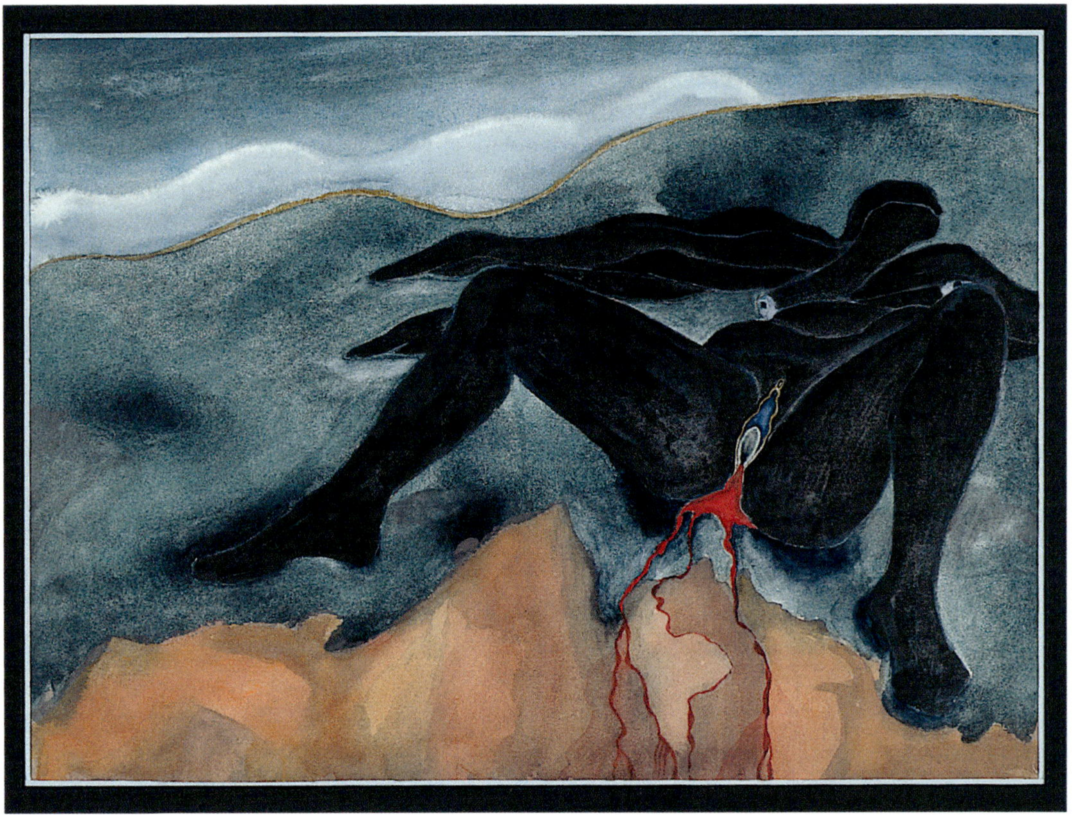

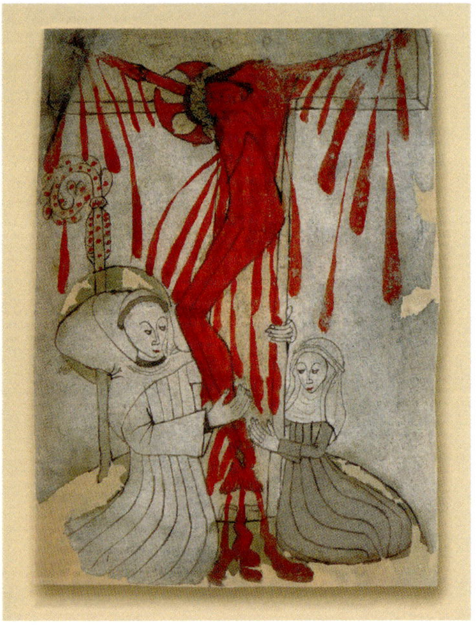

(ABOVE) *Woman Bleeding on Rocks*, c. 1981. Watercolor on paper, 10 × 14 in. (25.4 × 35.5 cm)

(RIGHT) Artist unknown, *The Vision of St. Bernard with Nun*, Lower Rhine, first half of 14th century. Pen and ink drawing on paper with color wash, 25¾ × 18¼ in. (25.8 cm × 18.2 cm). Museum Schnütgen, Cologne, Germany

(OPPOSITE) *Our Bodies, Our Selves*, 1971, printed on newsprint with stapled binding. This is the first edition (second printing).

CHAPTER SIX

THE BLOOD MYSTERIES

While living in Maine, I connected with women inspired by the women's health movement. *Women and Their Bodies* was a 193-page booklet self-published by a group of women in the Boston area in 1970. It dared to address topics of sexuality and reproductive health, including abortion. A year later, the title was changed to the now iconic *Our Bodies, Our Selves*—transforming the women's health movement worldwide. As of 2025, resources based on *Our Bodies, Our Selves* have been created in thirty-four languages.

In 1971, Carol Downer, Lorraine Rothman, and Belita Cowan were touring the country showing women how to view their own cervixes using a speculum, light, and mirror. Our group began holding similar meetings. Each evening culminated in one of us climbing onto a table and lifting our skirt (sans underwear) to display our cervix through a speculum for women in the audience to observe. My friends thought that my presence as an RN helped legitimize this unconventional "teach-in."[18]

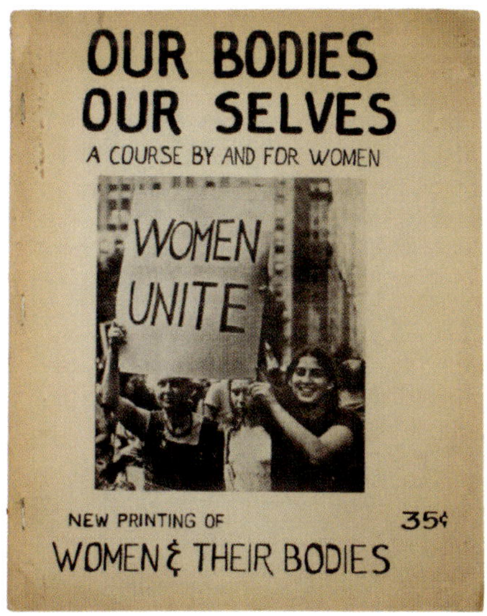

Liberating menstruation from the shadows was another aspect of the women's health movement. My ideas for menstrual-themed paintings emerged during this time of feminist activism.

The idea of the unfettered flowing of menstrual blood was the jumping-off point for many paintings in the series.

For most women, several days of monthly bleeding adds up to six to ten years of life spent menstruating. Yet the portrayal of this nonviolent bleeding in art is rare. Blood has been widely depicted throughout the history of art in battle scenes and in images of Christ bleeding on the cross.

The term "genre painting" is used to describe scenes of everyday life, such as cooking, bathing, and farming. Why not portray the colorful shedding of menstrual blood?

— In *Markings*, the woman is perhaps marking her territory with blood, as some animals do with their urine. Or maybe it's just a playful use of menstrual blood as body paint. Sometimes, I paint first and find out later what the painting is saying.

— In *Bleeding on a Sycamore Tree*, I continued my exploration of freely flowing menstrual blood, this time mingling the wine-red blood with the patchy, jigsaw puzzle-like pattern of the bark.[19]

— Not sure what I was thinking when I painted *Untitled*—perhaps a Lady Macbeth-ish "Out, damned spot!" scene but with menstrual blood?

— *Woman with Koala* evokes a multi-pawed, koala-like creature nuzzled on the shoulder of a menstruating woman.

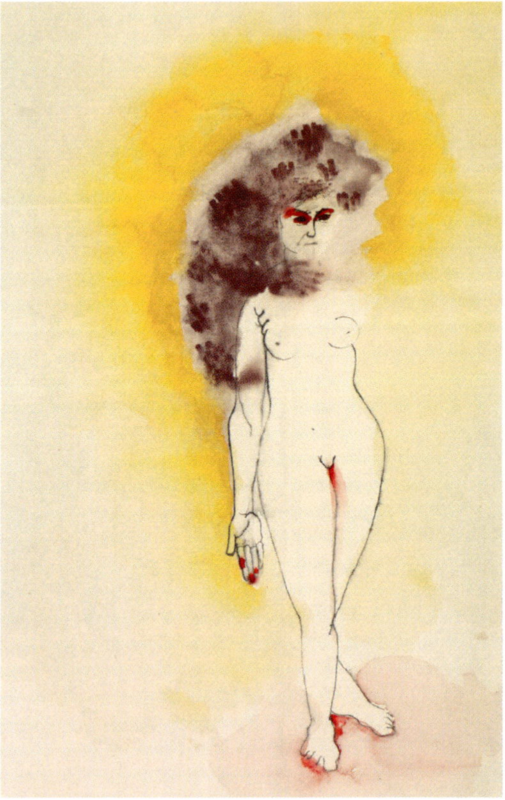

(RIGHT) ***Woman with Koala*,** c. 1980. Watercolor on paper, 15 × 9½ in. (38.1 × 24 cm)

(OPPOSITE LEFT) ***Bleeding on a Sycamore Tree*,** c. 1980. Watercolor on paper, 9½ × 5 in. (24.3 × 12.7 cm)

(OPPOSITE ABOVE RIGHT) ***Markings*,** c. 1980. Watercolor on paper, 13 × 11 in. (33 × 27.9 cm)

(OPPOSITE BELOW RIGHT) ***Untitled*,** c. 1980. Watercolor on paper, 13 × 8½ in. (33 × 21.5 cm)

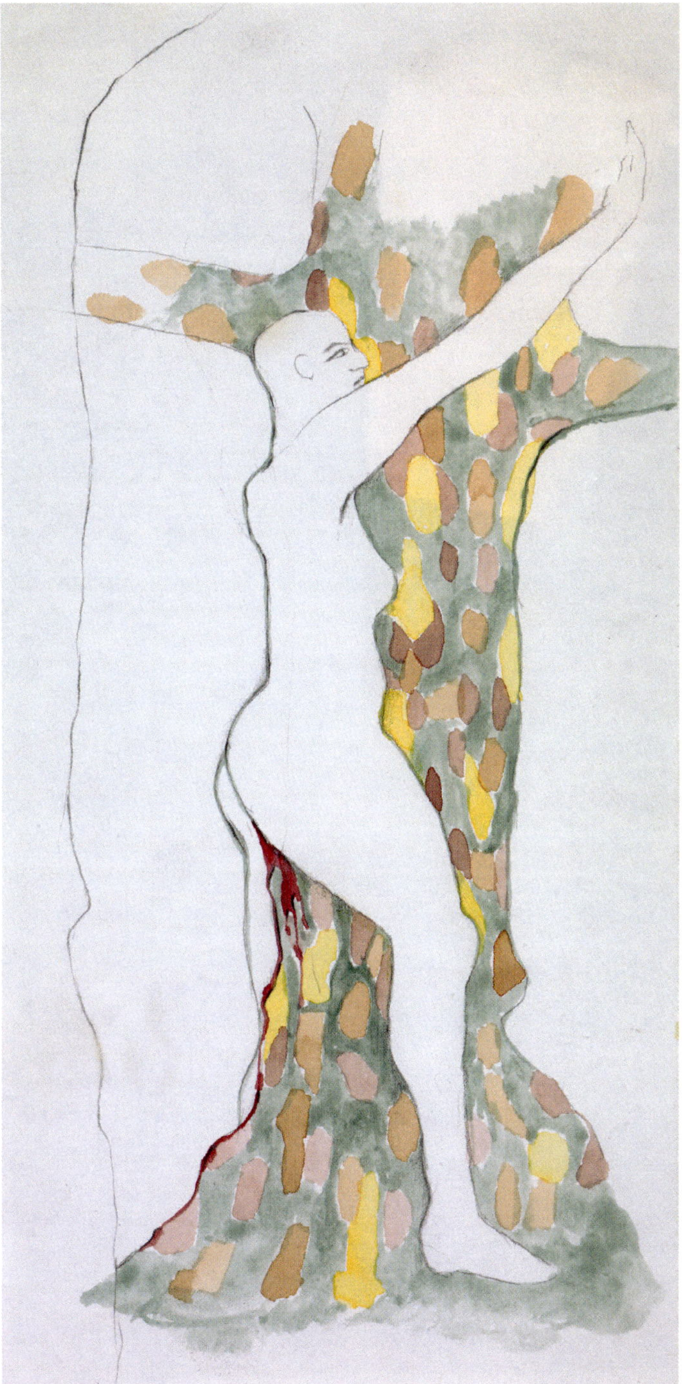

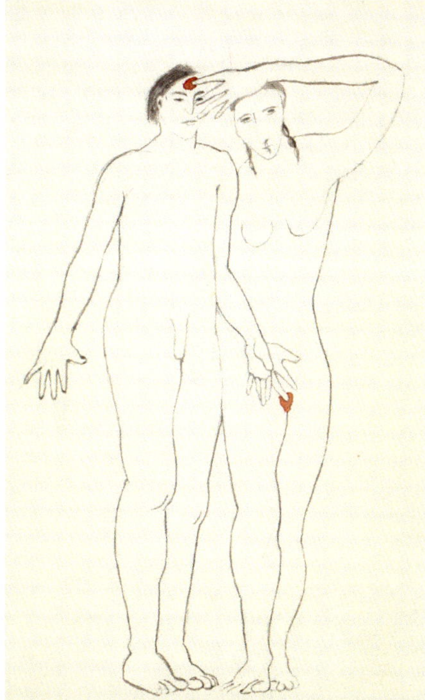

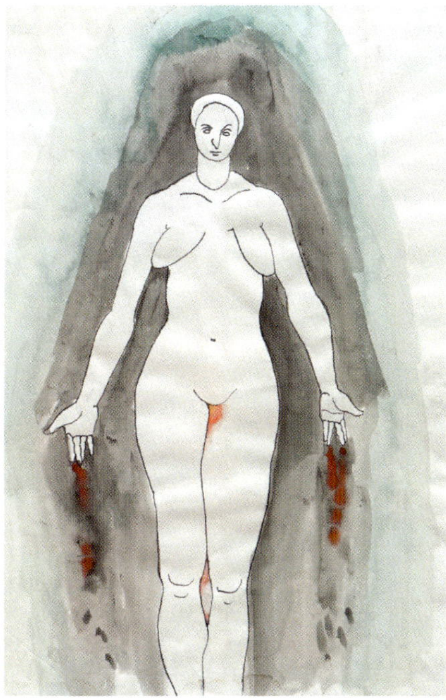

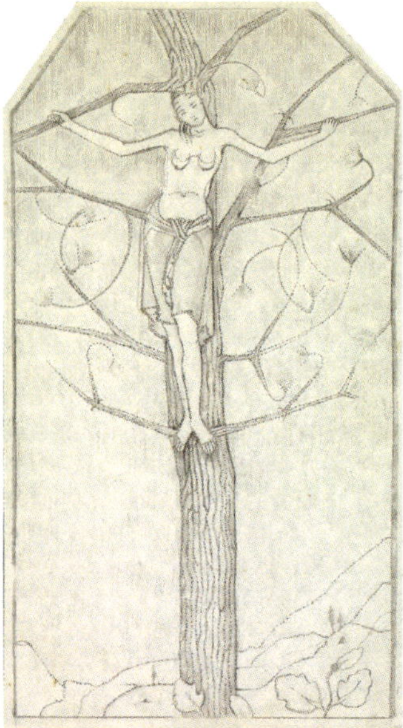

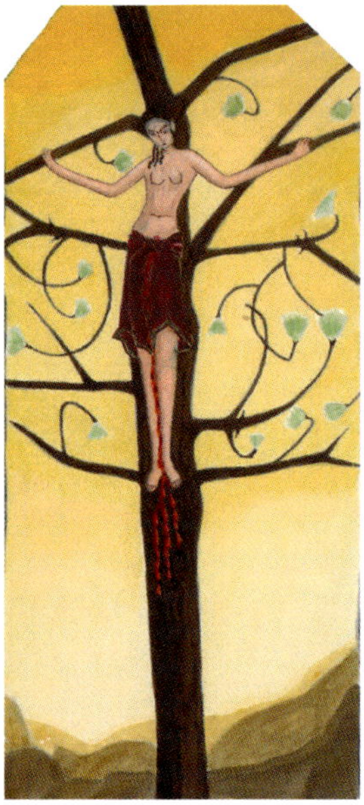

MADONNA OF THE MENSES

moon and stone
ancient accomplices
of femininity

—ILSE LEHNERT

I created additional menstrual art with inspiration from Christian imagery: the Virgin Mary and Christ bleeding on the cross.

The premise of *Madonna of the Menses* is that although Mary was a virgin, she must have menstruated like other women. While touring the Convent of San Marco in Florence, I became entranced by a fresco of Mary painted by Fra Angelico (or one of his assistants) on the wall of a monk's cell. I sat for hours copying the image in watercolor, later adding the blood oozing from under her garment.

Bleeding on a Pine Tree is an obvious allusion to Christ bleeding on the cross. But instead of the blood of suffering, I painted menstrual blood in a freely flowing, almost joyful manner. Pictured here are the preparatory sketches: a pencil drawing and a watercolor painting. The egg tempera version has been lost (see Chapter 12).

IN SPITE OF intense menstrual cramps and a heavy flow, I loved menstruating for the earthy smell, the rich palette of bluish reds, and the voluptuous sensations. I feared I would miss it after menopause, but I never looked back.

(ABOVE LEFT) *Bleeding on a Pine Tree*, c. 1984. Preparatory pencil sketch, 11 × 6 in. (27.9 × 15.2 cm)

(ABOVE RIGHT) *Bleeding on a Pine Tree*, c. 1984. Preparatory watercolor on paper, 9½ × 4 in. (24.1 × 10.1 cm)

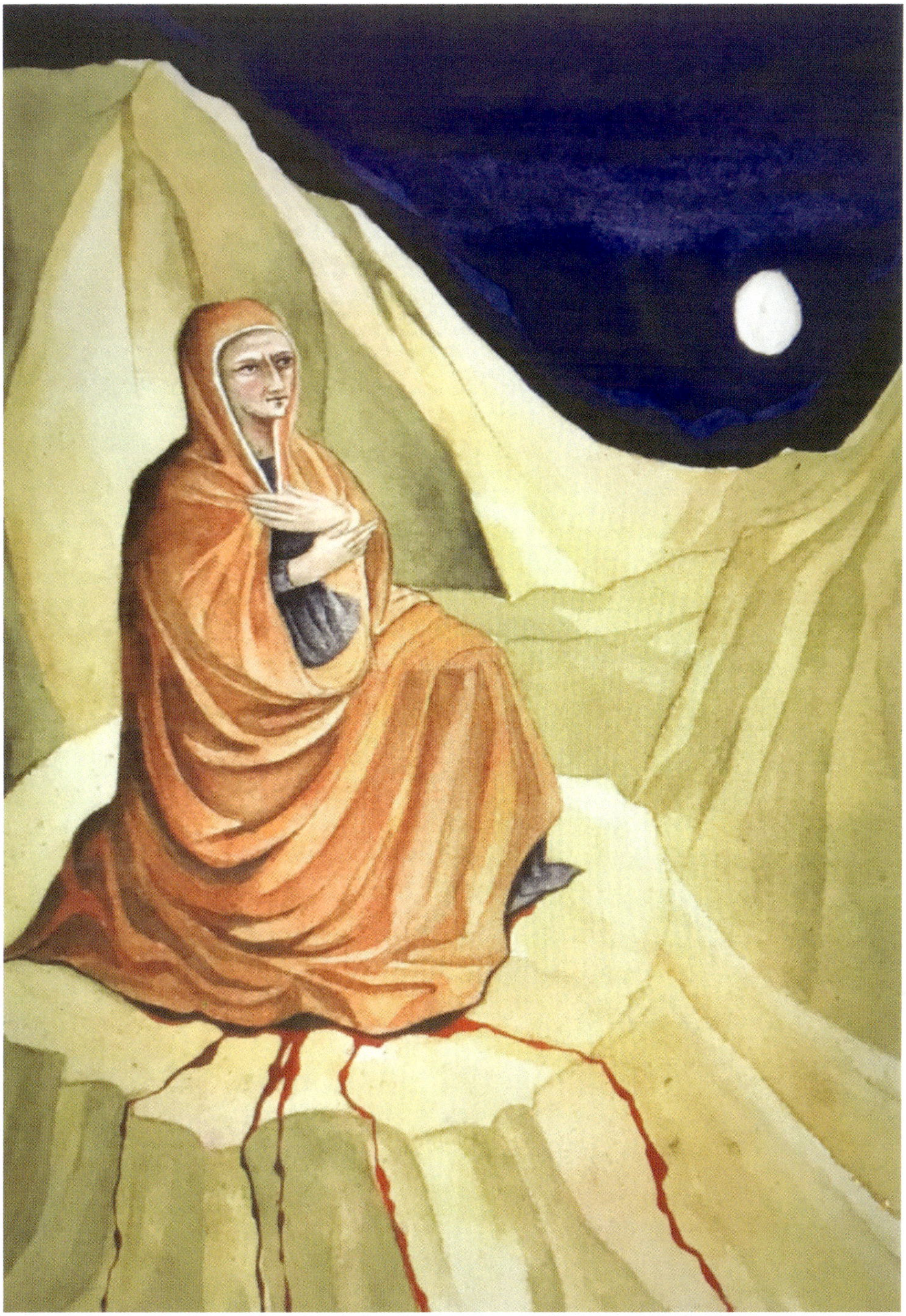

(ABOVE) *Madonna of the Menses,* c. 1981. (The original painting is lost and this reproduction was made from a low-quality scan of the original.) Gouache and watercolor on paper, 10 × 6 in. (25.4 × 15.2 cm)

(RIGHT) *Self-Portrait,* c. 1982. Ink wash with white watercolor on green-toned paper, 11 × 8 in. (27.9 × 20.3 cm)

(BELOW LEFT) In the hammock shop at Twin Oaks. Photo courtesy of twinoaks.org.

(BELOW RIGHT) Shal Loeser (left) and Valerie Renwick working in the hammock shop at Twin Oaks, 2017. Photo by David Holtzman.

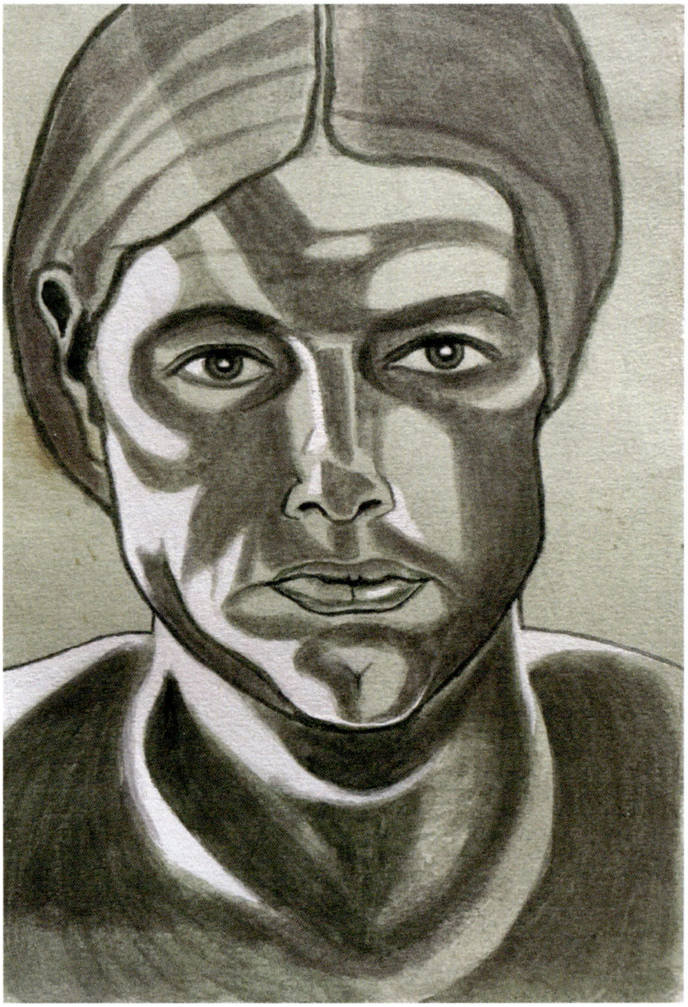

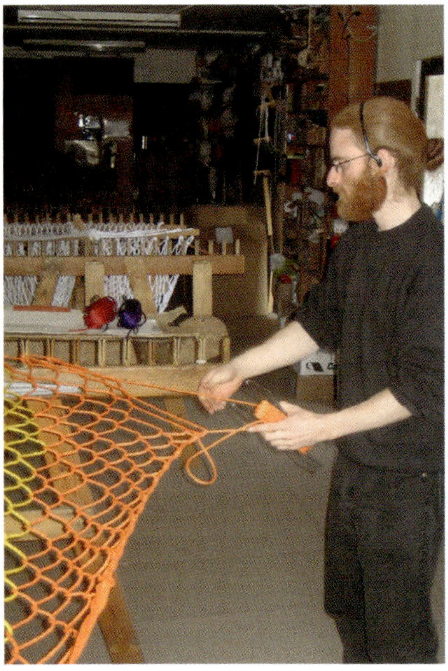

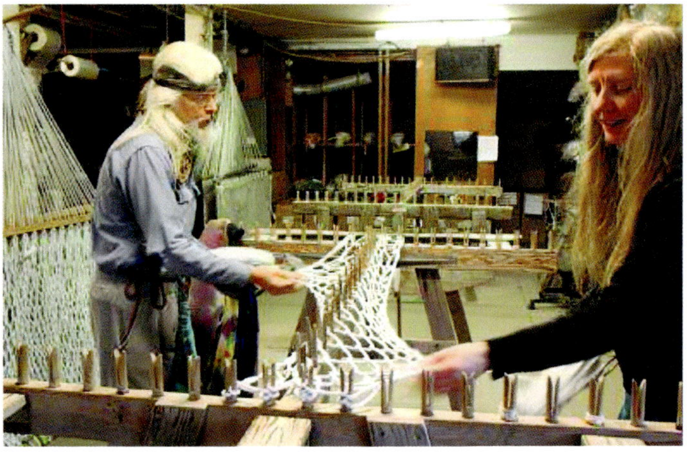

CHAPTER SEVEN

COMMUNES & CALIFORNIA

In 1979, I packed my tipi in kitty litter (to prevent mold) and stashed it in a friend's attic. I was ready to leave Maine.

I loved the summers of wild blueberries and lakes, the autumn magic, and the crystalline winters. But the dreary drawn-out mud season from March through May was depressing. Finally, warm weather would arrive in June, bringing out the vicious black flies that kept me indoors for another month.

Also, I was lonely and thought perhaps a community was what I needed. So, I drove across the country alone in my elderly blue Saab. I slept in the folded-down back seat, legs stretched into the trunk. For security, or at least the illusion of safety, I tied a blue coverlet to the seat backs to camouflage myself and my gear.

Hoping to find an intentional community to call home, I visited iconic groups Twin Oaks and The Farm, and a few lesser-known communes.[20]

Twin Oaks

Today, Twin Oaks is a community of about one hundred people living on 450 acres in Louisa County, Virginia.[21] I don't know what the population was when I visited, but it seemed to be roughly the same.

Many of their current systems were already in place: a communal kitchen, an organic farm, shared vehicles, and an effective structure of labor credits. Each member needed to earn forty-two labor credits per week. Every hour of work was worth one labor credit and could be fulfilled by working in the garden or kitchen, making tofu, performing childcare, or many other tasks. Their hammock-making and other businesses provided cash for the nearly self-sufficient community.

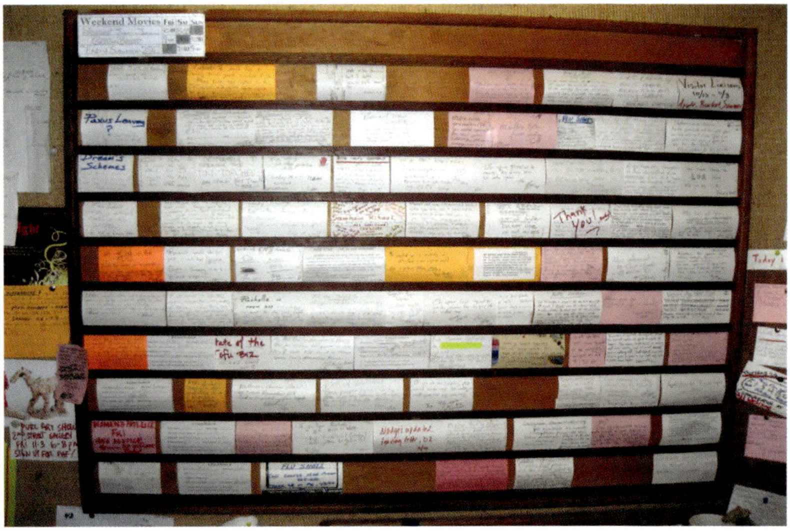

(RIGHT) I remember the so-called "3 × 5 Board" as an internal communication system at Twin Oaks using index cards. Valerie Renwick informed me via email (2024) that they still use the board but also use email and texting. Photo courtesy TwinOaks.org.

During my week-long visit, I mostly worked in the hammock shop doing some simple weaving. To entertain us worker bees, people read from books or played musical instruments, making the humdrum work almost pleasurable. I also helped in the kitchen, maneuvering large racks in and out of industrial dishwashers.

I found the Twin Oaks pragmatic counterculture values to be simpatico and envisioned myself living there. But I was turned off by the open-door bathroom policy; there were no locks, and I was told to just barge in without knocking. On that basis alone, I decided Twin Oaks was not for me. While writing this book, I asked Twin Oaks about their current bathroom policy. Their email response in November 2021 was: "It is true that we still have our open-door bathroom policy! It's waning a little, some bathrooms in the community do not observe this, but many do."

A Small Virginia Commune

Also in Virginia, a smaller commune stands out in my memory, though I can't recall its name. One evening, in the house where I was staying at with an older married couple, a tall, hefty younger woman bounced in through the door and soon departed with the older man. I was later told by another commune member that the man's wife suffered from severe arthritis and could no longer manage sex. Her husband was desirous of a sexual life and befriended this younger commune member for occasional trysts. This was totally out in the open and accepted. It was a welcome change from the "cheating" so pervasive in the dominant culture.

Another even more out-of-the-mainstream liaison I heard about (but did not witness) was an older man having a sexual relationship with a teenage (or perhaps even younger) boy. Apparently, the arrangement was accepted by the boy, the older man, and the boy's parents. This rattled my sense of proper consent and is, of course, unethical and in many situations illegal.[22] But I still marveled at the degree of openness in which these relationships and negotiations took place.

My final eye-opener at this commune was a sexual encounter with a woman—my first. I was not attracted to this woman—major mistake—but was interested in trying same-sex intimacy. All I remember was that she took off her numerous rings before lovemaking. I was neither turned on nor repulsed. Years later, I had a couple of sexual experiences with women I did find attractive. I found those experiences somewhat arousing but not memorable, so I decided to identify as straight.

The Farm

I was aware of Steve Gaskin's Monday Night Class, a weekly event in San Francisco in the late sixties, which some evenings was attended by upwards of 1,500 people. In 1971, Gaskin led a caravan of eighty school buses and other vehicles to found The Farm, near Summertown, Tennessee. Ina May Gaskin, wife of Steve, along with the midwives of the community, founded The Farm Midwifery Center, one of the first birthing centers in the United States where women could give birth in a non-hospital setting.

Although Ina May is pro-choice, as an alternative to abortion The Farm offered free medical care and housing to any pregnant woman or couple.[23] Many came, and some stayed, including many babies who were adopted into the community. As a result of this policy and a general welcoming philosophy, the population swelled to 1,600 people.

As the population expanded, the community could no longer financially support its many residents, and by the time I visited in 1979, it seemed to be in decline. In the house where I stayed, it was rumored that Ina May had just left the property to round up some teenagers who had run away. Another memory is of someone suddenly announcing, "The Store has toilet paper!" I made my way to the free store to find the shelves empty except for some rolls of toilet paper and a few miscellaneous items. It brought to mind the shortages happening in Eastern Europe about that same time.[24]

Years later, in 1985, Ina May Gaskin's book *Spiritual Midwifery* was the last of many pregnancy books I read, finishing it just as I was going into labor. I followed the advice to moo like a cow, a funny, effective way to get through contractions, which Ina May prefers to call "rushes."

Although the communes were sociologically fascinating, none inspired me to put down roots. So, I continued on to California, where I hoped to reunite with Richard, a lover with whom I had a relationship shortly before leaving Maine. Although the status of our relationship was ambiguous, I was still heartbroken to find him involved with someone new. But I reconnected with friends and rekindled my love of the Bay Area.

It had been six years since I'd left California after graduating from college, and art had been on the back burner for most of that time. This would soon change as I settled into my new life in San Francisco.

Haight Ashbury Free Clinic

A secondary goal of my cross-country sojourn had been to find an inspiring clinic to work in. My ideal health center would have an innovative atmosphere, be free of charge (or sliding scale), and provide compassionate non-rushed care. It would have a high standard of Western medicine and offer integrative therapies. I recall one clinic in Oregon had the words "We Deliver" painted on the van they used to attend home births. I did not find the clinic of my dreams, but once settled in San Francisco, I started volunteering and then was hired at the Haight Ashbury Free Medical Clinic (HAFMC).[25]

HAFMC was founded by David Smith, a twenty-eight-year-old physician responding to the influx of young people coming to San Francisco for the Summer of Love. It opened on June 7, 1967, with the motto "health care is a right, not a privilege."[26]

When I started working there in 1979, our patient population was mostly young people coming to the Haight in search of the sixties. We treated many sexually transmitted infections in addition to other ailments.

Toward 1980, we noticed our treatments, particularly for some sexually transmitted infections, were not working as well as they did before. Within months, we got word that a strange new virus was spreading in San Francisco.

The AIDS epidemic officially began in 1981. We were horrified to see young gay men appearing emaciated, old, and gray, walking with canes or in wheelchairs. Most died within six months. I lost many friends, acquaintances, and especially patients—it was heartbreaking.

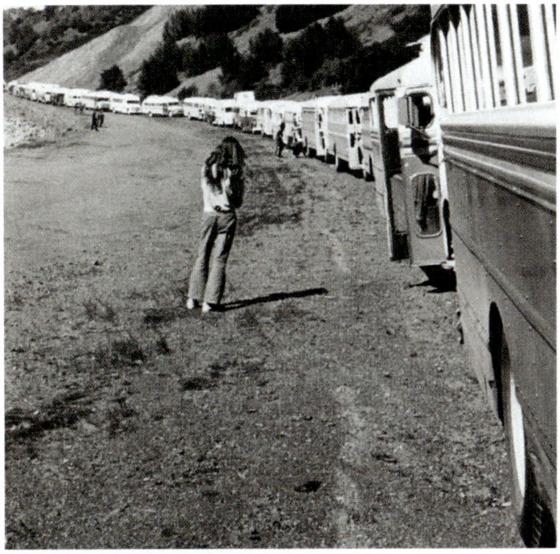

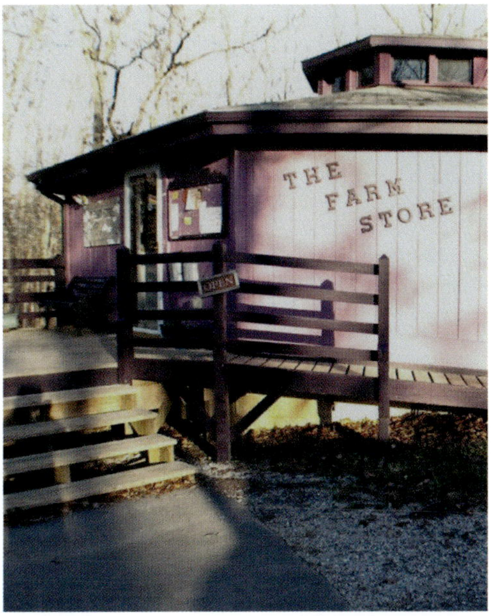

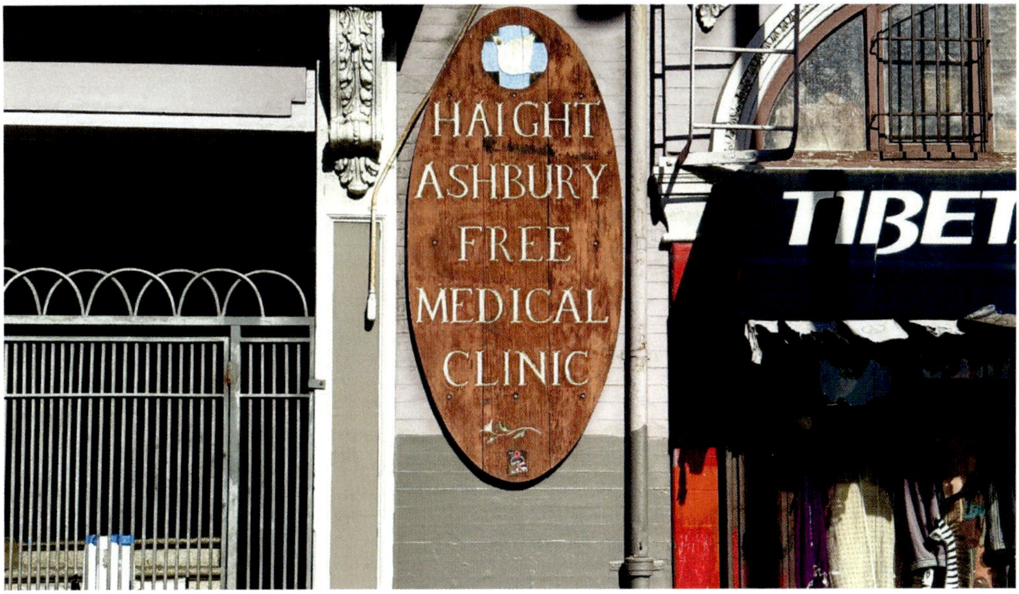

(ABOVE LEFT) A caravan of 320 hippie idealists landed on a farm in Tennessee in 1971. Photo by Gerald Wheeler.

(ABOVE RIGHT) The Farm Store at The Farm, Summertown, Tennessee. Date unknown. Photo by Douglas Stevenson.

(BELOW) Haight Ashbury Free Medical Clinic at 558 Clayton Street, San Francisco

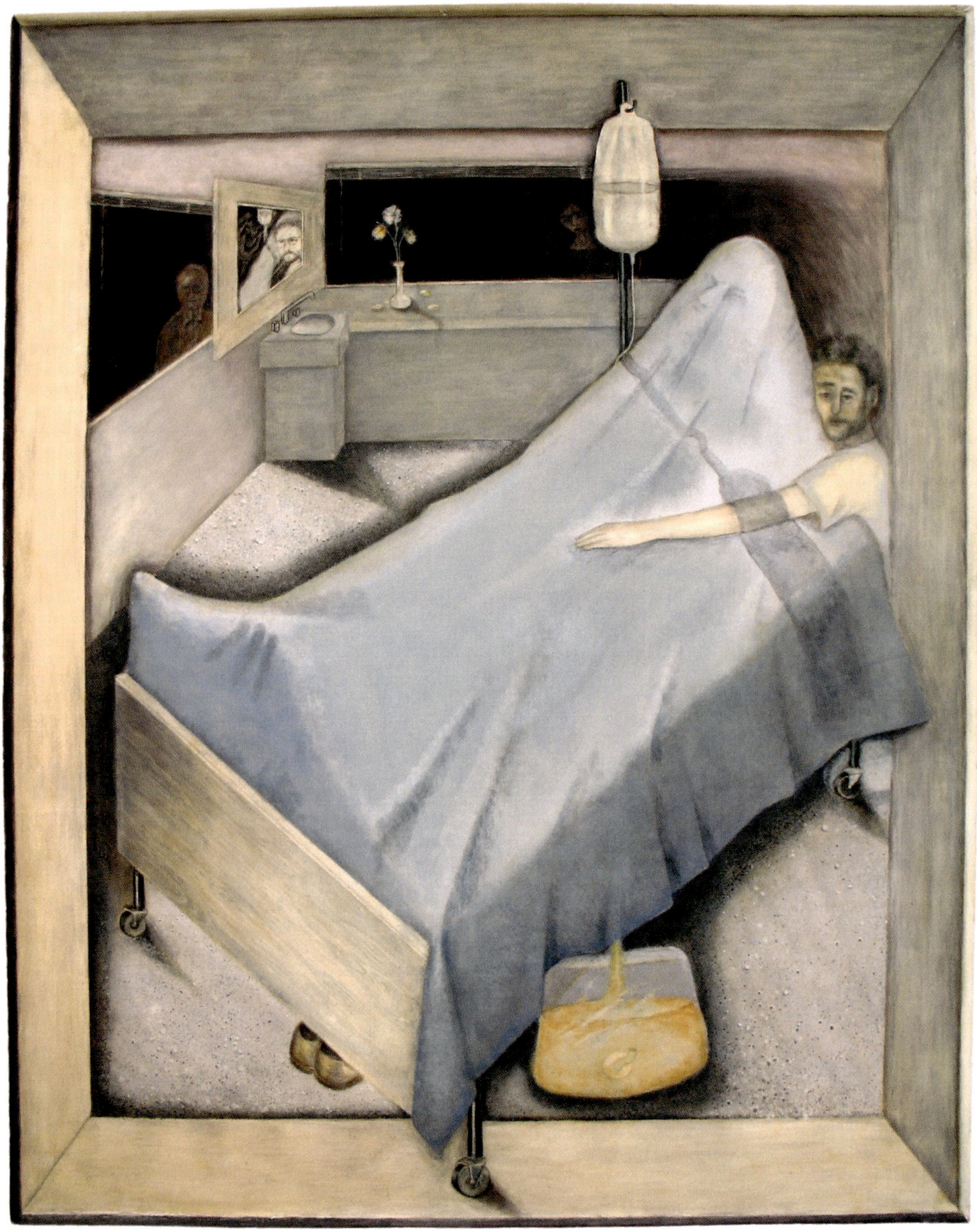

(ABOVE) *Don't Go My Friend: The Death of John Walsh, MD*, c. 1993. Egg tempera on gesso panel, 35 × 27 in. (88.9 × 68.5 cm)

(OPPOSITE) John Walsh in Grenada, c. 1989

CHAPTER EIGHT

WAYS OF DYING: A CHRONICLE OF THE AIDS EPIDEMIC

During those dark years of the epidemic, urgent images emerged from my psyche. They form the four paintings of the series *Ways of Dying: A Chronicle of the AIDS Epidemic*:

— *Don't Go My Friend: The Death of John Walsh, MD*
— *Bon Voyage: The Death of Tom Mabie*
— *No More Pollution; No More Somalia: The Death of Peter Ryan*
— *Birds of Pray* 🙏*: The Death of Greg Dubs*

Tragically, the effective antiretroviral medications used today were not available at the time these four men died.

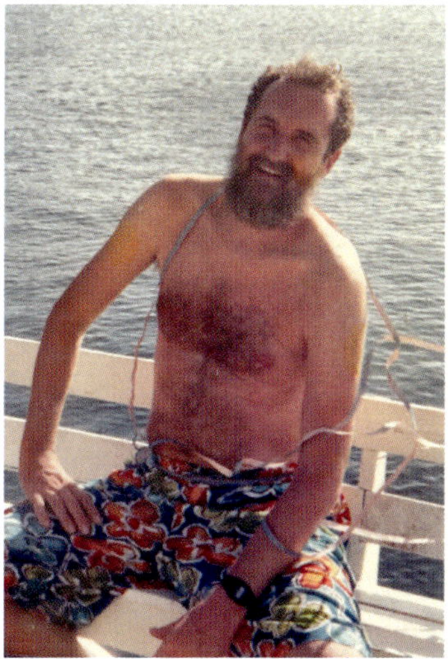

Don't Go My Friend: The Death of John Walsh, MD

At the Haight Clinic, a seasoned physician assistant named John Walsh became my mentor and friend.

John, or "Jacquot" (pronounced "Jocko"), his hippie name, was a legend in the Haight. He was often seen strutting down Haight Street in his pale blue denim jacket with a red muffler, and always a fresh gardenia in his lapel.

John was thwarted in his ambition to become a medical doctor and tried to make peace with the title of physician assistant. But in the mid-1980s, he left HAFMC and enrolled at St. George's University School of Medicine on the island nation of Grenada, where he earned his MD.

He had just started a residency at St. Vincent's Hospital in Manhattan when he was struck with pneumocystis pneumonia, an opportunistic infection that heralds the diagnosis of AIDS. I was devastated when he called to tell me he'd been diagnosed with full-blown AIDS. He moved back to his beloved San Francisco, where he died six months later in 1992.

I arrived at the hospital soon after John's passing. The image is true to the scene I found—his dear friend David Tuttle embracing him and repeating over and over, "Don't go my friend, don't go my friend." I knew at that moment I wanted to create a painting embodying what I felt and saw.

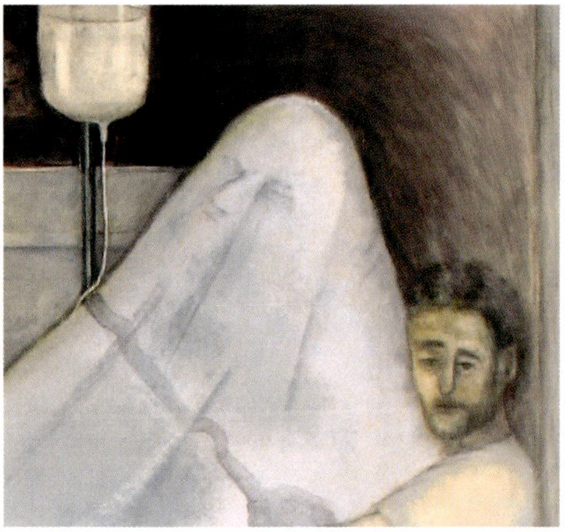

As I was painting, John's body seemed to rise up. I tried to lay the figure down on the bed without success. Finally, I embraced the metaphor of John's spirit rising.

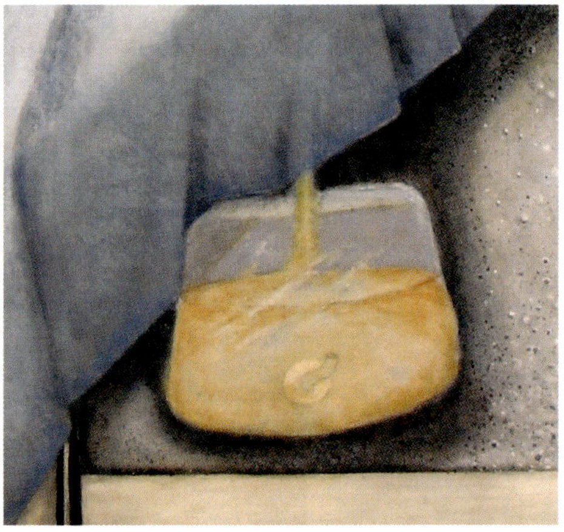

Even though John was declared dead, urine continued to drain into the collection bag. Nowadays, nursing staff remove drainage bags and other peripherals at the time of death.

In this detail, a healthy John is seen in the mirror above the sink, as if peering into the room from the threshold, witnessing his own death with a tongue-in-cheek expression. John was a practical joker—he would have appreciated a little humor in an otherwise mournful portrayal.

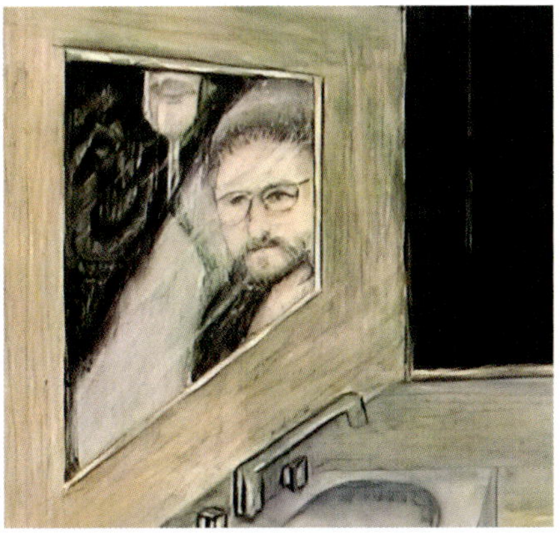

Flowers facing away from the light with dropping petals is another symbolic detail.

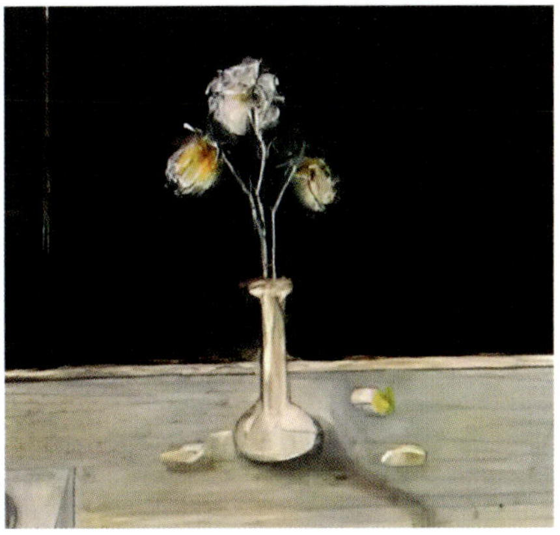

Peering through the window is an image of John's father, with whom he had a complex relationship.

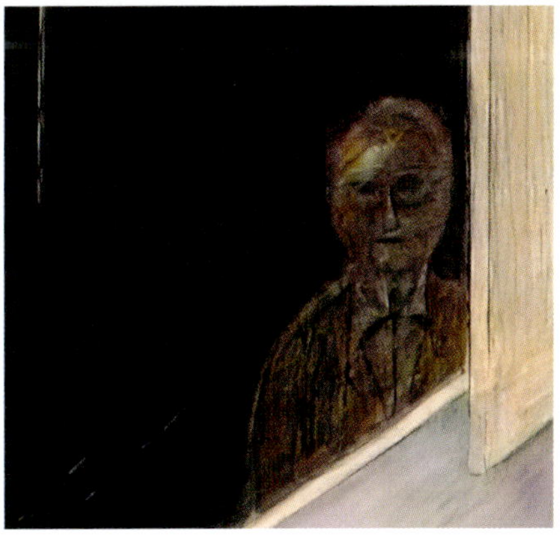

Don't Go My Friend: The Death of John Walsh, MD won first place in the *Art & Healing* exhibit at the Artwest Gallery in Jackson, Wyoming, in 1997. This validation boosted my courage to continue in the vein I was exploring.

Making Lapis Lazuli Pigment

The blue color in the painting *Don't Go My Friend* is a pigment extracted from lapis lazuli, a gem mined in Afghanistan and other countries. The intense blue seen on the stone is lazurite, and the golden streaks are pyrite (iron sulfide), also called "fool's gold." Lapis lazuli was the most expensive pigment in the Middle Ages—at one time more costly than gold. It was reserved to paint the robe of the Virgin Mary, giving this permanent pigment the power to impart divine love.

Manufacturing lapis lazuli pigment is an arduous process, more complicated than extracting pigment from other stones, but I wanted to attempt it just once. The first step for making any pigment is to pulverize the stone. In attempts at making pigments with other stones, such as malachite and azurite, I placed the stone in a plastic or paper bag and pounded it with a hammer. The bag often broke spewing particles.

Around that time, I was visiting my parents, and while I was talking on the phone, my eyes landed on a decorative container holding pens and pencils. I must have seen it many times, but on that day, I realized it was a heavy brass mortar and pestle—just what I needed. With my parents' permission, it went home in my suitcase.

I followed the historical recipe in Cennino Cennini's *Il Libro dell'Arte* (c. 1400), which purported to remove the fool's gold and other impurities. I combined the pulverized particles with beeswax, mastic tears (a tree gum), and pine rosin (same as used on violin bows) and rolled it into a bright blue Playdoh-like ball.

After a month of daily kneading, I immersed the ball in a bath of lye to extract the pigment. It somewhat failed, as the shade of blue I was left with resembled what's called "ultramarine ash," the dregs of the manufacturing process.

I found out recently that even if one selects a stone with the brightest blue and a minimum of fool's gold, there are other impurities, such as calcite, that are not always visible. This might be responsible for my failure to achieve a brighter blue. While it wasn't the vibrant blue I was aiming for, the hue has its own subtle gray-blue charm.

(OPPOSITE, ABOVE LEFT) My brass mortar and pestle

(OPPOSITE, ABOVE RIGHT) Lapis lazuli in its natural state with "fool's gold" striations

(OPPOSITE, BELOW LEFT) The results of my lapis lazuli pigment-making attempt: ultramarine ash

(OPPOSITE, BELOW RIGHT) Lapis lazuli pigment purchased from Natural Pigments company

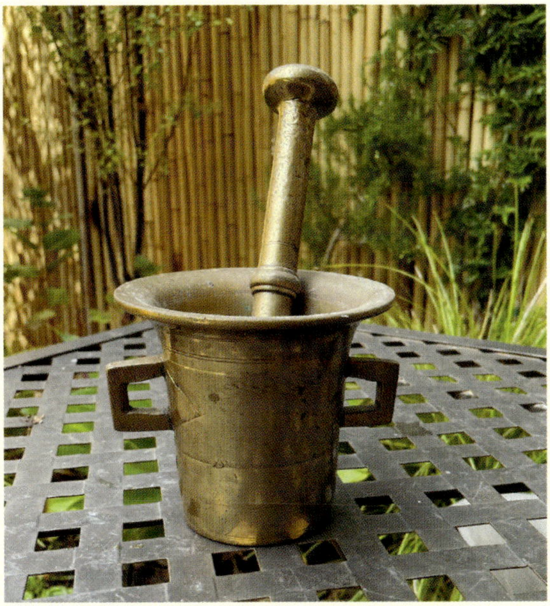

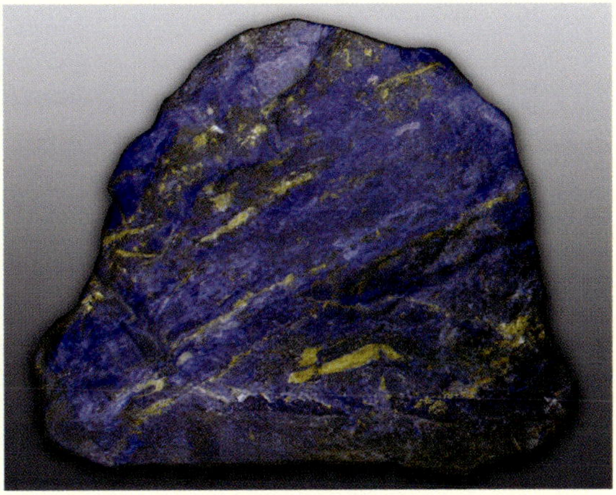

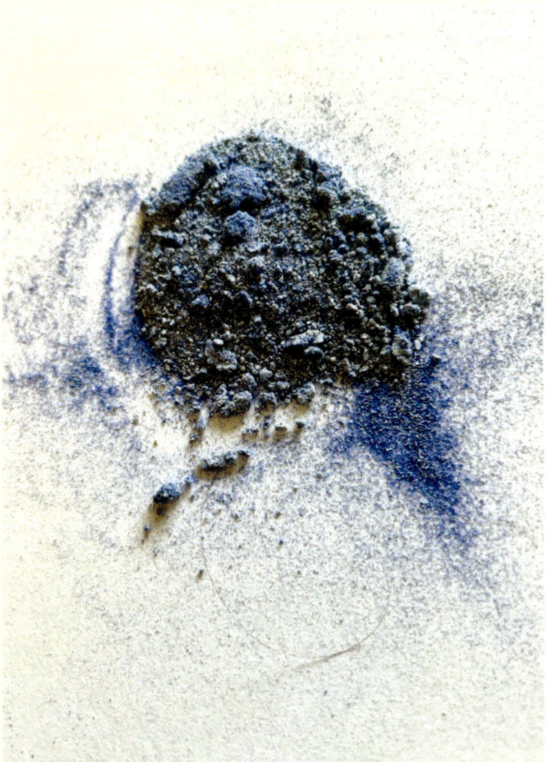

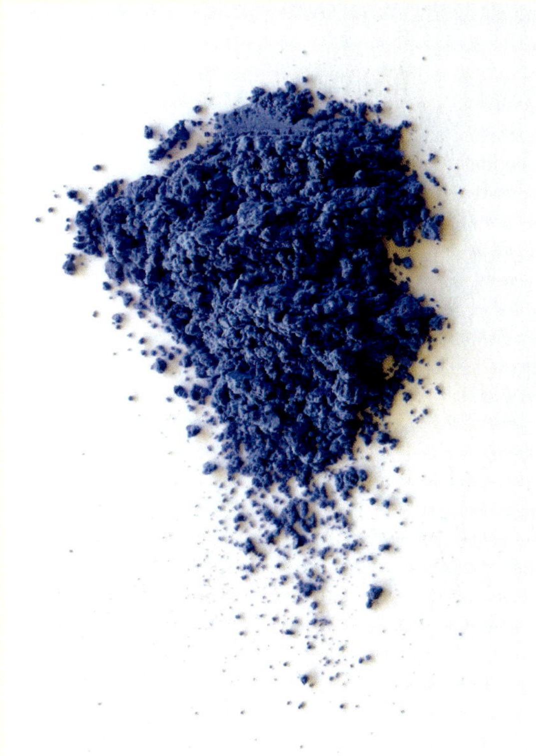

Bon Voyage: The Death of Tom Mabie

When the AIDS epidemic began, I was in awe of the healthcare professionals who jumped into the fray to care for the PWAs (Persons With AIDS). I was initially frightened to work around the virus, but providentially, shortly after John's death, I was offered a job in AIDS research at San Francisco General Hospital, and I felt ready to participate.

The purpose of the clinical trial was to test the effectiveness of a medication which was thought to be helpful in treating a nerve disorder caused by the virus. I enrolled approximately twenty men into my study. Tragically, at the end of the two-year trial, only one man remained alive. One patient, Tom Mabie, took his own life to intercept the horrific course of the disease.

Tom was in his early thirties and was an especially kind and gentle man. He was a gardener by profession and loved to travel—his favorite destination was the ancient pyramids of Egypt. One day, he said to me, "I'm dropping out of the study, and I'm dropping out of life." Those were his exact words. Then he added, "I'm having a going-away party, and I would love if you would come."

My first reaction was to try to talk him out of it, but he'd been through that with his physician, therapist, and friends. His mind was made up. He did not want to die in agony as he'd seen his previous lover and many friends do. Although weak, he was still able to function, but he was noticing that his mental state was declining.[27] He worried that in the future, he would not be able to make the decision he was making now.

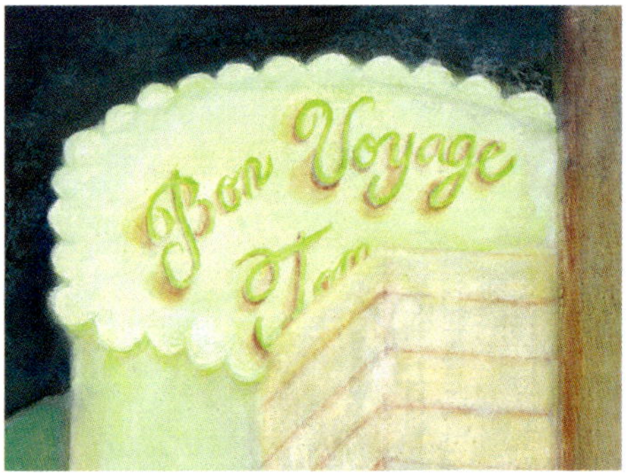

When I arrived at the party, Tom greeted me at the door with a big smile and a hug as he graciously took my coat. It seemed very strange for someone who was shortly planning to take his own life.

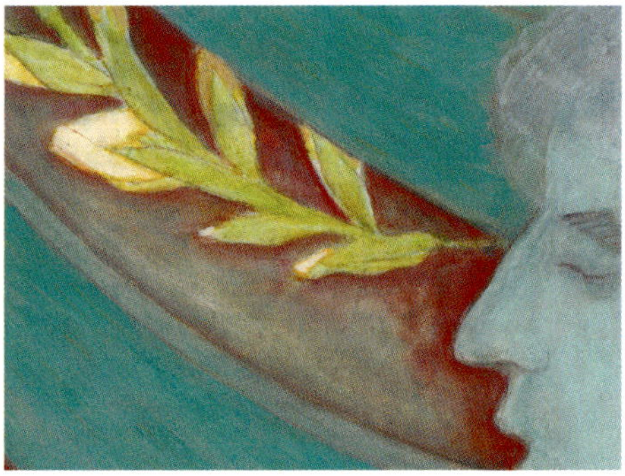

The party was amazing! People gathered in small groups, some crying (Tom comforting them!) and some laughing. Wine, liquor, and other substances flowed. Flowers and candles filled every available space. The food was opulent, complete with a cake inscribed "Bon Voyage Tom." This dramatic scene affected me deeply, and the idea for the painting *Bon Voyage* took shape soon after.

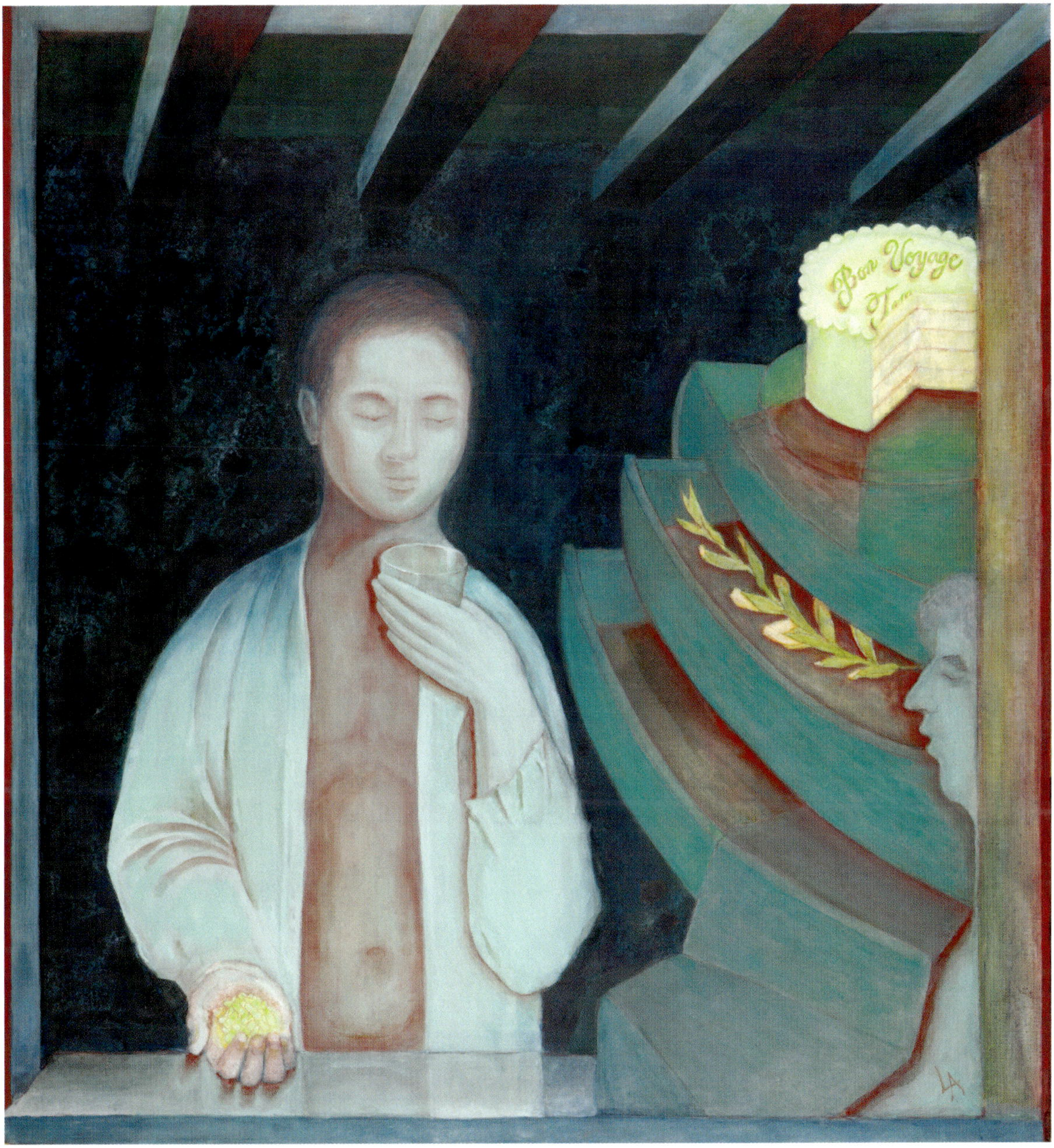

(ABOVE) *Bon Voyage: The Death of Tom Mabie*, c. 2002. Egg tempera on gesso panel, 39 × 35 in. (99 × 88.9 cm)
(OPPOSITE) Details: *Bon Voyage: The Death of Tom Mabie*

Rendering the Hands

I struggled mightily with the position of the hand that holds the pills. Hands are difficult to draw, and this particular hand, in addition to being in an awkward frontal position, was the main focus of the painting as it held the fatal dose of pills. I felt it needed to be expressive as well as accurate.

Rather than draw from a model or photograph, whenever possible I try to find an image in a book of art by one of my revered artists. In a book of Rembrandt etchings, I came across a hand that had a similar gesture.[28] It wasn't perfect, but I sense that communing with Rembrandt instilled the painting with a speck of his genius.

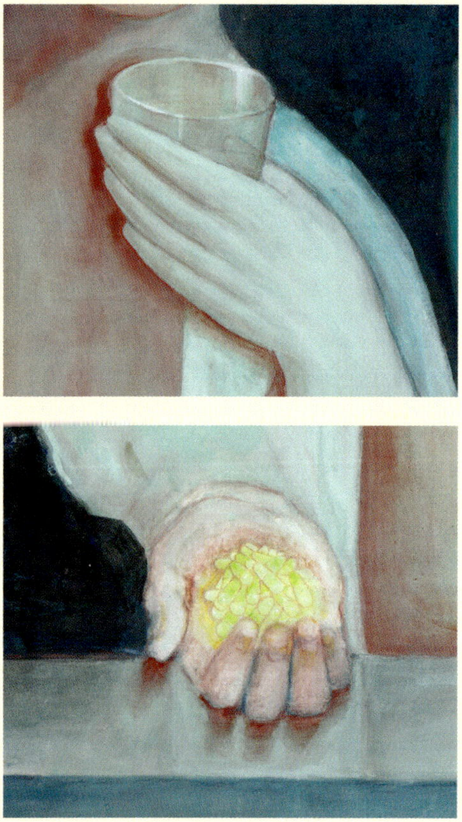

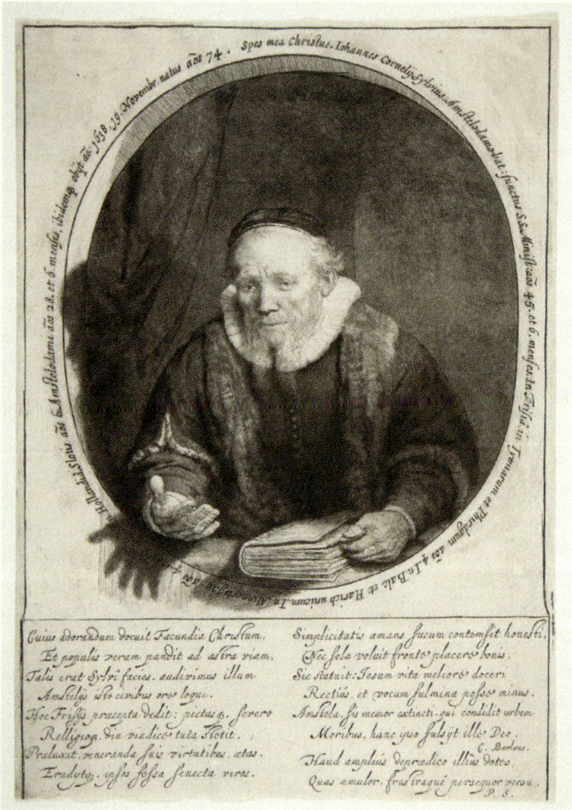

(ABOVE LEFT) Details: *Bon Voyage: The Death of Tom Mabie*

(ABOVE RIGHT) Rembrandt van Rijn, *Jan Cornelius Sylvius, Preacher*, 1646. Etching, 11 × 7 5/16 in. (27.8 × 18.5 cm). Metropolitan Museum of Art, New York

This was the plan: whoever remained at daybreak would be present at his suicide. I had decided not to stay but asked a close friend of his to call to assure me that that the process went smoothly. Two days later, I received a phone call. I don't remember her exact words, but this is the story she told me:

> *At dawn, seven people were present. All the flowers and candles were moved into Tom's bedroom. Tom lay back in the arms of a friend as his lover read him a "bedtime story." He then took the fatal dose of pills, washed down with vodka. He fell asleep within half an hour. In two hours, he was dead.*

Every aspect of the painting required thought and preparation, but most features came to me subliminally. I heard the command "paint furniture," so I painted a dresser—and later realized that the open drawer represented a coffin. I laid a spray of gladioli in the drawer since that flower is often present at funerals. The figure and furniture are squeezed close together, violating traditional principles of composition. I thought to fix it and then realized it symbolizes the narrowness between life and death.

I EXHIBITED THE PAINTING, fresh off the easel, at open studios in 2001. A friend, Stephani Lesh, took it home with the intention of purchasing it. The next day, I received this email from her:

> *We went to the beach today and it was sort of hard to leave the house because I kinda wanted to stick around and gaze at the painting. And I was really happy when we got home to see it again.*

She ended up returning the painting, nevertheless, her love for *Bon Voyage* has been dear to me.

A viewer at an exhibition told me that when he saw the painting from the doorway, he said to himself, "This painting called me. I had no choice."

I was not able to find an obituary nor any mention of Tom Mabie on the internet. I hope my painting and story find their way into the hands and eyes of someone who personally knew him. If that is you, please let me know!

With *Bon Voyage,* I felt I had turned a corner toward a sense of mastery. I knew that whatever technical weaknesses I had could be compensated for by a powerful portrayal. Now I long to acquire virtuosity, a level of technical skill that would leave the viewer breathless.

No More Pollution; No More Somalia: The Death of Peter Ryan

Peter Ryan and I became close when we lived together in a cooperative called New Moon House in the late 1980s.

Marty Goodman, Peter's hiking and hot spring explorer buddy, wrote: "Peter had the intellect of a Leonardo da Vinci and the soul of a Buddha. A self-taught high school 'dropout,' Peter could teach MDs about retrovirology [which includes HIV] and PhD engineers about electronic design and computer programming."[29]

After Peter learned that he was infected with HIV, he volunteered at Dr. Mike McGrath's Immunobiology Research Lab at UCSF (University of California, San Francisco), where Compound Q, a substance that halted HIV in the test tube, was being investigated.

"There his mechanical and intellectual genius became an invaluable asset to the everyday operation of the lab," wrote Marty. "Q" was not yet on the market, as the human trials were ongoing, but Peter was able to obtain the drug, which was being used in China to induce abortions and treat cancer. Peter invested all of his hope in "Q." When it did not pan out, he went from fiercely fighting the disease to a practical acceptance. One day, he spoke these words to me: "No more pollution, no more Somalia." At that time, Somalia was devolving into chaos. I understood this to mean that he would be leaving the problems of our troubled world behind. His words became the title of the painting.

During those last six years of his life, Peter was in a happy relationship with Susan Pete, who is portrayed in the painting together with her young daughter, Lizzie. Peter died of AIDS in 1993; he was only thirty-one years old.

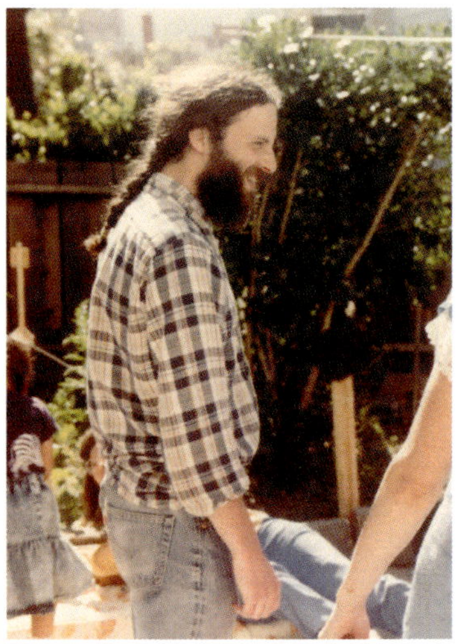

After he passed, Susan wheeled his gurney into a gazebo in the garden behind the hospital. Unlike the usual practice of pulling a sheet over the face of the deceased, Peter's face was gleaming in the sunshine. His body was covered with an afghan into which Susan had woven flowers. It was a gloriously unusual sight and sparked the concept for the painting.

I knew I could duplicate the somber tones of *Bon Voyage* to create an atmosphere befitting a death scene, but I wanted to challenge myself to evoke death using bright colors. I chose orange and blue, complementary colors that,

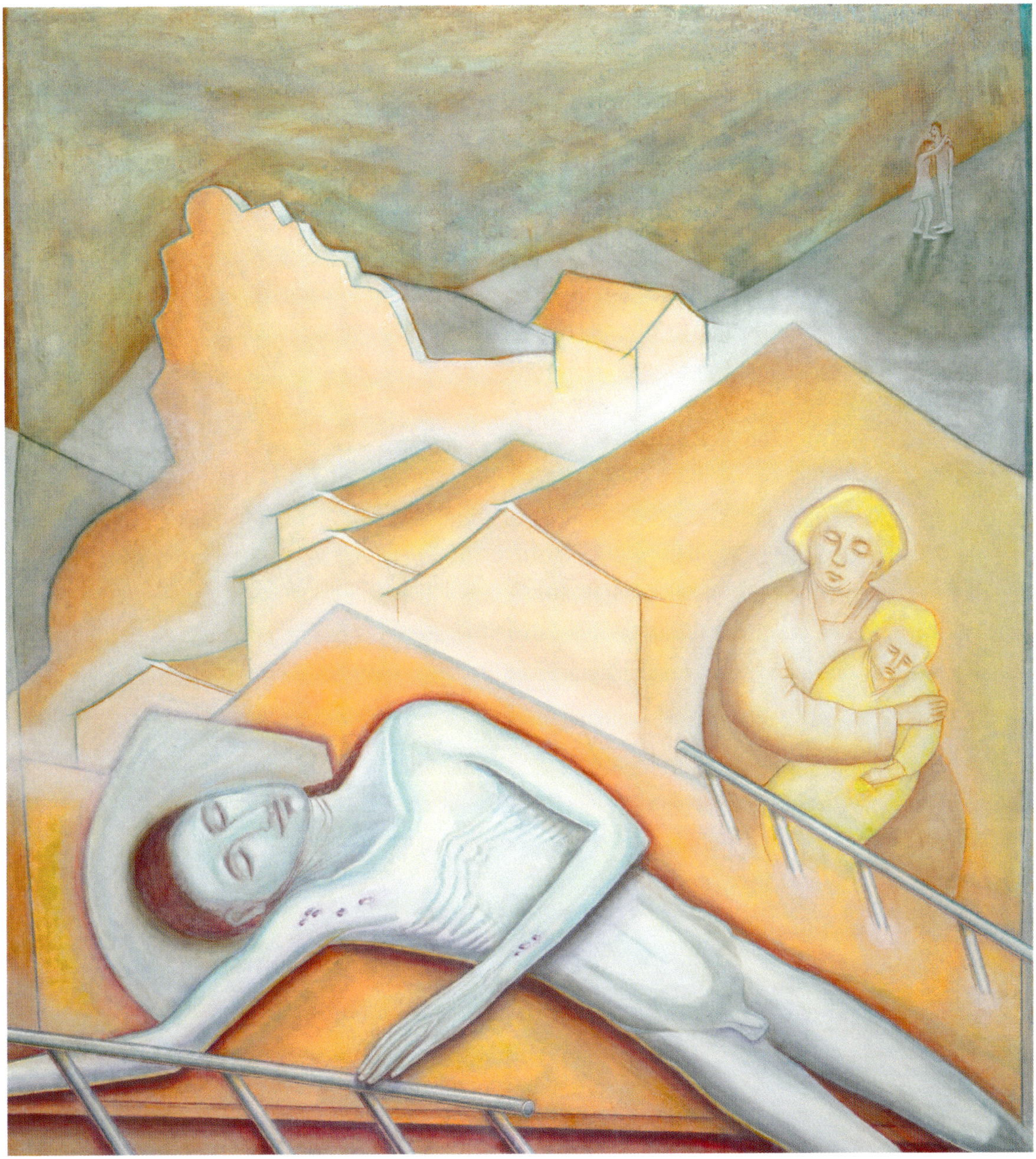

(ABOVE) *No More Pollution; No More Somalia: The Death of Peter Ryan,* c. 2015. Egg tempera on gesso panel, 54 × 48 in. (137.1 × 121.9 cm)

(OPPOSITE) Peter Ryan, c. 1987

when placed next to each other, create a sizzling vibration. Some of the elements, such as the afghan, flowers, and gazebo, were omitted in an attempt to simplify the composition and avoid cliché.

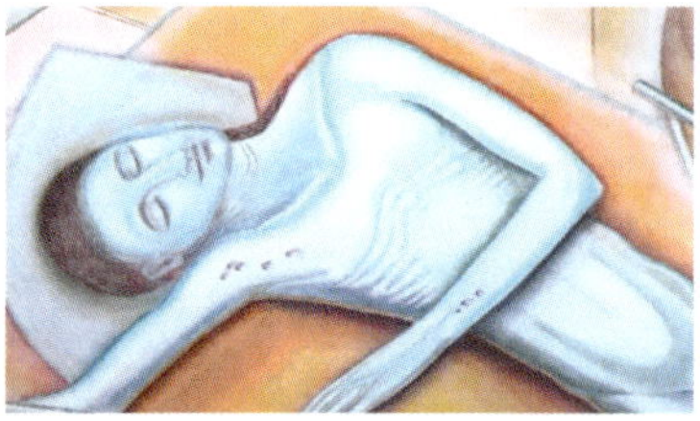

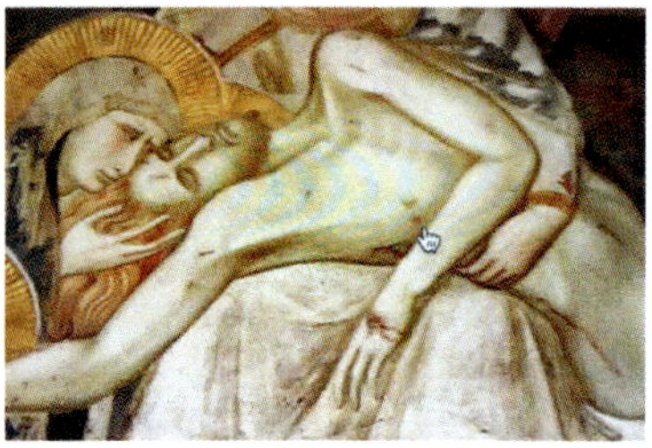

As I was painting, Peter seemed to be reaching for the railing and breathing imperceptibly, as if he was holding on to life. To my frustration, he was refusing to die!

In composing the painting, I appropriated the pose of Christ from Pietro Lorenzetti's fresco *Deposition of Christ from the Cross.*

It was never my intention to portray Jesus Christ, but when I sought reference material to design the deceased figure of Peter, Lorenzetti's dramatic pose came to mind.

Perhaps then I should not have been surprised that as the work progressed, several people commented that the figure resembled Christ. I am inspired by the teachings of Jesus and other spiritual masters, but this painting was to be about Peter Ryan, not Jesus Christ.

I spent considerable effort removing biblical references—to no avail. For example, Peter had long hair that he usually wore in a braid down his back. At one point, I gave him a haircut—which he would have hated! Even after I sheared off his long hair, viewers at open studios still commented on the resemblance to Christ, so I reinstated his signature braid.

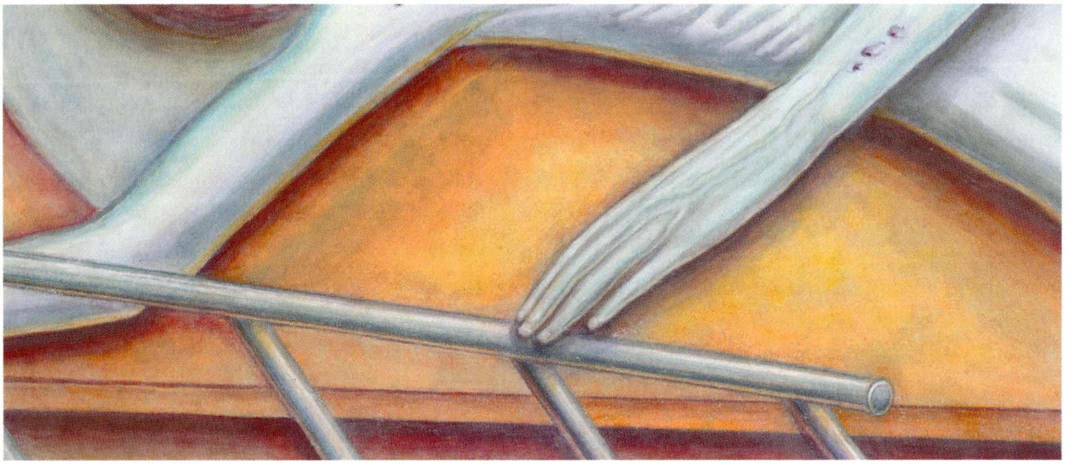

(TOP RIGHT) Lower image: Pietro Lorenzetti, *Deposition of Christ from the Cross*, c. 1320. Fresco. Lower Basilica of San Francesco d'Assisi, Assisi, Italy

(BELOW) Detail: *No More Pollution; No More Somalia: The Death of Peter Ryan*

Norwegian Pillow Painters

What may resemble a halo behind Peter's head was supposed to be a pillow. I'm capable of painting a realistic pillow, but when I tried adding some folds of fabric to read more "pillow," the painting resisted because it drew attention away from Peter's face. I settled for a shape that echoed the geometric shapes of the houses behind it. This abstraction contributed to a halo effect, once again suggesting an image of Jesus.

Then I came across the Norwegian "pillow painters," including Edvard Munch (famous for *The Scream*). Tuberculosis, or "consumption" as it was then called, took the life of Munch's mother when he was only five years old. *The Sick Child* portrays Munch's older sister, Sophie, who also died from tuberculosis, at the age of fifteen. The scene of her death haunted him—he painted six versions of it using different models. This version was painted when Munch was in his late forties.

Another Norwegian artist, Christian Krohg (Munch's teacher), also used the "pillow as halo" device in his painting *The Sick Girl.*

Whereas I was concerned that Peter's pillow resembled a halo, the "pillow painters" gloried in the association, emphasizing the sanctity of the soon-to-be-departed loved one. This put me in a bind: resist "pillow as halo" to avoid the Jesus reference? Or join the guild of pillow painters and embrace Peter's place in an ethereal realm.

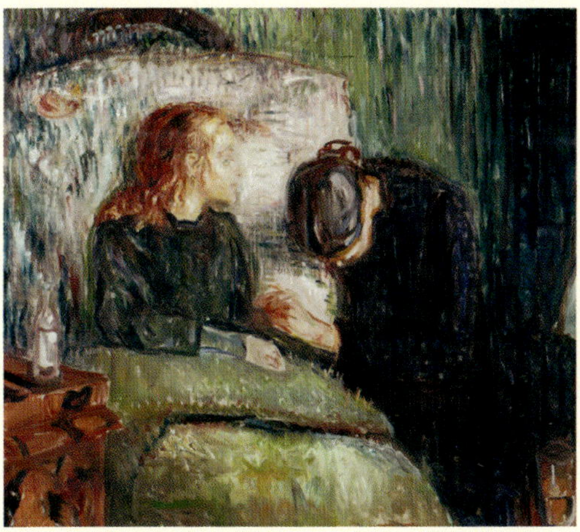

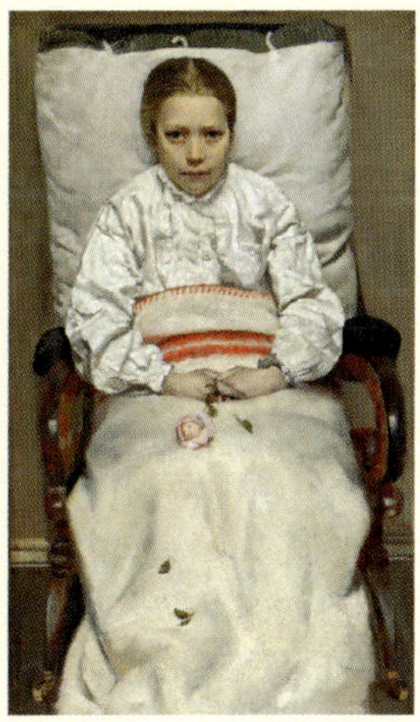

(ABOVE LEFT) Edvard Munch, *The Sick Child* (4th in a series), 1907. Oil on canvas, 54 × 54¾ in. (137 cm × 139 cm). Tate, London

(ABOVE RIGHT) Christian Krohg, *The Sick Girl*, 1880/81. Oil on canvas, 40¼ × 22¾ in. (102 × 58 cm). National Museum, Oslo. Photo by Jacques Lathion.

In another attempt to avoid the Jesus resemblance, I splashed the purple spots of Kaposi's sarcoma (KS), an AIDS-defining cancer, on Peter's arm and chest (although in reality Peter never had KS). This, too, backfired since the splotches are reminiscent of the stigmata of Christ, wounds that Jesus is said to have suffered during his crucifixion.

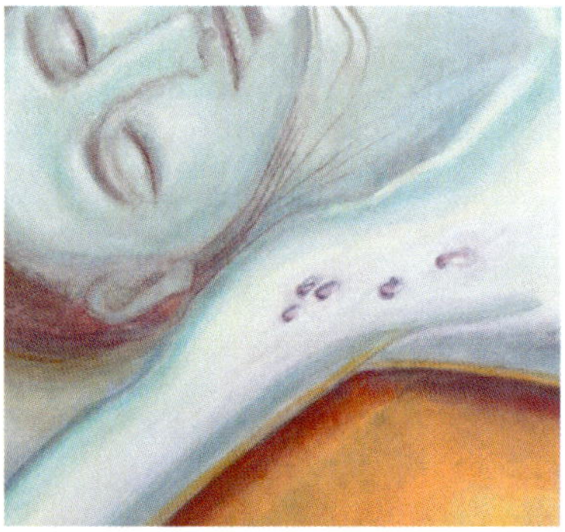

Eventually, another visitor at open studios advised, "Don't fight it!" and dubbed the figure "Saint Peter"—but not the Saint Peter of the Bible. It seems fitting; I like to think of Peter as a sanctified being.

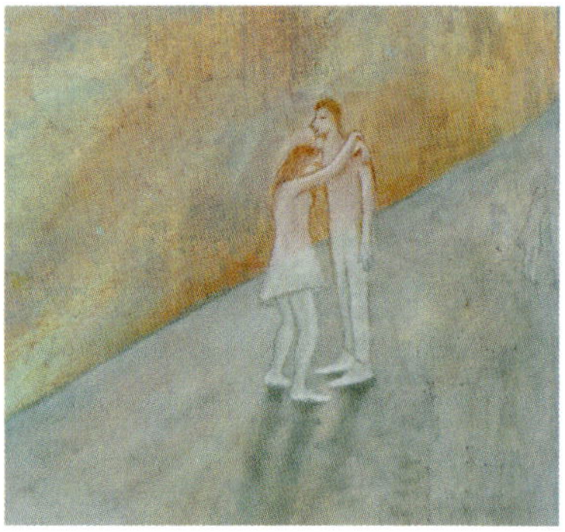

Another open studios guest blew me away with this comment: "Life around us is full of signposts, but they're all assembled here, pointing the way to where we're all headed."

The Spanish Revival-style building represents the old Laguna Honda Hospital in San Francisco where Peter died.

The tiny figures at the top right are me and a former lover. Out of touch for several years, we saw each other a few times when visiting Peter in the hospital during the last months of his life. Shortly after Peter died, I reached for a hug, but my ex-boyfriend felt cold and stiff. This incident etched a scar in my psyche that showed up in the corner of the painting.

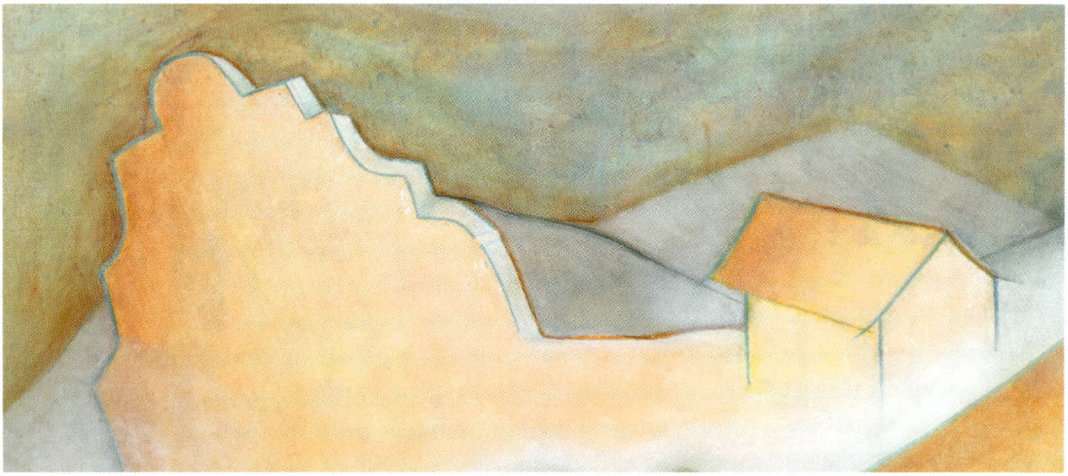

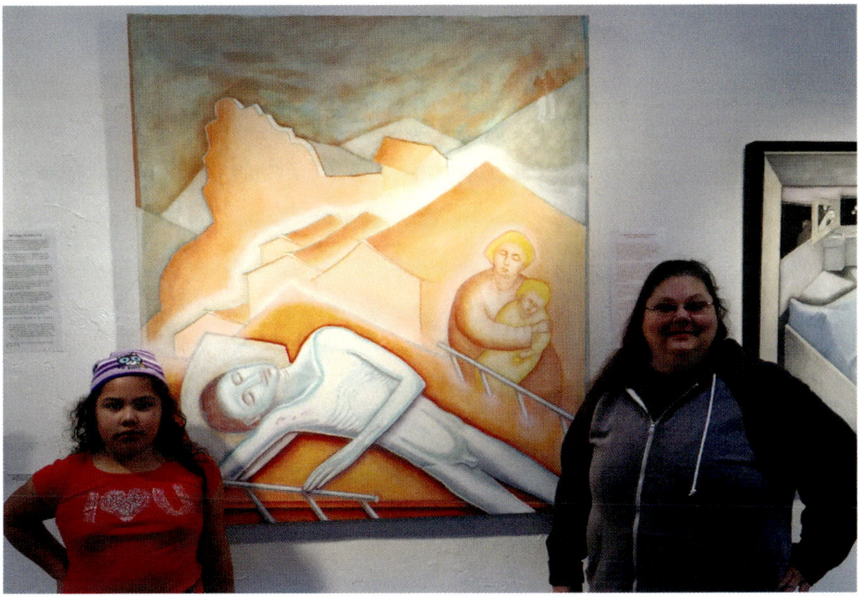

(ABOVE) Susan Pete and her granddaughter, Azalea (Lizzie's daughter), at the unveiling of *No More Pollution; No More Somalia: The Death of Peter Ryan* at open studios in the ICB Building, 2016
(OPPOSITE) Details: *No More Pollution; No More Somalia: The Death of Peter Ryan*

I labored away on the painting for seven years, unveiling it at open studios in 2016. Susan and Lizzie's daughter, Azalea (Susan's granddaughter), came to the exhibit. Decades later, Susan continues to mourn and miss Peter, as he was so supportive of her and Lizzie, and they had so much fun together.

In spite of the many challenges, viewers expressed that the painting held deep meaning about death. They viewed the Spanish mission as a gravestone, the diagonal placement of the figure as a symbol of Peter slipping out of life, and the bright orange as the fire of cremation.

I think of this painting as my "problem child." I remain disappointed, yet I refuse to abandon the painting and continue to try to improve it. But I fear the underlying structure is at fault, and I'm not sure if correcting and enhancing the superficial elements can ever make it right.

Birds of Pray 🙏: The Death of Greg Dubs

I met Greg Dubs, PhD, psychotherapist, psychology professor, and AIDS research administrator in 1993, when he hired me as a research coordinator for a study of NAC (N-acetylcysteine) at Stanford University. Laboratory studies showed that NAC could inhibit replication of HIV. Our study would be one of the first human trials of NAC, but sadly it failed as an effective treatment.

I was saddened to hear the news of Greg's death in 1998 at the age of forty-six, which was conveyed to me by another nurse who worked on the trial. We had not been in touch for five years, but I felt called to create a painting in his memory.

Unlike the other three *Ways of Dying* paintings, I had no knowledge of the circumstances of Greg's death, so I dreamed up a fictional scene.

Greg had close ties to the Native American community and had participated in the Sun Dance, the most sacred ceremony practiced by most of the Plains Indians. It's a time of renewal and cleansing for the tribe and the Earth. Since it was such an important part of Greg's spirituality and community, I was drawn to create a scene with reference to Native American culture.

I took many stabs at creating a composition with Native American elements, but they were all dismal failures. At one point, I even bought several leaves of pure copper foil on instinct, not knowing that Native Americans living around the Great Lakes were the first to mine copper and used it for toolmaking and arrowheads. But the copper idea also fell flat, and I was on the verge of giving up.

Eventually, I went to a fair of Native American artifacts, where I came across a photo of a "burial tree" in an old magazine. Tree burial is a custom previously common among some Native American tribes as an alternative to a grave.

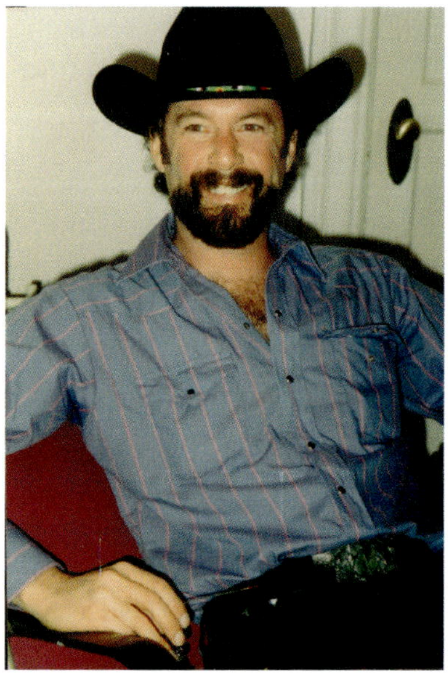

(RIGHT) **Greg Dubs, c. 1994**

(OPPOSITE) *Birds of Pray* 🙏: *The Death of Greg Dubs*, 2021. Egg tempera on gesso panel, 96 × 48 in. (243.8 × 121.9 cm)

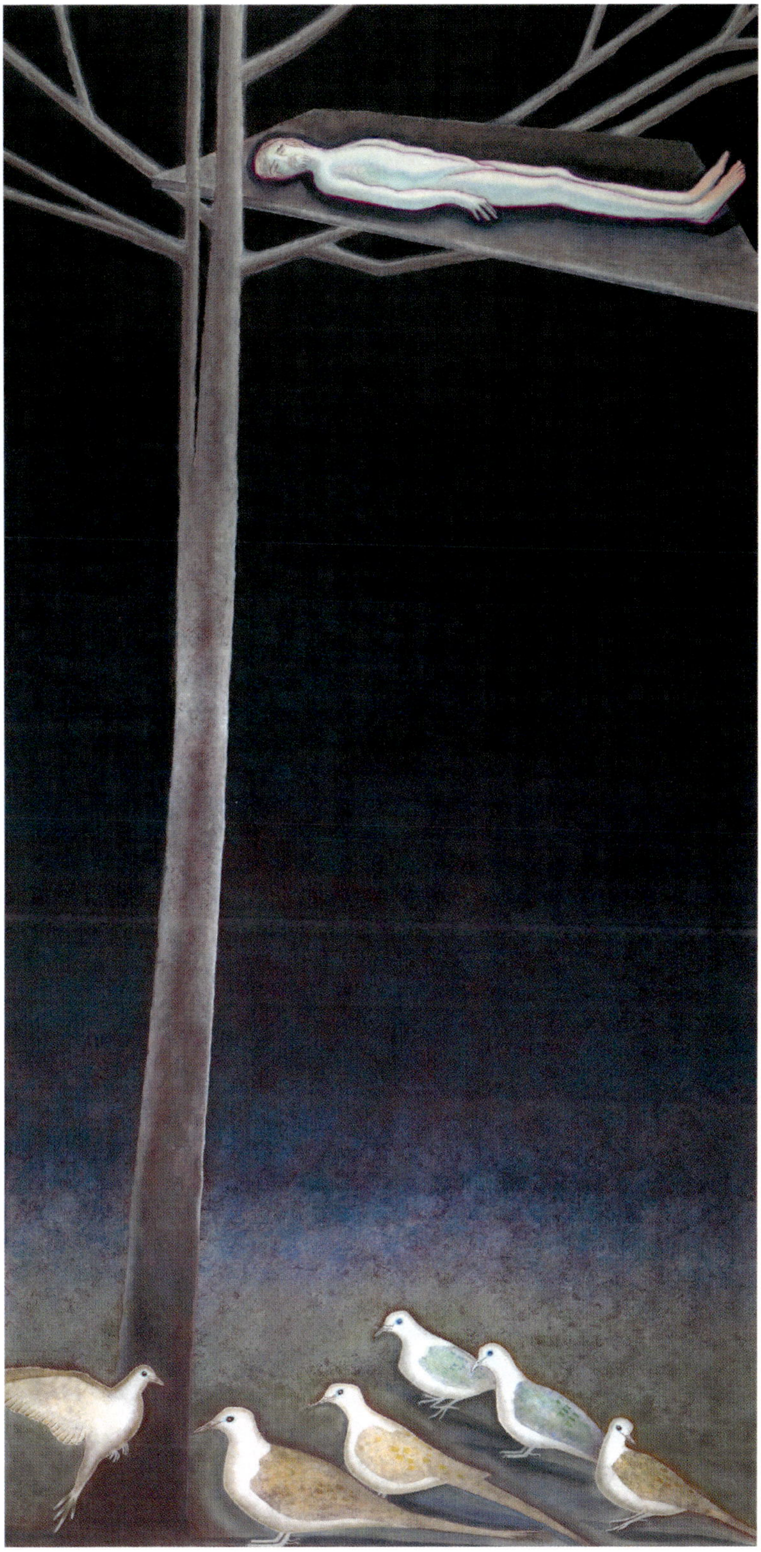

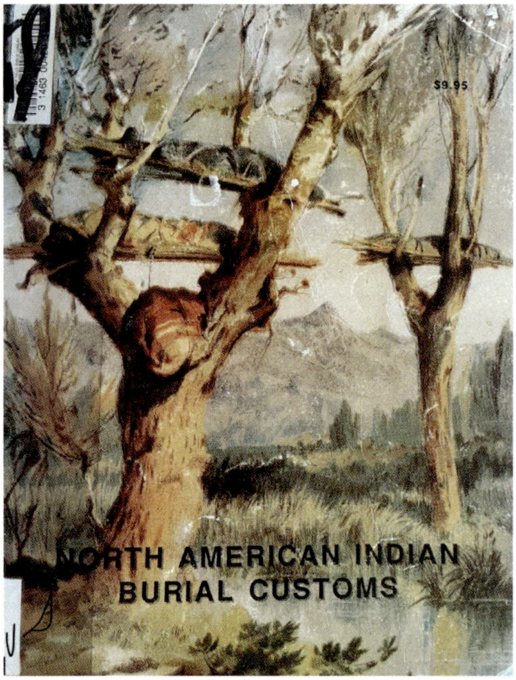

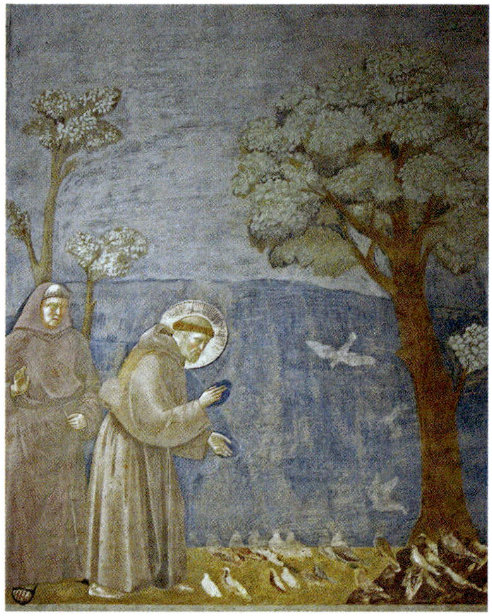

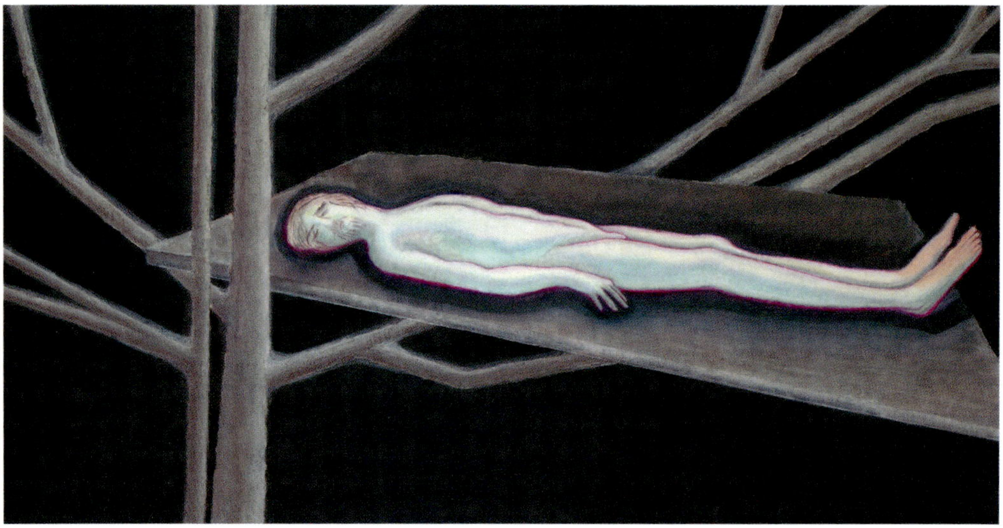

(ABOVE LEFT) *North American Indian Burial Customs* by H. C. Yarrow, 1987. The cover image is based on an undated drawing by Dr. Washington Matthews.

(ABOVE RIGHT) Giotto di Bondone, *Saint Francis Preaching to the Birds,* 1297-99. From the *Legend of St. Francis* cycle, Upper Church, Basilica of Saint Francis of Assisi, Assisi, Italy.

(BELOW AND OPPOSITE) Details: *Birds of Pray* 🙏: *The Death of Greg Dubs*

Tree burial is akin to sky burial, a practice in which the deceased is placed on a mountaintop to decompose or be eaten by scavenging animals. Although still practiced in parts of China, Mongolia, Bhutan, and India, sky burial is now often banned, ostensibly for reasons of hygiene. One concern is that scavenged human remains may contaminate groundwater. Not enough uninhabited land and diminishing populations of vultures are also factors leading to the decline of sky burial.

By combining elements of tree burial and sky burial, I came up with a concept that resonated with artistic and emotional possibilities. I sketched many versions to determine the best arrangement of the figure, tree, and birds.

In working out the composition, I sketched birds of prey—falcons, hawks, and vultures—but these felt too violent. What came to mind were mourning doves, birds I've loved for their gray humility and mournful coo. It turns out the coo is the mating call of the male dove and has nothing to do with mourning.

The arrangement and spirit of the birds were inspired by my favorite Giotto fresco, *St. Francis Preaching to the Birds.* Giotto captured an intimacy between St. Francis and the birds.

I tried to bring out the individual personality of every dove by painting a slightly different expression on the face of each one.

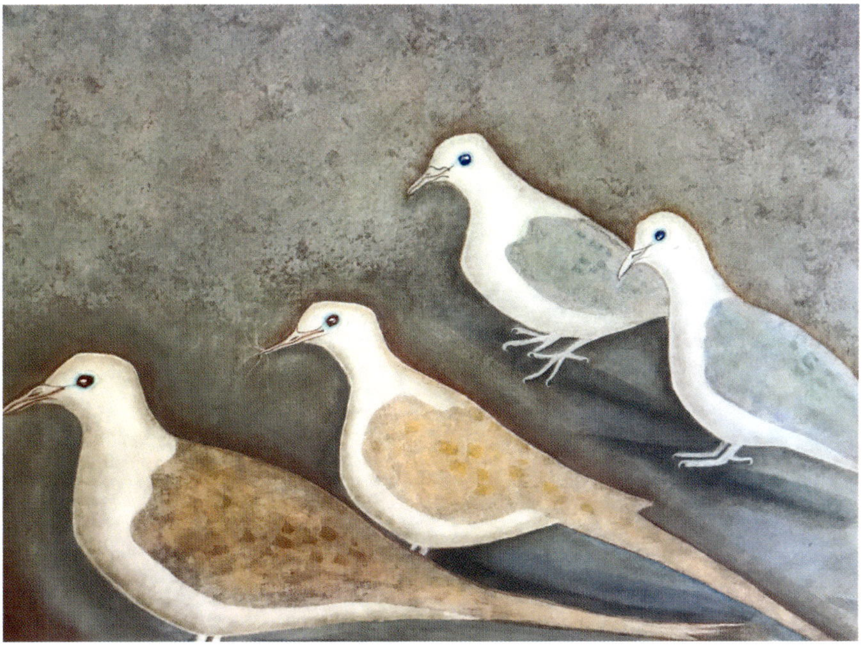

The title of the painting became *Birds of Pray* 🙏. I included the prayer emoji because people thought I was misspelling "prey." With the 🙏 emoji, my intent is clear.

The image demanded a seriously large format, so I prepared a four-by-eight-foot sheet of hardboard, tapering two inches off each side at the very top to draw the viewer's eye upward, contributing to a sense of awe. The paint was applied with full-size low-nap paint rollers, a giant sea sponge, and large brushes. And I used lots of eggs!

In *Birds of Pray* 🙏, I violated academic precepts of composition that recommend "a center of interest." I purposefully left the middle of the painting almost blank, forcing the eye to look way up and way down to piece together the meaning of the image. Paradoxically, the middle of the painting really *is* the "center of interest," since nothingness may capture the essence of death.

I DID NOT get to communally mourn Greg's death as I had with the other three subjects of my paintings, but I take solace in the peaceful presence of the mourning doves and having given Greg an imaginary Native American-style "burial."

Sometimes I wonder what John, Peter, Tom, or Greg would have thought about the paintings I made in their honor. Although I tried to capture something of their essence, the paintings are not meant to be biographical. For the most part, the person and their story are just jumping-off points for flights of artistic imagination.

Prior to the AIDS epidemic, I never thought much about the variety of ways in which people confront death. Some fight to live until their last breath, while others wish to intervene sooner in order to have more control. Witnessing several deaths prompted me to think about and perhaps plan my own inevitable passing.

(OPPOSITE) Standing with *Birds of Pray* 🙏, 2021

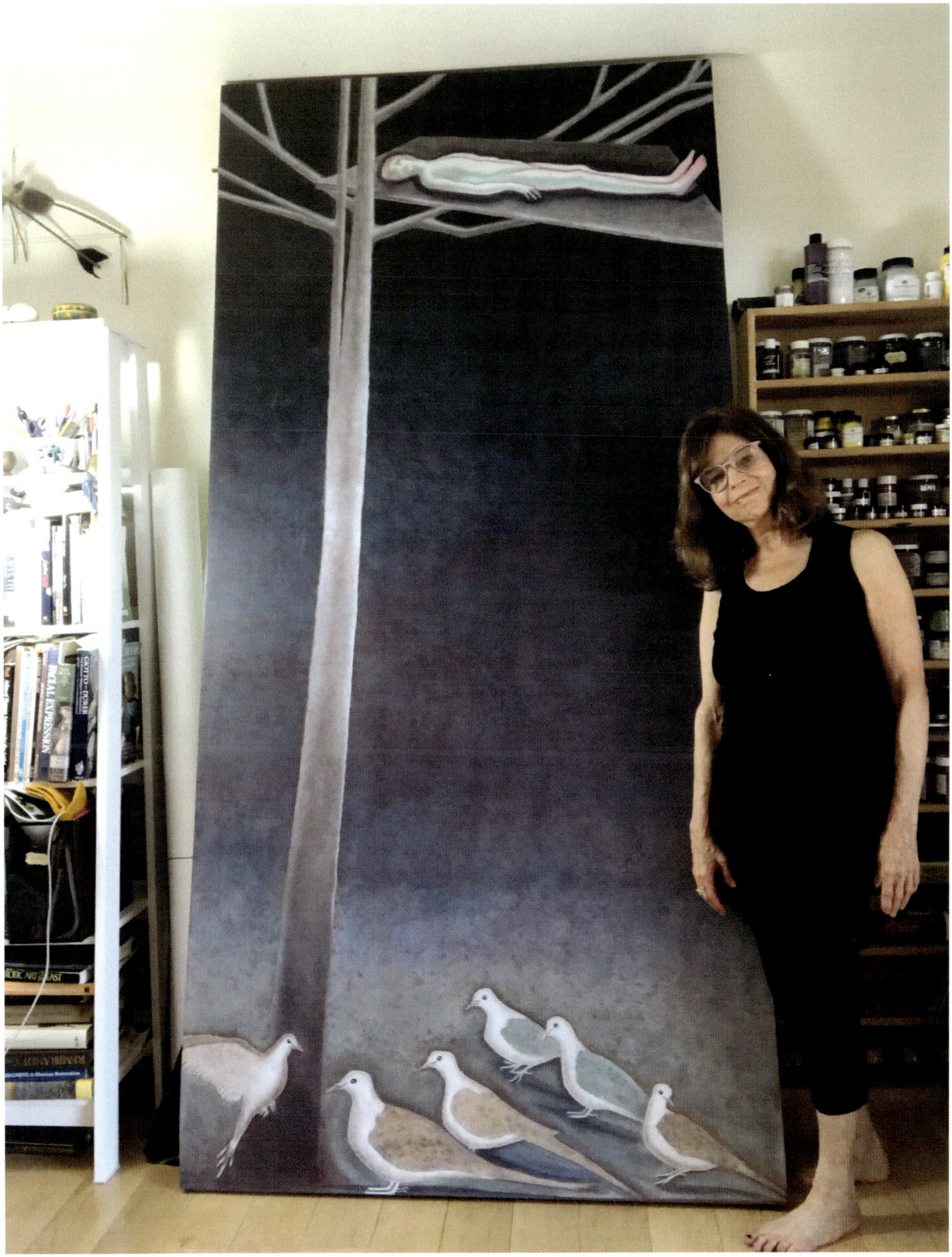

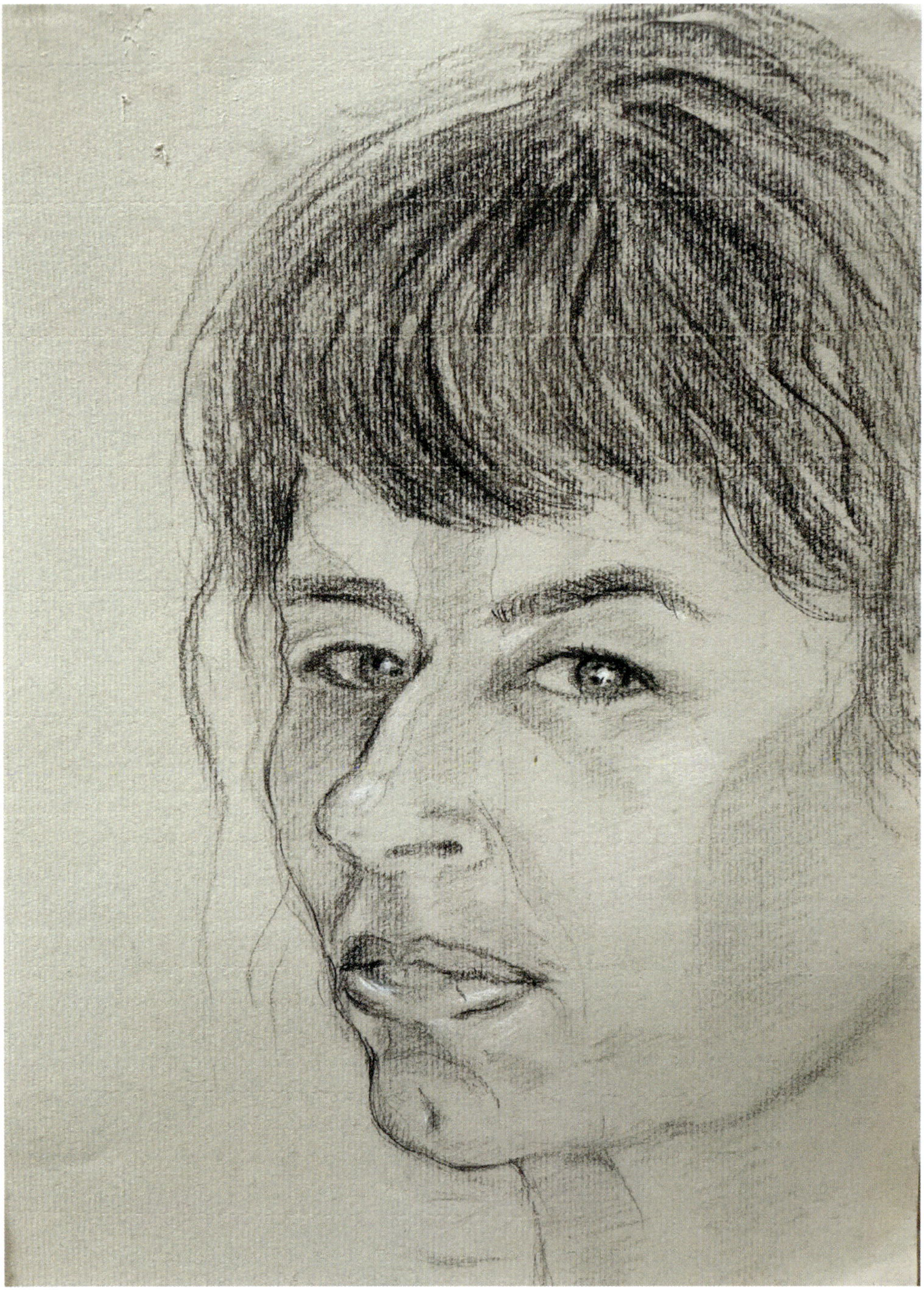

(ABOVE) *Self-Portrait*, 1978. Charcoal pencil and white chalk on gray paper, 8½ × 11 in. (21.5 × 27.9 cm)

CHAPTER NINE

ART & LOVE COME TOGETHER

Before the dark days of the AIDS epidemic, I had befriended Janet, a premed student who was volunteering at the Haight Ashbury Free Clinic as a medical assistant. She was aware that I lived in a roach-infested studio apartment overlooking a noisy street, so when a vacancy turned up in her building, she encouraged me to apply. It was a lovely apartment in the Mission District, but I wasn't sure if I could live with the wall-to-wall carpets—a slightly nauseating dusty rose color. After a couple of visits, I succumbed, and once I settled in, Janet took me on a tour of the neighborhood.

At that time, the population of the Mission was largely Central American, but there were remnants of the Italian and Irish presence from prior decades. Two of Janet's favorite spots were Lucca Ravioli and Dianda's Italian American Pastry, famous for their rum-soaked cake.

One evening, she brought me to a commune in the neighborhood to meet some of her "interesting" friends. The layout consisted of a classic Victorian home connected to a giant warehouse and an even bigger garden space, a parcel of land that the Southern Pacific Railroad used to run through. Combined, the property took up about a third of a city block.

As we entered the cavernous, industrial-looking kitchen, I recall seeing several young men. There was also a much older man who was slowly pacing the floor. He was very short, with a salt-and-pepper beard and long hair—I immediately typecast him as the charismatic guru holding sway over the younger men.

One man was standing at the sink washing dishes. He turned his head to see who had entered the room, and I felt an immediate affinity as my eyes alighted on his kind, deep face. We chatted a bit and discovered that as teenagers Ben and I had lived in neighboring twelve-story apartment buildings back in The Bronx.

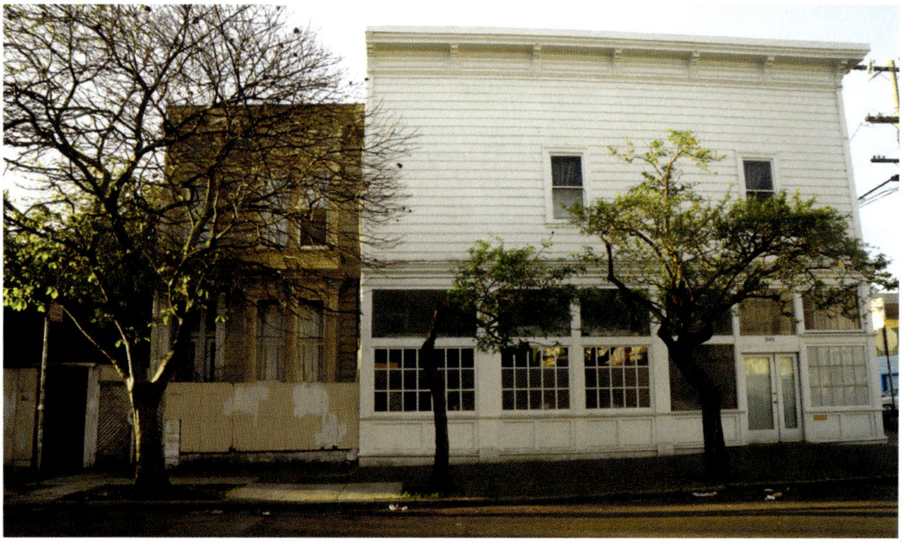

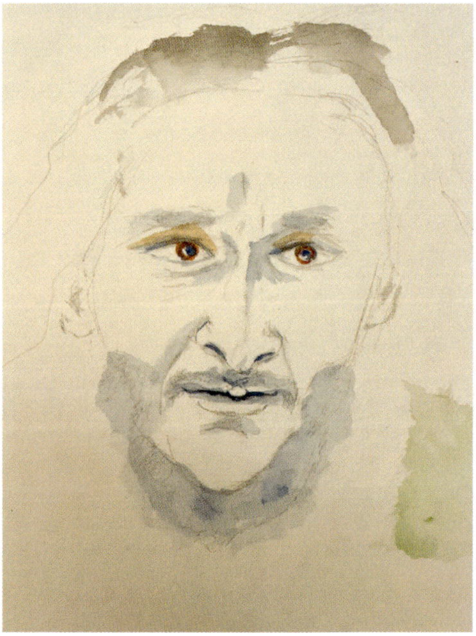

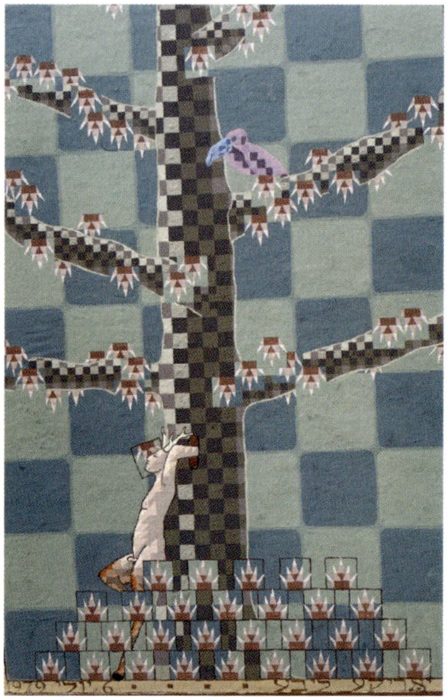

(ABOVE) Kaliflower Compound in the Mission District, San Francisco. Photo by Joseph Johnston.

(BELOW LEFT) *Ben*, c. 1983. Watercolor on paper, 8 × 10 in. (20.3 × 25.4 cm)

(BELOW RIGHT) Ben made this sublime painting for my thirtieth birthday. His style was not always geometric like this one.

A few days later, with trepidation, I knocked on the door of the Victorian house. The elfin older man, whose name was Irving Rosenthal, opened the door and subtly scowled at me. I asked if I could see Ben, and he ushered me into a room off the front hallway and then disappeared.

The room was sparsely furnished with a platform that served as a bed—it could not have been wider than two feet. There was a table and chair with some art supplies including an airbrush. The setup was ascetic, to say the least. Ben seemed happy, if not a little surprised, to see me and asked if he could paint my portrait. I recall many dark colors, and instead of hair, he painted snakes all around my head.

I came back a few times, and we got to know each other. He introduced me to his fellow communards and shared some of the beautiful things about the group. There was an atmosphere of creativity and innovation. One man was a master organic gardener who wrote love songs about whales. Two others, David and Peter, were ace mechanics, and, of course, Ben was a consummate artist and one of the members who operated the commune's printing press.

I also learned more about Irving, which helped me to understand the esteem in which he was held by the group members. He was almost fifty by the time I entered the scene, but in 1958, while a graduate student at the University of Chicago, he had been the editor of *Chicago Review*, a highly respected student-run literary journal. He courageously published excerpts from the not-yet-published novel *Naked Lunch* by William Burroughs. Writing in the *Chicago Daily News*, Jack Mabley referred to the issue as "one of the foulest collections of printed filth I've seen publicly circulated." University administrators insisted that Rosenthal's next issue be "completely innocuous." In the now-famous episode, Rosenthal protested the university's censorship by resigning and was joined by all but one member of the editorial staff. He took galleys from the planned next issue of *Chicago Review* and published them in the inaugural issue of *Big Table*, a journal he founded with the other staff members who had resigned.

Ten years later, Irving's autobiographical novel *Sheeper* was published and is considered a minor classic in the beat literary genre. I read it but found it to be a stream of consciousness that barely held my interest. Donald Stanley, in the *San Francisco Examiner* when it was published in 1967, wrote:

> *There is no plot. Instead, what he uses for plot—is the recurrence over and over and over again of the details of Sheeper's homosexuality.*

Stanley went on to say:

> *But leaving the question of morality to better moralists than I, one is stuck with the conviction that this approach, this startling frankness, this violation of old taboos will become commoner before it becomes rarer.*

Irving had a reputation for being extremely controlling, and Ben confided in me that he was in a contentious relationship with him, perhaps on the verge of a falling-out.[30] My heart sang with optimism when I heard this, and I grew hopeful that he might someday leave this cult-like group. I did not have long to wait. Within weeks of our meeting, Ben left the commune and moved into El Capitan, a cheap hotel on Mission Street. He spent a lot of time at my apartment, and we started a relationship that felt magical and rekindled my love of art. While I slept, he often stayed awake, and in the morning, I would be delighted to find a beautiful watercolor painting.

JUST BEFORE MEETING BEN, I had started taking an art class at City College of San Francisco. Ben praised my drawings, and we talked a lot about art. He opened my eyes to the classical Greek aesthetic and to the Art Nouveau-inspired work of Berkeley artist David Lance Goines. Ben had met Goines and absorbed some of his style into his own art. Starting then, and in future years, Ben encouraged and believed in my artistic yearnings and became a kind of mentor to me.

We decided to look for a place together and found a flat near Precita Park owned by Cosimo and Antonella, an elderly Sicilian couple who lived in the flat below.

We spent hours working on our art, and I began experimenting again with egg tempera. In one of my first efforts, *Friend Reading a Book,* my intention was to portray a woman who, while reading or studying, is distracted, thinking about her lover. However, a friend interpreted the image as the breaking of water in pregnancy heralding the start of labor.

BEN HAD HIS HEART SET on traveling to Europe to absorb the great art of the Western world. I was reluctant to leave my friends and job at the Native American Health Center. And since I'd already experienced a magical three-month solo trip to Europe when I was twenty-one, I was not particularly interested in traveling there again.

But with an intense desire to stay with Ben, I packed up my life for what turned out to be an eight-month adventure.

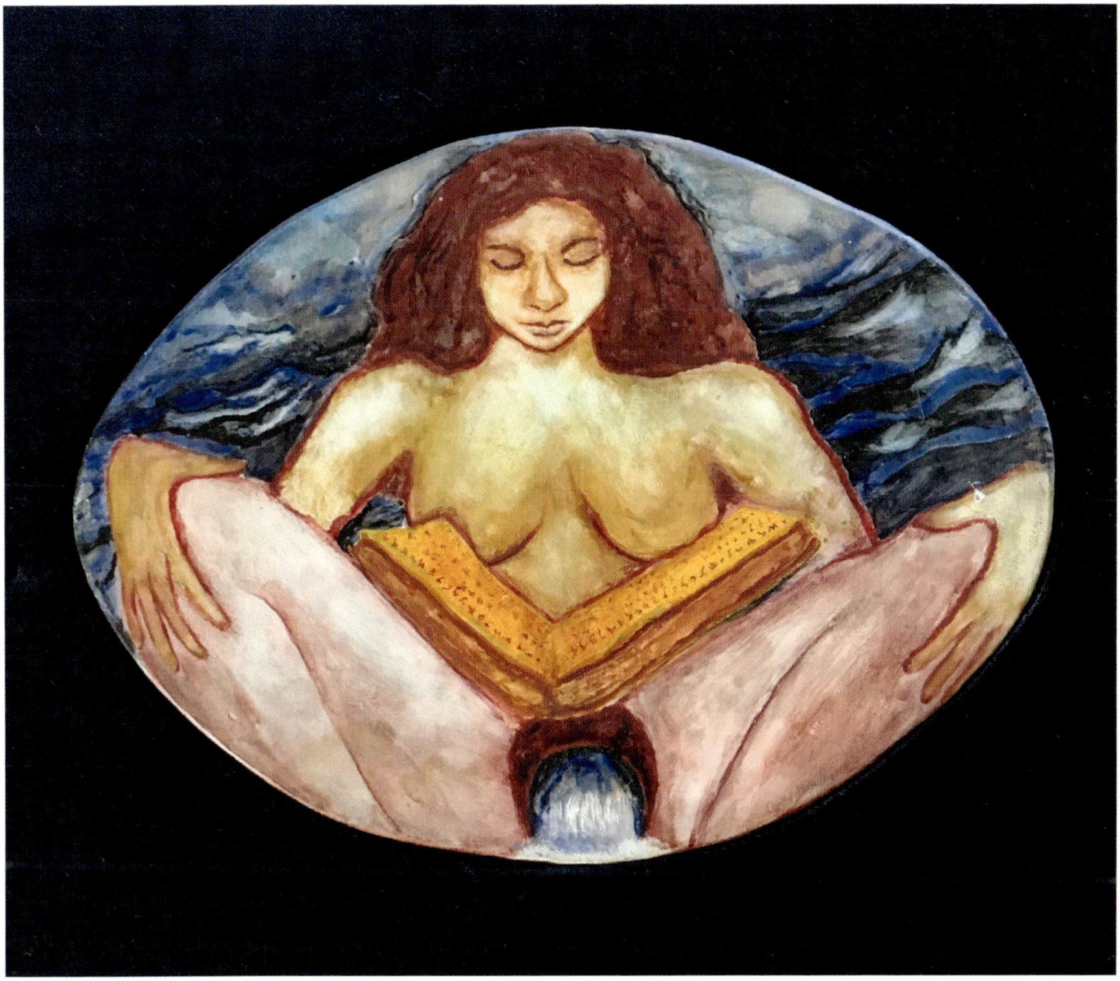

(ABOVE) *Friend Reading a Book,* 1979. Egg tempera on oval-shaped gesso panel, 10 × 9 in. (25.4 × 22.8 cm)

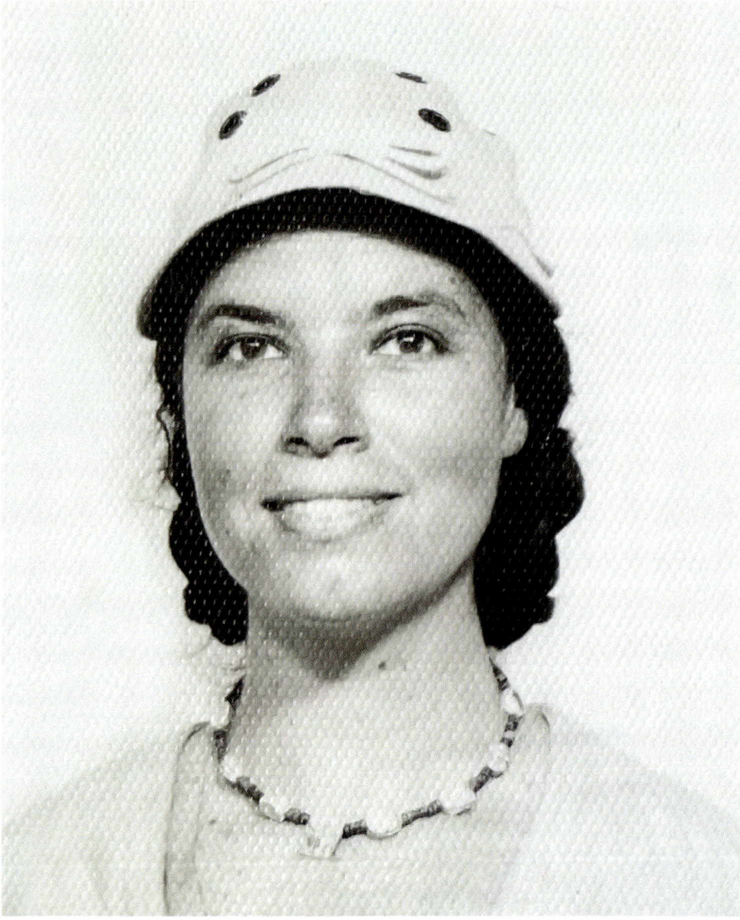

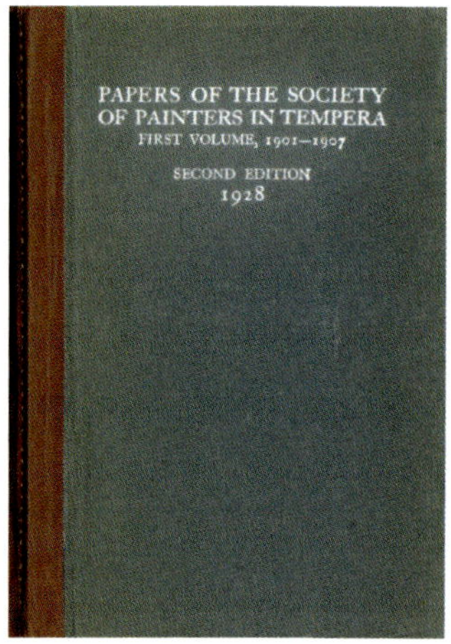

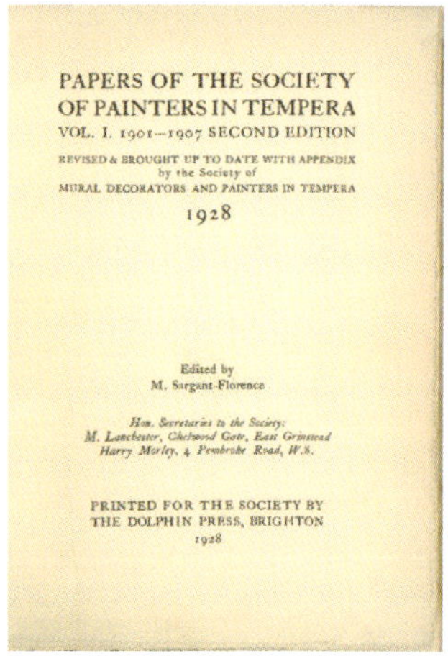

PAPERS OF THE SOCIETY
OF PAINTERS IN TEMPERA
VOL. I. 1901–1907 SECOND EDITION

REVISED & BROUGHT UP TO DATE WITH APPENDIX
by the Society of
MURAL DECORATORS AND PAINTERS IN TEMPERA

1928

Edited by
M. Sargant-Florence

Hon. Secretaries to the Society:
M. Lanchester, Chelwood Gate, East Grinstead
Harry Morley, 4 Pembroke Road, W.8.

PRINTED FOR THE SOCIETY BY
THE DOLPHIN PRESS, BRIGHTON
1928

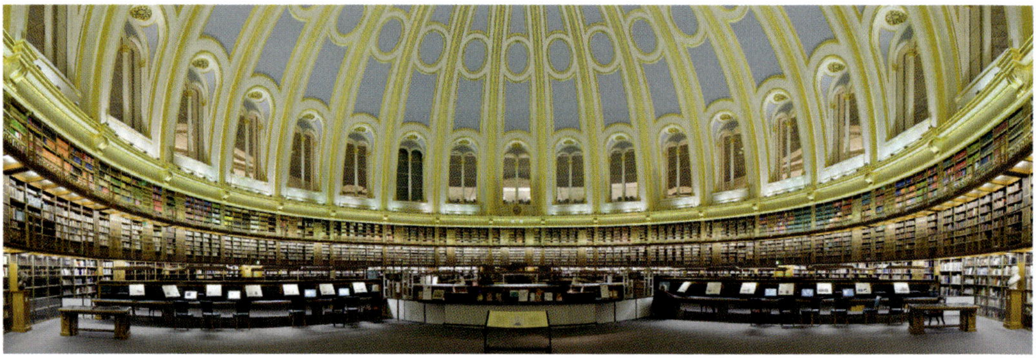

(ABOVE LEFT) In Paris, 1981

(ABOVE RIGHT) Cover and title page of *Papers of the Society of Painters in Tempera, First Volume, 1901–1907,* second edition, 1928

(BELOW) The British Museum Reading Room, c. 2006. Photo by Diliff.

CHAPTER TEN

TRAVELS IN EUROPE & BEYOND

We landed at Heathrow Airport in the middle of winter 1980. My first impression of London was of the omnipresent patrolling bobbies in their iconic helmets, armed only with nightsticks.

During our three weeks in London, we stayed with a woman in a council flat in Hackney, where we fed shillings into a meter to dispense a timed amount of heat.[31]

Ben and I gained permission to enter the Prints and Drawings Study Room of the British Museum, where we literally touched, and sometimes copied, drawings and etchings of the great masters.

What a thrill it was when an original drawing by Leonardo, Rembrandt, or Dürer was set before me on the table where we sat. Protective gloves were not required at that time, and I've since learned that white cotton gloves are no longer recommended for handling archival paper—clean dry hands are safest.[32]

I researched egg tempera history in the glorious British Museum Reading Room, becoming familiar with the *Papers of the Society of Painters in Tempera*. This sparked the idea to revive this venerable society, which was founded in England in 1901 by Christiana Herringham and a group of egg tempera painters. Years later, this dream would become a reality (see chapter 16).

And so, I became doubly obsessed: learning the egg tempera painting technique and delving into thousands of years of tempera history.

We had just missed an exhibit of paintings by egg tempera pioneer Joseph Edward Southall at the Fine Art Society. The paintings had been returned to the Birmingham Museum of Art, so we hitchhiked to Birmingham in the snow. The director of the museum graciously gave us a private showing of Southall's work in the basement storage area. Southall's sublime technical skill and elegant imagery approached egg tempera perfection.

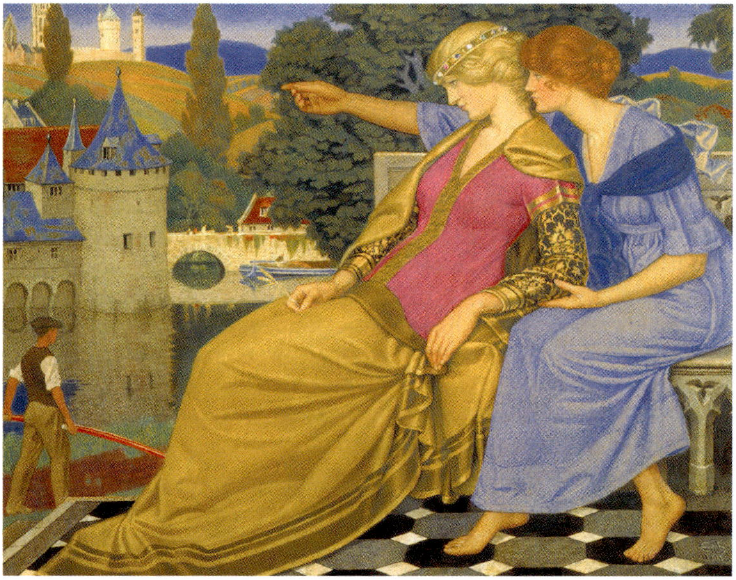

(ABOVE) Joseph Edward Southall, *Belgium Supported by Hope*, 1918. Egg tempera on linen, 12½ × 16 1/8 in. (31.8 cm × 41 cm). Tate, London. Photo: Tate.

Southall did very little painting during the First World War, devoting most of his time to the cause of pacificism, a tenet of his Quaker faith. Despite the ravages of the war, in *Belgium Supported by Hope,* Southall, speaking through the figure of Hope (in the blue dress), seems to be encouraging Belgium (the figure in pink) to renew and rebuild her country.

After a rough ferry ride across the English Channel, we spent our first night in Paris in a cheap tourist hotel. In the morning, while I slept, Ben scouted out less expensive lodging, and by the time I awakened, he had located an even cheaper hotel in Belleville, a Vietnamese-Moroccan neighborhood, several metro stops out of the central area.

The mattress was so soft that Ben removed the closet door from its hinges and placed it under the mattress. To stretch our money during the eight months of travel, we bought a miniature pressure cooker and camping stove, shopping at local markets to create our own meals. For entertainment, we took turns reading *Moby-Dick* to each other in the evenings.

Feeling deprived of Parisian cuisine, I spent an afternoon searching out French pastries. I sampled many, but they all tasted "off." I finally surmised that they may have been made with margarine instead of butter.[33]

From Paris, we hitchhiked to the Netherlands.

Amsterdam

Camping in winter is not for delicate types. In Amsterdam, after a night trying to sleep in frost, we rented a room at Hotel My Home.

At this time, I was becoming depressed. I was carrying a heavy backpack and suffered from chronic heel pain caused by plantar fasciitis. Ben tried to encourage me by saying, "You walk very slowly... but you never stop." I recall he bought me a flower to cheer me up. I had written to a friend back home telling her what to do with my possessions. She became alarmed and notified her friends in Italy to look out for me when I got there. But by that time, the mood had passed—I had never seriously planned to end my life.

I had been ambivalent about the trip in the first place; then traveling in winter and the ascetic manner of our travel wore me down. I don't recall arguing with Ben, but in hindsight I can see that I was gradually losing myself to his charisma and lifestyle, which was heavily influenced by the commune he had left. When my grandmother Reizel died on March 29, 1981, I did not fly home for the funeral, which I still deeply regret.

On the other hand, I was terribly excited by the art we were experiencing. Ben had no interest in egg tempera but was supportive of my fascination and more than willing to go off the beaten track in search of obscure tempera artists.

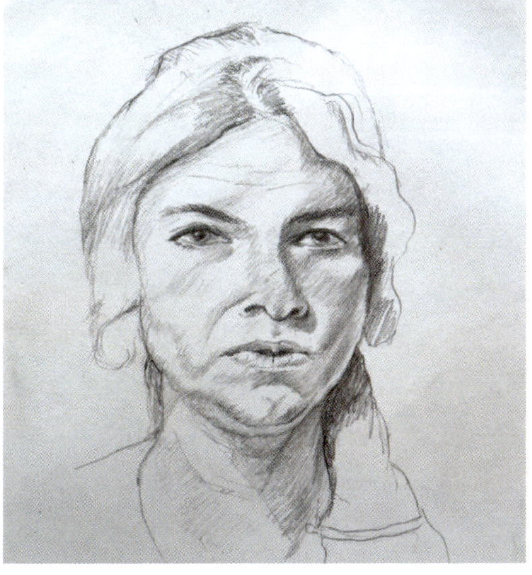

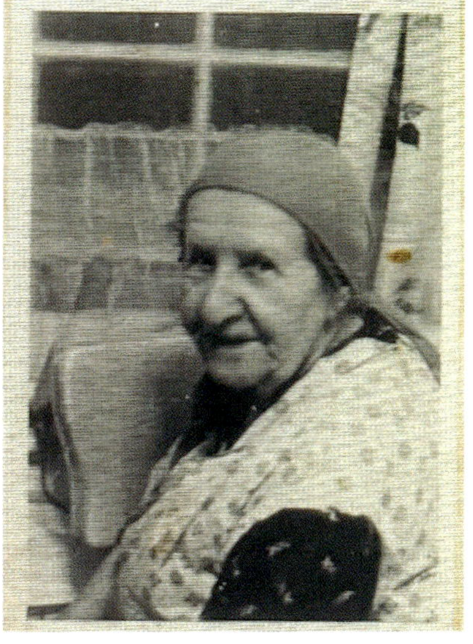

(ABOVE LEFT) *Self-Portrait in Europe,* c. 1981. Pencil on paper, 7½ × 5½ in. (19 × 14 cm)

(ABOVE RIGHT) My paternal grandmother, Reizel Goldbaum. Photo by Ruth Goldbaum.

Paula Modersohn-Becker

From Amsterdam, we hitchhiked to Germany, where we made a pilgrimage to the northern city of Bremen and to the artist colony Worpswede to soak in the art and times of Paula Modersohn-Becker. Not long before, I had come across a book of her art and was blown over by the expressively intense, simplified portraits.

Paula Becker was born in Dresden in 1876, but her family moved to Bremen as she entered her teenage years. After studying art in Bremen, London, and Berlin, in 1898 she moved to the rural village of Worpswede. She had been inspired by the work of a group of artists who had settled there, drawn to the pastoral setting and distance from the stifling art academies. She studied with Fritz Mackensen and met and later married fellow painter Otto Modersohn.

THE WORPSWEDE ARTISTS focused on landscape painting, but Modersohn-Becker said, "Painting people is indeed more beautiful than painting a landscape."[34] I was deeply moved by the portraits she drew of peasants and people living in the local poorhouse.

While living in Worpswede, she met the sculptor Clara Westhoff and her fiance, the poet Rainer Maria Rilke. Both became life-long friends.[35]

Although the artists in Worpswede, including her husband, were content to paint traditional subject matter, Modersohn-Becker was drawn to the exciting work of the breakthrough modernist painters working in Paris: Gauguin, Cézanne, Van Gogh, Degas, and Rodin. Modersohn-Becker first went to Paris in 1900 to study at the Académie Colarossi.[36] She would make three more transformative trips to Paris. In addition to the modernists, she was also influenced by Japanese, Old Master, and ancient Greek and Egyptian art, which she spent hours copying in the Louvre Museum. But far from being derivative, she broke new ground, writing to her sister Milly in May 1906, "I am becoming somebody—I'm living the most intensely happy period of my life. Pray for me.... Never lose faith in me."[37]

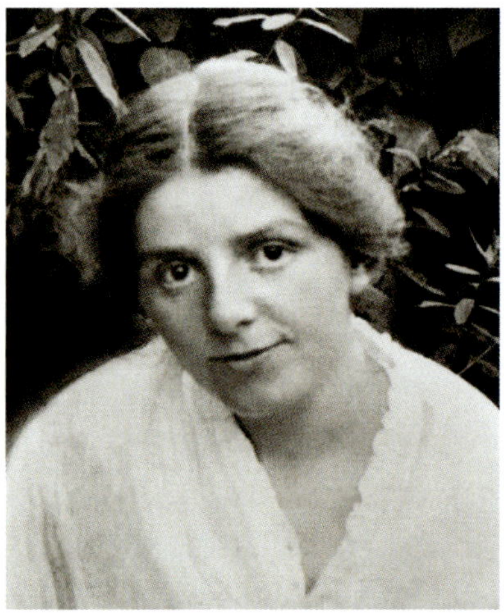

(RIGHT) Paula Modersohn-Becker, c. 1905. Paula Modersohn-Becker Foundation, Bremen, Germany. Photographer unknown.

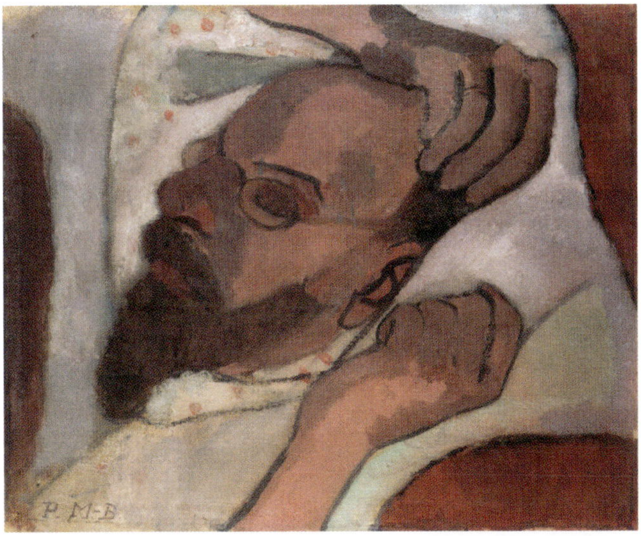

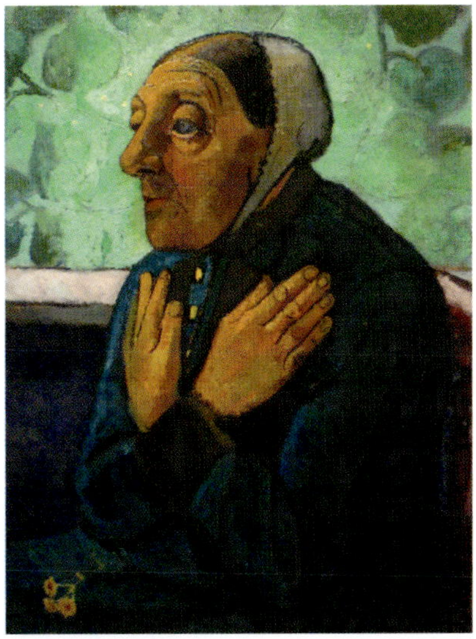

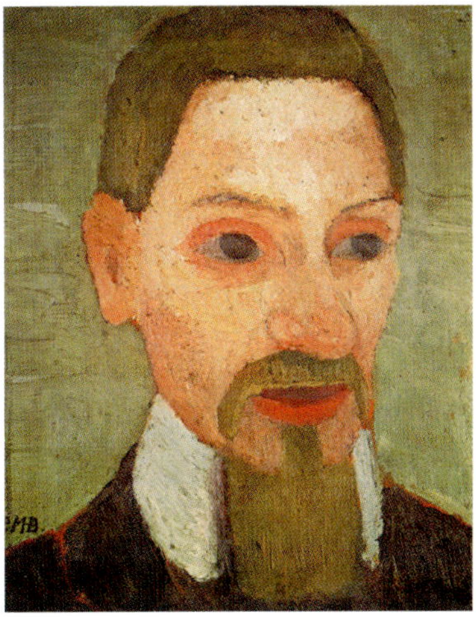

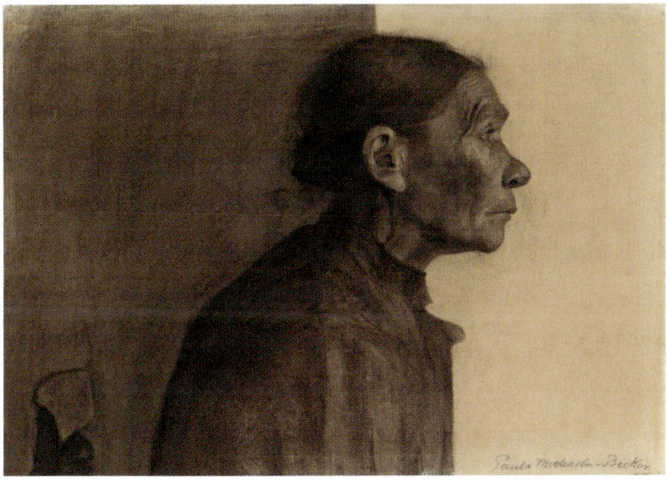

(ABOVE LEFT) Paula Modersohn-Becker, *Otto Modersohn Sleeping*, 1906. Tempera grassa (egg-oil) on canvas, $15\frac{3}{4} \times 18\frac{1}{4}$ in. (40 cm × 46.5 cm). Paula Modersohn-Becker Foundation, Bremen, Germany

(ABOVE RIGHT) Paula Modersohn-Becker, *Old Peasant Woman*, 1905. Oil on canvas, $29\frac{3}{4} \times 22\frac{3}{4}$ in. (75.6 × 57.8 cm). Detroit Institute of Arts

(BELOW LEFT) Paula Modersohn-Becker, *Portrait of Rainer Maria Rilke*, 1906. Oil and tempera on cardboard, $12\frac{3}{4} \times 10$ in. (32.3 × 25.4 cm). Louisiana Museum of Modern Art, Denmark

(BELOW RIGHT) Paula Modersohn-Becker, *Woman in Profile, Turned Right*, 1898–99. Charcoal on paper, $18\frac{3}{8} \times 25\frac{3}{4}$ in. (46.7 × 65.4 cm). Art Institute of Chicago

Her husband, Otto, was at first in awe of her talent and vision, but later commented on her work in his journal in 1903:

> *Paula hates to be conventional and is now falling prey to the error of preferring to make everything angular, ugly, bizarre, wooden.... Her colors are wonderful, but the form? The expression! Hands like spoons, noses like cobs, mouths like wounds, faces like cretins.... She overloads things.... It is difficult to give her advice, as usual.*[38]

In researching this book, I was surprised to learn that she frequently combined egg tempera with oil paint in order to achieve the simplicity she aspired to.

Many years after her death, Modersohn-Becker's work was included in the Degenerate Art (*Entartete Kunst*) exhibition organized in 1937 by the Nazi Party. The accompanying text read:

> *Her vision is so lacking in femininity and so vulgar.... Her work is an insult to German women and to our farming culture.... Where is the sensitivity, the essence of the feminine-maternal spirit?... A revolting mixture of colours, of idiotic figures signifying farmers, of sick children, degenerates, the dregs of humanity.*[39]

Self-Portrait at 6th Wedding Anniversary is the first full-figure nude self-portrait by a woman in Western art. Actually, Modersohn-Becker was not pregnant at the time she painted this but became pregnant soon after.

In 1906, she stayed in Paris an entire year. By that time her marriage was strained, but Otto came to Paris to see if their relationship could be repaired. They reconciled and she returned to Worpswede pregnant.

Two to four weeks of bed rest after childbirth was recommended at the time, which we now know encourages the formation of blood clots in the veins of the leg, which can be fatal if they break off and travel to the lungs or heart. In 1907, she died of a massive pulmonary embolism eighteen days after giving birth, when she was first allowed to stand.[40][41] I was deeply struck by her tragic death at age thirty-one, exposing the obstacles and hazards that women faced—and still do today to some extent.

Although she had been painting for less than ten years, she completed 400 paintings and 1,000 graphic works, which her daughter, Mathilde, lovingly preserved and promoted. Ironically, her tragic story has been twisted into a legend that purports that, had she lived, she might have been the next Cézanne, or some such melodramatic conjecture.

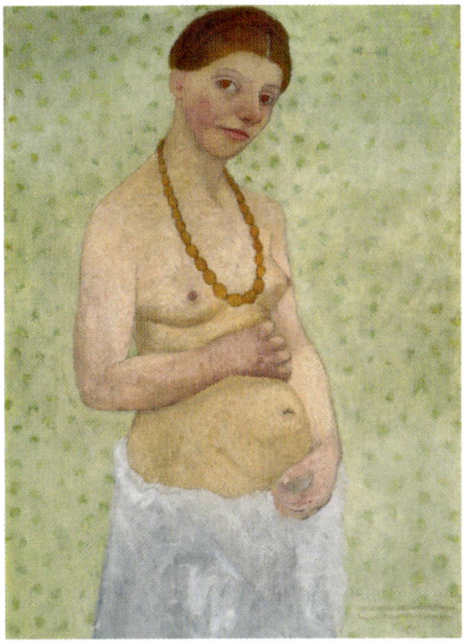

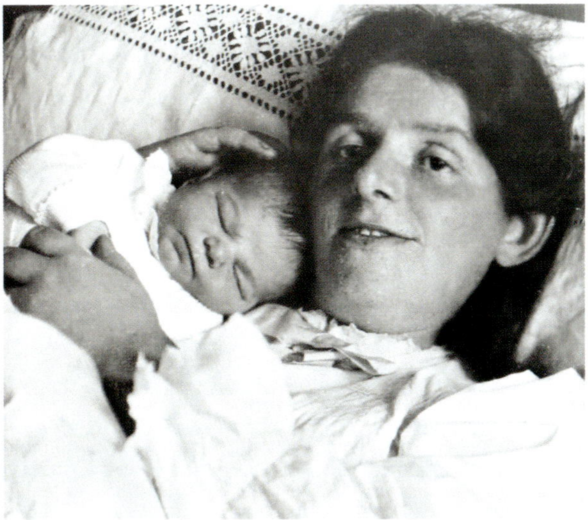

(LEFT) Paula Modersohn-Becker, *Self-Portrait at 6th Wedding Anniversary*, 1906. Tempera on canvas, 40$^{1}/_{16}$ × 27$^{5}/_{8}$ in. (101.8 × 70.2 cm). Paula Modersohn-Becker Museum, Bremen, Germany.
(ABOVE) Paula Modersohn-Becker with her daughter, Mathilde, November, 1907. Photo by Hugo Erfurth.

Male artists who die young are viewed as having a complete body of work, such as Egon Schiele, whose output is similar to Modersohn-Becker's—330 paintings and 3,000 drawings.

But this is changing as art historians are bringing to light her unique vision and contribution to the history of art.[42] She is revered in Germany, where we visited the Paula Modersohn-Becker Museum in Bremen, the first museum in the world to be dedicated to the work of a female painter. Her style is now considered part of the foundation of modern German art.

Traveling South: The End of Hitchhiking

Next, we hitchhiked south through Germany, Austria, and the Italian Alps. A brawny Italian truck driver, upon learning I was childless at thirty, offered to help impregnate me, noting that obviously Ben was not up to the task. I had a fleeting fear of impending rape but opted to see it as a humorous offer, even though this man seemed quite serious!

I put a halt to hitchhiking after a frightening joyride in Italy. The driver, his companion snuggled under his arm, was singing at the top of his lungs while speeding down the *autostrada* in a tinny little car. It so frightened me that I whispered to Ben, "I'm going to pretend to be sick," and proceeded to feign nausea, motioning a request to stop the car. We sat in the grass near a service station, and I continued my sick charade until the couple drove off. After that, we mostly took trains and buses and walked a lot.

We were disappointed that Botticelli's colossal egg tempera *The Birth of Venus* was being restored and so was absent from its usual spot in the Uffizi Gallery in Florence. But we saw the work of other virtuoso egg tempera painters, including Fra Angelico in the National Museum of San Marco in the hilltop town of Fiesole.

Fra Angelico is described by Giorgio Vasari, one of the first art historians, as having "a rare and perfect talent" and that his panels were "painted by a saint or an angel."[43] Writer and critic William Michael Rossetti wrote, "It is averred that he never handled a brush without fervent prayer and he wept when he painted a Crucifixion."[44]

Fra Angelico was beatified on October 3, 1982, by Pope John Paul II and in 1984 was declared patron saint of Catholic artists. I was impressed when the taxi driver who took us to Fiesole referred to Fra Angelico reverentially as "Beato." I thought, "Even taxi drivers in Italy revere their artists," but I've since learned that in modern Italian, he is called "Beato Angelico" (Blessed Angelic One).

From Italy we traveled to Spain where, in Barcelona, the Sagrada Família, Antoni Gaudí's towering, unfinished cathedral, was a beehive of activity. Cranes and workers were buzzing around the elaborate structure that seemed like a cross between a living organism and a crusty sandcastle.

Gaudí spent his last years actually living in the church so he could devote all his time to the project. When asked how he felt about the massive amount of work still needed, Gaudí replied, "My client is not in a hurry." I am adopting Gaudí's words as my mantra whenever I feel my painting, or this book, is taking too long to complete.

At the time of his death, less than a quarter of the project was completed. As of this writing, in 2025, the cathedral is projected to be structurally complete in 2026, but work on decorative details and a controversial stairway may continue until 2034.

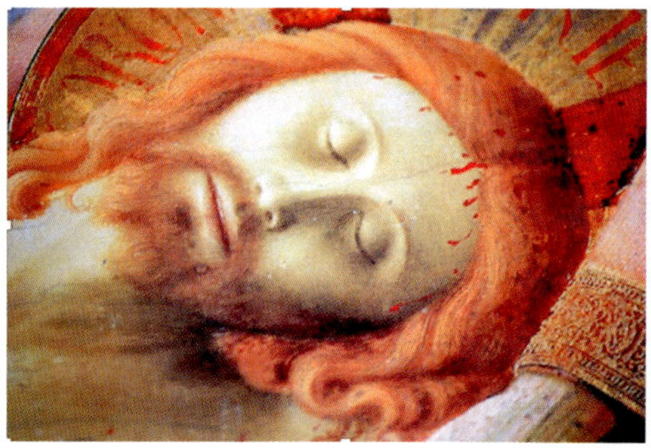

(RIGHT) Detail: Fra Angelico, *Deposition of Christ*, 1432–34. Egg tempera on panel. 18⅜ × 25¾ in. (46.7 × 65.4 cm). National Museum of San Marco, Florence

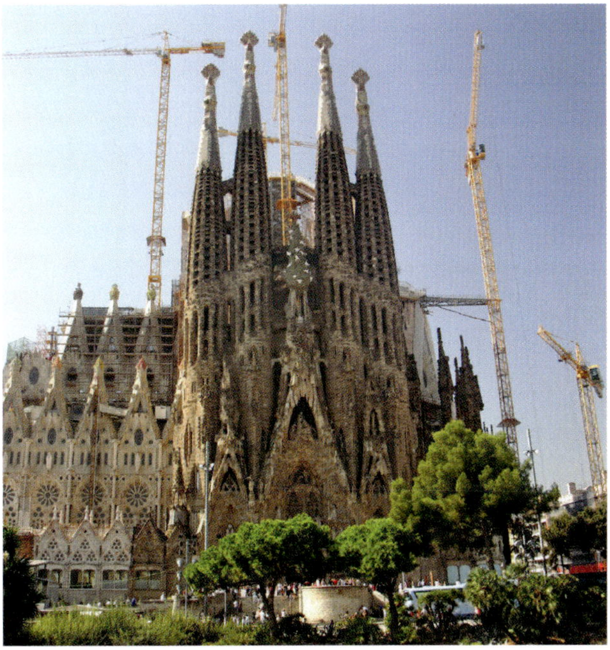

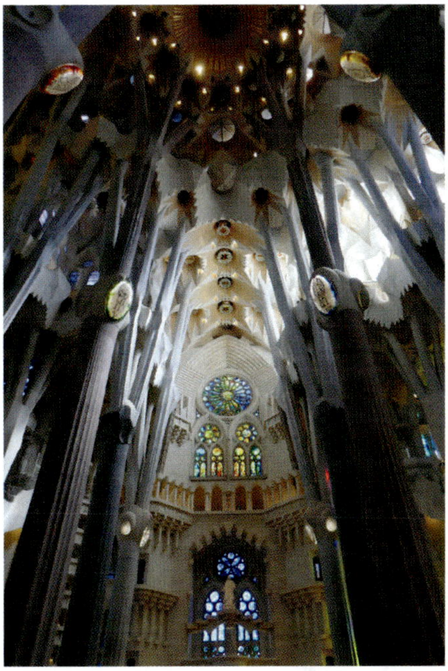

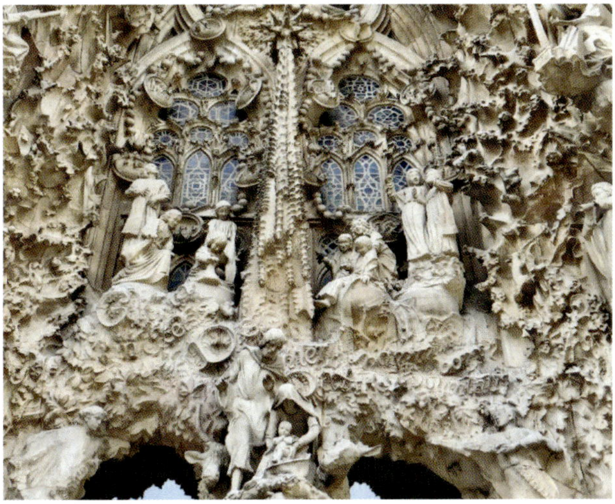

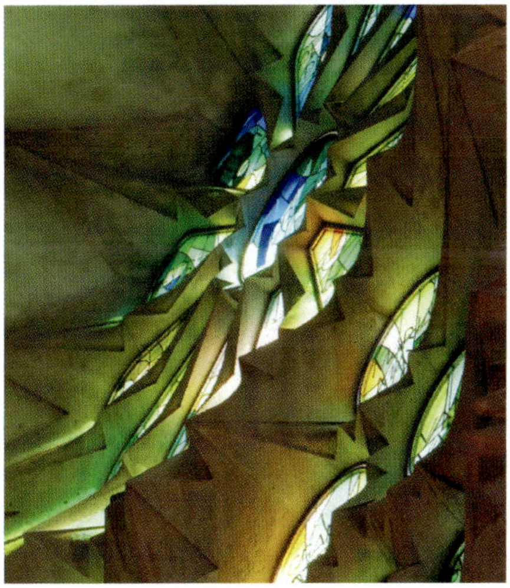

(ABOVE LEFT) La Sagrada Familia, designed by Antoni Gaudí, Barcelona, Spain. Photo by Greg Balfour Evans, 2011.

(BELOW LEFT) Exterior of La Sagrada Familia. Photo by Neil Steinberg, *Chicago Sun-Times*, 2022.

(ABOVE RIGHT, BELOW RIGHT) Interior of La Sagrada Familia: vaulted ceilings, modeled after a canopy of trees; morning light casting colors from the stained glass windows onto white interior walls. Both photos by Domini Dragoone, 2019.

Morocco

From Spain, we crossed the Strait of Gibraltar into Tangier, Morocco. The call to prayer over a loudspeaker and the overwhelming smell of peppermint in the streets heralded entrance into another world. The ubiquitous peppermint tea contained so much sugar that a man in a cafe entertained us by encouraging a swarm of bees to alight on his tea-soaked tongue.

While in Fez, we stayed in the medina, the walled-off old part of the city with narrow, maze-like streets. Our room had no bathing facilities, so we went to the neighborhood bathhouse. I was surprised when an elderly woman bathed me as she would a young child. It seemed the entry fee included this service. My watercolor sketch entitled *Moroccan Woman* was not intended to be an exact portrayal of the woman but more of a feeling of her.

The weight of our backpacks was always an issue, and in Spain we delighted some Roma people (derogatorily called gypsies) when we gave them our tent.

I had schlepped my banjo across six countries but never played it. Finally, I became willing to part with it and created a scene in Fez when competing vendors vied to purchase it.

In the marketplace where we bought produce for our meals, I noticed some of the women wore veils with only their eyes exposed, while others were not veiled at all or only held their headscarf in their mouth to partially cover their face. These women often had mysterious, black-patterned tattoos on their faces. I learned that these were Berbers, an indigenous people of North Africa.[45]

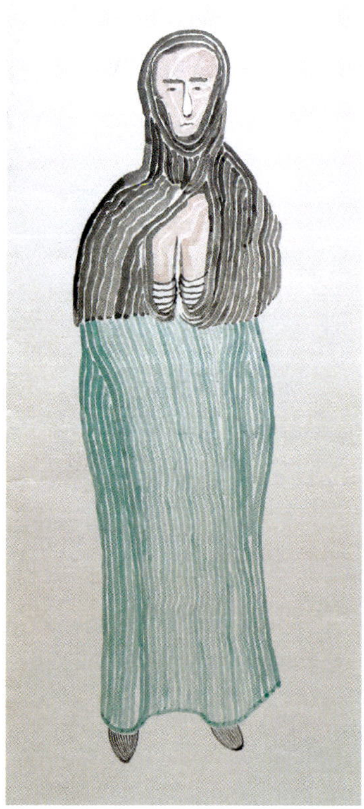

In order to experience more Berber culture, we left Fez and walked from Berber village to Berber village. Along one footpath, we watched a young man open a melon with a swift karate chop of his hand. Up to that time, I'd been meticulously careful to avoid getting sick, but he offered me a glass of water, and although I was not thirsty, I felt I could not refuse his kind gesture.

Two weeks of dysentery ensued. Thankfully, when I got up from my sickbed at our hotel, the intense heel pain that had plagued me the entire trip had vanished, never to return.[46]

Amazigh (Berber) Women

The term "Berber" was given to them by the Romans and is viewed as derogatory, so many Berbers refer to themselves as "Amazigh" (singular) or less frequently "Imazighen" (plural), which translates as "free men."

Prior to the Arab conquest in the late seventh century, Morocco was inhabited by mostly Amazigh people. With Arab rule, many Berbers converted to Islam.

Some Amazigh tribes from the fourth through sixth centuries were likely matrilineal, and the women played significant roles in local communities. Kahina was a legendary Amazigh female military leader who fought against the Arab expansion into North Africa.

The tattoo tradition dates to pre-Islamic times, when it helped nomadic Amazigh tribes distinguish between members of different groups. The designs are symbolic and are believed to cure illness and infertility, protect against evil spirits, and promote health and beauty. The markings are made as a rite of passage into womanhood, although there are many reports of forced tattooing.

The tattoo custom started to decline during France's occupation in 1907–1934 and with the rise of radical Islam in Morocco in the twenty-first century.[47] Tattoos are seen mostly in elderly women who were born at a time when tattoos were celebrated, but they have now become a source of shame. However, some younger women are reclaiming the tradition but usually confine their tattoos to non-facial areas of the body.

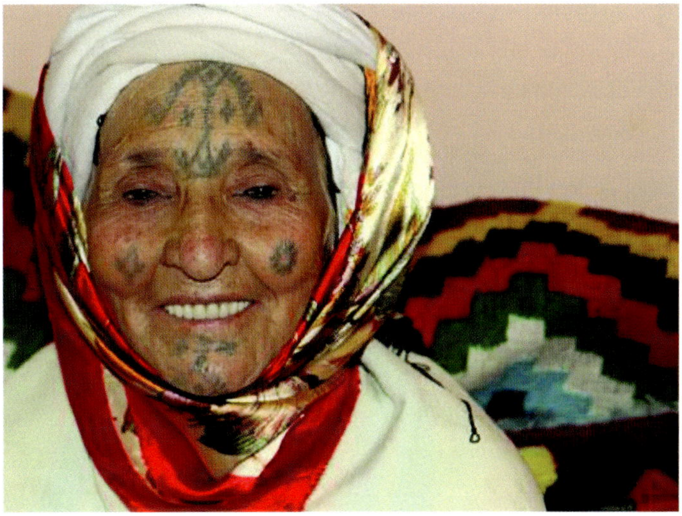

(OPPOSITE) *Moroccan Woman*, c. 1981. Watercolor on paper, 5 × 8 in. (12.7 × 20.3 cm)

(LEFT) Berber woman with tattoos, Sefrou, Morocco. Photo by Skye Hohmann. We did not carry a camera with us, but this photo is reminiscent of many Berber women we met.

Study of Anatomy

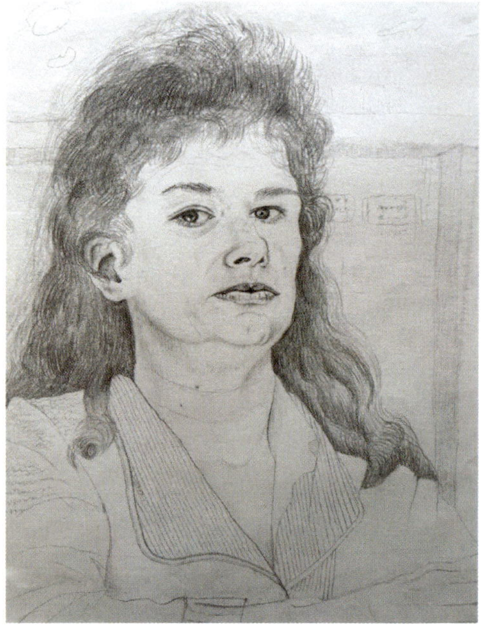

After eight months, I became weary of traveling and leery of the overland journey through Africa we were planning to undertake. Although we had not been arguing and had a close and creative bond, I impulsively broke up with Ben and left him in Morocco.

I then traveled to London to complete the return leg of my round-trip ticket back to San Francisco. While in London, I took the train to Windsor Castle, where I spent a day in the Print Room of the Royal Library perusing the original anatomical drawings of Leonardo da Vinci. Aside from the librarian, I was the only person in the room, intensifying the sublime experience.

I learned anatomy in nursing school and studied it again as an artist, first from books and later with expert instructor Rob Anderson. Sadly, Anderson passed away from AIDS in 2014.

John Walsh, my friend from the Haight Free Clinic (and the subject of my painting *Don't Go My Friend*), suggested I meet Gary Faigin, co-founder of the Gage Academy of Art in Seattle. He would later write *The Artist's Complete Guide to Facial Expression* (1990).

Gary suggested that I deepen my knowledge of anatomy by drawing every bone in the body to learn where the tendons and ligaments attach. For this study, he advised me to buy a disarticulated human skeleton. I purchased a twenty-five-year-old female skeleton for $300 and gave her the name Petra.[48] I wondered what country she came from and how she died so young. While writing this book, I contacted Gary Faigin, who put to rest my curiosity concerning Petra's origin:

> *And you don't have to wonder about the original home of 'Petra'; it was India, without a doubt. At the time of your purchase, there was a brisk trade in bones from there, and only there. In general, unclaimed bodies could be acquired by bone merchants, who would then sell them to preparers for export. Sometime in the '80s (or so), there was a scandal suggesting more nefarious ways certain merchants were "finding" their bodies, and the Indian government decided to pull the plug on the whole business—bad for its image as a modernizing, Western-aspiring country.*[49]

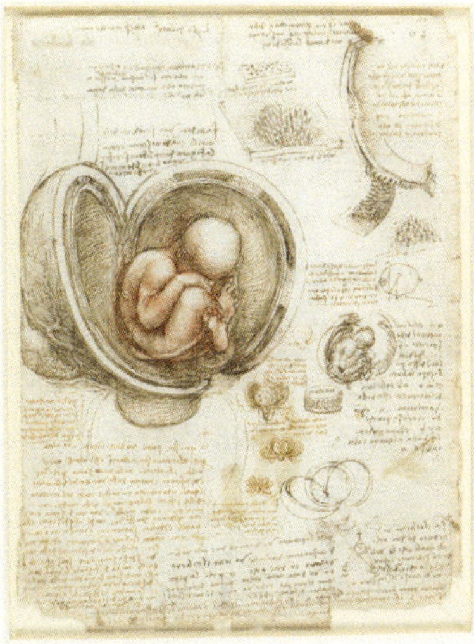

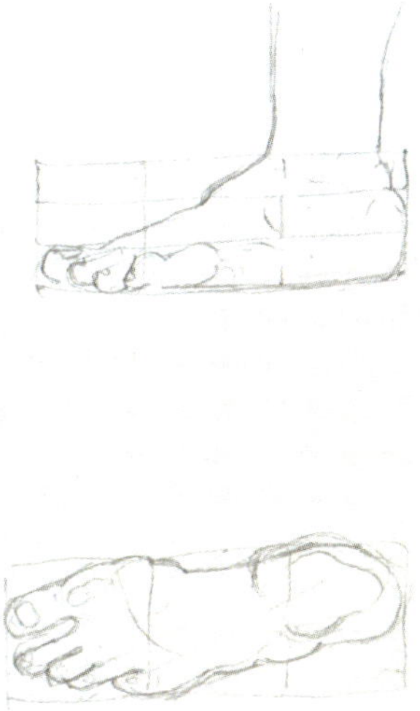

(OPPOSITE) *Self-Portrait,* c. 1981. Pencil on paper, 12 × 8½ in. (30.4 × 21.5 cm)

(ABOVE LEFT) Leonardo da Vinci, *Studies of the Fetus in the Womb,* 1510–12. Brown ink over black and red chalk on paper. Print Room of the Royal Library, Windsor Castle, Windsor, United Kingdom

(ABOVE RIGHT) My pencil sketches of a foot, c. 1981. Pencil on paper, 8 × 4 in. (20.3 × 10.1 cm)

I never did get around to drawing the individual bones, but I brought Petra to my son's school a couple of times for an educational presentation around Halloween. The children enjoyed spreading the bones out on a blanket and assembling them from head to foot. On one occasion, a boy said he was offended by the presence of a real skeleton. At the time, I felt put off, as it dampened the enthusiasm of the other children. I always treated Petra with respect and considered her box to be her grave. Mysteriously, Petra disappeared—I have no idea how it happened. I searched the school and my home but could not find the box. I thought perhaps the offended student had taken her, but I could not see how. I'm not sure what I would have done with Petra if she had not disappeared. Maybe build a beautiful box to keep her in, or return her to India for a proper burial in her tradition.

Every one of my paintings contains at least one figure, so anatomy is a constant concern. Although I revere virtuoso anatomy masters such as Michelangelo and Leonardo, my artistic vision does not cleave to strict realism. I include enough accuracy so that the anatomy reads correctly, but then simplify, distort, or otherwise transform the body to create a being that is not of this world.

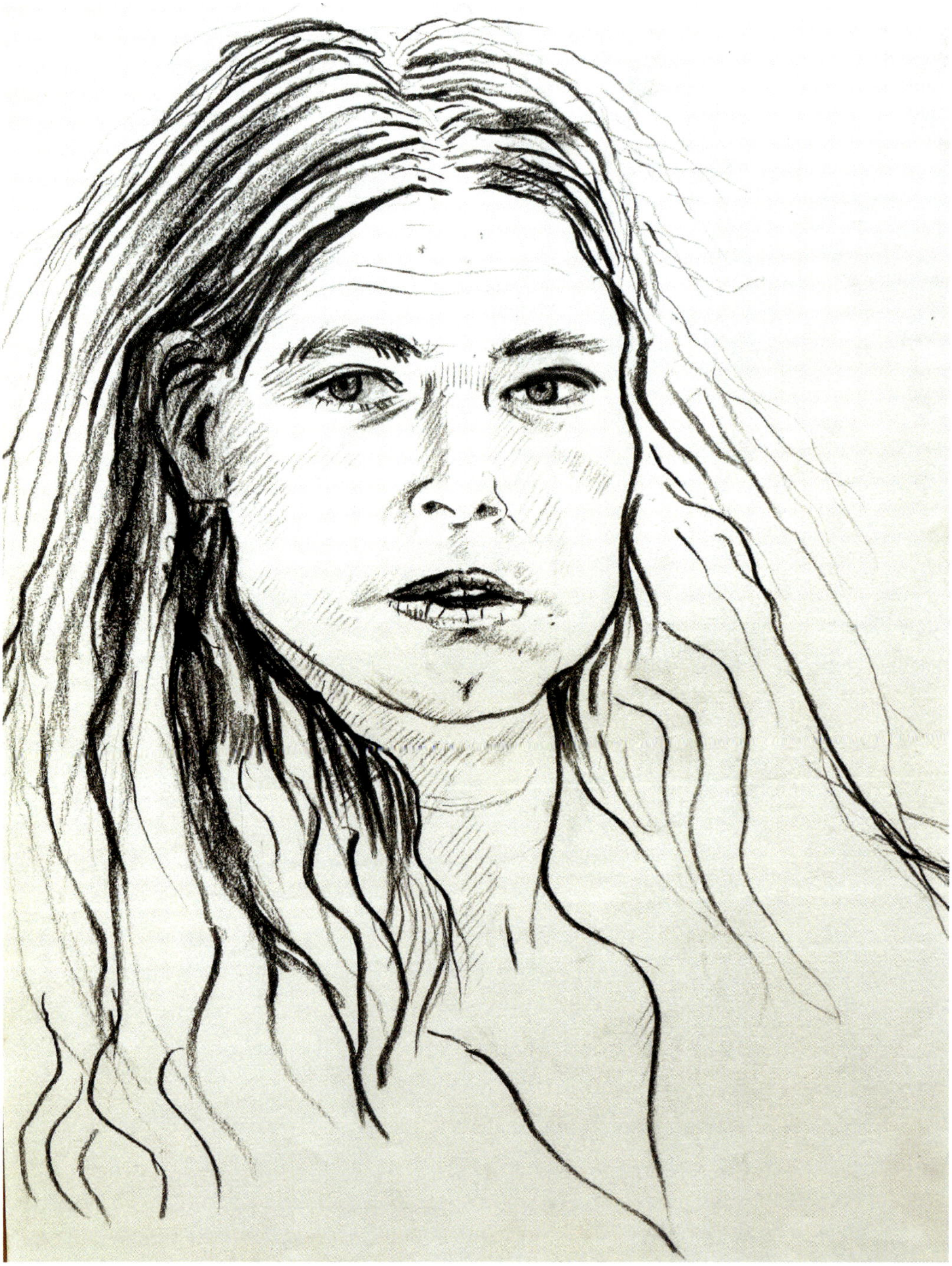

(ABOVE) *Self-Portrait,* 1983. Pencil on paper, 11 × 8½ in. (27.9 × 21.5 cm)

CHAPTER ELEVEN

LIFE IN THE KALIFLOWER COMMUNE

When I arrived back in San Francisco, I rented a tiny room in the home of a friend. I was depressed over the breakup with Ben and thought about him all the time. I was quite surprised when only weeks after we had parted in Morocco, I heard from him—he had returned to San Francisco! He said that he had received mail from the commune about an urgent matter that required his presence. Along with the business letter, Irving had written an ardent note to Ben reminding him of the beauty of the commune they had built together and entreating him to "come home."

When Ben called, he was already living back at the commune and asked me to join him there, saying he wanted to show me "the beauty of the way of life." I felt trepidation and a pang of revulsion at the thought of living at the commune. But my love for the tender and artistic Ben was the stronger emotion, quieting my ordinarily questioning mind. Within a matter of days, I had moved in.

While living at the commune, I learned that many of the beliefs and practices were derived from three sources: the nineteenth-century Oneida Community of silverware fame, and two different groups called "Diggers."[50] The earliest Diggers were a seventeenth-century English group who had challenged the oppressive feudal system of land ownership (see sidebar). Inspired by the English Diggers, the San Francisco Diggers of the 1960s appropriated the name and evolved their own expansive practices of freedom.

From Oneida, Kaliflower adopted the principles of common property, group marriage, and daily meetings. And from both Digger groups, they embraced the concept of "free," which became their central credo. While writing this book, I've found it helpful to read about these historical groups and observe how their beliefs and practices played out in my new home.

English Diggers of the Seventeenth Century

The English Diggers challenged the oppressive feudal system of land ownership by cultivating crops on the common wastelands of manors. "The earth was made a common treasury for all," wrote Gerrard Winstanley, a cloth merchant, Protestant religious reformer, and mystic, in *The True Levellers Standard Advanced* (pamphlet *1649*).

The English Diggers arose in response to the enclosure movement, in which fenced-off common lands had been turned into private property.[51] The lord of the manor owned an estate (actually the king owned it), but "the commons" was an integral part of the manor, and peasants had the right to "peaceful enjoyment." This might include grazing livestock, cutting wood, drawing water, or growing crops.

As medieval England progressed to modernity, wealthy landowners wanted to privatize the common lands to improve agricultural efficiency. Through various means, they were able to fence off or "enclose" large parcels of common lands or wastelands, which were then no longer available to peasants. Improved farming methods meant less labor was needed, so poor people were forced to migrate to cities and towns to seek work in factories and mines. This was one of the main causes of the Industrial Revolution.

The situation became dire during the English Civil Wars (1642–1651). Harvests were failing, and food prices were high. In response, on April 1, 1649, Gerrard Winstanley, along with William Everard, began cultivating crops on common wastelands of manors in order to feed themselves and others.

The group occupied these lands, pulling down hedges, filling in ditches, then planting crops and even constructing houses. They called themselves "True Levellers"—the term "Diggers" was used by both their supporters and opponents.

Local landowners reacted to the Diggers' activities by hiring armed men to beat the Diggers and destroy their colonies. Their crops were pulled up, their tools destroyed, and their houses set on fire. Local magistrates imposed heavy fines. Winstanley protested to the government, but to no avail. After only one year, by 1650, the colonies were abandoned.

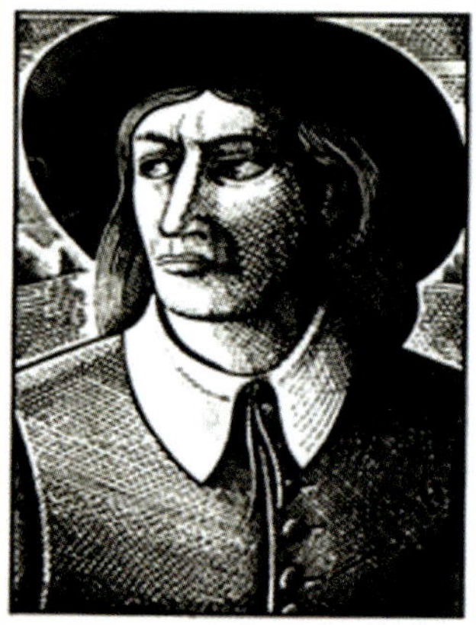

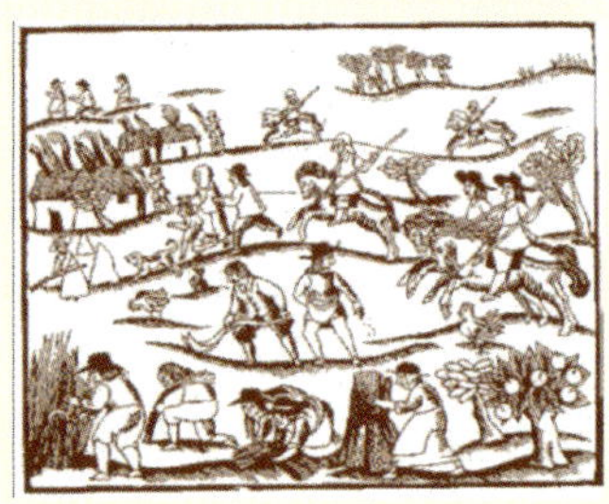

(ABOVE) *Gerrard Winstanley*, illustration by Clifford Harpur

(BELOW) ***Beginning to Plant and Manure the Waste land upon George-Hill, in the parish of Walton, in the County of Surrey.*** This woodcut first appeared in the 1649 pamphlet *The True Levellers Standard Advanced* by Gerrard Winstanley.

Oneida and Christian Perfectionism

The Oneida Community was founded in 1848 by John Humphrey Noyes and lasted for more than thirty years. Its underlying doctrine was Noyes's interpretation of Christian Perfectionism, which was based on the biblical Book of Revelation. He instructed that because Jerusalem was destroyed in 70 AD, the second coming of Christ had already taken place. Noyes wrote that Christ's appearance was not visible because "the second coming was an event in the spiritual, and not in the natural world."[52] Since heaven on earth had already arrived, Noyes preached that the community must manifest what God's reign would look like here on Earth. He declared himself free of sin and maintained that because he had surrendered his will to God, everything he chose to do was perfect, because his choices "came from a perfect heart."[53]

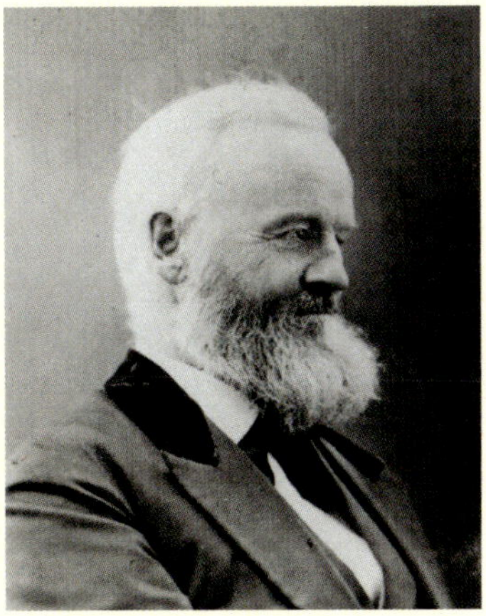

(LEFT) John Humphrey Noyes in profile, undated. Oneida Community Collection, Syracuse University Libraries, Syracuse, New York. Date and photographer unknown.

Friends of Perfection

When I joined in 1982, I learned that the official name of the commune was Friends of Perfection. Not knowing that Oneida was based on Christian Perfectionism, Friends of Perfection sounded like we were expected to be perfect, and I did feel an atmosphere of nitpicking scrutiny.

A bedrock principle of Oneida was the abolition of personal property. Likewise, the custom for a new member of Kaliflower was to donate all of one's worldly possessions. Many members were very young when they joined and had few possessions and little money, but I was a thirty-year-old professional with some of the trappings. I wanted to join in good faith and give it a wholehearted try, so I donated everything to the commune: books, stereo, artwork, clothing, and other items. It felt cult-like, but I appreciated the Zen sensibility of non-attachment to my possessions.

I was permitted to keep my car, as they did not want the expense and bother of maintaining it. I did not drive it much, and I recall someone helping me attempt a tune-up in the commune shop.

After traveling for eight months, I had no money to donate, but I had started a new job at Lyon-Martin Health Services and dutifully turned over my first and future paychecks to the communal treasury. There was a box containing small amounts of cash that everyone had access to. Everything was shared—even our clothing and laundry. As the only woman, it was easy for me to find my clothes in the communal drawers. I was the only member with a job—everyone else lived on forms of government assistance. It was justified, or rationalized, by the belief that the government should support people who are making art and doing service to the community.

At first, it was beautiful. I was with my beloved while fulfilling my dream of communal living. Irving seemed to be in the background, and I was happy. I was preparing to paint in egg tempera and had constructed boxes, made from recycled oak floorboards, to hold my jars of pigments. I also made rustic paint daubers by gluing pieces of sponge onto wooden blocks. These turned out to be a prototype of a refined sponging technique I would adopt in later years. And with the guidance of a commune carpenter, I was constructing a four-by-eight-foot panel that I planned to use for a large egg tempera painting. The panel was put aside. The painting never happened.

Complex Marriage

Noyes wrote that because there is no marriage in heaven, there should be no traditional family bonds in the community, and that "his new relationship with God canceled out his obligation to obey traditional moral standards."[54] Thus, he established "complex marriage," in which each member was married to every other member. Irving promoted a similar philosophy of relating "each to each."

I first heard about "each to each" while traveling with Ben in Germany. We were sitting in a cafe chatting with an earnest young woman. I was mortified when Ben impulsively reached for her hand. I questioned him about it later, and he explained his belief in relating "each to each." I was not happy with this, but it did not come up often and I was able to put it aside.

During my time at Kaliflower, I did not witness complex marriage. I only saw romantic pair bonds, and I was never told that I could not be in an exclusive relationship.[55]

The Communal Bedroom

To help me understand my time at Kaliflower, while writing this book I interviewed several ex-members. They told me that in the early days of Kaliflower, members slept together in a communal bedroom. Ex-member Stanley said that there was quite a bit of sexual experimentation, and long-term relationships were discouraged. But the overall atmosphere of the communal bedroom was a feeling of family, in keeping with other customs, including eating together, wearing clothes from the communal bins, and sharing money.

When I joined in 1981, I was not aware of people sleeping in a communal bedroom, but soon we were hard at work installing a recycled oak floor in a gargantuan space that seemed the size of an Olympic swimming pool. Once our new communal bedroom was finished, Ben and I slept there a few times along with two other couples and a few individuals. I never heard sounds of lovemaking—the communal bedroom felt rather chaste to me and, if anything, seemed to repress or hinder lovemaking.[56] I sensed one purpose of the communal bedroom was a way for Irving to keep tabs on members' intimate relationships. But ex-member Stanley did not agree that romantic surveillance was on Irving's radar.

I sidestepped the communal bedroom by setting up a nest for Ben and myself on the roof of the warehouse, claiming truthfully that I preferred sleeping outdoors. Perhaps Ben also liked the urban camping aspect, but we never discussed it, and I assume he would have been okay sleeping in the communal bedroom.

"Third Person" at Kaliflower

At Oneida, an invitation for sex was initiated by a man in the presence of a third party (see "Sex at Oneida" sidebar). Inspired by Oneida, Kaliflower had a custom called "third person" but the purpose was more expansive:

> *Our commune started using Third Persons as messengers between people wanting to sleep together.... The use of a Third Person in beginning a sexual relationship elevates it from a private affair to part of the communal marriage.... We started to experiment, using Third Persons in other areas where interpersonal relationships needed communal aid—especially where two people were having difficulties with each other which they couldn't resolve themselves.... It adds a touch of grace and gentleness to communications that could otherwise be harrowing or hysterical.*[57]

Sex at Oneida

In contrast to the communal bedroom at Kaliflower, there was never a communal bedroom at Oneida. Sex was considered a spiritual practice that generated magnetic energy essential to group coherence. Sexual activity took place in small rooms used only for lovemaking. Most Oneida members had a small, spartan room to themselves, and after sex, the two people were required to retire to their own rooms.

At Oneida, an invitation for sex was initiated by a man in the presence of a third party, who recorded the interaction in a logbook to assure that no favoritism occurred. The woman could accept or decline; however, it was considered "uncommunal" to refuse.

On the other hand, if two people were found to favor each other in what was called a "sticky relationship," the Central Guidance Committee would not permit them to have sex with each other until the intense feelings passed. Often, one member of the pair was banished for a time to their satellite site, the Wallingford Community in Connecticut. Sometimes, the woman would be "invited" to have sex with Noyes in order to cure her of this undesirable "special love." The wish of many members to pursue romantic love was one reason for the breakup of the Oneida community in 1881. Noyes also claimed the role of "first husband," deflowering each virgin after the start of menstruation as early as age twelve. Eventually, he fled to Canada to avoid charges of statutory rape.

In addition to reading works by Noyes and other books that discuss Oneida, I read primary sources, such as the few diaries of Oneida members that still exist. In the 1940s, when Oneida had transformed itself into a corporation and was trying to sell silverware to brides, they tried to suppress the colorful sexual history of the community. They even held a "burn" in 1947, in which most of their archives were destroyed. But much material survived the destruction and is now mostly housed in the Oneida Community Collection at the Syracuse University library.

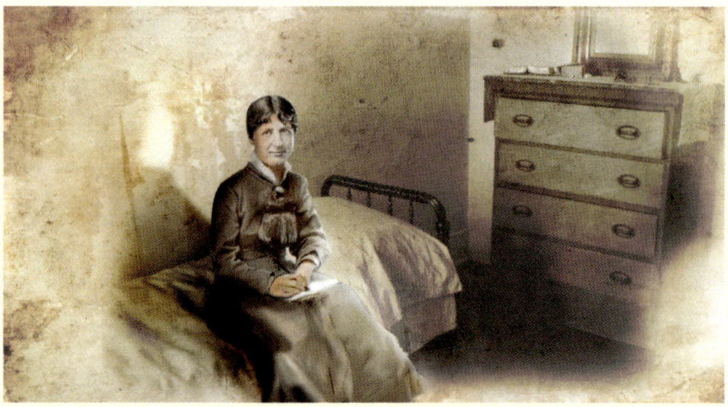

(RIGHT) Tirzah Miller in her room, digital recreation by Emmanuel Bazin, using an archival photo of Tirzah Miller and a photo of her former room in the Oneida Community Mansion House in Oneida, New York. Miller was Noyes' niece and favorite lover. Her bedroom was typical of most Oneida members. I read her revealing diary, *Desire and Duty at Oneida: Tirzah Miller's Intimate Memoir* (2000).

Was Oneida Feminist?

Oneida and Noyes have been called "proto-feminist." Noyes, himself an abolitionist, equated the status of women in marriage to that of slaves. Oneida women wore shorter dresses with bloomer-style pants in order to expand work roles and they were encouraged to cut their hair short. They were mostly free of childbearing due to the practice of male continence, and there was a children's house freeing them from the burden of childcare.

However, Noyes did believe in the superiority of men, and "much of the literature on Oneida has seen Noyes as a seriously disturbed individual who vacillated between extreme license and excessive concerns for sexual control."[58] The endlessly fascinating history of Oneida is beyond the scope of this book, but the academic literature is robust and easily accessed.

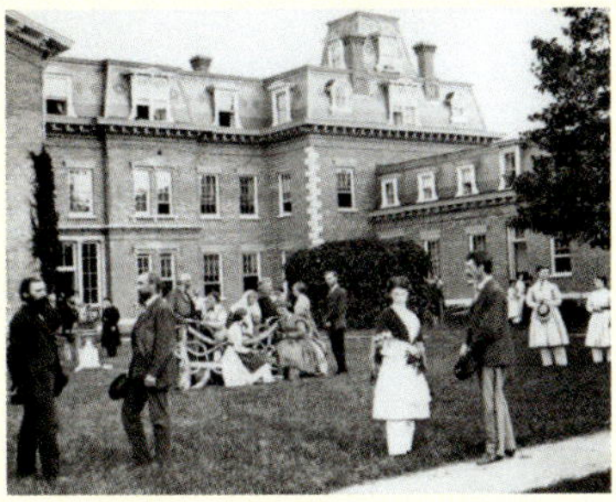

(LEFT) Mansion House Quadrangle, c. 1870. This may have been a staged photo put out by the community to counter "free love" rumors: the women avert their gazes, and the men have removed their hats. Oneida Community Collection, Special Collections Research Center, Syracuse University Libraries, Syracuse, New York. Photographer unknown.

Communal Mailbox

In addition to the communal bedroom, another source of surveillance that I felt, but cannot prove, was the communal mailbox. After reading our mail, we were encouraged to place it in the communal mailbox for anyone to read. This seemed like a warm and fuzzy custom until I got the impression that Irving was especially interested in correspondence between members and their families of origin.

I can envision Irving standing at the wall of mailboxes encouraging me to put my mail into the communal box. At one point, my parents removed me from their will, fearing I would turn over any inheritance to the group. Oddly, none of the ex-members I spoke with remember a communal mailbox.

Work at Oneida and Kaliflower

Work was a dominant feature of life both at Oneida and Kaliflower, and from the start, Irving stated that he wanted a "work commune." Although members did not need to work at a "straight" job, in my experience, there was little leisure time for personal projects. If one's passion happened to dovetail with communal needs—for example, someone who loved gardening—then the need for personal time was not an issue. And for some members, prosaic tasks were meaningful or enjoyable if carried out with a "Zen mind." But if one had interests not directly related to commune goals, there was a vibe to "get with the program." We weren't directly told we could not pursue non-communal passions; there simply was little free time.

Many were young when they joined and did not have a clear idea of their life's work, or were attracted to the commune because of the variety and types of projects happening there. In contrast, I joined mostly to be with Ben. My personal passions and direction were already set, although I was open to trying new things that directly contributed to the communal direction.

For example, I was concerned about our vegan diet and had an idea to propagate spirulina for its protein content. I acquired a fish tank and began experimenting; I don't remember what happened except that it was a failure. Another time, I must have complained about not getting enough exercise, and someone, maybe Irving, suggested that I harness the energy of exercise for a productive outcome. I purchased a stationary bicycle that simultaneously milled flour from the energy of pedaling. But this also failed, as only a small amount of flour was ground from my time on the bike and the exercise component was clunky and uncomfortable. These were interesting projects, but I longed to make paintings.

There were no days off at either Oneida or Kaliflower. The Oneida Community believed that every day was a sabbath, so there was no need to set aside a specific day; most Oneida members worked only four to six hours per day.[59] Kaliflower did not have any spin about every day being a holy day, and although we could skip work any time we wanted to, I remember working most days. I recall a lovely young man, Nanyar, who objected to the never-ending treadmill of work. He declared Sundays a sabbath for himself and refused to work. He was not castigated or pushed out, but he soon left, along with dozens of other people I witnessed who joined mostly because of the free rent, food, and counterculture vibe but sooner or later became disenchanted with the oppressive environment—nonstop work being one factor.

The Kaliflower complex was a sprawling property requiring constant repair and upkeep: gardening, carpentry, cooking, cleaning, and many other tasks. I despaired as I watched Ben's amazing art talent go unrealized as he was taken up with maintenance of the

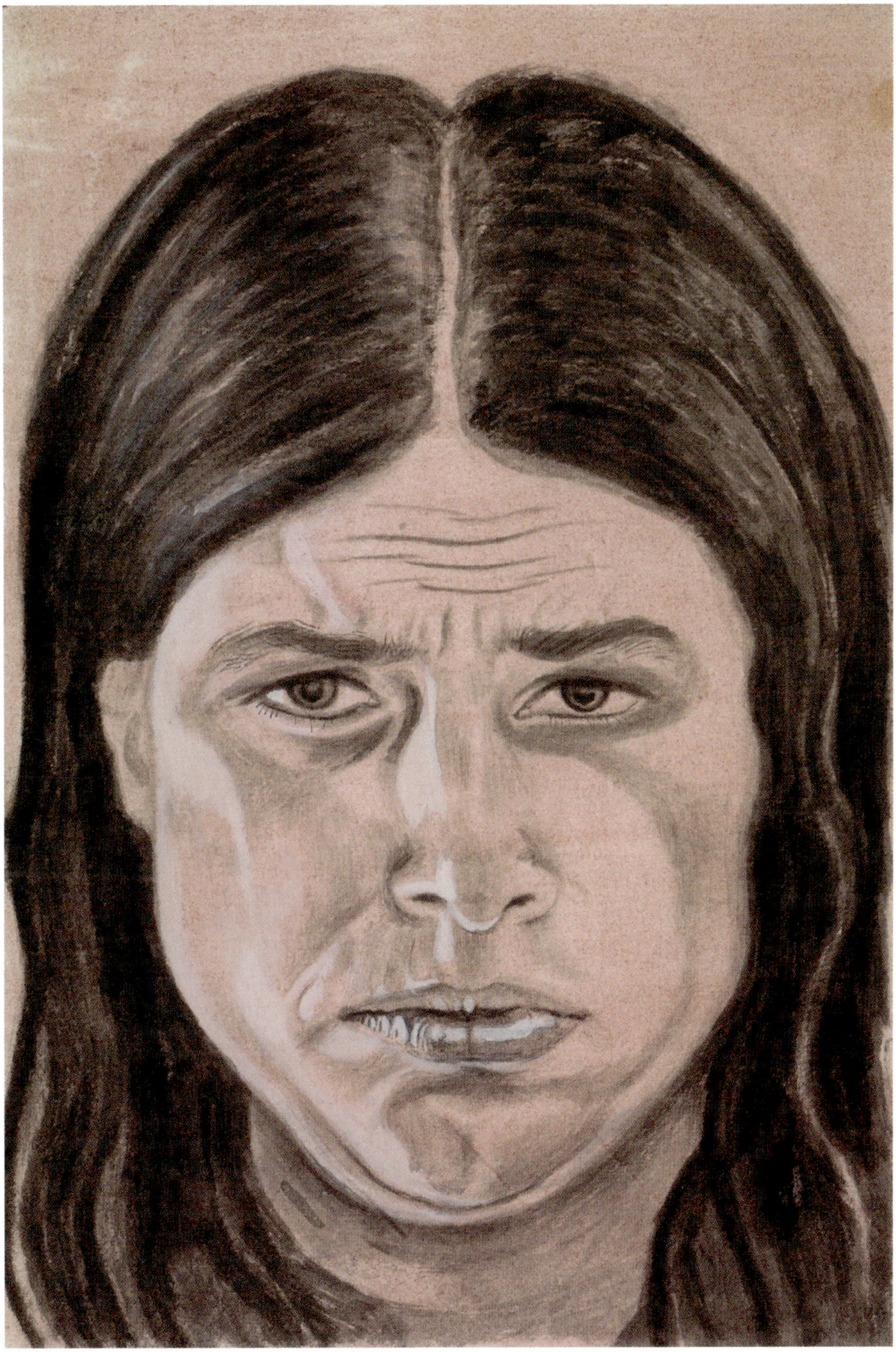

(ABOVE) *Self-Portrait*, c. 1984. Charcoal pencil on pink paper, 11 × 8½ in. (27.9 cm × 21.5 cm)

property. He never complained, but he told me that, at times, he woke up at 4 a.m. to do some personal artwork—I never saw any of it.

Still in my mind's eye, I see Irving standing at the kitchen island, leisurely reading the *San Francisco Chronicle* or, at other times, sorting little items. I rarely saw him doing any of the essential tasks, but he had his finger in everything, meting out coveted praise and feared criticism.

Oddly, the focus on work is a Kaliflower custom that has stayed with me. I find meaning and satisfaction in work and have trouble fully enjoying recreation or even social events. I always feel a strong pull to work on my paintings. This does not apply to my nursing work, which I would give up in favor of full-time art if I had the financial means.

Criticism and Self-Criticism

The Oneida Community and Kaliflower both held daily meetings that included the practice of criticism and self-criticism. Noyes learned mutual criticism from his time in seminary—the practice was based on biblical verse Matthew 18:15.[60] A similar practice was later adopted by authoritarian regimes, starting with Stalin, and also practiced by Mao Zedong and at Jim Jones's People's Temple.[61] Criticism/self-criticism can be an effective practice for personal growth and group cohesion, but even in its milder forms practiced at Oneida and Kaliflower, the process has, at times, resulted in unhelpful putdowns or suppressive tactics. I experienced this myself, as I will soon share.

Follow the Leader

Oneida was unambiguously authoritarian; members believed that Noyes was a prophet of God, and "although each member was encouraged to speak out, Noyes's divine authority could not be challenged."[62]

I was never told that Irving was the official leader of the commune, but it was obvious to me that his opinion held more weight and was often the final word.

In contrast to Kaliflower and Oneida, the San Francisco Diggers were staunchly anti-authoritarian, rejecting any formal leadership. Although the early members respected and even revered Irving, several former members told me that they assumed Kaliflower to be based on democratic values and consensus decision-making. An ex-member recalled overhearing Irving telling another member that he was not interested in a democratic

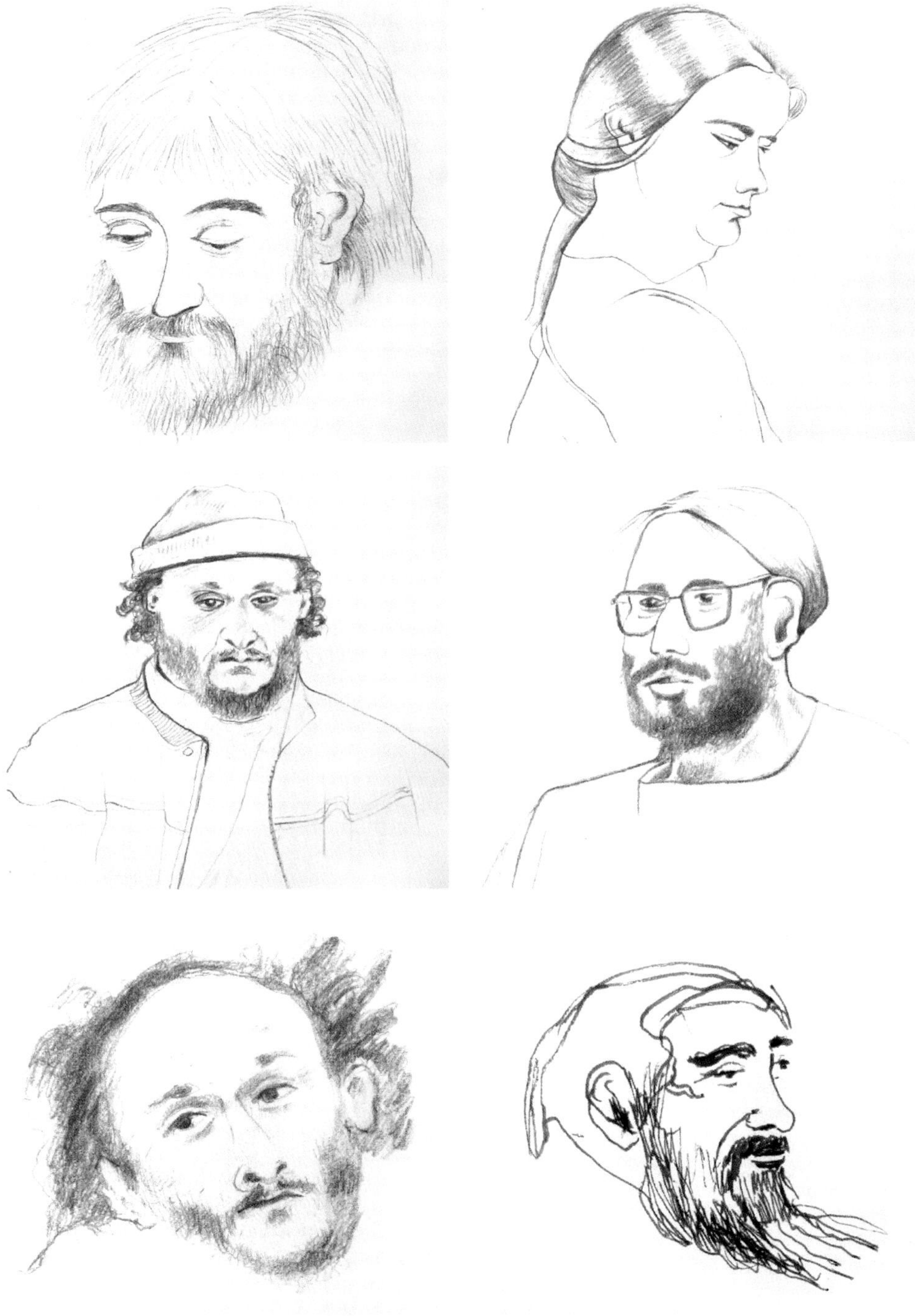

(ABOVE) **Sketches of commune members drawn at daily meetings**

commune and was toying with the idea of being a spiritual leader. But apparently that never happened, at least not in any transparent way.

A few ex-members continue to revere Irving, while others are intensely ambivalent yet credit him with changing the trajectory of their life path in a creative direction. Here are some recollections of Irving I recently collected from former members who lived at Kaliflower in the early days:

Stanley mentioned that in the first years of Kaliflower, "Irving instigated the art, he attracted amazing people, and thanks to him people were having a great time." He added, "Irving had a great aesthetic sense and a great understanding of literature. He saw the potential in people and helped them a lot with their own artistic things."

Ricky described his years at Kaliflower this way:

> *The commune, with all its work projects, inspired by Digger philosophy, felt constantly on the vanguard of a social revolution. Irving played an important role as mentor, but the incredible talents and personalities of the group created a unique synergy, with the whole being greater than the sum of its parts.*

But Stanley said, "Creative geniuses are not always nice people. Look at what they say about Picasso." Stanley lived at Kaliflower from the age of seventeen to thirty-four and told me that "over the years, the commune became more and more serious and ideologic."

That explains the somewhat ossified and rigid atmosphere that I encountered. Stanley said that he was very enthusiastic in this beautiful little bubble, but as years went on, he felt "we were intentionally cutting ourselves off because no one comes up to our standards." He decided, "Gotta see the rest of the world," and left.

Another ex-member, David Parkhurst, described incidents in which a friend or neighbor wanted to borrow a tool or bicycle and Irving refused, saying that the outside person was not "pure" enough. There was an air of superiority, David said, like the Kaliflower way was the best way and the only way to be in the world. After thirteen years living there, one day he had an epiphany: "I realized that I had a very different set of ethics and could never win an argument." He was not willing to accept the situation, so he left.

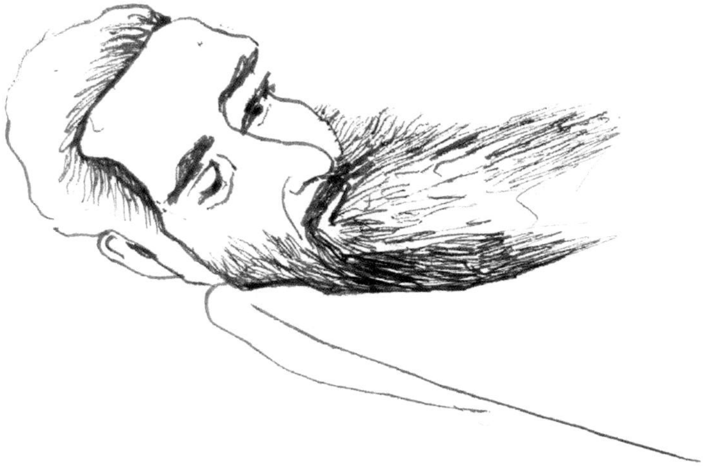

(ABOVE) I drew this impression of Irving while living at the Kaliflower commune, probably at a group meeting, c. 1984. Pen and ink on paper, 5 × 8 in. (12.7 × 20.3 cm)

But, like other ex-members, David had mixed feelings about Irving:

> *Something that impressed me about Irving was his gift of perception; his ability to understand the subtleties of personalities and sense what people were really trying to communicate despite whatever difficulty they may be having in expressing themselves. I felt fortunate to have been accepted by someone so interesting and resourceful, possessing such incredible gifts and, as I gradually was to learn, equally arresting flaws.*

In my attempt to provide a balanced view of Irving, I may have leaned more positive than was my experience. I neglected to mention the dozens, perhaps hundreds, of people who stayed only a short time after tasting the tyrannical flavor of Irving's rule. My feelings toward Irving remain negative, bordering on traumatized. In my experience, his dogmatic sureness and sometimes cruel demeanor set an oppressive tone.

I only know of one member who consistently stayed—a five-decade span of loyalty. That person is Ben. But even Ben left once for a year and at other times lived only part-time at Kaliflower. Ben, assisted by some ex-members, cared for Irving during his last months until he passed away on April 22, 2022, at the age of ninety-one.

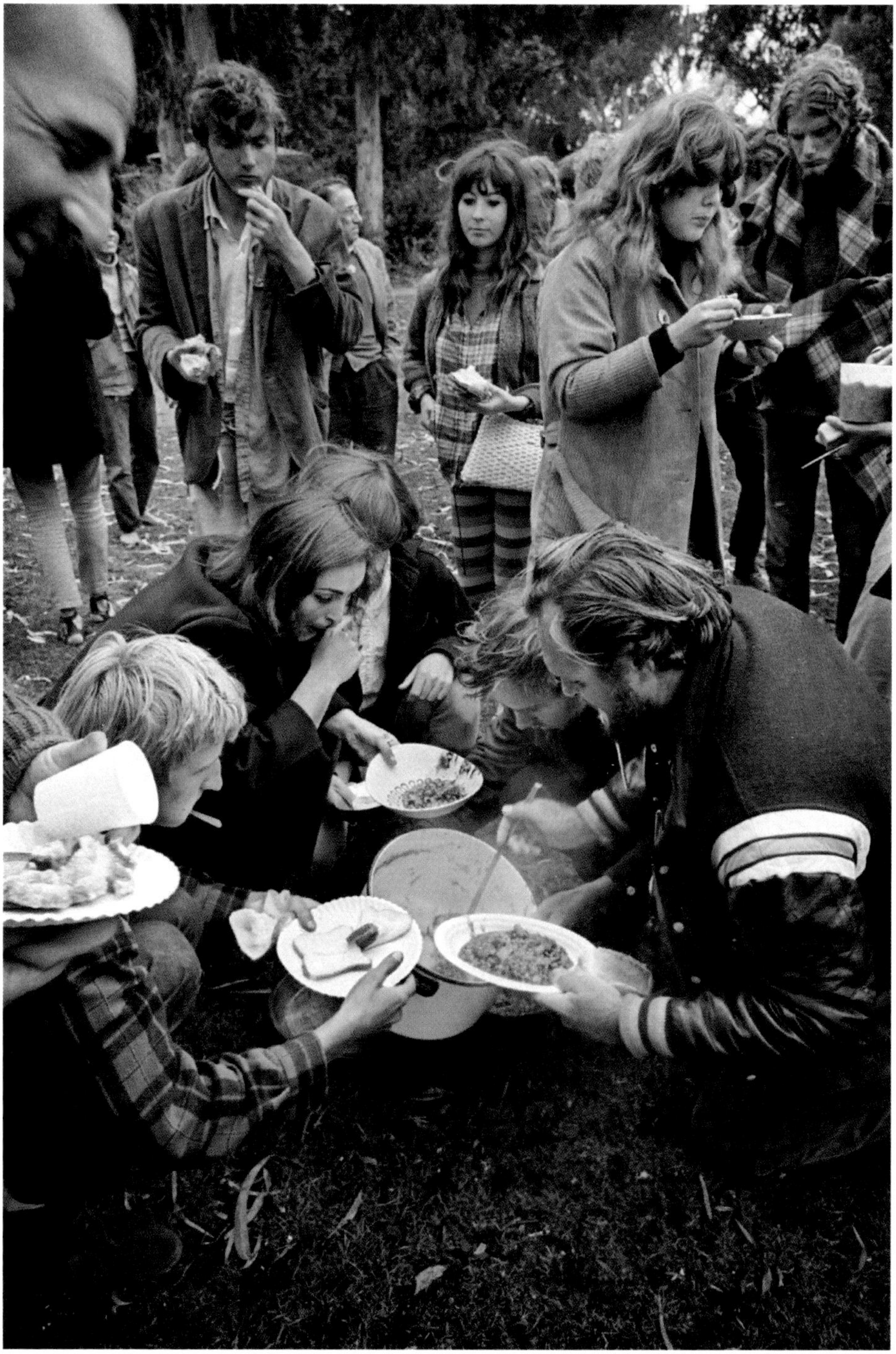

(ABOVE) Diggers giving out food in the Panhandle of Golden Gate Park, 1966. Photo by Jim Marshall, LLC.

CHAPTER TWELVE

THE CONCEPT OF FREE

The overarching credo of the Kaliflower commune is the concept of "free," which they adopted from both the San Francisco Diggers of the 1960s and the English Diggers of the seventeenth century (see sidebar in Chapter 11).

1960s Diggers of San Francisco

The Diggers of the 1960s were an offshoot of the San Francisco Mime Troupe, an audacious political satire theater company founded in 1959.[63] This spinoff group named themselves "Diggers" and set off to upend even alternative theater by totally erasing the boundary between actor and audience. They called this "life acting" and created provocative participatory events such as the Death of Money Parade in December of 1966.

The Free Frame of Reference

The Diggers created many service programs, including free food in the park, free stores, and free medical care that preceded the Haight Ashbury Free Medical Clinic. But these were not projects in the sense that a conventional social service agency might provide. According to Digger Peter Berg: "The idea was not just to give away things for free, but to create a theater where people could explore this notion of a free store. What would it be like if things didn't cost money?"[64]

They called this the "Free Frame of Reference." To partake of the 4 p.m. daily meal in the Panhandle of Golden Gate Park, one had to step through an actual "Free Frame of Reference," a giant yellow wooden

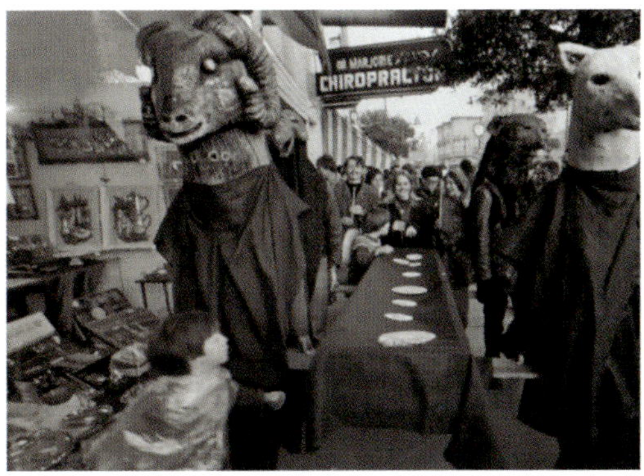

(ABOVE) Death of Money Parade, 1966. Photo by Gene Anthony.

rectangle. All of these events, services, and their underlying philosophy came to be known as "Digger Free."

"The Diggers were dedicated to freedom; not simply political freedom, but personal freedom as well," explained Digger Peter Coyote.[65] In my experience, the Kaliflower commune's vision of "free" did *not* include personal freedom; quite the contrary, it seemed to constrain it. But several ex-members I spoke with said that they did not feel their freedom was compromised. The activities they enjoyed dovetailed with the commune's vision.

I am of two minds about "free." On the one hand, I want everyone to have free access to food, clothing, shelter, health care, art, entertainment—everything! But what is most important to me is not that everything is free, but that people who do not have enough or any money are not denied these basics. Things *do* need to get paid for, so people who can afford to pay should and may even want to contribute extra funds if they have the resources.

Digger Free economy was based on the excesses of capitalism; the free food and free store items were scavenged or acquired from resources that might otherwise have gone to waste. This holds true today to some extent, but for many necessities and services, money is needed and has to come from somewhere.

It is ironic that the Kaliflower anthology, *Kaliflower Volume Five*, initially given away for free, now sells for high prices on the internet and is only available for in-library use at the San Francisco Public Library.

Kaliflower took to heart the message of the San Francisco Diggers and clung religiously to the tenets of "free." Their most influential project was the Free Print Shop.

Free Print Shop

By the fall of 1967, in the burgeoning counterculture, so many people were calling themselves "Diggers" that the Diggers "gave away their name" and started calling themselves the Free City Collective. Free City spread from the Haight Ashbury neighborhood throughout the city holding events such as free poetry readings on the steps of City Hall. The Kaliflower Commune, then called the Sutter Street Commune, entered the Digger orbit during the Spring of 1968 at one of the gatherings on the City Hall steps. Two Diggers pulled Irving aside and proposed that he move his New York City printing press west to help launch a Free City print shop. One of them even offered to travel cross-country to assist in the relocation. Irving, by then fully committed to "Digger Free," was delighted. That chance encounter gave birth to the Free Print Shop.[66]

Over the next several years, the Free Print Shop published a variety of materials, but by far the most creative and influential project was the intercommunal newsletter *Kaliflower.*

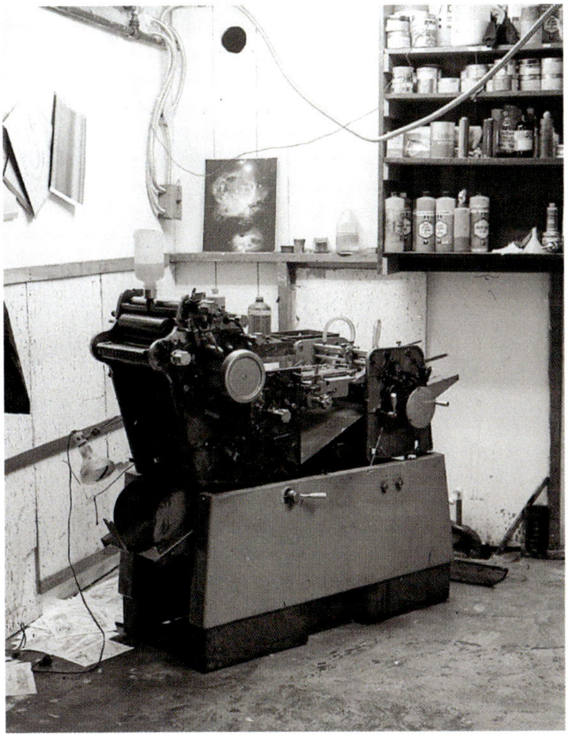

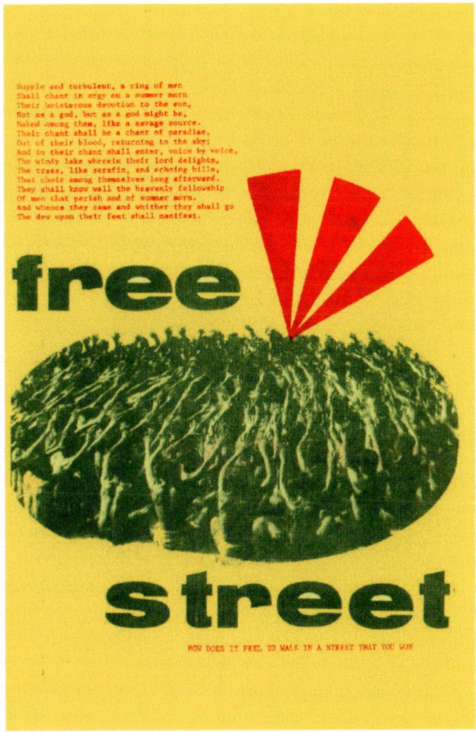

(ABOVE LEFT) Chief 15 offset printing press. Photo by Miriam Bobkoff.

(ABOVE RIGHT) *Digger Free City News* sheet, February 24, 1968.

Kaliflower Newsletter

The first issue of *Kaliflower* was printed and distributed in April of 1969. The name *Kaliflower* comes from Kali Yuga, the age of Kali, the darkest period in human history. The idea of pairing Kali with the word "flower" was to plant a seed of positivity growing out of the darkness.

At its height in 1971, *Kaliflower* was hand-delivered every Thursday to more than 300 communes throughout the Bay Area. *Kaliflower* kept many communes in touch and helped spread the word about myriad free activities, projects, and services. The publication continued until the spring of 1972, when the editors realized that they were losing contact with their commune-based readers as the sixties counterculture went increasingly mainstream.

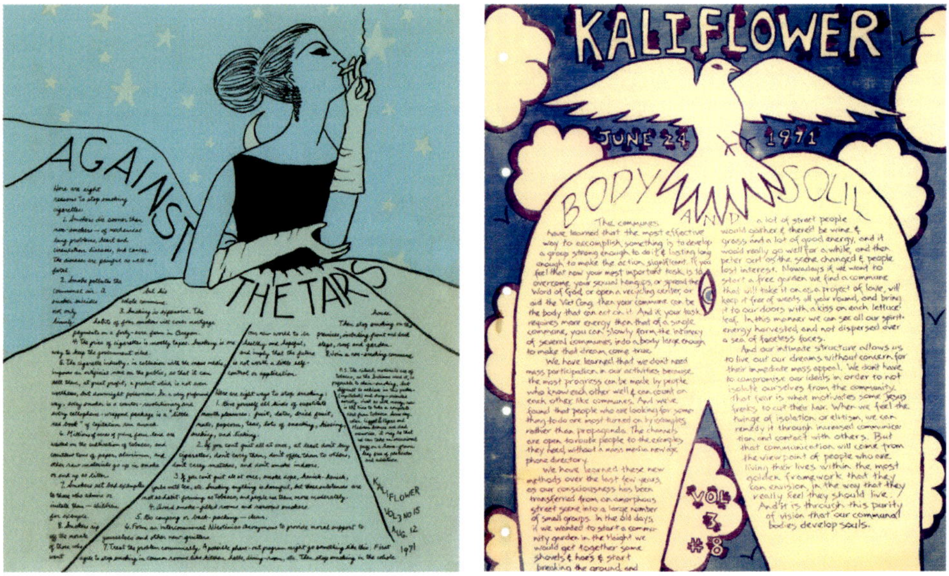

(ABOVE) "Against the Tars," *Kaliflower* Vol 3, No. 8, June 24, 1971, and "Body and Soul," *Kaliflower* Vol. 3, No. 15, August 12, 1971.

By the time I joined in 1982, ten years had elapsed since the final regular issue of *Kaliflower* had been printed. I felt an atmosphere of stagnation and did not sense big enthusiasm for anything. For several years, the members had been working on compiling selected writing and artwork from past issues of *Kaliflower,* plus some new material, into an anthology. Many pages had already been printed but not yet assembled or bound.

In addition, the commune had purchased a humongous Miehle printing press in hopes of printing large format projects.[67] But the power supply for the Miehle needed to run through the basement of the warehouse, and the section of basement below the press was just dirt. It needed a concrete floor and new foundation before it would be safe for wiring. I heard no talk of repairing the foundation, so I assumed there was no money for such an expensive undertaking.

Our frugal lifestyle suggested a philosophy of voluntary poverty, so I was curious to know how much money we actually had. Although my track record with my own finances was not sterling, I volunteered to be the group treasurer, with the ulterior motive of finding out how much money we had in our bank account. I suspected a hypocritical discrepancy, and my suspicion was confirmed when I learned there was $27,000 in savings—equivalent to more than $85,555 in 2025. This was enough money to rebuild the foundation and simultaneously drain our bank account of what I felt was an amount incompatible with our values. We hired a construction company headed by a competent man with a lovely personality.

Ben worked alongside the crew, and a beautiful new basement was constructed. I overheard Irving telling someone on the phone, "Lora is spearheading the basement project." I felt pride in his praise. This was the golden era of my life at Kaliflower. It did not last long.

I started noticing how Irving would build a person up by praising their brilliance or artistic talent and then, at other times, put them down with hypercritical comments. I felt myself falling prey to this dynamic while, at the same time, I retained the ability to dispassionately observe the insidious manner in which he controlled us.

I also noticed how some members minimized, apologized for, or even enabled his behavior. Once, I witnessed Irving harshly criticize someone in the presence of another member. I later asked the member if he had observed the punishing treatment that I saw. He minimized my concern, saying, "It's not so bad... You're exaggerating." Apparently, others did not see the oppressive dynamic or were able to rationalize Irving's behavior. I started feeling like I was living in a mindfuck situation.

Perhaps I experienced a more intense version of Irving because he had a reputation for disliking women, especially Jewish women, stemming from being abused by his mother. I was also a threat because I had won the affection of one of his closest disciples. I had lured Ben away once, so was capable of doing it again.

After several months, I became disgruntled with the suppressive atmosphere and lack of time to work on my personal art. I left the commune and rented a small, shabby, neglected warehouse. Ben and I broke up for the second time but stayed in touch sporadically. After several months of work, I was close to transforming the warehouse into a sweet art studio and home.

Kaliflower: Take Two

During the time I lived away from the commune, the members had succeeded in self-publishing their anthology, *Kaliflower Volume Five* (1980), and had embarked on several nationwide road trips to give away many of the 2,000-plus copies to communes and others.

When Ben returned from the last trip, we decided to give our relationship another try. I was sad to leave the space I had lovingly prepared to create art in, but after almost a year away, I returned to the commune.

When I moved back in 1983, I was pleased to find the commune in an upbeat mood—perhaps a taste of the glory days of the Kaliflower commune of the 1970s. We created a free restaurant called A Small Free Inn, which offered elaborate vegan meals to the public once a week. Some former members returned to help, and we dressed up in bizarre costumes, creating quite a spectacle. The restaurant became very popular and crowded.

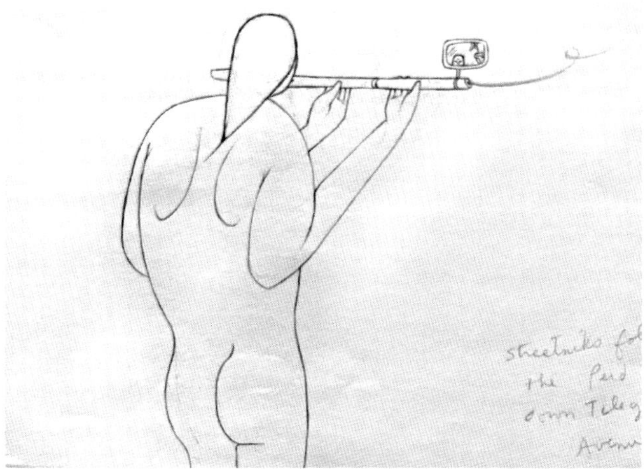

(ABOVE) *Pied Piper*, illustration for *The Book of Dau* by Dau Freitag. This is the only drawing I have from the book, which was printed but never distributed.

A Small Free Inn also had a lodging component. We had been taking in stranded travelers and other homeless people from our listing with Traveler's Aid at the San Francisco International Airport. One evening, when we were expecting a guest, I opened the front door to a tall burly man with huge, blazing, scary eyes. He was obviously psychotic, and I was alone in one of the buildings. I became deathly afraid that he would murder me. I spoke with him for a few minutes, then excused myself and went for help. Fortunately, no one was harmed, but looking back, I can see that we were unprepared for emergencies, especially situations that might have needed security.

During this second chapter of living at Kaliflower, I again felt frustrated that I could not find time to pursue my personal artwork. I set up an inconspicuous painting nook next to the humongous Miehle press, and by eking out small blocks of time, I managed to complete a very small egg tempera painting called *Bleeding on a Pine Tree* (see Chapter 6). I believe the painting is still somewhere in the Kaliflower compound, but I have asked and was told they cannot find it.

At this time, the commune decided to publish a book by Dau Freitag called *The Book of Dau*. Ben was sympathetic to my desire to do more artwork and enlisted me to draw illustrations for the book. Ben and Irving loved my drawings and were very encouraging. Being praised by Irving, especially for my art, had the dopamine effect of softening my hostility toward him and drawing me closer to the commune.

Commune or Cult?

One day, a dear childhood friend, the late Merry Kassoy, came to visit me at Kaliflower. She had been writing her master's thesis in psychology on the topic of cults. She said to me point blank, "Lora, this is a cult!" I reflexively said, "Of course it isn't."

But she planted a seed that would later be instrumental in understanding my involvement with the group. Although I had smelled "cult" even on my first visit to Kaliflower, it took years to make sense of my five-year association with the group.

The word "cult" can be used as a slanderous accusation, but academic psychologists and sociologists agree that some groups can be problematic. However, they disagree over the extent of harm the groups can cause. Young people, or anyone at a transitional time in their life, can be drawn in and derailed from moving forward with their life's purpose. In my case, it was the romantic involvement with Ben that created the opening for my vulnerability.

Here are some characteristics of cults that matched my experience at Kaliflower:

— Charismatic authoritarian leader with intense influence
— Extreme work ethic; control of personal time
— Surveillance of one's former or outside life and romantic life within the group
— Encouragement to turn away from conventional society and family
— Narrow, simplistic belief system with only one way to think: we are right, they are wrong
— Air of superiority to dominant culture
— Undermining self-confidence; no allowance for real input or criticism[68]

I don't mean to imply that all communal living amounts to a cult. And many groups are on a continuum—certainly Kaliflower does not compare to, for example, the Unification Church (the "Moonies") in the extent of social control. I also believe that some groups with non-elected leaders, such as many religious groups, are not necessarily cults if the leadership style is transparent and participants freely join.

Most humans long for community of some sort, and the art of communal living has come a long way. There are now very successful communes, often called "intentional communities," that thrive without authoritarian leaders; Twin Oaks and East Wind are two examples. Plus, other forms have evolved, such as the "cohousing" movement.

I now live in a cooperative development in which the group owns the property together, but each family or individual has their own apartment. We have a social hall where monthly meetings take place and social activities are organized. For me, it is a good balance between privacy and community.

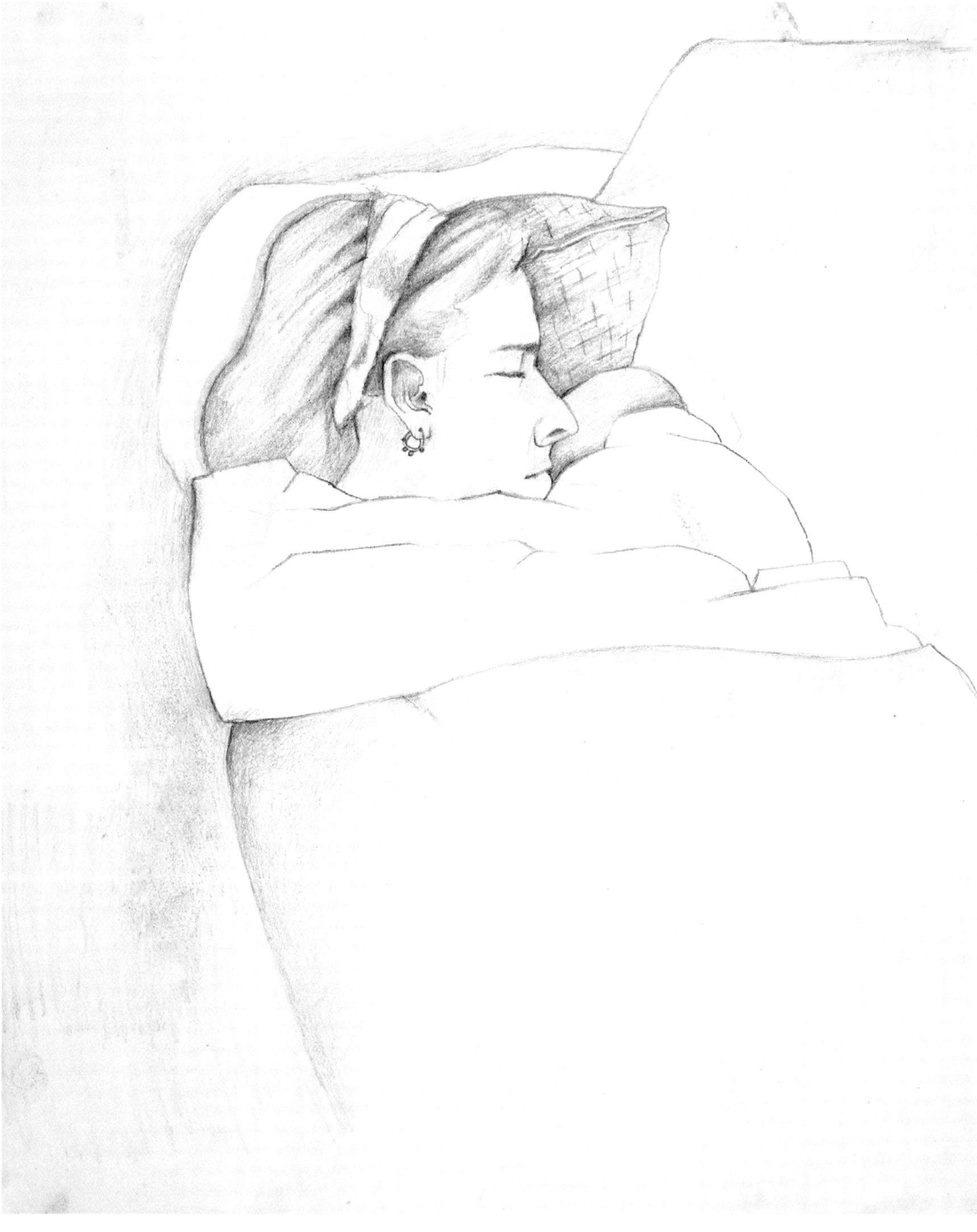

(ABOVE) *Meryl & Elena*, c. 1998, Pencil on paper, 13½ × 11 in. (34.2 × 27.9 cm)

CHAPTER THIRTEEN

MOTHERHOOD CALLING

For many years before I met Ben, I had a deep yearning to become a mother. At times, I found it painful to be in the presence of a baby or young child because my desire for motherhood was so intense.

My previous lover had two children and definitely did not want more, so I promised myself that in future relationships, I would make my intention clear early on.

I talked to Ben about this at the start of our relationship and recall him saying that he was open to having a baby. With that assurance, I wholeheartedly gave myself to the relationship. But a year or so later, when we discussed it again, he said his recollection was that he said he wanted one "at some point in his life," which apparently had not meant any time soon. I had interpreted his words through an optimistic lens.

Soon after, when we were traveling in Morocco, he did agree, but I did not want to be pregnant in a developing country without the support of family or friends.

During this second period of living together at Kaliflower, Ben was again open to the idea but said that Irving was against it.

Having reached the age of thirty-five, I was becoming increasingly frustrated. My periods had always been regular, but at this time, they were somewhat irregular, so I consulted a gynecologist. She asked if I'd ever been pregnant, and when I said no, she said, "I think you are probably sterile." I protested, "I'm just very good at birth control—I know my cycles and when I'm ovulating, I take precautions."

I left the doctor's office, went straight to Ben, and said, "I've waited so long and now I may be infertile, all because Irving won't allow us to get pregnant." I then marched off to see Irving and was very surprised when he said, "I never told you you couldn't have a baby. The worst thing that could happen is if we don't get along, you'll have to get your own apartment." I went back to Ben and told him what Irving said.

Then I told Ben, "I'm not going to use birth control anymore; you're now in charge of contraception," implying the use of condoms.

We didn't talk about it again, but I initiated lovemaking soon after. I figured, based on what the gynecologist said, I was probably not fertile, and in any case, because of my age, it would take a while to get pregnant. Due to my study of natural birth control, I knew my cycles extremely well, and we made love during ovulation—the most fertile time.

While making love, I thought, "Does he even know what we're doing?" He did not seem to, and I did not say anything. Then I said to myself, "You're going to be a single mother."

Two weeks later, my period was late, and the pregnancy test was positive. When I told Ben, he was truly shocked and not at all happy, which broke my heart.

The commune had a custom called "quarantine": whenever a person had a cold, they stayed in a separate room where meals were brought to them. It happened that on the day I told Ben I was pregnant, he was in quarantine and was not supposed to touch anyone.

The classic scenario where the wife tells the husband that she is pregnant and the husband draws her to him in an embrace and says "Oh, darling!" did not happen. I'm sure I imagined it, but his face seemed to turn gray. I begged for a hug, which he reluctantly gave. I blame myself for not being more upfront while we were making love, but we both now agree that, in retrospect, it was a colossal miscommunication.

The next morning, at our daily meeting, I announced that I was pregnant. Irving's immediate comment was "abort, *abort, ABORT!*" Ben became very conflicted—one minute saying, "I have to stay with you," and the next minute saying, "I can't leave the commune."

My trial—it felt like a trial—went on for several days until it became clear that if I was not willing to have an abortion, I would have to leave. I am pro-choice, but this was a planned pregnancy, at least on my part, and in any case, I wanted the baby. I took almost nothing with me and left.

Pregnant and Homeless

Two things I never thought would happen to me—being homeless and being a single mother—were now both a reality. I was thrilled to be pregnant and at the same time devastated that I would be a single mother and my child fatherless.

An acquaintance said, "God is your child's father now!" Another person said, "Some men bolt when their girlfriends become pregnant—it's nothing new." I called a close friend and asked if I could stay with her. She said she needed to ask her partner, Joe. This was, of course, reasonable, but I was devastated that she did not say yes without hesitation. I hung up the phone and burst into tears. After that, I did not ask anybody for help.

I told my parents I was pregnant, and to my surprise, they were delighted. I'm sure they would have been happy for me to move back to New York, but I never considered it, perhaps because I maintained hope that Ben would change his mind and decide to be with me.

I had very little money because I always turned my paychecks over to the communal treasury, but I would have access to future paychecks. I could have asked my parents or friends for money, but, woozy from morning sickness and deep into my personal tragedy, I wasn't thinking practically.

I drove to Merced, where my best friend from nursing school, Carol Cruickshank, was having a baby. I stayed with her for a couple of days, then drove back to San Francisco and lived in my car for a few more days. I continued working at the Lyon-Martin Clinic, crying in the lab in between seeing my patients. One day, I told my coworker, "I'm still miserable, but there just aren't any tears left."

On a rainy night around Christmas, I saw a sculpture of the Virgin Mary with baby Jesus. Even though I am Jewish, I identified with her and found strength—and a bit of welcome melodrama.

One afternoon, I knocked on the door of St. Elizabeth's Home for Unwed Mothers, with the idea that they could take care of me during my pregnancy, and in exchange, I could help care for the girls living there, since I was older and a registered nurse. Peering through the door, I was shocked to see a child with a pregnant belly. I received a call back responding that I could either live there as an unwed mother or possibly work there, but not both.

I was still in touch with Ben, and he suggested that I go to a shelter. I probably did not need a shelter, but in my mournful and dramatic state of mind and with the desire to please him, I rang the doorbell at Raphael House. Raphael House was established in 1971 to care for homeless families. I was pleasantly surprised that it was clean and felt safe.

They told me that I would be assigned a single room because of my psychologically precarious condition. I was provided counseling to discuss options for my next step.

After about a week, on their recommendation, I moved to the Civic Center Residence in the seedy Tenderloin district. I felt an intense mixture of joy and misery. Looking back, I wish I'd been able to focus more on the delight of becoming a mother.

Since my psychological state was shaky, I threw myself into optimizing the physical aspect of pregnancy. I took long walks and attended prenatal yoga classes with Judith Hanson Lasater, a physical therapist, longtime yoga teacher, and mother of three.

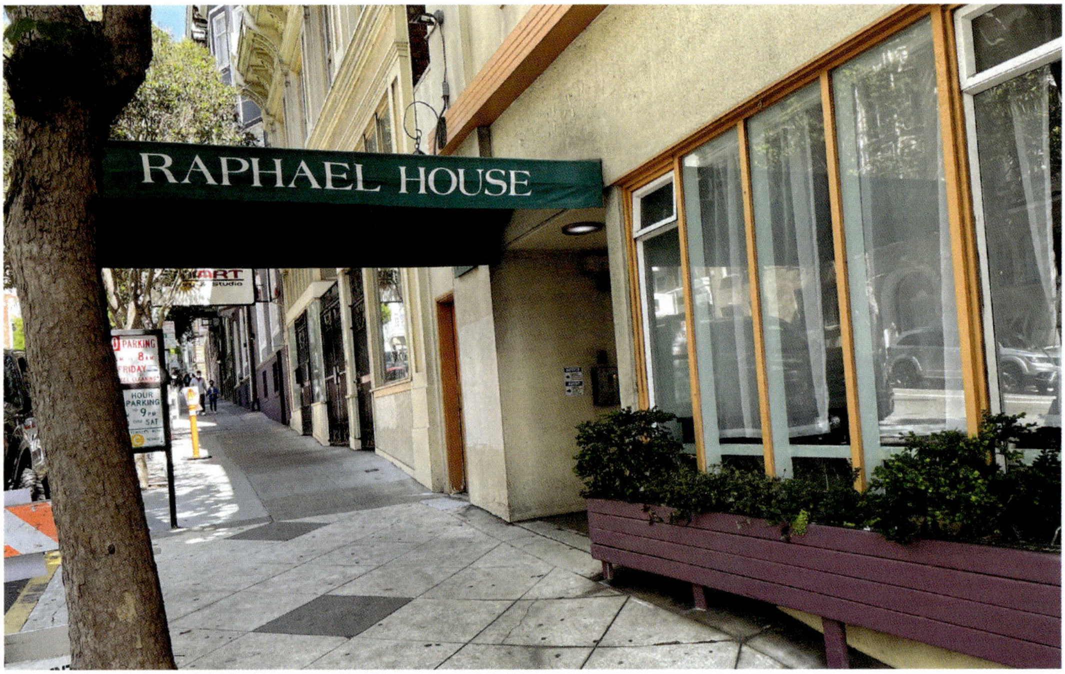

(ABOVE) Raphael House in San Francisco

(RIGHT) Felipe Azira with Amos, 1985

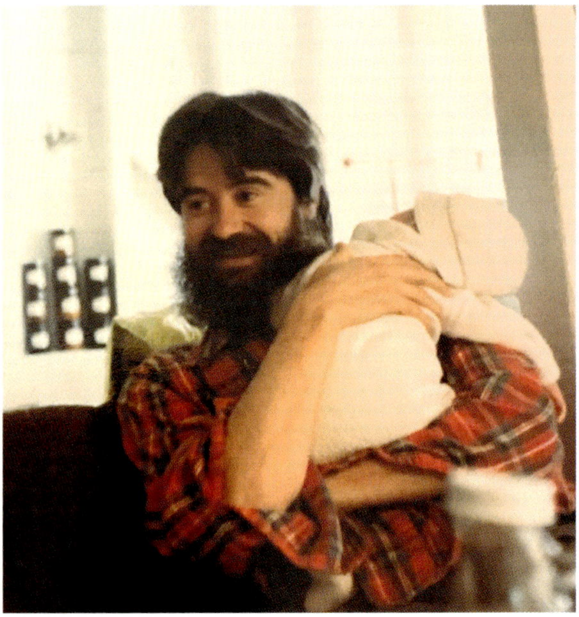

One day, I spontaneously approached her after class and said, "I feel really bad that I'm going to be a single mother." Without skipping a beat, she looked me in the eyes and said, "Every mother is a single mother!"

From Civic Center Residence, I rented an unfinished basement on the west slope of Bernal Hill. It seemed crazy to rent a space with no bathroom or kitchen and only a spigot near the floor for water, but the price was right—$250 per month. I did not have the money, so Ben paid for it. By this time, I was five months pregnant.

One night, an inebriated couple living upstairs cursed me, saying, "How can she live like this? It's disgusting!"

I felt frightened, especially since some of the windows were broken. I'd been using the bathroom at El Patio restaurant, where I ate humongous burritos—the only food that filled my bottomless hunger. And for bathing, I had taken a membership at Osento, a nearby and somewhat shabby but endearing Japanese-style women's bathhouse.

Felipe to the Rescue

That night I called Felipe, a close friend from Kaliflower. Felipe was angry that I had been forced out of the commune due to my pregnancy, and he had left in protest. He was house-sitting for a friend in the posh Marina district and told me to take a taxi there.

Starting that night, he chivalrously cared for me during my pregnancy and helped me in every possible way. We were already close friends, and the urgency and intimacy of the situation brought us closer, and we became lovers.

He moved in with me and helped transform the basement into an ersatz apartment. We had a toilet installed by a carpenter friend, created a makeshift kitchen, and eventually acquired a recycled blue bathtub.

As I neared the final weeks of my pregnancy, someone asked, "Are you going to have a shower?" (meaning a baby shower). I replied, "Well, I hope to at least have a bathtub!" I spent hours in the blue bathtub while in labor, helping to ease the pains. I never did have a baby shower.

Felipe grew up on a farm in Montefrío, a town in Andalusia, Spain. Sometimes, in the evening, he would regale me with stories about the sounds various animals made while giving birth. He had never witnessed a human birth but was present when my son, Amos Felipe Goldbaum, was born at home on July 5, 1985.

Afterwards, somebody asked Felipe what he thought about the birth, and he replied in his charming Spanish accent, "I think it is very painful!"

If ever there was a "knight in shining armor," Felipe fulfilled this vision. On a spiritual and psychological plane, I will always feel that he saved my life.

Milk Mystery Series

The experience of pregnancy and lactation emerged from my pencil the day after Amos was born. I was surprised that after going through labor and birth, I would want to draw so soon, but images just poured out and became what I call the *Milk Mystery* series. I found the experience of having milk in my breasts animal-like, and I felt a kinship with all female mammals.

— I drew *Childbirth* as a general expression of the exuberance of childbirth, but in my personal experience, intense pain was the dominant feeling—euphoria and relief only once the baby was safely in my arms. And although the pose is celebratory, her expression is not happy, perhaps because of the dangerous position of the baby.

A birth with the baby's hand presenting first is extremely rare and would necessitate a Caesarean delivery. Art gives me the opportunity to fantasize a hazardous birth without the dire consequences of dangerous reality.

— We exploit animals for their milk, but we don't reciprocate. In *Milking Cycle,* an animal and a human provide sustenance for each other.

— I drew *Milk Rollups*, a take on Fruit Roll-Ups (or fruit leather), a popular snack at the time.

In *Man Nursing a Baby,* I pose the question: Can a man nurse a baby? Yes, but it may require hormone supplements and other interventions. Now, with the surge in trans and nonbinary people considering parenthood, the issue of lactation has become complex and multifactorial.

— *Milk Flowing into an Urn* (FOLLOWING PAGE) is a rendering of an imaginary low-tech breast pump with a classical aesthetic; perhaps I was thinking Grecian urn? I did not use a breast pump; my imagination pumped out this image.

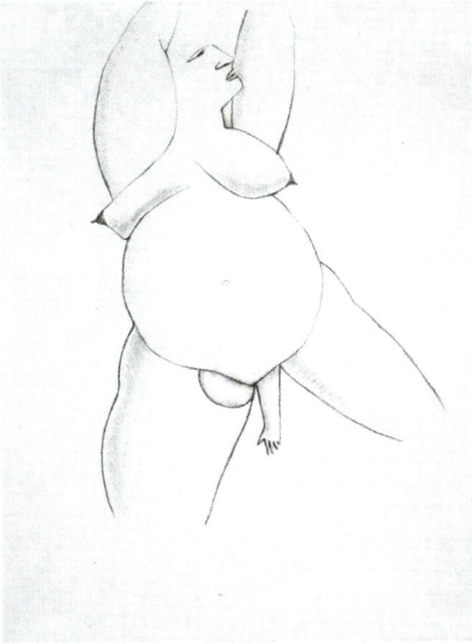

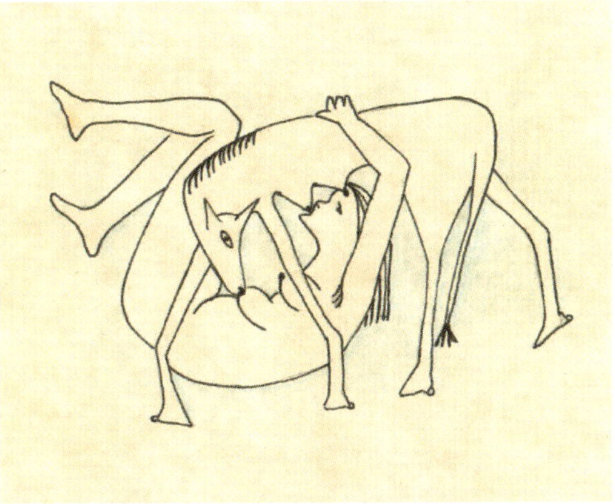

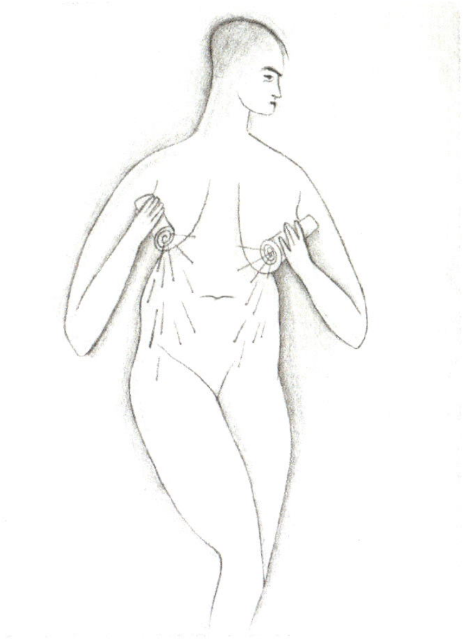

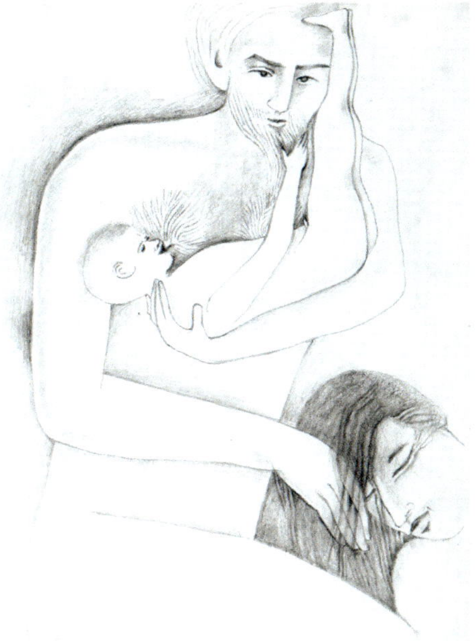

(ABOVE LEFT) ***Childbirth,*** c. 1985. Pencil on paper, 11 × 8½ in. (27.9 × 21.5 cm)

(ABOVE RIGHT) ***Milking Cycle,*** c. 1985. Ink and colored pencil on paper, 8 × 11 in. (20.3 × 27.9 cm)

(BELOW LEFT) ***Milk Rollups,*** c. 1985. Pencil on paper, 12 × 9 in. (30.4 × 22.8 cm)

(BELOW RIGHT) ***Man Nursing a Baby,*** c. 1985. Pencil on paper, 17 × 14 in. (43.1 × 35.5 cm)

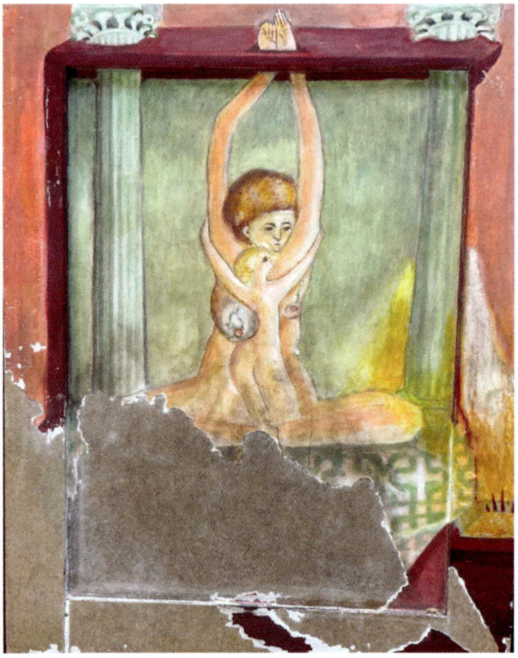

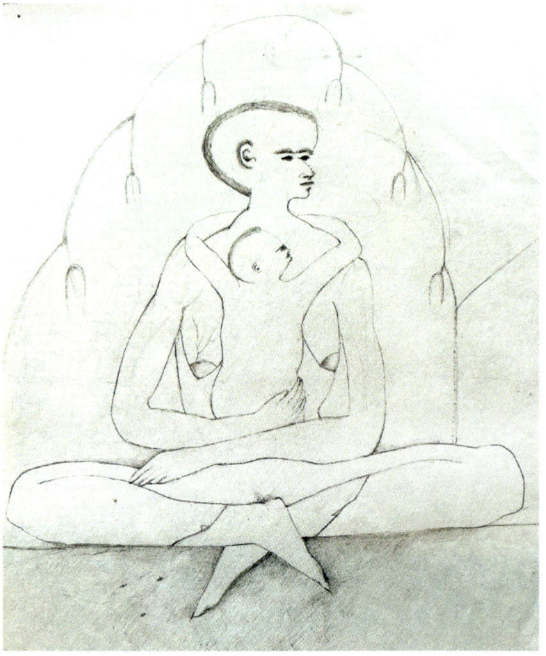

(ABOVE LEFT) Detail: *Engorgement,* c. 1986. Egg tempera on gesso panel, 16 × 12 in. (40.6 × 30.4 cm)
(ABOVE RIGHT) *Baby between Breasts,* c. 1994. Pencil on paper, 11 × 8½ in. (27.9 × 21.5 cm)

In general, my painting *Engorgement* represents a mother feeling chained to the needs of her baby. Most nursing mothers have experienced engorgement, painful pressure from excessive milk in the ducts. I never experienced severe engorgement and did not feel oppressed by motherhood—not every portrayal is autobiographical!

Egg tempera paintings should never be stored horizontally, but I had stored this painting laid flat in a closet that developed a water leak, causing some of the gesso to lift off and take the paint along with it. Once egg tempera has a chance to polymerize or cure, the paint film is water-resistant but not waterproof. However, I like how the damage created an archaic fresco-like effect.

Even a small baby would not fit between a woman's breasts, as it does in my drawing *Baby between Breasts*, but artistic license allows me to rearrange anatomy.

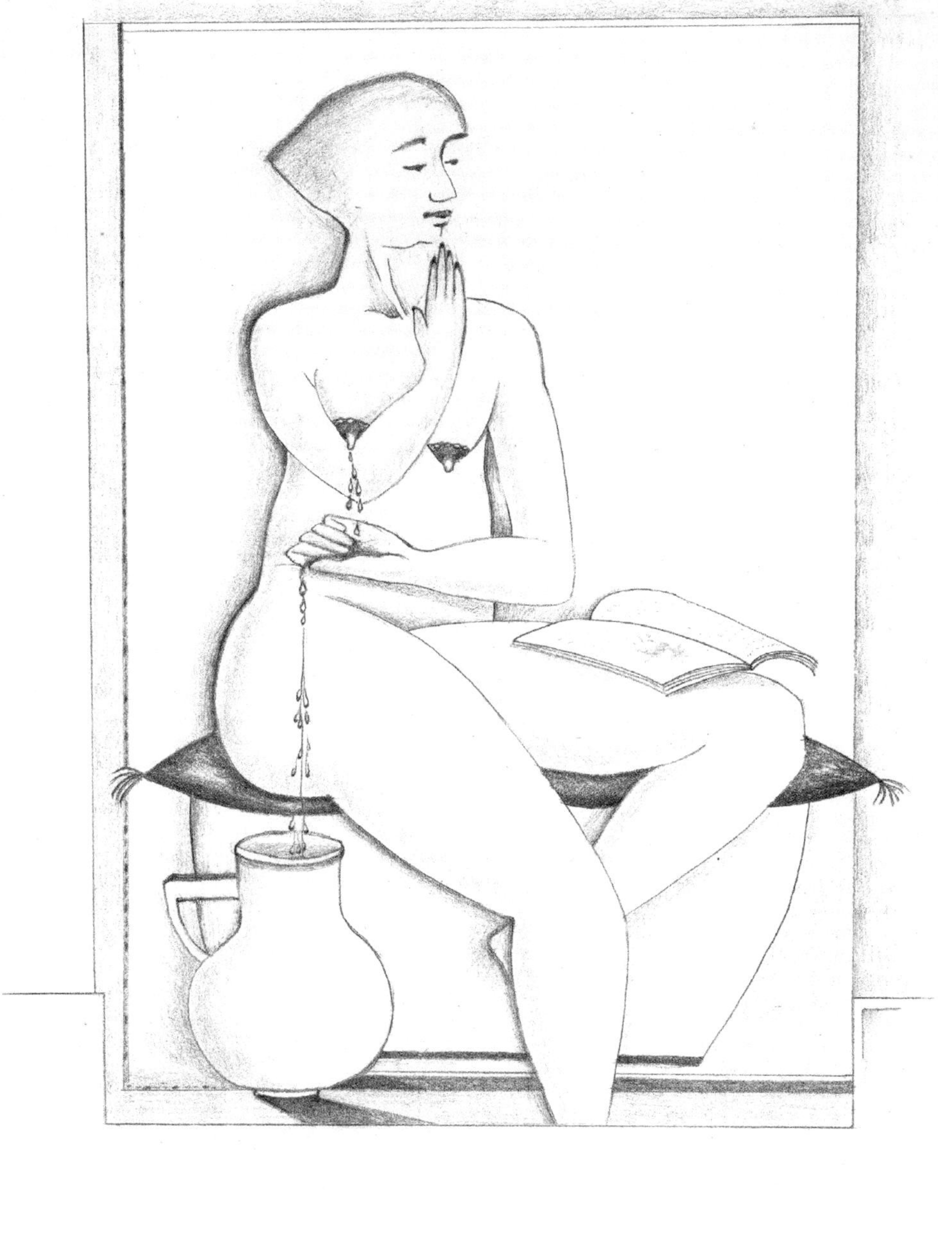

(ABOVE) ***Milk Flowing into an Urn***, c. 1985. Pencil on paper, 16½ × 14 in. (41.9 × 35.5 cm)

Amos as Artist

I had a hunch that my child might have a heavy dose of art genes, given that Ben, my mother, and I were all active in the arts. When he was about nine months old, I set him down on a paper larger than his little body and gave him giant bulb-shaped crayons to scribble with. As he grew, we would draw together, and when he was fussy, instead of a toy or candy, I handed him pencil and paper. When he was about ten, well-meaning adults would ask, "What do you want to be when you grow up?" Amos's reply was always "I *am* an artist."

Amos is now a well-known and beloved artist in San Francisco (www.amosgoldbaum.com). His murals, drawings, and wearable art are all over the city and beyond. We have a strong bond, and I am extremely grateful that he is such a fine human being and phenomenal artist. His life is enriched by his remarkable life partner, Christina Briegleb. I am so relieved and happy that my painful relationship history has not carried into the life of my child. Seeing them together warms my heart.

(OPPOSITE, ABOVE LEFT) ***Amos, Age Fourteen***, **1999. Conté crayon on colored paper, 14 × 10 in. (35.5 × 25.4 cm)**

(OPPOSITE, ABOVE RIGHT) **Amos Goldbaum, *Drawing Machine*, 2019. Gouache and pen on paper, 18 × 24 in. (45.7 × 60.9 cm). This painting was exhibited at the de Young Open exhibition at the Fine Arts Museums of San Francisco in 2020.**

(OPPOSITE, BELOW) **Amos Goldbaum, *Gantry House / Opera Crane*, 2020. Enamel paint on metal, 9 × 9 ft. The Box Shop, San Francisco**

(RIGHT) **Amos and Christina**

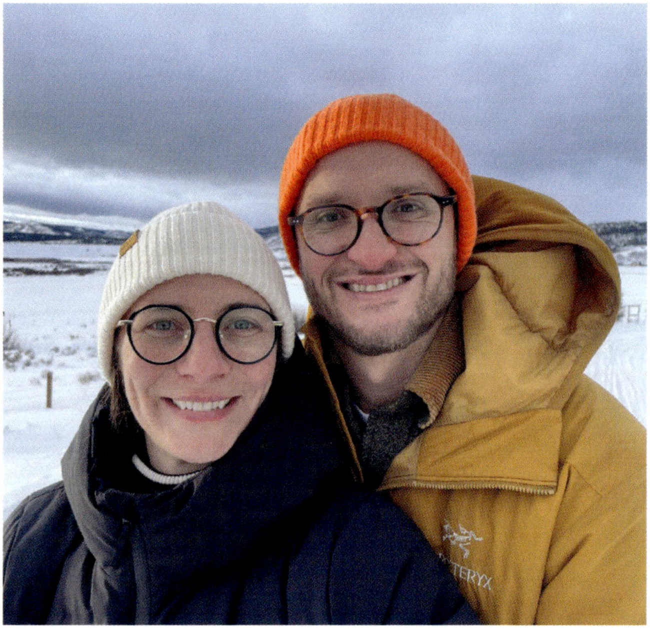

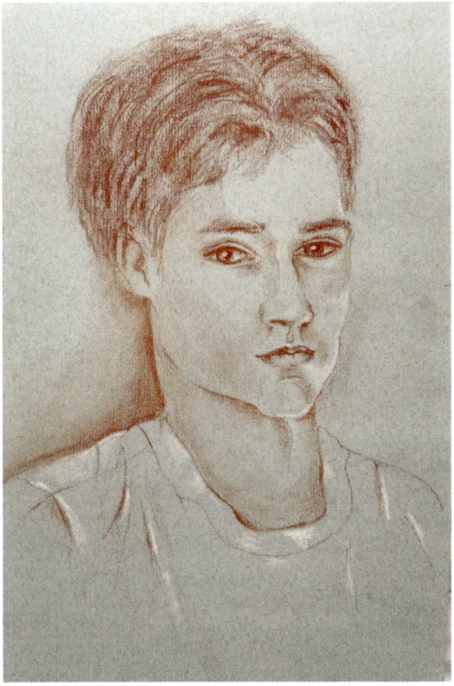

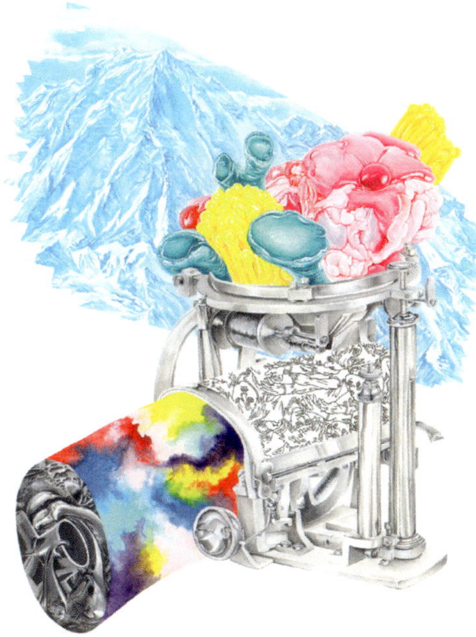

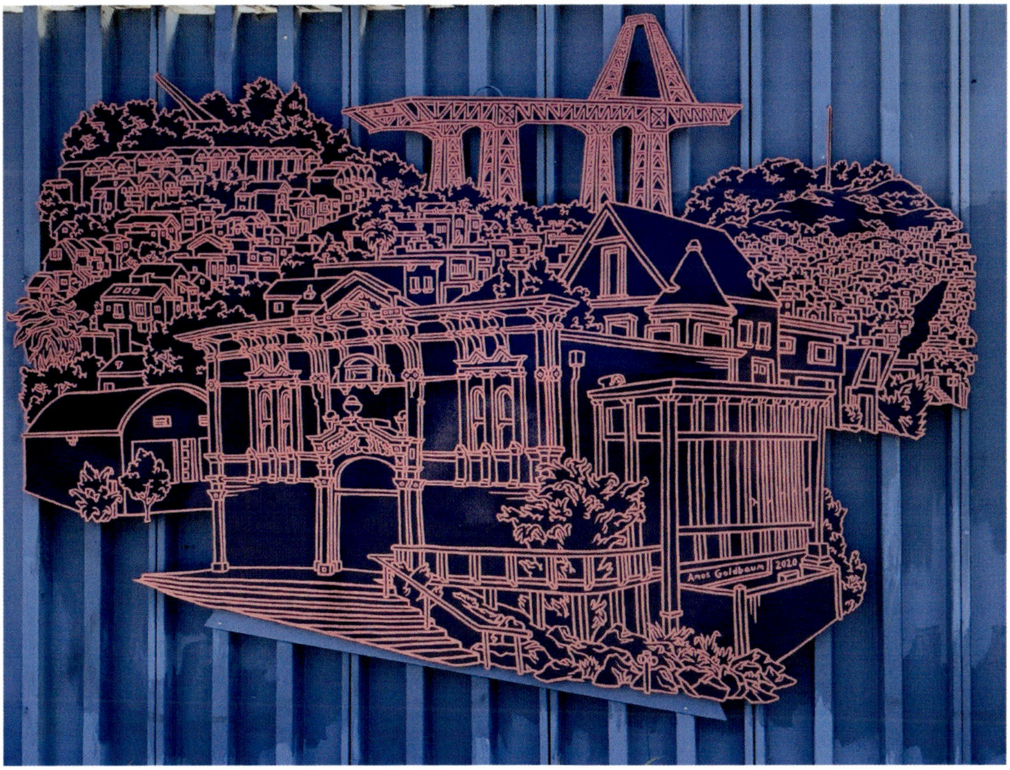
Amos Goldbaum
2020

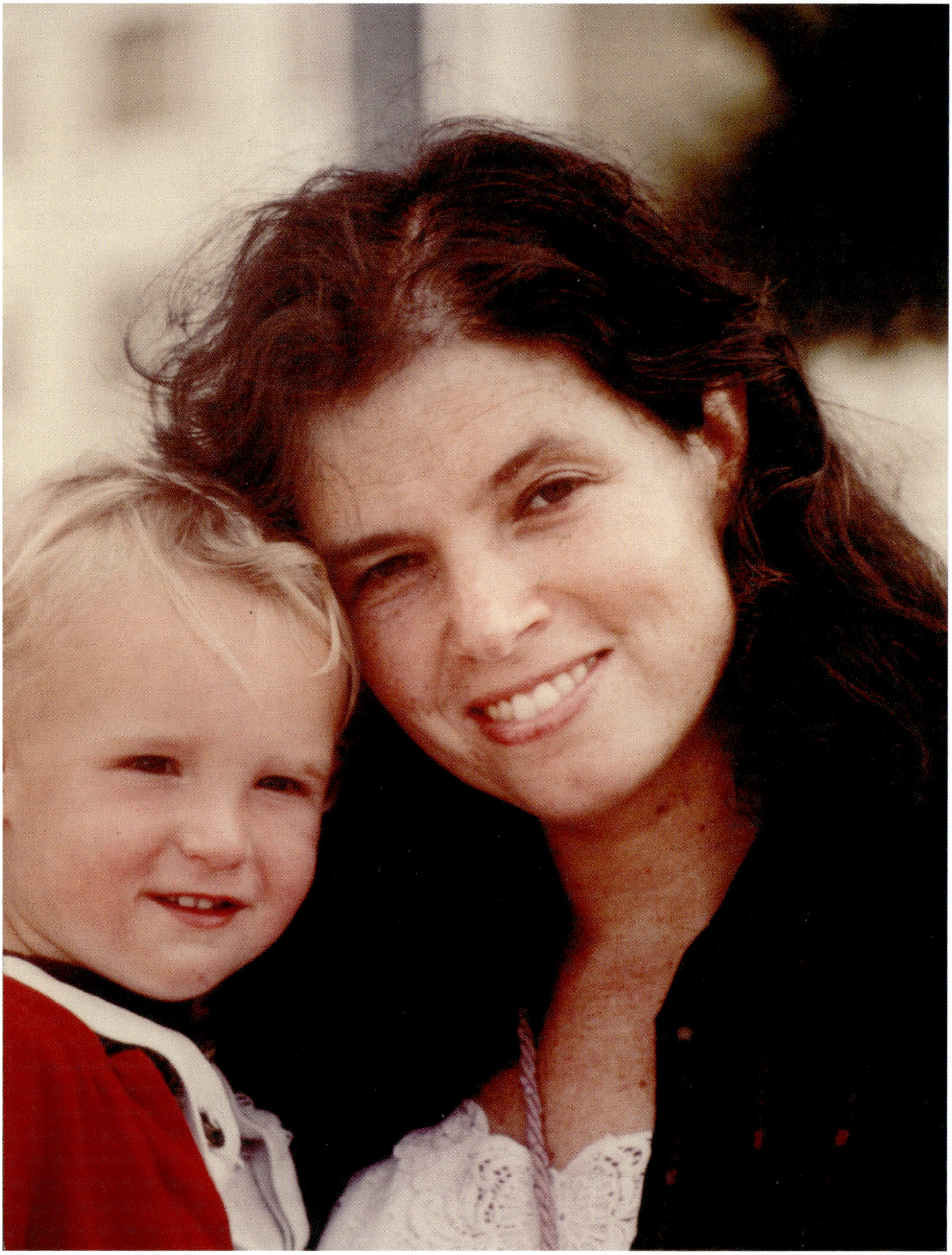

(ABOVE) Me and Amos, 1985. Photo by Felipe Ariza.

CHAPTER FOURTEEN

REFUGE FOR A SINGLE MOTHER

When Amos was about one year old, I separated from Felipe. I think I hurt myself more than I hurt him, as I had turned my back on someone who was unconditionally there for me and Amos. However, we have remained friends to this day.

I moved into New Moon House, a cooperative oriented toward parents and children—a godsend for an inexperienced mother like myself.

A Space for Art-Making

An artist in the cooperative, George Brooks-Hutton (www.huttonio.com), advised that it was important to have a dedicated painting area. He cleared a space for me in the basement, and while my son was in playgroup or napping, I immersed myself in the creation of egg tempera paintings.

Sometime after I left home, my father gave me the book *Italian Painting: The Creators of the Renaissance* by Lionello Venturi and Rosabianca Skira-Venturi. The book explores the roughly 200-year period from the more abstract and static icons of the Byzantine era to the virtuoso realism of Michelangelo, Leonardo, and other artists of the High Renaissance. This transitional epoch is now called the Proto-Renaissance (1280–1400). These artists were pejoratively called "Italian Primitives" until the 1970s, when art historians came to revere the unique beauty of this period. The book made no reference to egg tempera, but I discovered that these were the painters who inherited Byzantine iconography and the craft of egg tempera painting.

I was mesmerized by the stylized icon-like imagery, simplified yet with human emotion, more realistic than its medieval predecessors, yet retaining some of the otherworldly feeling. This marriage of the egg tempera medium and the Proto-Renaissance style

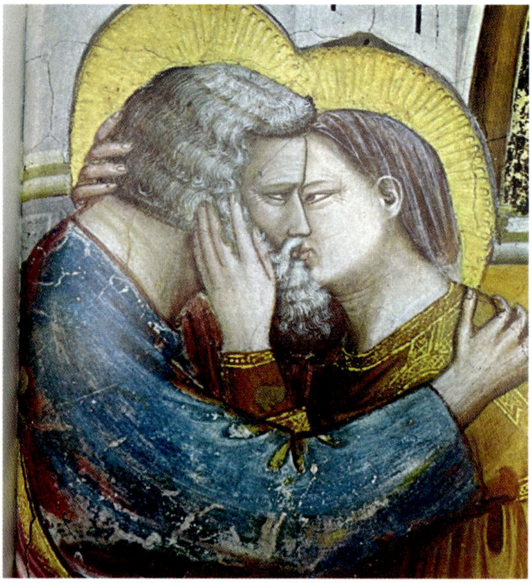

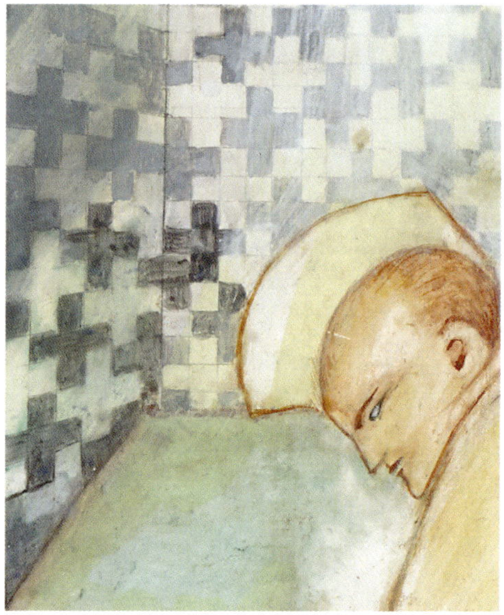

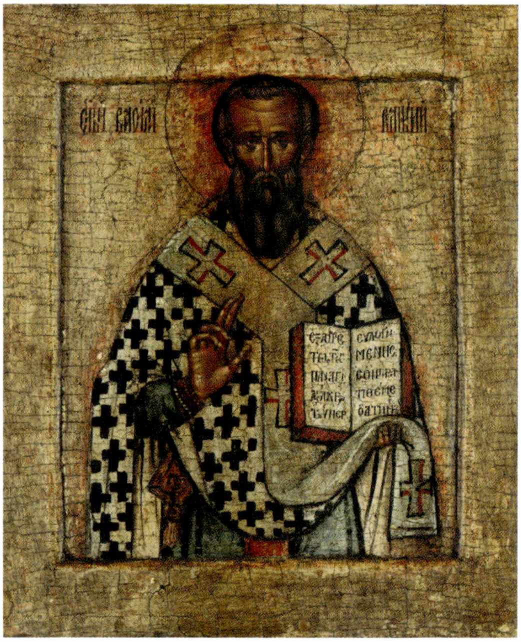

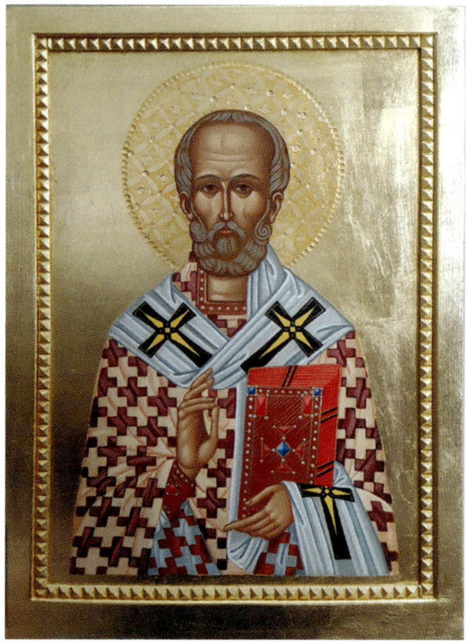

(ABOVE LEFT) Detail: Giotto di Bondone, *Meeting at the Golden Gate*, 1305. Fresco, $78\frac{3}{4} \times 72\frac{7}{8}$ in. (200 × 185 cm). Scrovegni Chapel, Padua, Italy

(ABOVE RIGHT) Detail: *Scene from Surgery I*

(BELOW LEFT) *Saint Basil the Great*, late 1500s–1600s. Egg tempera and gold leaf on gesso panel, $12\frac{1}{4} \times 10\frac{3}{4}$ in. (30.9 × 27.4 cm). Icon Museum and Study Center, Clinton, Massachusetts

(BELOW RIGHT) Maria Miteva, *St. Nicholas the Wonderworker,* 2023. Egg tempera, acrylic, and gold leaf on gesso panel, $15\frac{3}{4} \times 11\frac{3}{4}$ in. (40 × 30 cm)

cemented my devotion to both. I gradually adopted Giotto, Cimabue, Fra Angelico, Giovanni Bellini, and others as my stylistic mentors. This became the sweet spot I chose to live in with my art and is perhaps what may be called my style or artistic voice.

One of my favorite Giotto paintings depicts the legend of St. Joachim and St. Anne meeting at the Golden Gate. The great leap that Giotto took from his predecessors was the portrayal of human emotion. To me, this detail of a kiss is a timeless expression of love and connection that resonates through the ages.

As my work evolved, I've been equally inspired by artists outside of the confines of the Proto-Renaissance: Rembrandt, de Lempicka, Gauguin, Magritte, Kahlo, de Kooning, and many others.

Surgical Surrealism

While at New Moon House, I completed my two *Surgical Surrealism* paintings. They were inspired by my friend Janet, who, after completing medical school, announced to her friends that she intended to become a surgeon. This was unusual in the early 1980s, when most liberal-minded aspiring physicians enrolled in family practice residencies. She began a residency at an inner-city hospital and was the first woman ever to complete the program.

During the early weeks of training, Janet had trouble using the bone saw and sensed an unspoken attitude: "Of course you can't handle it—you're a woman."

Observing that she was shorter than the male physicians, a sympathetic physician assistant lowered the operating table. Once the table was adjusted, she had the leverage needed to manipulate the saw effectively.

In *Scene from Surgery I* (FOLLOWING PAGE), the first of the two surgery-themed paintings, the patient and surgeon are both naked, symbolizing their equal status.

Originally, the painting had an infant suckling while the surgeon was performing surgery to show that she could be a mother and a surgeon too. But I removed the infant because it seemed too literal a statement and seemed to take away from the image as a whole. I'm a bit regretful, as the painting has lost some deeper meaning and has an unintended violent aspect.

I appropriated a pattern of crosses typically seen on the robes of saints and other clergy in Byzantine icons and arranged them into an Escher-like undulating wavy mind-play that helps evoke the feeling of disorientation and dread a patient may experience when entering an operating room.

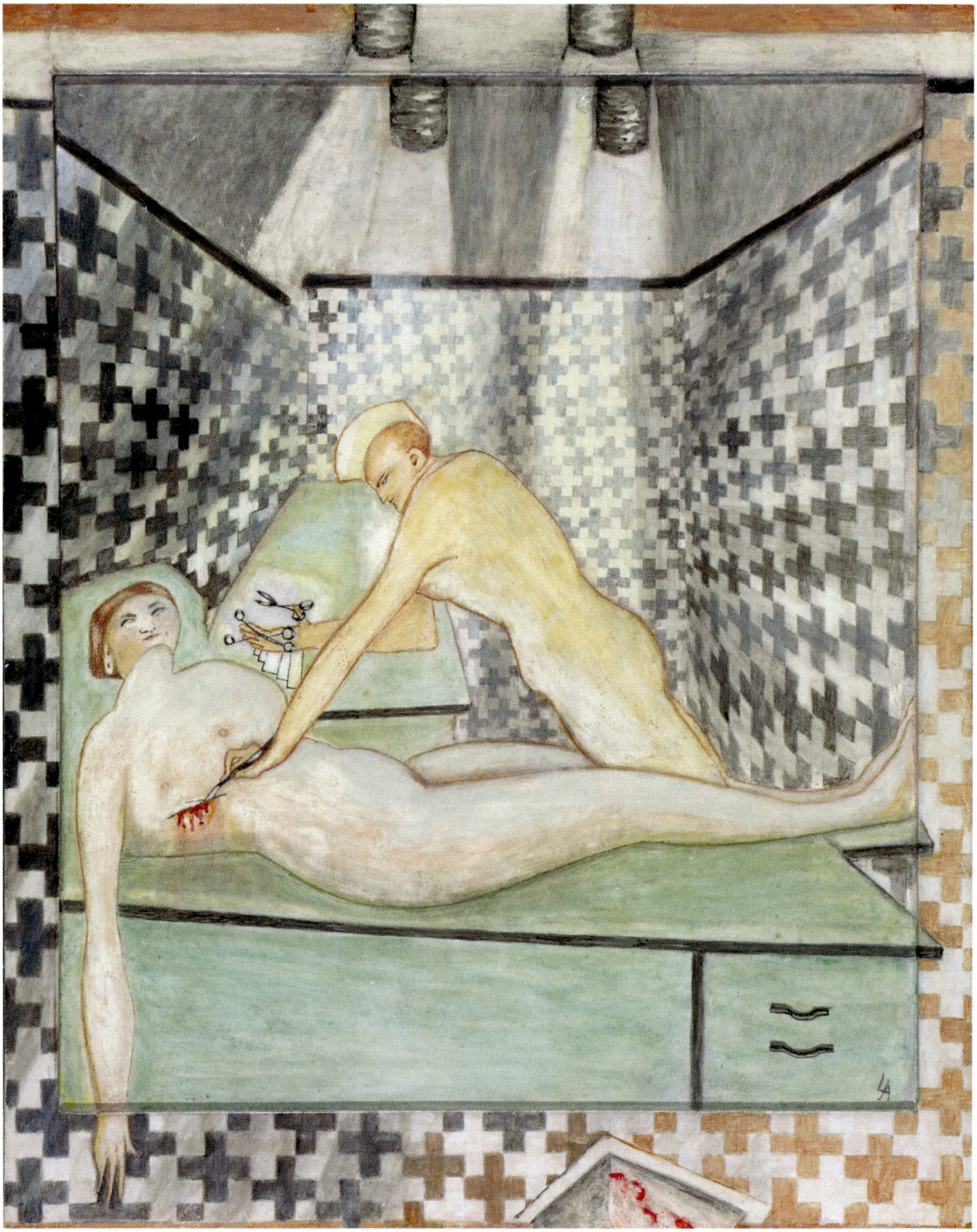

(ABOVE) *Scene from Surgery I,* c. 1986. Egg tempera on gesso panel, 15 × 12 in. (38.1 × 30.4 cm)

The Byzantine Empire & Byzantine Design

In 324 BC, the Emperor Constantine moved the capital of the Roman Empire to a town called Byzantium. It had been a Greek colony and was strategically located on the Bosporus Strait. Constantine officially gave it the name Constantinople and commissioned art and architecture with Christian imagery. Constantinople is today the city of Istanbul in modern Turkey.

Although there is evidence that egg tempera was practiced in the early Byzantine Empire, encaustic (wax) painting was the primary painting medium of icon panels. The infamous periods of Iconoclasm, when icons were banned and many were destroyed, was a setback for Byzantine art. However, when icons were permanently restored in 843 AD by Empress Theodora, egg tempera superseded encaustic as the preferred panel painting technique because it was easier to use. In the centuries that followed, egg tempera was brought to high levels of artistic and technical achievement, especially during the ninth to fifteenth centuries of Byzantine rule.

Byzantine design is highly stylized; the aim was to portray the timeless and spiritual nature of the figures, not strict realism. In Byzantine perspective, the figures lack depth and are two-dimensionally arranged on a single plane without the illusion of three-dimensional space. Byzantine icons feature religious themes with figures in frontal poses against ornate gold backgrounds.

The second *Surgical Surrealism* painting is *Compassion: Scene from Surgery II* (FOLLOWING PAGE). It was initially simply titled *Scene from Surgery II* until a gallery owner renamed the painting *Compassion.* Here, I combine both titles.

This painting is my attempt to humanize an area of medicine known for its cold, harsh environment. The patient's arm wrapped around the shoulder of the surgeon signals connection and empathy.

As in *Nature's Call* (see Chapter 5), I planned a full-color rendering, but the underpainting became so intricate and labor-intensive that I didn't have the courage to obliterate the delicate markings, so I declared the work finished as a black-and-white study.

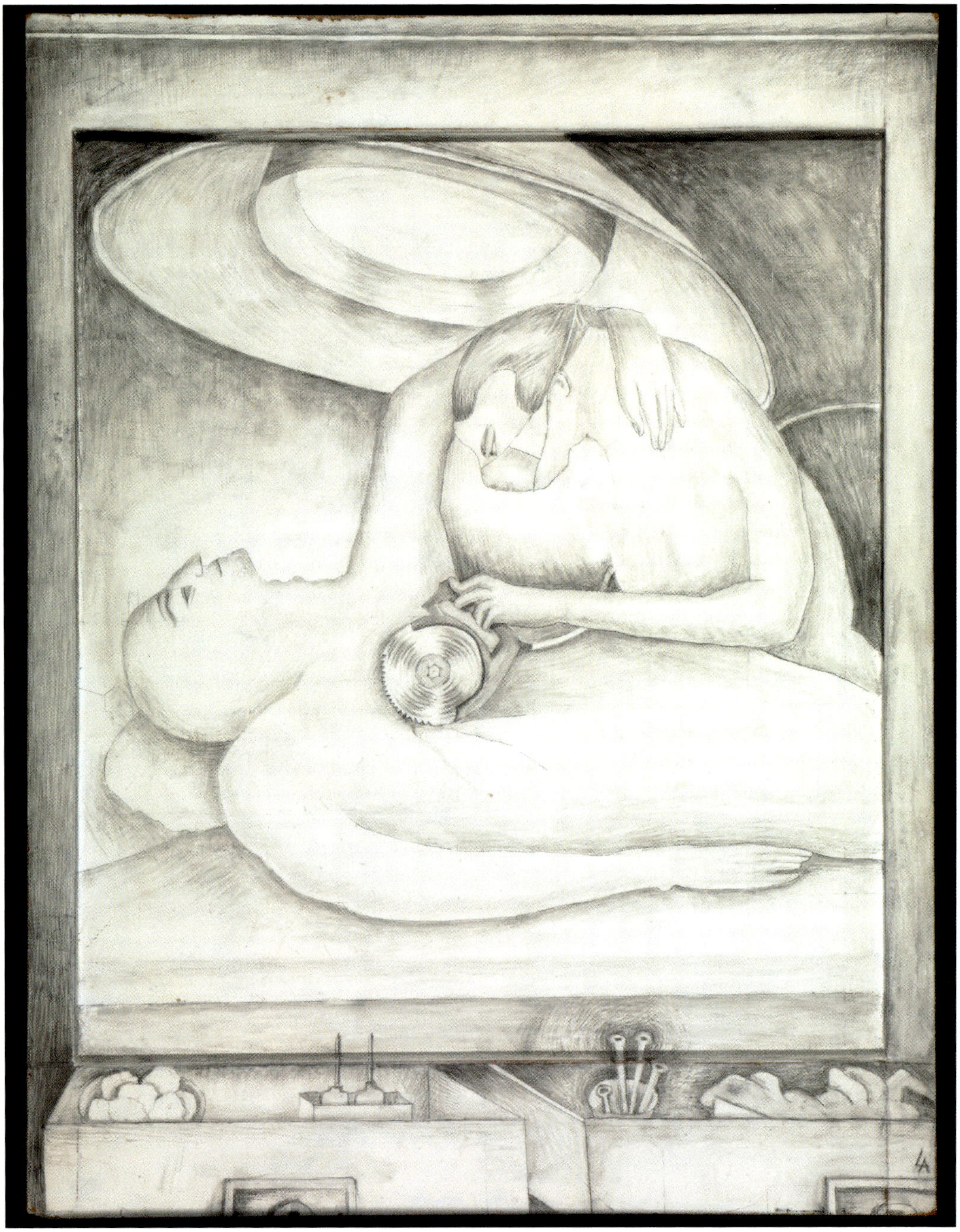

(ABOVE) *Compassion: Scene from Surgery II*, c. 1987. Chinese ink stick on gesso panel, 15 × 12 in. (38 × 30.4 cm)

Making Paint from Malachite

I rarely manufacture my own paint from gemstone.[69] However, in *Scene from Surgery I,* the green pigment of the examining table was ground by hand from malachite.

While you can buy malachite at a gem store, it can be less expensive and more fun to purchase a pre-owned necklace from a thrift store or eBay. This necklace would have been perfect for paint grinding, but I decided to keep it in my jewelry collection, at least for now.

After breaking down the stone into particles in my brass mortar and pestle, I further ground it into paint consistency using a glass slab and muller. I then washed the pigment several times to float off impurities, a process called levigation. Finally, when combined with egg yolk, it became paint.

(RIGHT) Malachite mineral with markings called "bandings"

(MIDDLE LEFT) A malachite necklace purchased on eBay

(MIDDLE RIGHT) Wearing a malachite necklace, 2023

(BELOW) Muller and ground glass slab

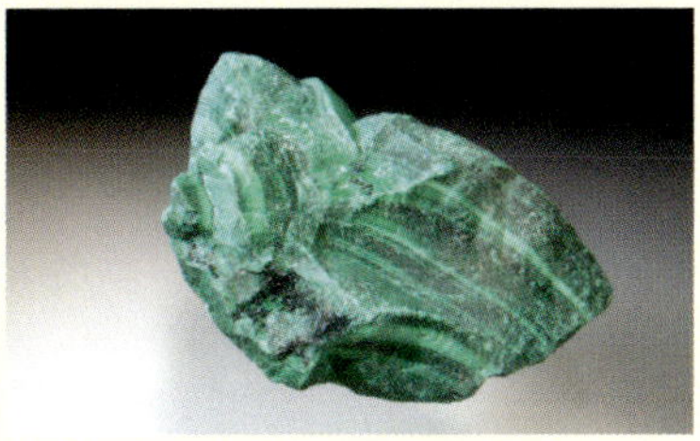

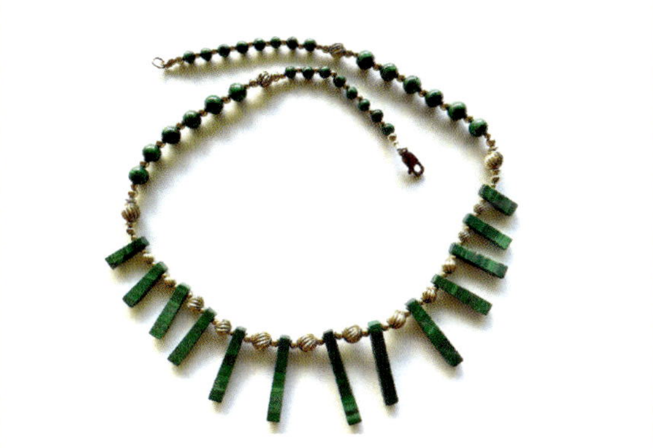

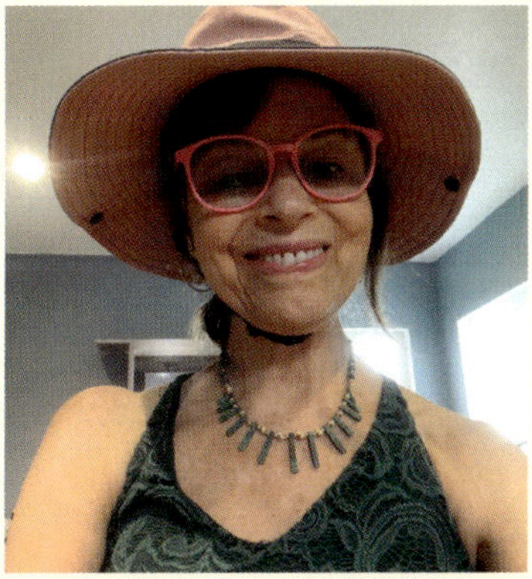

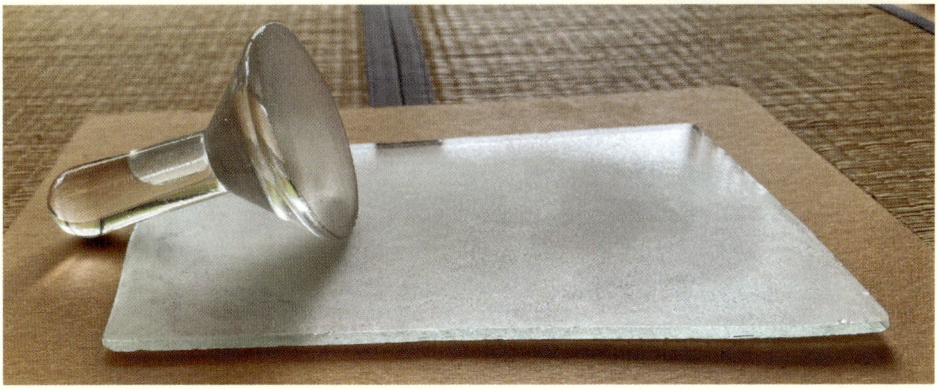

Brainwashed?

Even two years after I'd left Kaliflower, it still had a hold on me, and I started yearning to go back. You feel like you are in the vanguard, like it's the most creative and only cool way to live. Everything outside is boring and meaningless. I was able to recognize this as a pathological thought process but was not able to free myself from this desire.

On the recommendation of a friend, I contacted Arlene Noble, a psychologist who had helped my friend free his daughter from a cult. I shared with her that I was having feelings of longing to rejoin the commune but was resisting the urge to contact them. Surprisingly, instead of bolstering my resolve to resist communication, she encouraged me to send the letter to Irving I had planned to write.

I received a reply back, accusing me of stealing Felipe from the commune. Irving wrote that unless I admitted my nefarious intent, he could see no way to reconcile. The tone was so paranoid and bizarre that it immediately broke the spell. I never had a desire to rejoin the group after that.

SCENE FROM SURGERY I

colors
in the dark basement
of the house on Guerrero
crosses
flow black and white
onto canvas
words
hammered into black & white
remington rand[70]

—ILSE LEHNERT

Pete Arrives at New Moon

In 1987, Pete Arkes, an energetic twenty-one-year-old, barefoot with scraggly dreadlocks, arrived at New Moon House.

We had met once or twice at Kaliflower, and he heard that I was now living at New Moon House. At thirty-eight, I was seventeen years older, but I fell for him, and he befriended two-year-old Amos. When my dad met him and learned he was my boyfriend, Pete's appearance and age so appalled him that he said, "I want to commit suicide."

During the three years we were together and beyond, my father and the rest of my family came to appreciate Pete's love and devotion to Amos.[71] "Pa" and Amos remain close to this day.

Pete's ex-wife, Meryl Juniper, was and still is a devoted stepmother, and their two children, Eli and Elena, are Amos's beloved siblings.

Pete encouraged my desire to grow as an artist and cared for Amos while I attended evening classes at the Atelier School of Classical Realism.

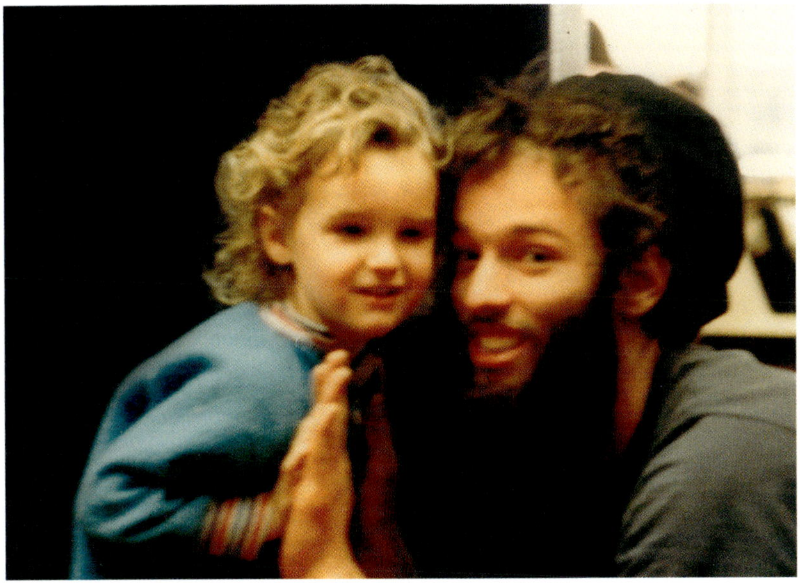

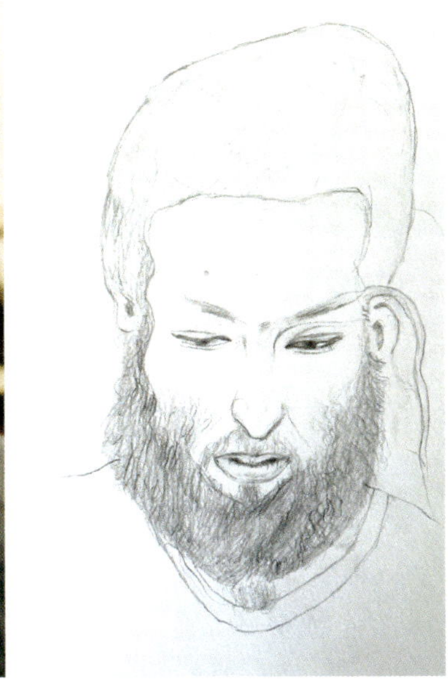

(LEFT) Amos and Pete, c. 1987

(RIGHT) *Pete*, c. 1988. Pencil on paper, 8½ × 11 in. (21.5 × 27.9 cm)

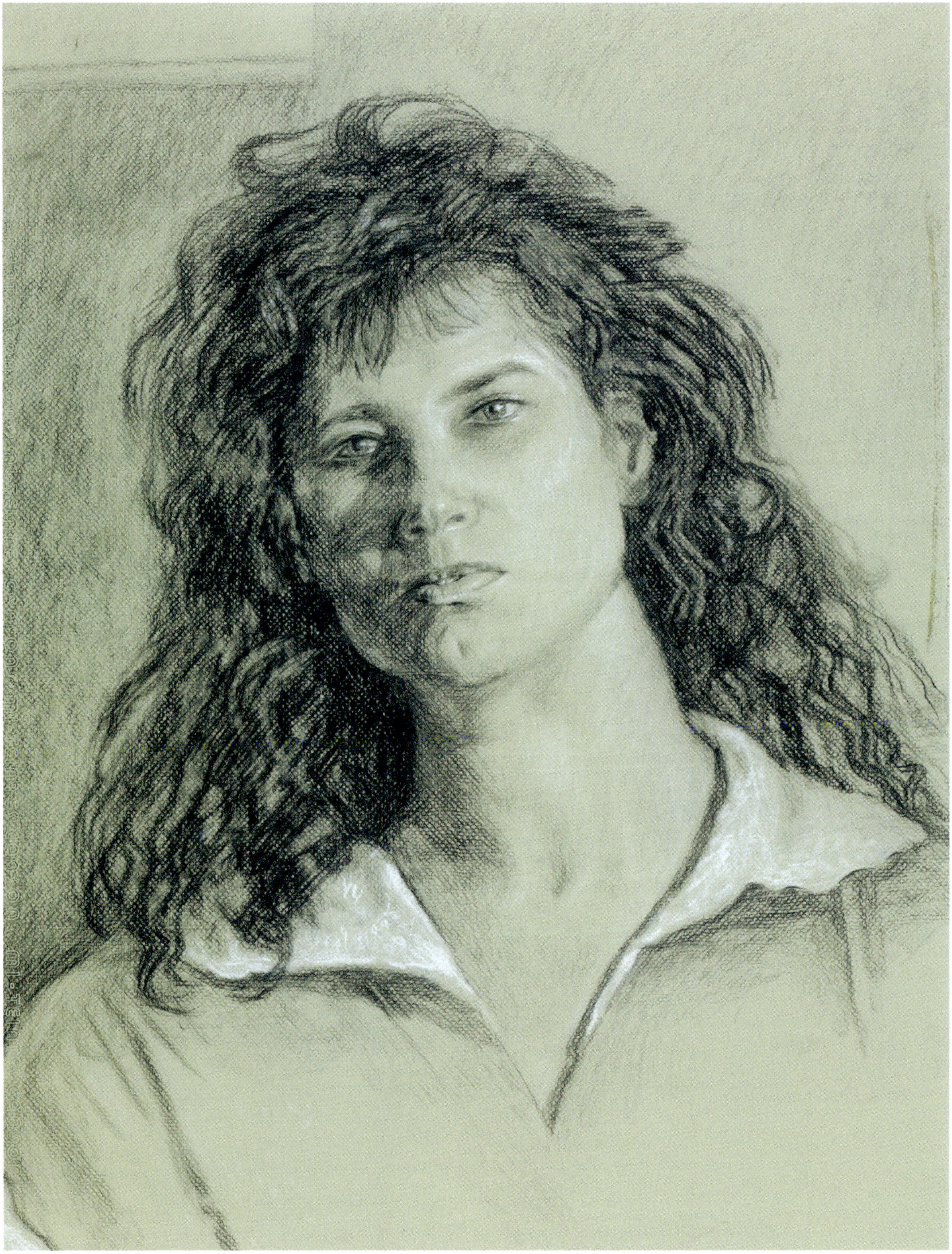

(ABOVE) ***Self-Portrait***, c. 2001. Charcoal pencil on green-toned paper, 25 × 19½ in. (63.5 × 49.5 cm)

CHAPTER FIFTEEN

CLASSICAL REALISM: MORE REAL THAN REALITY

In 1988, I was still struggling with aspects of egg tempera, so when I saw an announcement for a class in Renaissance painting techniques at the de Young Museum School of Art, I arranged to meet the instructor. After reviewing my work, he said, "You already know egg tempera—your problem is you don't know how to draw!" He advised me to seek "the master"—David Hardy. To my astonishment, he then invited me to be a guest instructor in his course, saying I knew more about tempera than he did!

I did teach his egg tempera class and also contacted David Hardy at the Atelier School of Classical Realism. David's teachings were handed down from the great art academies of Europe and were exceedingly stringent. We were required to spend two years drawing in charcoal pencil before being permitted to touch paint. It was torturous to observe the advanced students painting in oils to alluring effect. David later relaxed his rules and allowed novice pupils to work in color sooner.

David Hardy was also a master portrait painter. In fact, he was a society portrait painter in Dallas early in his career but left that line of work because he felt the clients were too demanding. But he was very helpful guiding students who wished to draw self-portraits in his class. The self-portrait on green paper on the opposite page and the one on blue paper on the following page were both drawn under his guidance.

I fell in love with David's painting *A Special Time* when I first saw it in his home. It was so enticing—it appeared more real and beautiful than reality, the epitome of what Classical Realism can do. I offered to buy it but could not afford the $3,000 price. Although David paints in oils, he loves working on the traditional gesso panels used by egg tempera artists. He was very excited to learn that I knew how to prepare traditional

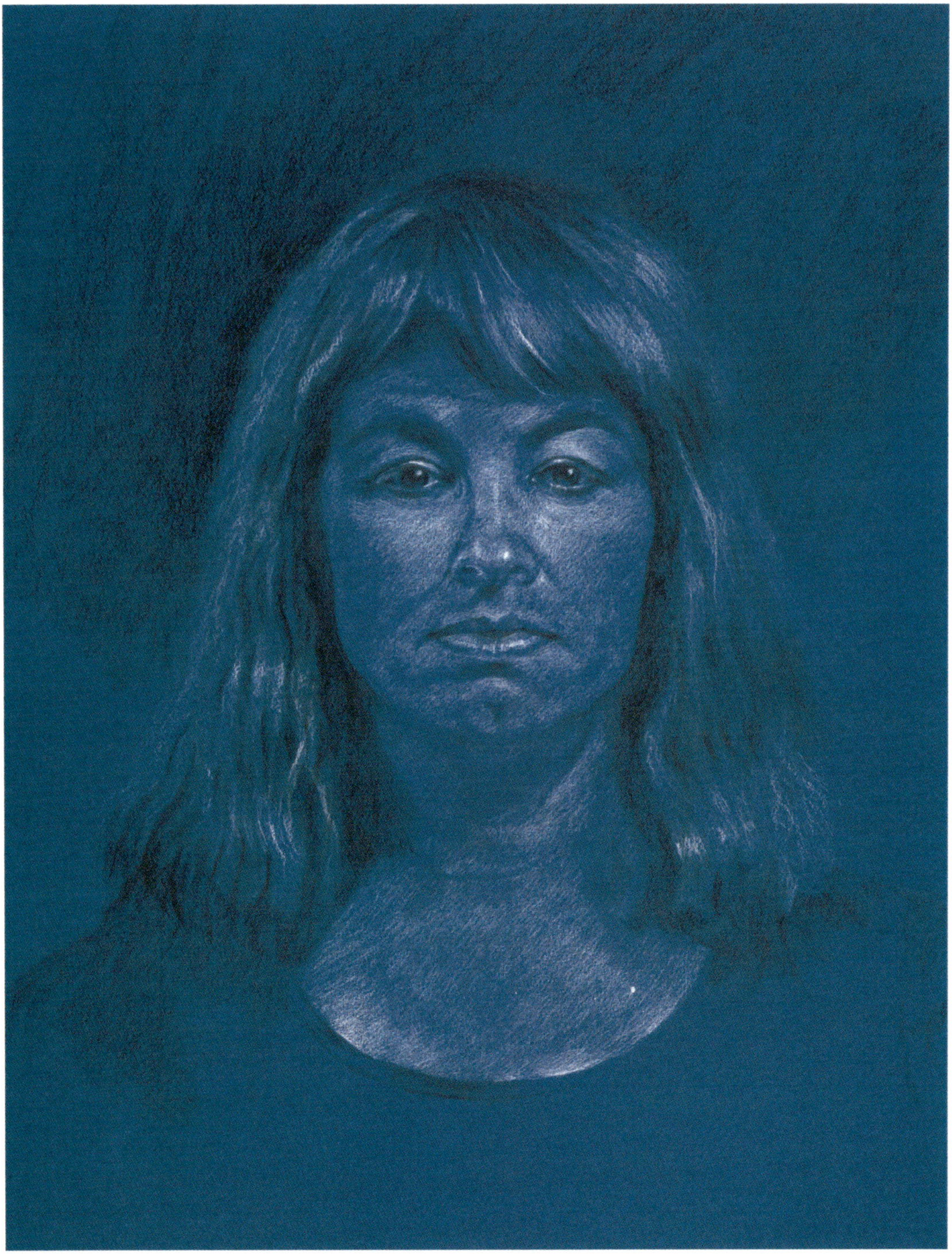

(ABOVE) *Self-Portrait*, c. 2001. Charcoal pencil on blue-toned paper, 25 × 19½ in. (63.5 × 49.5 cm)

gesso panels and agreed to accept panels in lieu of cash. Traditional gesso grounds are too absorbent for oil painting, so David would seal the surface with a coat of rabbit skin glue to prevent the oil colors from "sinking."

After a couple of years, the barter transaction was complete. I picked up the painting and organized a party to unveil it. David and his wife, Sally, and many of my friends came. I covered the painting with a cloth, and when everyone had assembled, I dramatically pulled away the cloth to reveal the beloved painting. Everybody oohed and ahhed, and David was very touched.

A Special Time still hangs in my bedroom at a vantage point where I can admire it while lying in my bed.

The classes met two evenings per week. Students would study at their own pace, often for years, forming bonds from our mutual struggles and artistic epiphanies. David also took us on trips to museums and on landscape painting jaunts. He was then, and still is, a very dear person with very stringent standards and expectations.[72]

Using photographs as reference material was verboten in David's class. Instead, he taught us how to use our eyes as a camera. He encouraged wearing brimmed hats to dilate the pupils of the eyes, which helped in discerning lights from darks. These value changes, when

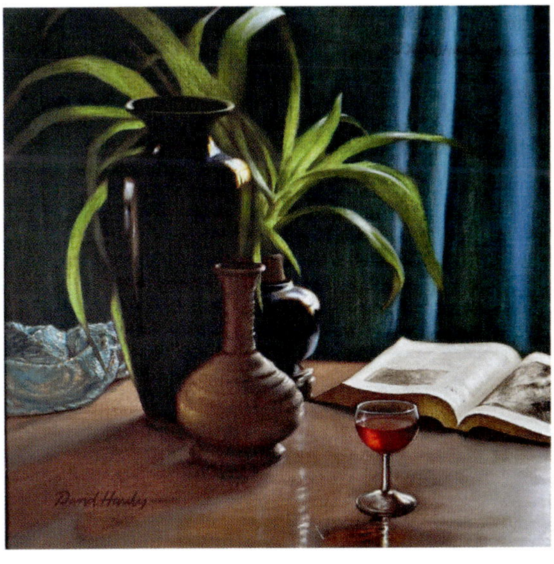

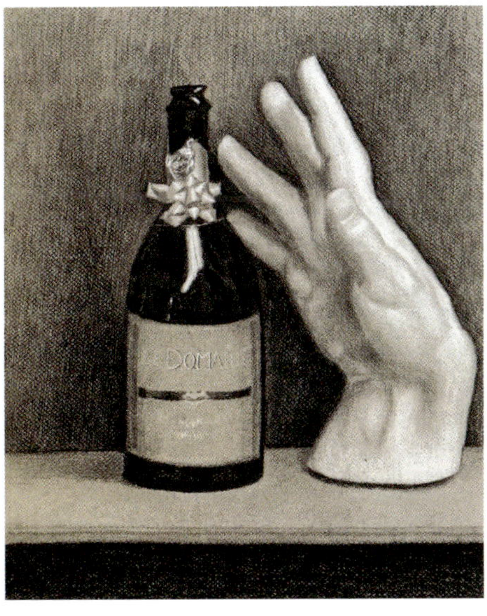

(ABOVE LEFT) David Hardy, *A Special Time*, date unknown. Oil on canvas, 19½ × 19½ in. (49.5 × 49.5 cm)

(ABOVE RIGHT) *Plaster Cast with Bottle*, c. 1988. Charcoal pencil and white chalk on gray paper, 20 × 13 in. (50.8 × 33 cm)

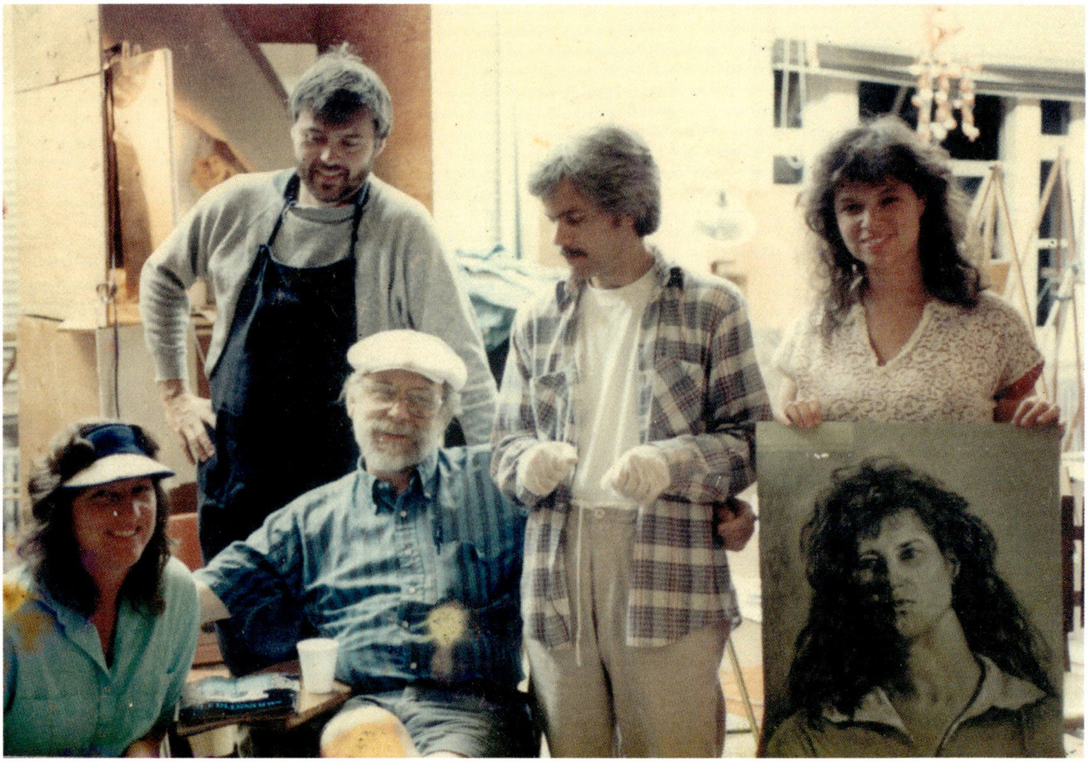

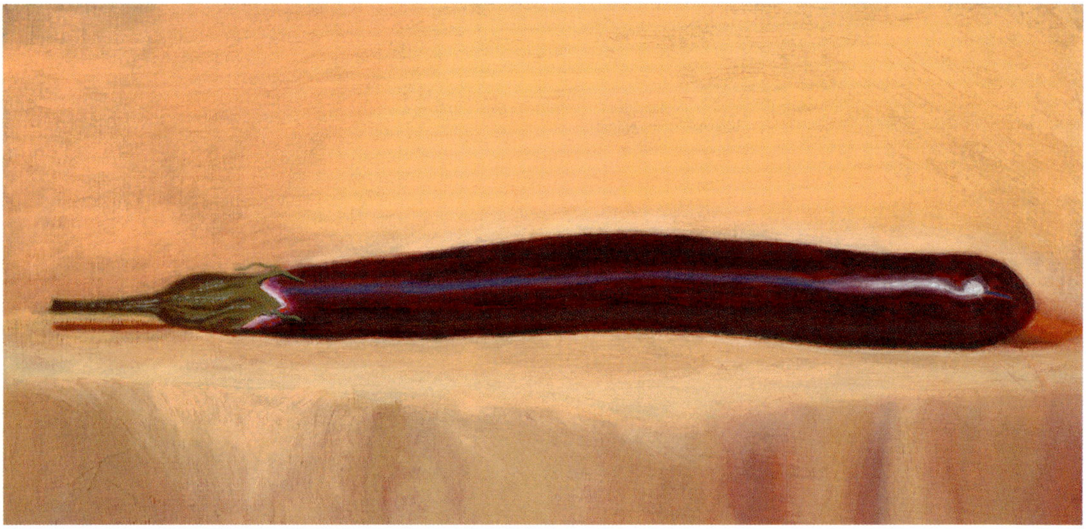

(ABOVE) David Hardy's class c. 1988, Alameda, California. LEFT TO RIGHT: unknown person in visor hat, Mathew Kenny (standing) David Hardy (seated), Gary Bennet, me. Photographer unknown.

(BELOW) *Japanese Eggplant*, c. 2000. Oil paint on traditional gesso panel, 17 × 14½ in. (43.1 × 36.8 cm)

Color Temperature Theory

According to color temperature theory, warm colors are reds, oranges, yellows, and browns; cool colors are blues, violets, and greens. But color temperature is relative. For example, although blue is a cool color, it can lean warmer if it has a lot of red in it. Or it can lean cooler if it has more green—for example, the color turquoise.

Warm colors advance or come forward, and cool colors seem to recede or go back into space. As the play of alternating warm and cool hues washes over objects, the transitioning tones create a sublime realism that photography cannot capture. Different moods are revealed depending upon the color temperature of the light source. For example, a warm light (the sun) casts a cool shadow, and a cool light (the moon) produces a warm shadow.

However, not every system of color temperature is the same. I learned about a different theory from egg tempera artist Koo Schadler. She explained in a 2023 email to me that the "Old Masters used an archetypal idea of illumination as given by the full spectrum, balanced light of the sun. In this system, halftones are painted relatively cool and deep shadows appear relatively warm."

rendered skillfully, produce a startling effect of realism. Other techniques were squinting, peering through sheets of tinted plastic, and using a "black mirror."[73] We drew still lives, plaster casts, and self-portraits. After two years of study, I began instruction in oil painting.

Realistic drawing was difficult, but oil painting even more so. I was happy with the painting I made of a Japanese eggplant, though, because I feel it captured its unique beauty.

Color temperature theory is at the heart of David's teaching and is responsible for transporting the viewer into a magical world that somehow seems even more real than reality.

I was an anomaly in class because, unlike the other students, I did not aspire to realism in my personal artwork. However, these techniques can also be applied to nontraditional art, helping me to create the otherworldly-scapes of intensity that I strive toward.

I'm also grateful to David for helping me overcome my insecurity as an artist. David preached that passion can be a substitute for talent, an asset of which I feel I am in short supply.

Fortunately, my passion for painting is immense, carrying me through times of self-doubt. At its most intense, this passion feels like I possess godlike powers. The concept for a painting comes from an unknown source, like dipping into a deep well of mysteries from which I draw out seductive colors and dangerous arrangements of elements. But it depends on my training and labor to bring it to fruition.

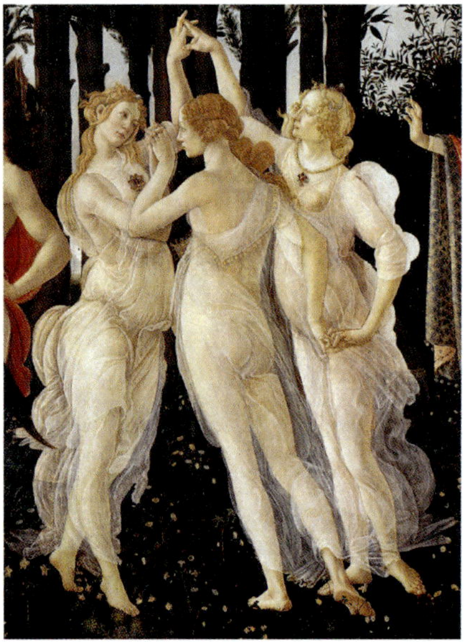

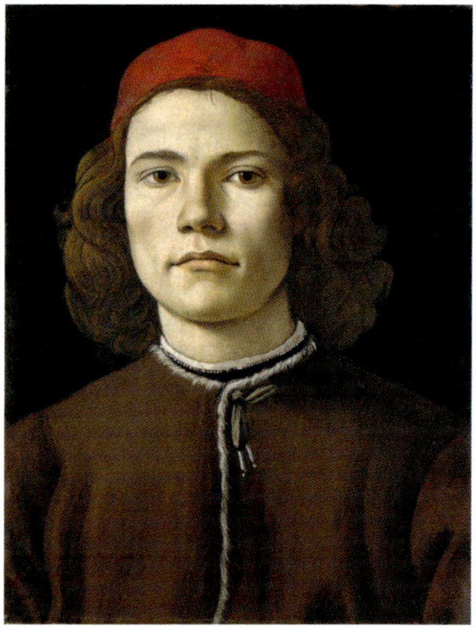

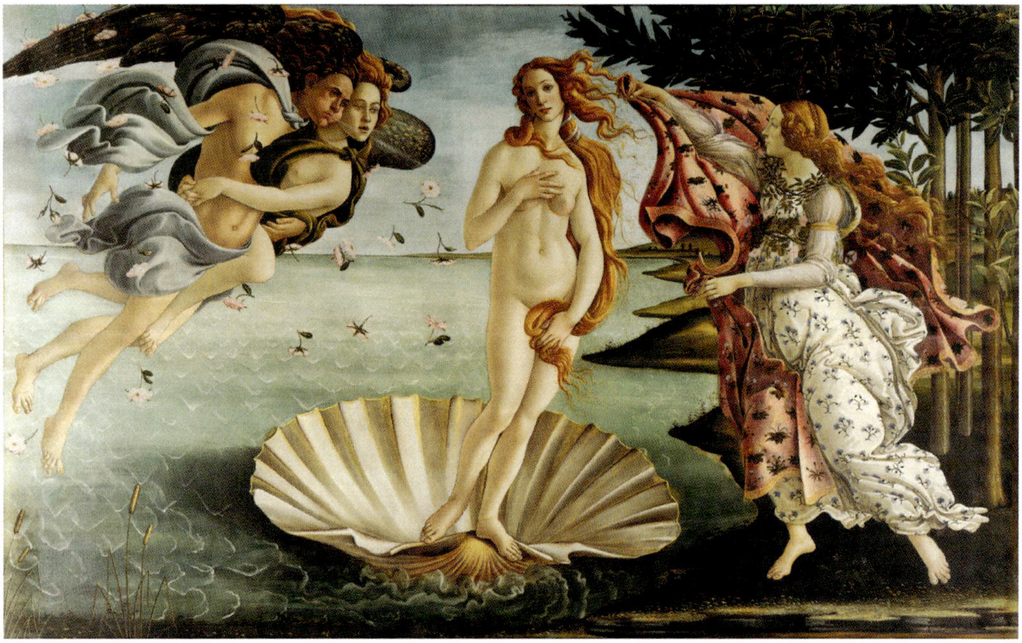

(ABOVE LEFT) Sandro Botticelli, *Primavera* (detail showing The Three Graces), c. 1482. Egg tempera (with some oil) on panel, 80 × 124 in. (202 × 314 cm). Uffizi Gallery, Florence

(ABOVE RIGHT) Sandro Botticelli, *Portrait of a Young Man*, c. 1483. Egg tempera (with some oil) on panel, 14⅞ × 11⅛ in. (37.5 × 28.2 cm). National Gallery, London

(BELOW) Sandro Botticelli, *The Birth of Venus*, 1486. Egg tempera on canvas (with some oil), 67⅞ × 109⅝ in. (172.5 × 278.5 cm). Uffizi Gallery, Florence

CHAPTER SIXTEEN

FIVE THOUSAND YEARS OF EGG TEMPERA HISTORY

Classical Realism harkens back to nineteenth-century academic models, which in turn breathed inspiration from the Renaissance and the classical Greek era. My foray into Classical Realism helped me to sharpen my skill in drawing and learn about color temperature theory, but my artistic soul remained true to egg tempera and its fascinating history.

The Birth of Venus by Sandro Botticelli is a widely known painting, but few people know the medium is egg tempera.

Botticelli eventually switched to oil painting after a transitional period when he used both oil and tempera on the same painting.[74]

In 1995, a friend who worked at the Johnson Museum at Cornell University invited me to speak about egg tempera at their lecture series. I developed the presentation "Botticelli's Forgotten Medium: Egg Tempera Past and Present," and in the years following, shared it with a variety of groups.

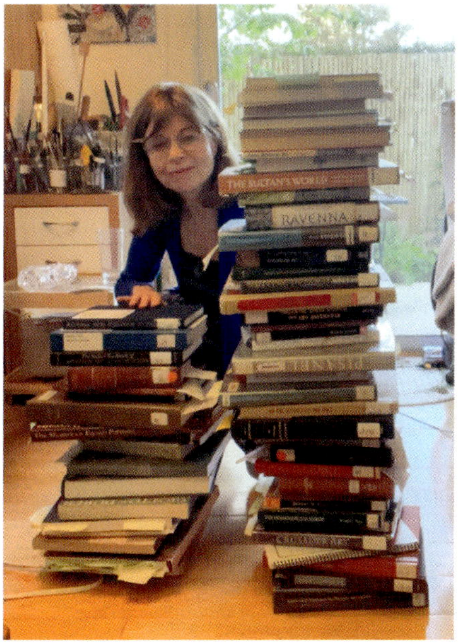

(RIGHT) Seated behind a tower of books related to egg tempera, some from my own collection and many from the public library

The Society of Tempera Painters

The deep dive into egg tempera history I took while preparing the Cornell lecture rekindled my long-harbored desire to revive the Society of Painters in Tempera, whose papers I had discovered at the British Museum Library during my travels in 1981.

STP

The improvement in the art of Tempera Painting by the interchange of the knowledge and experience of the members.

The Society of Painters in Tempera
London, 1901

(ABOVE) Society of Tempera Painters logo (1997) with the mission statement of the original Society of Painters in Tempera, London (1901)

The group was founded in England in 1901 by Christiana Herringham and several British artists. In 1912, it merged with the Mural Decorators' Association, becoming the Mural Decorators and Painters in Tempera Society. The last papers of the society I could find were published in 1924.

In 1995, I took my first step and consulted an attorney at California Lawyers for the Arts. He advised that in order to revive the old society or even to use the original name, I would need to obtain permission from any surviving members.

Next, I purchased the domain name www.eggtempera.com. The fact that the web address was available is indicative of how little interest there was in egg tempera at that time. Indeed, Dianne Mitchell (who would become my egg tempera teacher in 1990) used to say, "Egg tempera artists are as rare as hen's teeth!" I built a website devoted to all things egg tempera, including a forum, gallery, lists of resources, a timeline of egg tempera painters throughout the ages, and the revival of the Society of Painters in Tempera.

While working on the site, I came across an internet post by Michael Bergt, a masterful and imaginative figurative egg tempera artist living in Santa Fe, New Mexico (michaelbergtart.com). To my utter surprise, he too was working on starting an egg tempera society! I immediately responded to his post; his reply was "great minds think alike."

Michael's approach to finding members was to organize an egg tempera exhibit in Santa Fe. He was excited by our joint vision, and we joined forces. I preferred to rekindle the old society and use the original name, but Michael thought it was less cumbersome, with fewer potential legal issues, to call it "Society of Tempera Painters." I agreed, and STP was founded as a nonprofit organization in 1997.

We held a few meetings in San Francisco, with members sharing their artwork and techniques. A branch of STP was established in the UK, and a lively exchange of information took place on the website forum. A paper newsletter was published from 1997 to 2007, and museum shows, lectures, and demos brought greater awareness of egg tempera and support to its practitioners.

I dropped out of the leadership after about a year but remained a member. As of this writing, in 2025, STP is dormant. I maintain hope of reviving STP, but it will need fresh energy and enthusiasm from egg tempera painters. Please contact me if you are interested!

UNRELATED TO STP, there is a 2,500-plus-member (as of 2025) Facebook group, Artists and Patrons of Egg Tempera, which brings tempera artists together to share images and information.

Through the years, I've continued my study of egg tempera history and have extensive notes for a comprehensive book. But writing this memoir has taken me away from painting for far too long, and my priority is to create paintings. So instead of completing the history book, I've included a bonus chapter at the end of this book called "Which Came First? A Taste of Egg Tempera History." It is my compact overview of 5,000 years of egg tempera history.

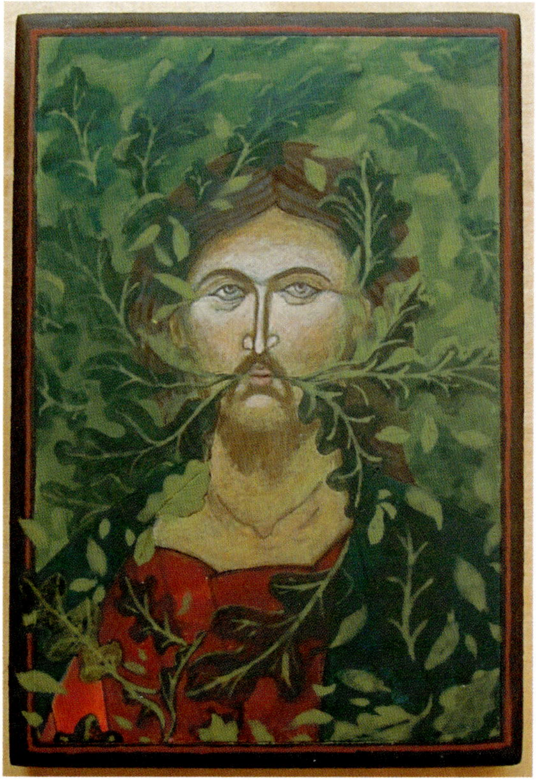

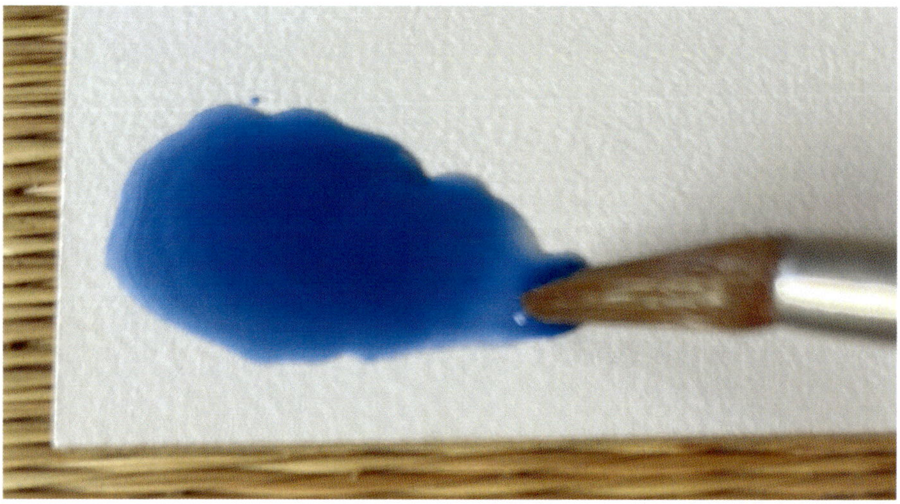

(ABOVE LEFT) *Petit lac* technique, first step: create a puddle

(ABOVE RIGHT) Christopher Castle, *Green XC,* 2014. Egg tempera on gesso panel, 8½ × 5¼ in. (21.5 × 13.4 cm)

(BELOW) *Petit lac* technique, second step: tease out puddle with brush. Traditionally, the brush should float above and not touch the panel.

CHAPTER SEVENTEEN

AT LAST! THREE EGG TEMPERA TEACHERS

In the period that followed, I was fortunate to study with three egg tempera masters: Christopher Castle, Dianne Mitchell, and Koo Schadler.

Christopher Castle

The first teacher I connected with was Christopher Castle, a modern icon painter who uses ancient techniques.

I especially loved learning about the *petit lac* (little lake) technique in which the artist places a small pool of color on the gesso panel and then teases it out into a wider space. I've heard it called "flooding" or "pushing a puddle around." It is akin to, but actually quite different from, a watercolor "wash."

Dianne Mitchell

In 1992, I came across an article, "One Egg, Over Medium: The Struggle to Master Egg Tempera Painting," by Dianne Mitchell.[75] I immediately called the author, who fortuitously would be teaching a five-day workshop the very next week.

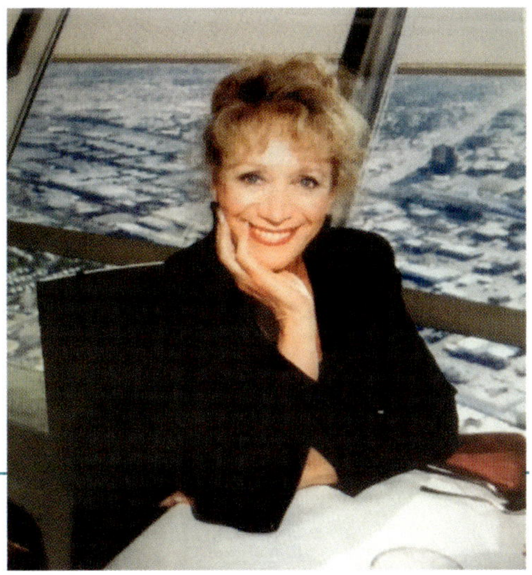

(RIGHT) Dianne Mitchell. Date and photographer unknown.

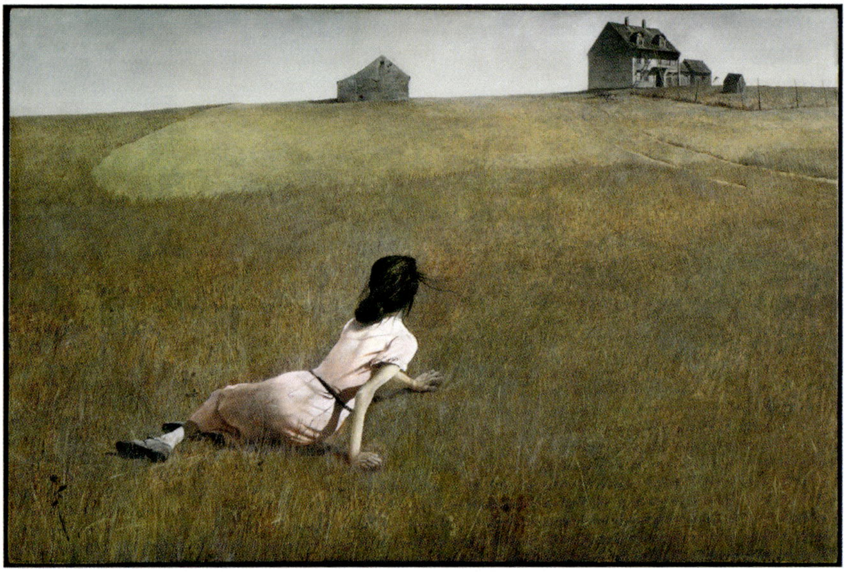

(ABOVE) Andrew Wyeth, *Christina's World*, 1948. Egg tempera on gesso panel, 32¼ × 47¾ in. (81.9 × 121.3 cm). Museum of Modern Art, New York City. Digital Image/Museum of Modern Art.

Dianne had been captivated by *Christina's World*, the famous egg tempera painting by Andrew Wyeth, and had left her home in California to study with egg tempera master Rudolph "Rudy" Zallinger at the University of Hartford in Connecticut.

I had seen *Christina's World* at the The Museum of Modern Art many times growing up in New York but never realized it was painted in egg tempera until years later.[76]

Zallinger learned egg tempera from Prof. Louis York at the Yale University School of Art. Yale was an epicenter of the American egg tempera revival that took place from 1930 to 1950. Zallinger is remembered for his gargantuan murals, *Age of Reptiles* and *Age of Mammals*, at the Yale Peabody Museum of Natural History.

Dianne's painting *Virgil* illustrates the high level of skill in egg tempera she attained, combining her native talent with the expert instruction of Zallinger.

Studying egg tempera with Dianne was revelatory, solving dilemmas I had been grappling with for years. The essential challenge of painting in egg tempera is building up the layers of paint. Most historical and modern egg tempera artists apply the paint in tiny linear brushstrokes called "hatch marks." In expert hands, like those of Duccio, it is dazzling. The hatch marks follow the shape of the object being defined, and the spaces between the marks allow some light to beam up from the gesso board, creating an inner glow.

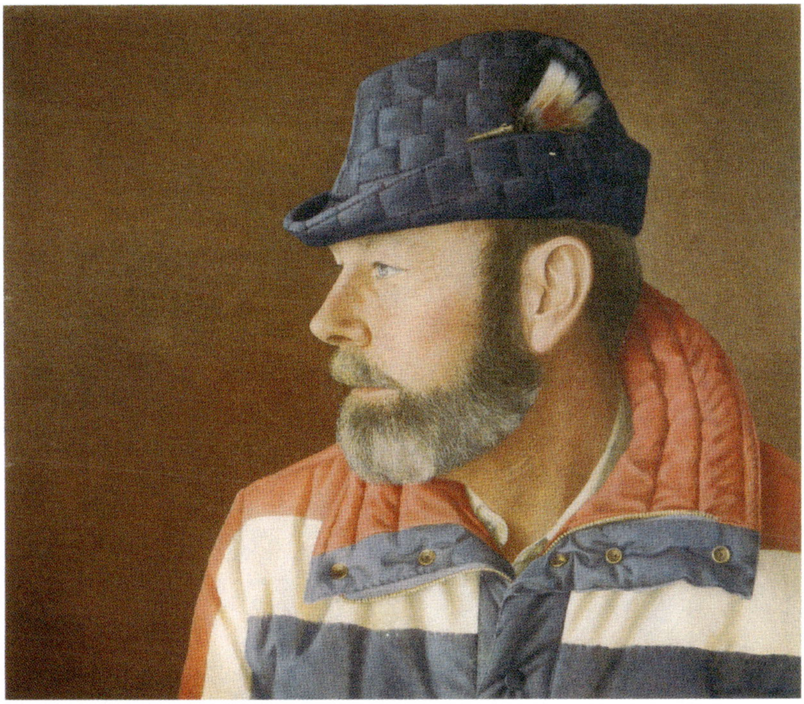

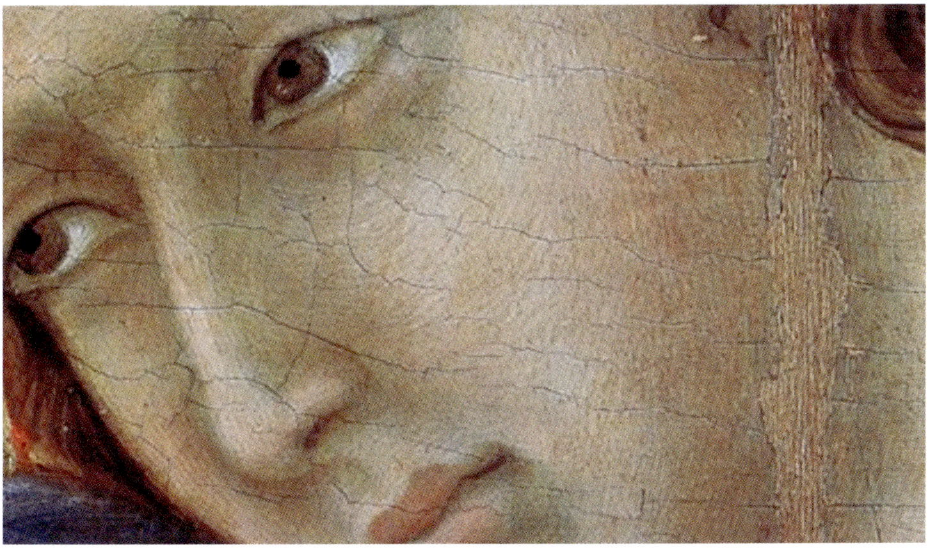

(ABOVE) Dianne Mitchell, *Virgil*, 1984. Egg tempera on gesso panel, 19½ × 22 in. (49.5 × 55.8 cm).

(BELOW) Detail: Duccio di Buoninsegna, *Madonna and Child* (Rucellai Madonna), 1290–1300. Egg tempera and gold on wood, 175 × 114 in. (445 × 290 cm). Uffizi Gallery, Florence

From the start, I had an "allergy" to hatching; I found it unbearably laborious and did not like the results, which, in my hands, looked stiff or fussy.

Instead of hatching, Dianne favored a stippling technique. An old brush is repurposed by cutting off the bristles at the top like a blunt haircut, and the paint is dabbed on with a light pecking motion. This technique retains the same luminous effect as hatching.

A common complaint of beginning tempera artists is the phenomenon of paint lifting. If my paint is too watery, a tiny blob is deposited at the end of each brushstroke. These blobs take longer to dry and are easily picked up with subsequent brushstrokes, lifting off layers of paint that I'd carefully laid down. This can be avoided by wiping the brush on a rag or paper towel before applying each stroke. Dianne romantically called this "dressing down one's brush." It sounds daunting to wipe the brush with every stroke, but it becomes automatic, like the steps of a familiar dance.

Each student made the same little painting of a still life set up by Dianne, designed to demonstrate her various techniques.

AT THE TIME, I was worried about the cost of the workshop and where I would stay in Lake Tahoe. Lola, the owner of Lakeside Gallery, where the workshop took place, graciously allowed me to sleep there in a rollaway bed. I left my six-year-old in the care of his adored stepmother, Meryl Juniper. I sent him a card every day with a drawing and when I got home, bound them together into a little book with a ribbon.

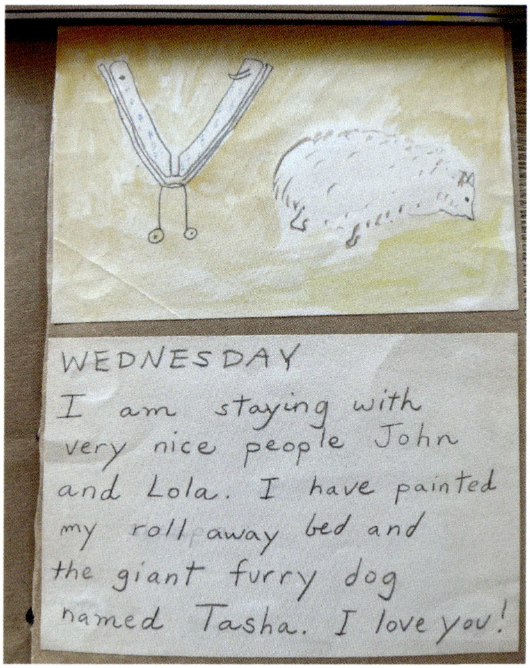

After the workshop, I stayed in Dianne's condo for one night. Her kindness and openness are probably the reason we became close and continue to be to this day.

Tragically, Dianne lost her home and most of her paintings in the Camp Fire blaze in Paradise, California, in 2018. Fortunately, she has photos of most of her work. As of 2025, she is building a new life and starting to create art again.

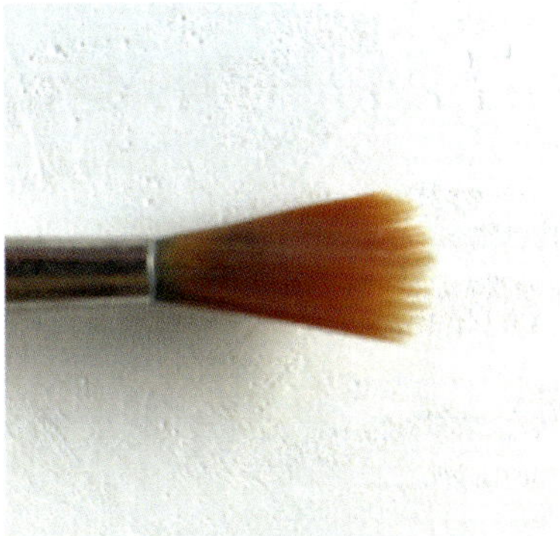

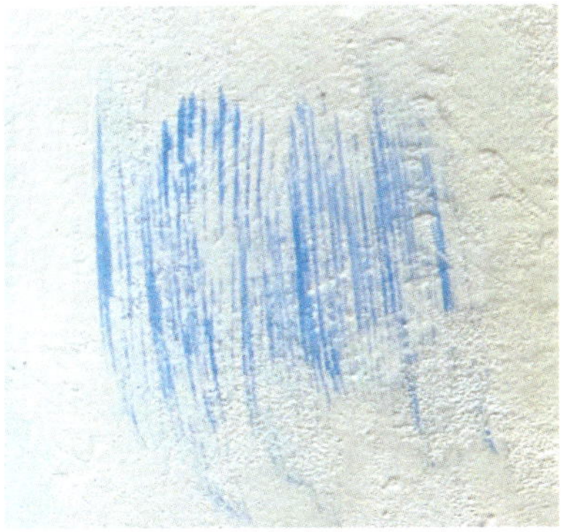

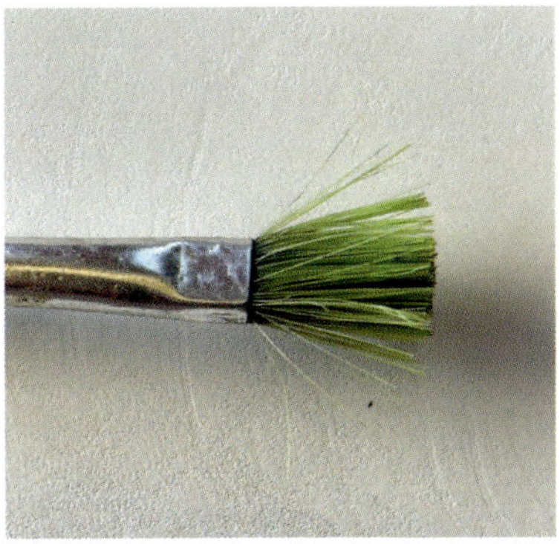

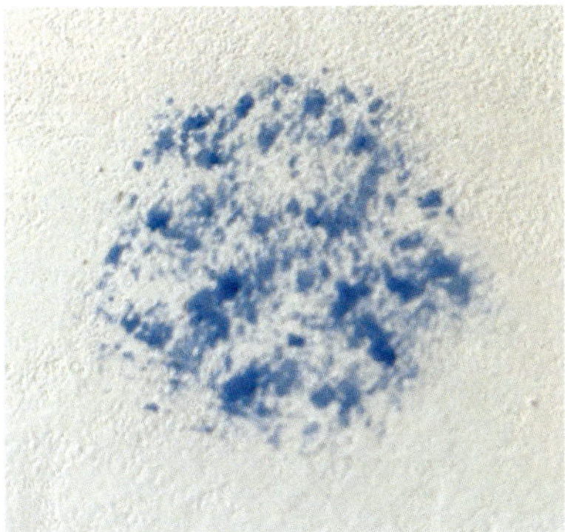

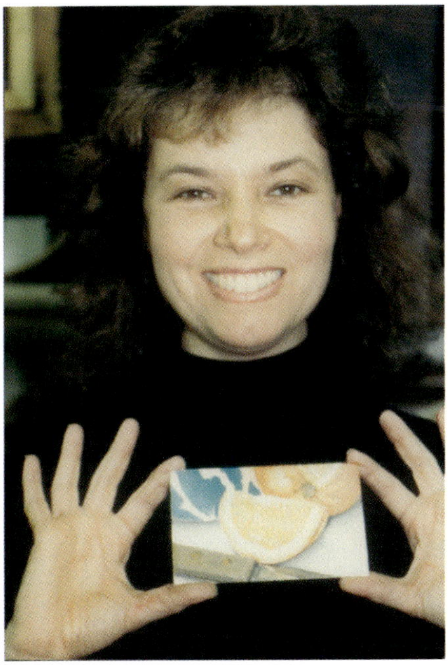

(TOP ROW) A brush can be "splayed" or "fanned" so that multiple hatch marks are accomplished with one stroke, expediting the paint application

(MIDDLE ROW) A brush with a blunt "haircut", and stippling markings made with the brush

(LEFT) In Dianne Mitchell's class, 1992

(OPPOSITE) Pages from the booklet I made for Amos

Koo Schadler

One of the delights of the Society of Tempera Painters was meeting some of the most committed and knowledgeable practitioners of the medium. When Koo Schadler joined the board of STP, I immediately recognized an artist with vast expertise, someone even more immersed in the technique than I was.

Schadler is a superb artist who has explored every facet of and written in depth about egg tempera. When I found out she would be teaching in Boston, I signed up and booked a flight. That first workshop was in 2004, and in later years, I participated in two others. Her magnanimous teaching dissolved many of the remaining gaps in my knowledge of tempera painting.

The stippling technique that I'd learned from Dianne Mitchell was an improvement over hatching but still did not suit my painting personality. Koo invented a technique that is as inscrutable as it is glorious. She champions the use of high-end cosmetic sponges (pharmacy brands will not do), which deposit a lace-like layer of paint. This subtle texture is obliterated when successive layers are sponged on, eliminating any trace of sponge marks or brushstrokes. With patience, beautiful cloud puffs of paint appear.

Koo also employs brushwork but uses very diluted paint with only a whisper of color. To offset some of the time-intensive effort her technique requires, she first applies a fairly thick base coat of paint before the fairy-dust deposits of sponging begin.

Koo shares hundreds of tips and techniques in her book *Egg Tempera Painting: A Comprehensive Guide* (2021). At nearly 300 pages, it is chock-full of detailed instructions, rarefied knowledge, and anecdotes from the egg tempera universe. This is, and most likely will remain, the bible of all aspects of egg tempera painting. Attending her workshops was a true life-changing experience for me.

(OPPOSITE, ABOVE LEFT) Koo Schadler, *Illuminated Self Portrait II,* 2007. Egg tempera on traditional gesso panel, finished with oil, 11¼ × 8⅝ in. (28.5 × 21.9 cm)

(OPPOSITE, BELOW LEFT) Koo Schadler, *Ama Nesciri with Apples*, 2020. Egg tempera on traditional gesso panel, 7½ × 7½ in. (19 × 19 cm)

(OPPOSITE, ABOVE RIGHT) Cover: *Egg Tempera Painting: A Comprehensive Guide* by Koo Schadler, 2021

(OPPOSITE, BELOW RIGHT) Foreground: cosmetic sponges, one with sharp edges trimmed. Background: "sponge daubers" in two sizes

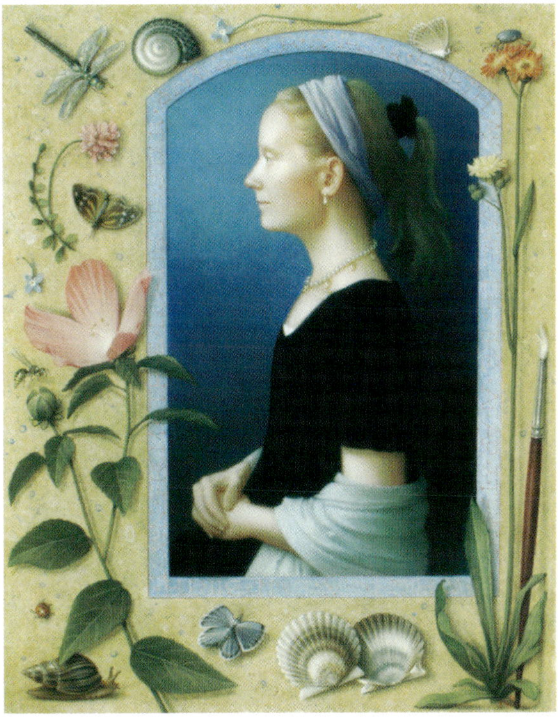

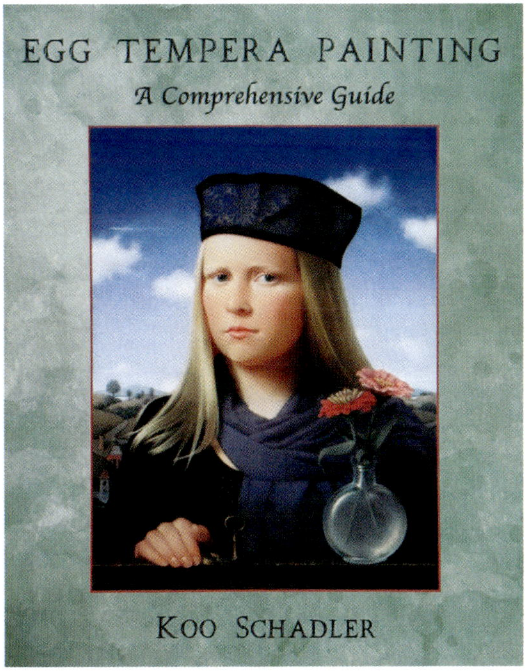
EGG TEMPERA PAINTING
A Comprehensive Guide
KOO SCHADLER

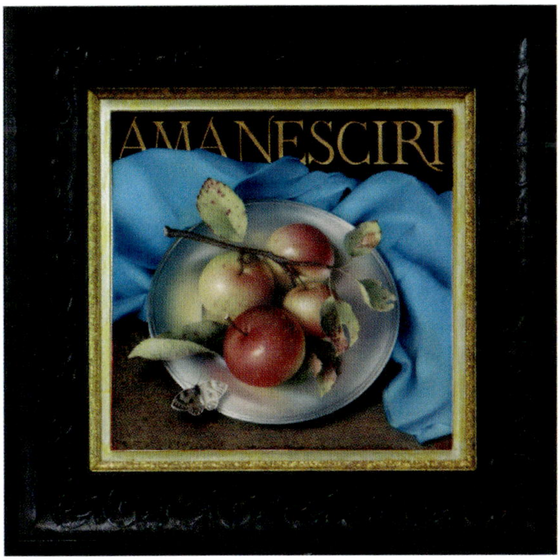
AMANESCIRI

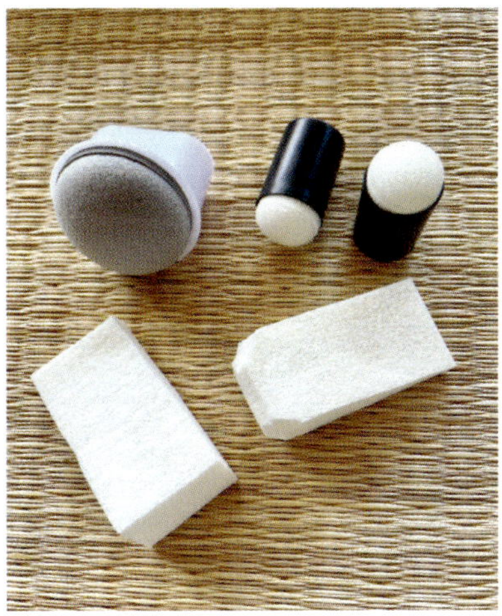

Formal Flexibility—The Yoga Series

The *Formal Flexibility* series reflects techniques I learned from both Dianne Mitchell and Koo Schadler. I first learned yoga in the late 1960s, before it became trendy. There were no yoga mats; we practiced on thick wool blankets. I eventually had to give up yoga due to injuries caused by a condition of hypermobility. Drawing yoga poses enabled me to connect with the aesthetic shapes without harming myself.

Hand to Foot Pose (Padahastasana)

I was told to bring a sketch that could be used to practice egg tempera technique in Dianne Mitchell's workshop, and I drew *Hand to Foot Pose*. Dianne taught us how to underpaint in a complementary color, which sets up a sizzling vibration. I planned to paint the background in cerulean blue, Dianne's favorite blue pigment, but she advised me to first underpaint in orange (the complementary color of blue). You can see some orange peeking through the blue, especially in the areas surrounding the limbs.

Triangle Pose (Trikonasana)

Triangle Pose (FOLLOWING PAGE) speaks to geometry, marrying the mathematical construct with the organic forms of the body. The background pattern was appropriated from an Art Nouveau design. Art Nouveau was a style inspired by the curved and sinuous lines of plants and other natural forms. Many psychedelic concert posters from the 1960s were actually inspired by Art Nouveau posters—which might explain my attraction to Art Nouveau patterns.

Eagle Pose (Garudasana)

Eagle Pose (FOLLOWING PAGE) was conceived in Laughing Horse Inn, an adobe lodge built in 1887 in Taos, New Mexico. I was visiting the area with my sister, Ruthie, and was excited to absorb the colors and culture of the Southwest. By chance, we were assigned the room that Georgia O'Keefe was purported to have stayed in. Of course, we made a pilgrimage to Ghost Ranch, where the reclusive painter spent her summers in a hidden spot.

I was disappointed in my color choices for *Eagle Pose*, as they do not broadcast "Southwest" as I'd hoped, but I adapted to the painting's own voice. Not fun to be bossed around by a painting—surrender is the only option.

Although hatha yoga originates in India, the figure is standing on a Navajo carpet with a classic eagle pattern. It's a play on India, the birthplace of yoga, and Indian, as in Native American.

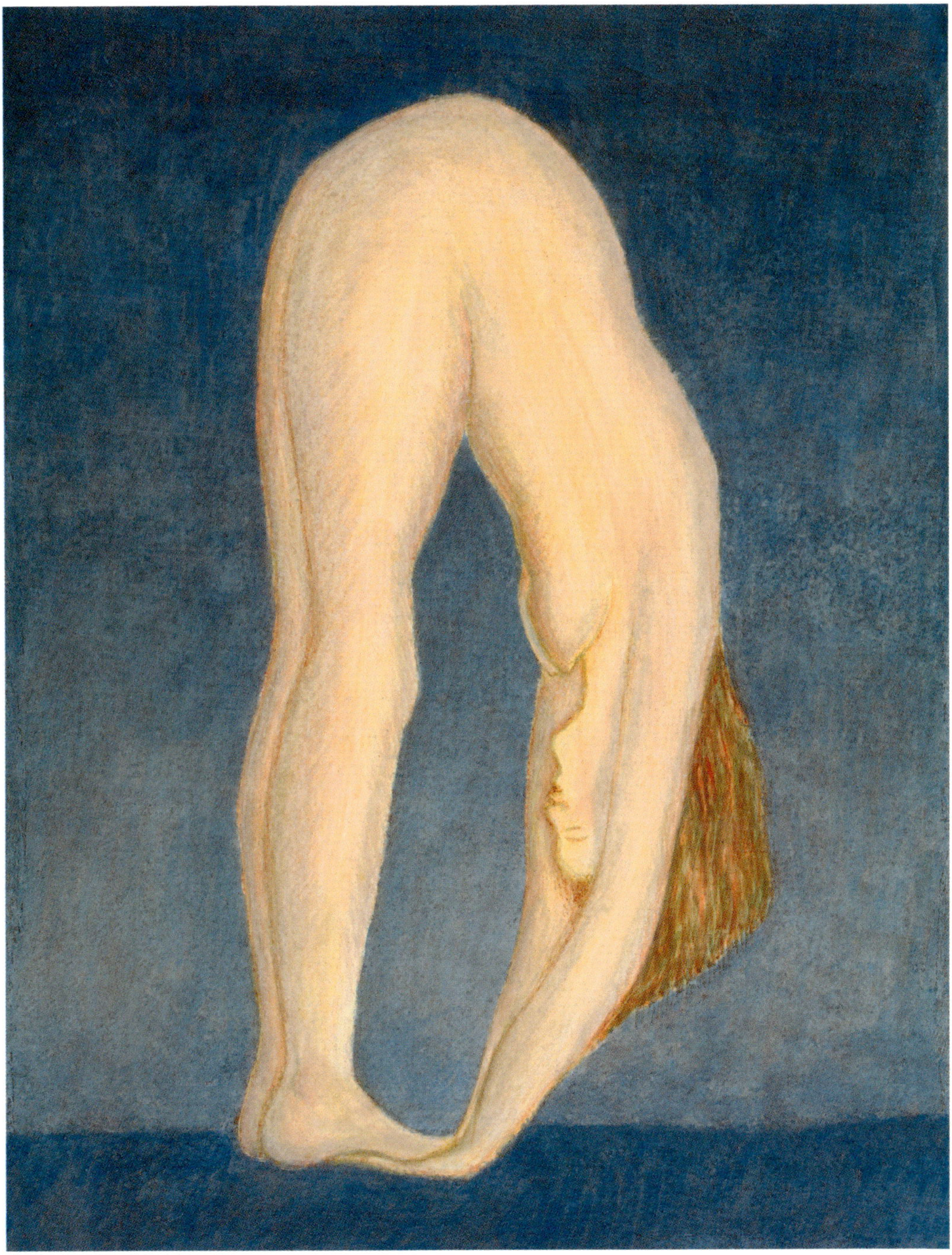

(ABOVE) Detail: *Hand to Foot Pose (Padahastasana)*, c. 1992. Egg tempera and palladium leaf on gesso panel, 11 ½ × 10 in. (29.21 × 25.4 cm)

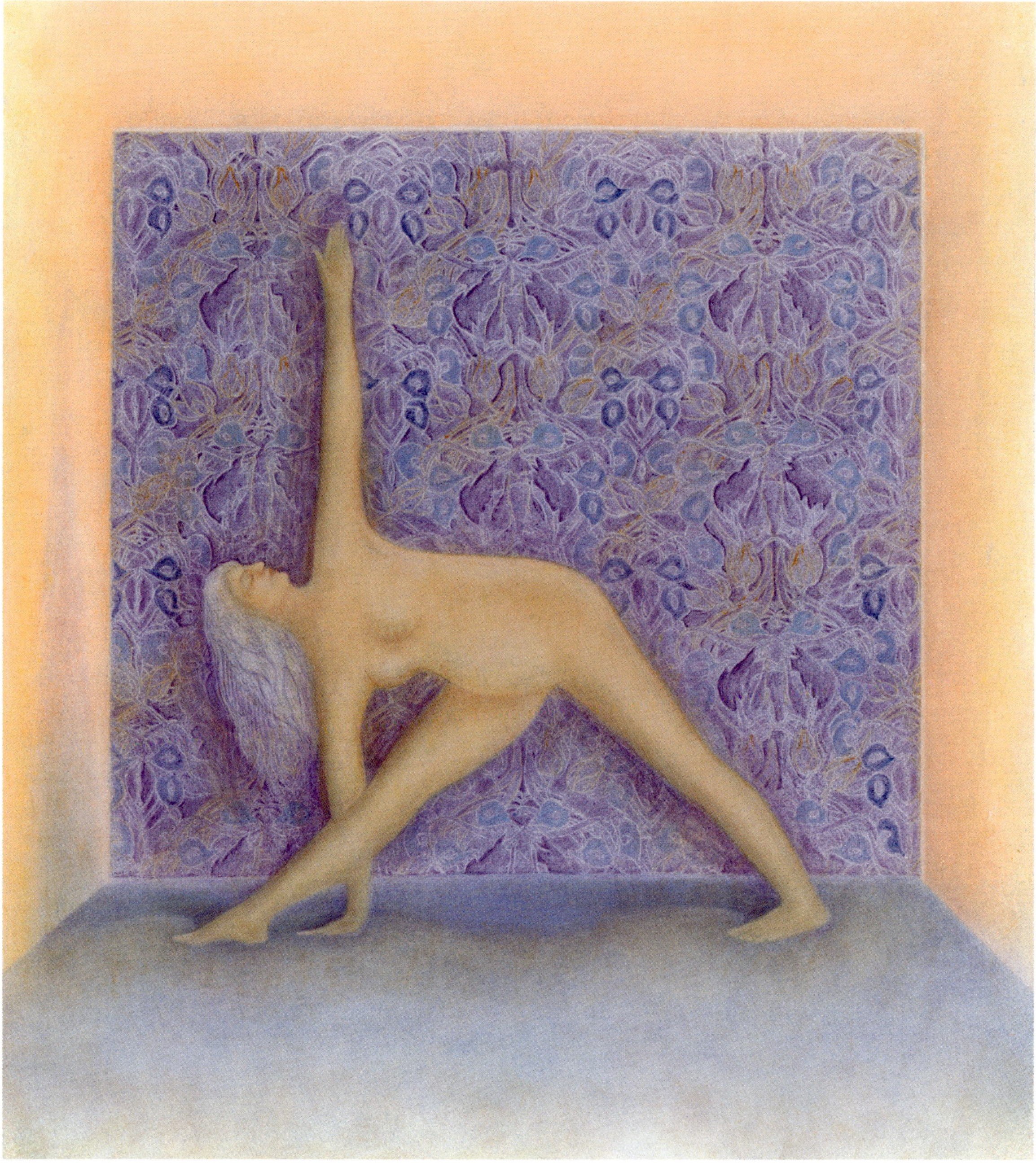

(ABOVE) *Triangle Pose (Trikonasana)*, c. 2006. Egg tempera on gesso panel, 16 × 12 in. (40.6 × 30.4 cm)
(OPPOSITE) *Eagle Pose (Garudasana)*, c. 2008. Egg tempera on gesso panel, 9½ × 6½ in. (24.1 × 16.5 cm)

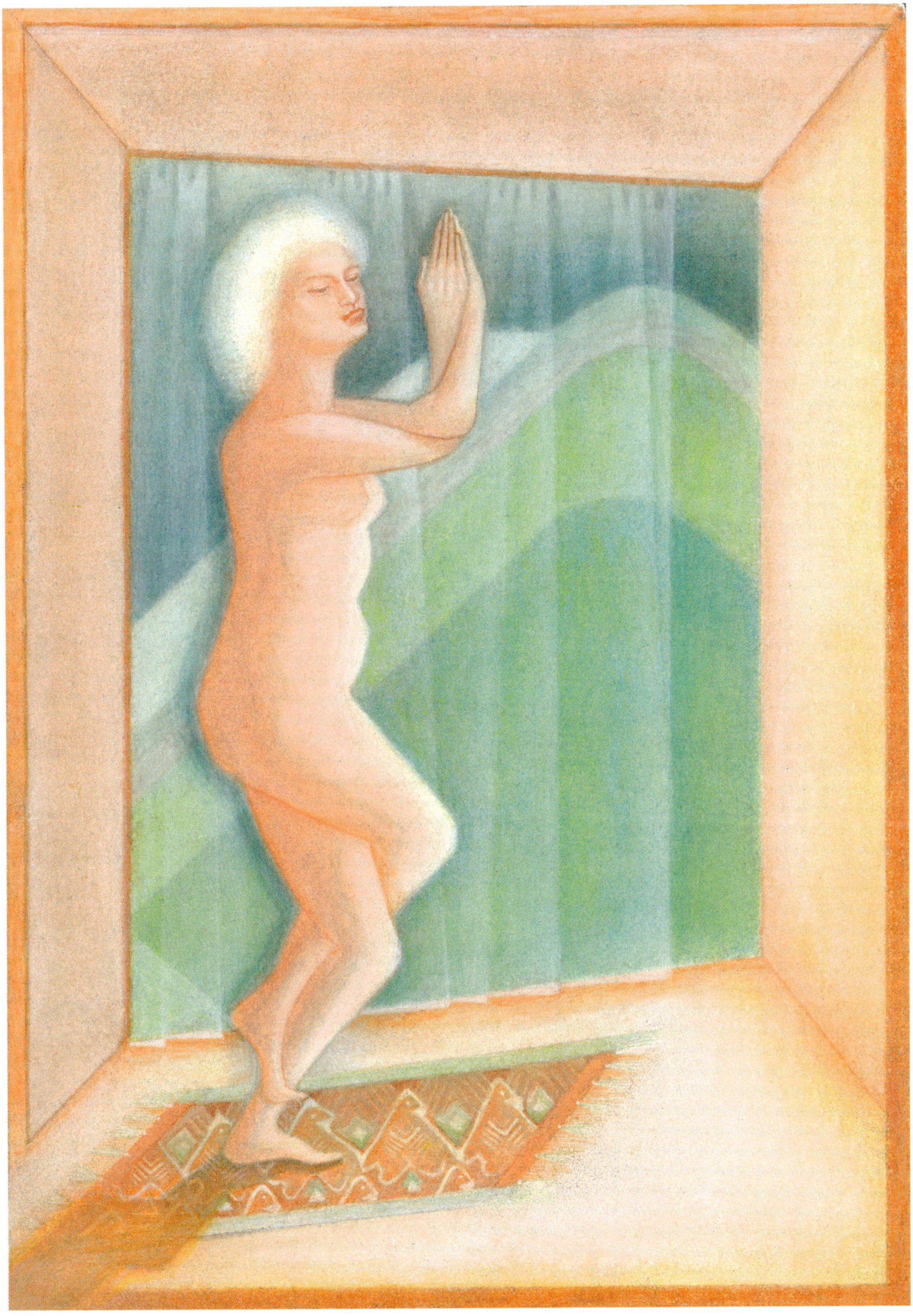

Tree Pose (Vrksasana)

In *Tree Pose*, the woman's belly can be viewed as either a little pregnant or a little fat. I like to challenge the viewer to see how their judgments surface when confronted with this image. The background pattern was adapted from an advertisement promoting a Persian carpet.

I started this painting in Koo's class, and as Dianne had instructed in *Hand to Foot Pose*, Koo advised underpainting in a complementary color—I think it was blue. In addition to cosmetic sponging, she shared a wonderful technique of transferring complex patterns with pigmented transfer paper called Saral. I often dip into her book to deepen my understanding of the medium and find solutions to technical and aesthetic challenges..

Making Money From Art?

Starting in the early 2000s, yoga was becoming extremely popular, so I decided to create a line of greeting cards that might generate some income, allowing me to cut back on my nursing job to provide more time for painting.

I reproduced my yoga paintings as greeting cards and shopped them around to yoga studios. I was surprised when they were criticized for their nudity. One owner suggested I paint gym shorts on them! My objective was to reveal the forms of the body uninterrupted by cloth—not to promote "naked yoga," although I am not opposed to that!

Making money from my art continued to be an exercise in frustration and disappointment. I saw how much time many artists spend in marketing and made peace with my dual identity of artist/nurse. As I write in 2025, I still work part-time as a nurse.

In spite of the prudish reaction of the yoga studios, I felt my yoga paintings were more conventional than my usual subject matter. But I came to view them as devotional art, in keeping with the spiritual underpinnings of egg tempera, the medium of Orthodox Christian icons. I would soon be returning to more daring themes.

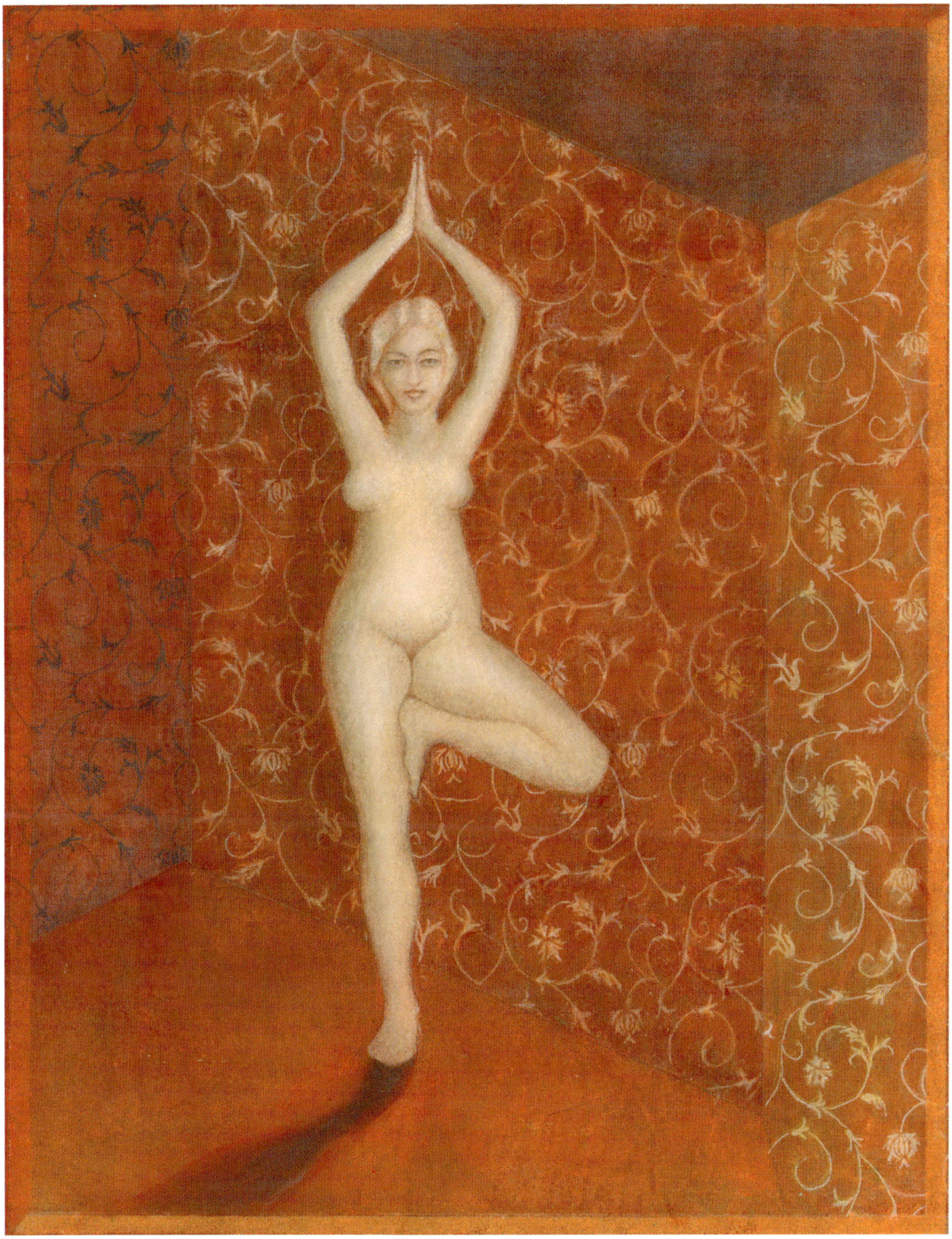

(ABOVE) *Tree Pose (Vrksasana)*, c. 2004. Egg tempera on gesso panel, 16 × 12 in. (40.6 × 30.4 cm)

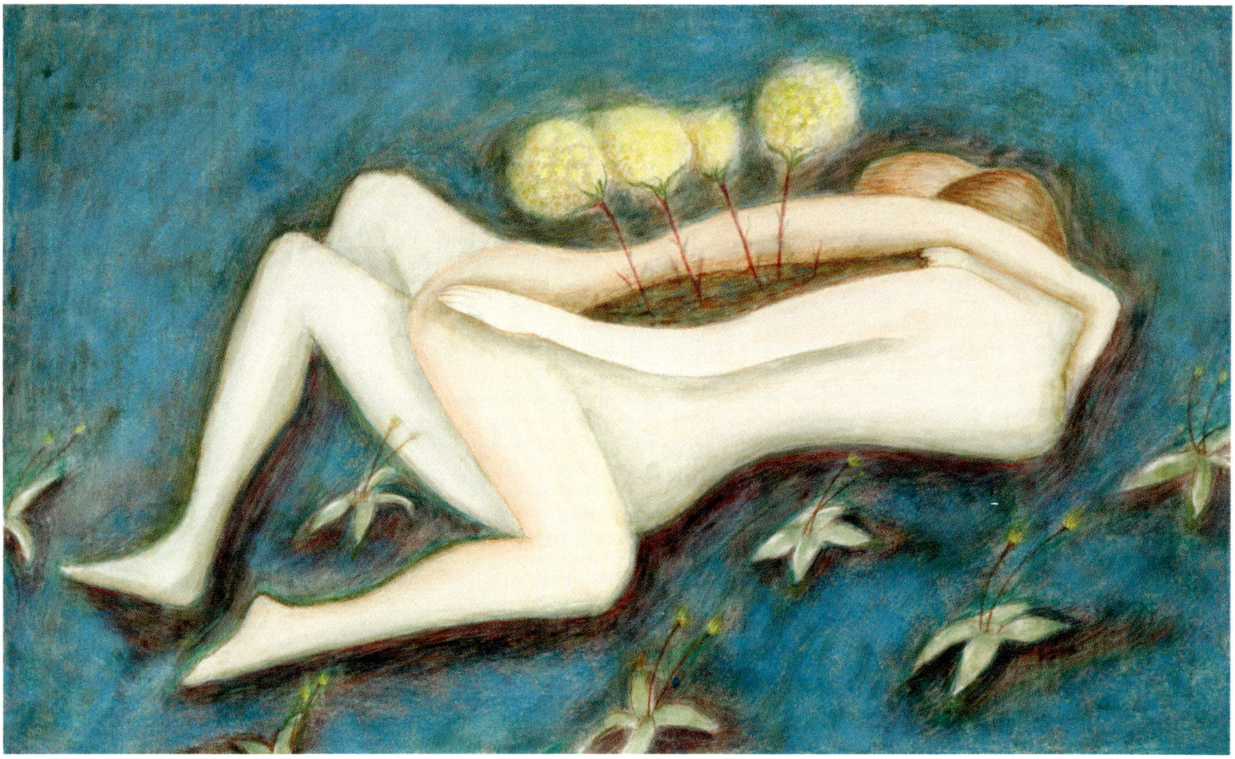

(ABOVE) *The Blossoming of Love,* c. 1995. Egg tempera on gesso panel, 12 × 19 in. (30.4 × 48.2 cm)

CHAPTER EIGHTEEN

ON THE EDGE: FINDING MY SENSUAL SELF

"I like your pornography," my mother once said. However, an erotic art dealer deemed my art non-pornographic on the grounds that it is "non-titillating."

The erotic art dealer had it right. I'm not after "titillation" or sexual arousal; rather, my artistic mission is to reveal the aesthetic and emotional beauty of our intimate relating.[77] Of all my paintings, perhaps *The Blossoming of Love* best embodies this elusive aesthetic. The painting expresses the delight and fertile creativity that a synergistic love relationship can bring.

When women were portrayed at their baths by Degas, Courbet, and other artists, it was at first considered scandalous, but now it is commonplace—even boring. I choose to see my portrayals of sex as neither pornography nor erotica but as genre painting—scenes from everyday life, like gardening or reading a book. But even this gentle painting has shocked some viewers. Perhaps naively, I like to think that egg tempera, the sacred medium of the Byzantine icon, has the power to sanctify seemingly profane imagery.

Finding My Sexual Self

Although somewhat liberated in the sixties atmosphere of "free love," I felt that a limited understanding of my sexuality may have contributed to my failure to form a stable romantic partnership.

There may also have been a biological explanation. Years before, due to a hair loss condition, my doctor measured my testosterone. My levels were so low that she inquired, "Do you even have a sex drive?" I replied, "Enough to get into a little trouble!" It's occurred to me that my quest for erotic intensity may have been an instinct to bolster this flagging hormone. Testosterone is a major contributor to sex drive in women as well as men—although, in general, men have fifteen times more![78]

My family was somewhat open about sexuality. Once, as an adult, I asked my dad what my grandmother Reizel thought about sex. I imagined it might be negative, since I knew her to be in a loveless arranged marriage with my grandfather Wolf.[79] He translated from her Yiddish, "If it wasn't healthy, the doctors wouldn't do it, and if it wasn't holy, the rabbis wouldn't do it."

LOVE ON A BLACK SHEEP FARM

clasping flesh
a light breeze
smell sound taste
who is the billy goat?

—ILSE LEHNERT

This traditional maxim portrays the perhaps less repressive culture of Judaism; still, I absorbed the repressive message from the dominant culture.

The *Pastoral Romantic* series is a celebration of sensuality, born of a hard-fought struggle to understand my erotic nature. I don't think people talk enough about sex and what it means to have a fulfilling sensual relationship. This may result in sex becoming something dirty and furtive, a source of unhappiness or even relationship breakdown. This chapter reveals (maybe too much!) the bumpy path I followed and how it surfaced in my art.

Explicit Paintings

The idea for *Love on a Black Sheep Farm* came to me while visiting an actual black sheep farm with a couple who were newly in love. I did not witness their lovemaking—that came from my imagination, along with the sheep that looks like a goat! Like *The Blossoming of Love*, the setting is pastoral, but this image crosses the line from the sensual into the explicitly sexual.

Even though *Afterglow* and *Sweet Feeling* are explicitly sexual, I painted them with no intention of arousing the viewer. I've observed that most erotica and pornography depict "action" scenes, but in *Afterglow* I tried to capture the moments of bliss or rest a couple may experience after making love (specifically oral sex).

Paradoxically, in *Sweet Feeling*, I sense that the focus on emotion may have inadvertently triggered arousal (in myself and the viewer). And that is fine—authentic emotion may be the aphrodisiac missing in much of pornography. I'm not into pigeonholing my art into artificial categories but rather wish to remain open to wherever creativity wanders. And I enjoy hearing the experience of the viewer—you![80]

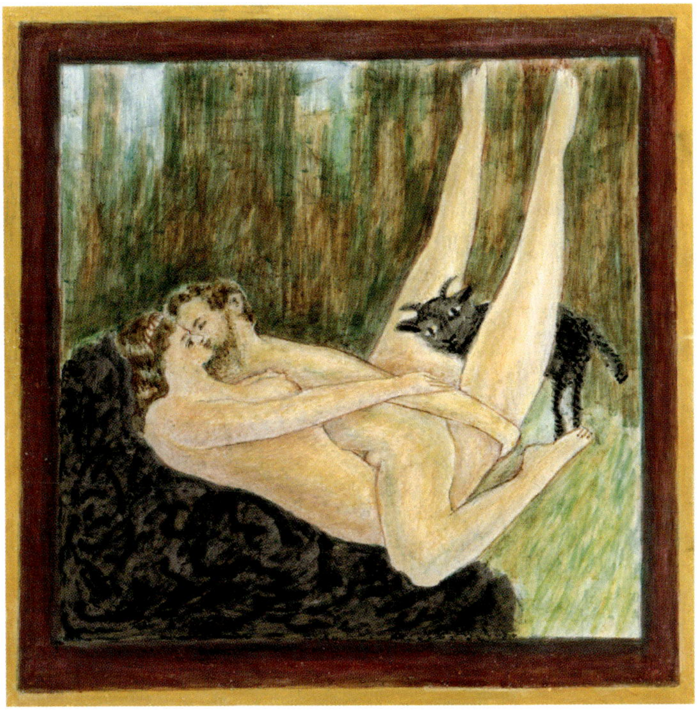

(ABOVE) *Love on a Black Sheep Farm*, c. 1989. Egg tempera on gesso panel, 6 × 6 in. (15.2 × 15.2 cm)

(BELOW) *Sweet Feeling*, c. 1992. Pencil on paper, 11 × 8½ in. (27.9 × 21.5 cm)

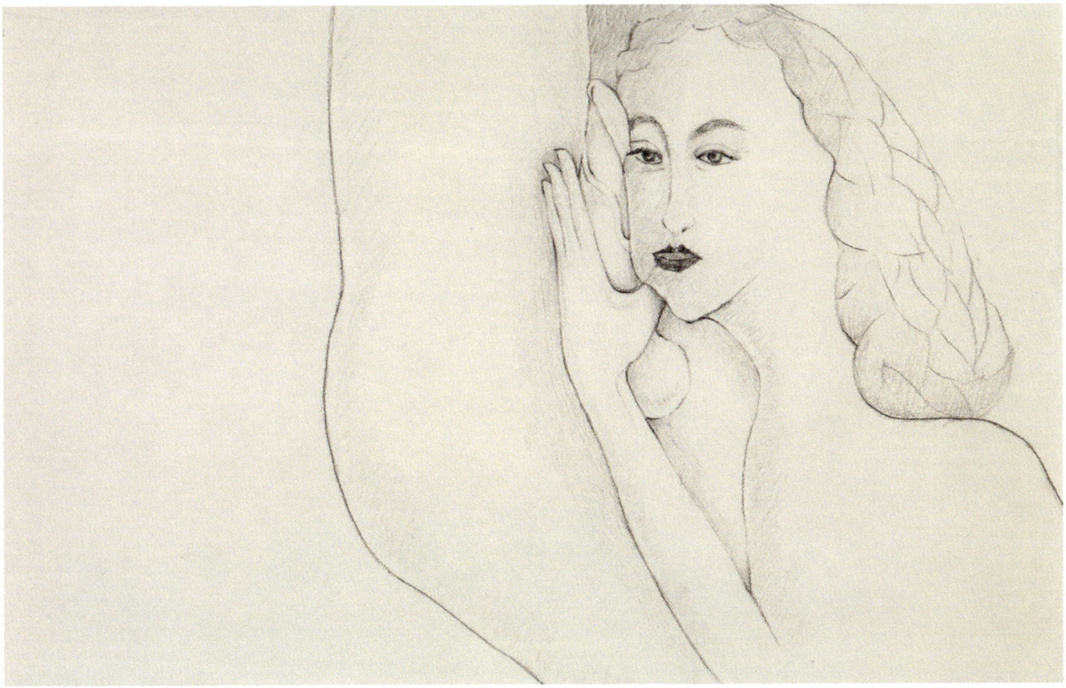

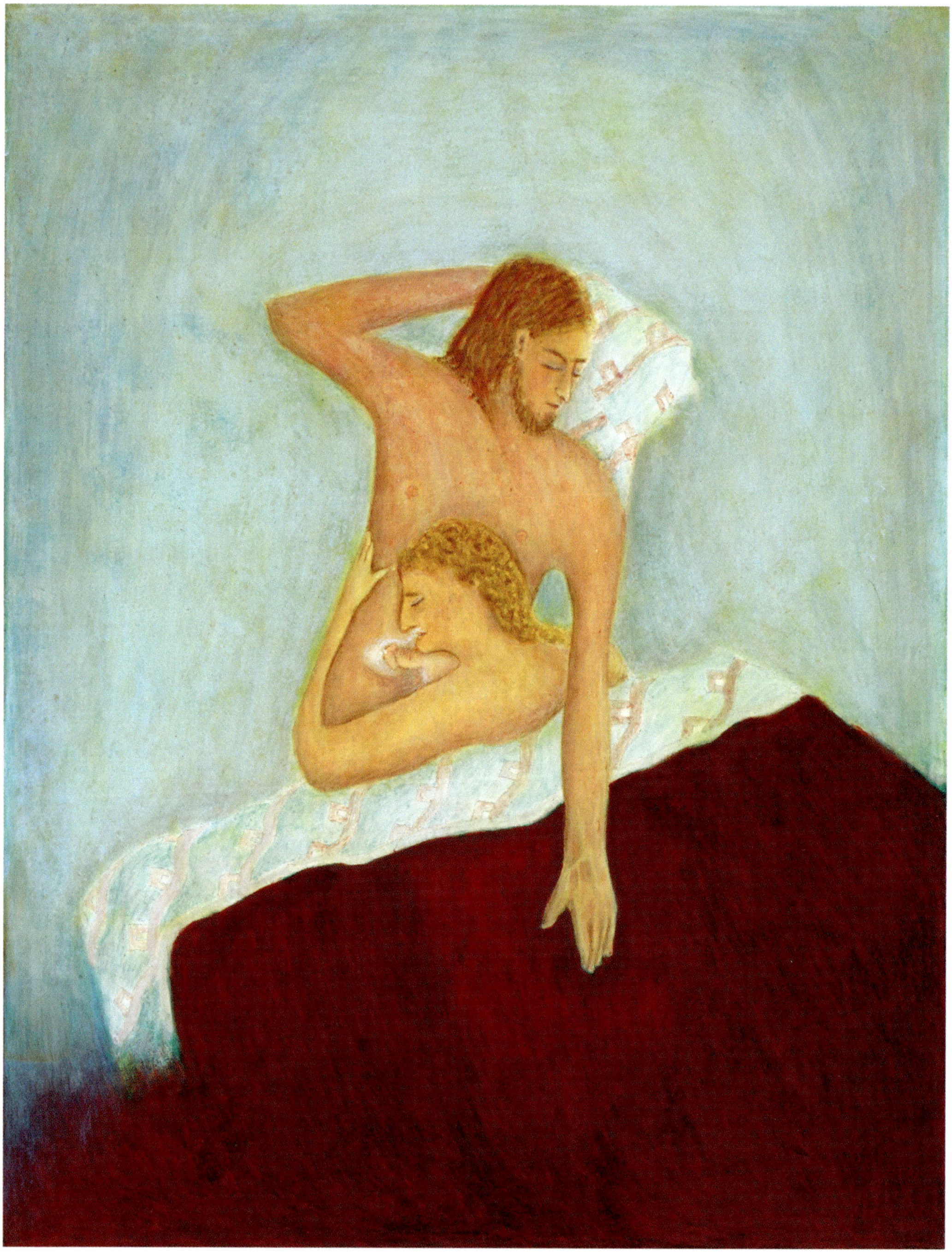

(ABOVE) *Afterglow,* c. 1990. Egg tempera on gesso panel, 15 × 12 in. (38.1 × 30.4 cm)

Magic and Ceremony

Back in 1968, I participated in a summer program where students lived together in a dorm and chose one intensive course. I selected Magic & Ceremony.

At that time, I had sworn off intimate relationships because they had become too frustrating. However, a handsome man in the class, Harry, took an interest in me. I told him outright that I did not want to have sex, and he accepted that limitation and may have even been intrigued by it.

The course project was to form a partnership and create a ritual and costume for each person. Harry and I became partners. The rituals would be presented on the last day of a camping trip at the Navarro River.

We were naked in a circle on the sandy bank of the river in the hot sun. Each duo, in turn, entered the circle to present their rituals to their partners. As I stepped into the circle, Harry released a live snake at my feet! It was about a foot and a half long, and an inch thick, with brown, black, and green scales. It was obvious that his intention was to help me overcome my fear of the male organ. I danced around the snake—it did not bite me. After a minute or two, it slithered away.

That evening, at dusk, when Harry and I were camped in our tent, he said to me, "Let's play a game—I'm a bear and I'm going to chase you through the woods." I said okay and playfully ran off into the woods. He quickly caught up with me and said, "No, I want you to pretend that it's real. Run away as if your life depended on it." So, I ran as fast as I could, and he soon overtook me. That's how I had my first orgasm with a partner. After that, I became very responsive with him, and it no longer involved playing chase. I remained in love with him for many years, even after he had moved on to other women.

San Francisco Sex Underground

Although the bear chase scenario could be seen as a classic dominant/submissive roleplay, at the time I did not apply the label "kinky" to my responsiveness with Harry. But in the years that followed, I noticed I was more orgasmic under intense situations, such as being rejected by a lover. I also had a pattern of being interested in sex for the first few weeks of a relationship, then totally losing interest for months and even years while still in the relationship—not great for building trust and intimacy.

Years later, in my early forties and still stymied by relationship failures, the opportunity arose to explore the San Francisco sex underground of the 1980s. A friend confided that a man she had a crush on, Dan, had offered to tie her up and cook waffles for her. This intrigued me—I do love waffles!—but it was of no interest to her, so, with her consent, I telephoned Dan. He never did cook waffles for me, but at our first meeting, he tied my hands behind my back, threw a coat over my shoulders, and walked me around Lake Merritt. It did not turn me on, but it was exciting and interesting to experience this taste of kinky culture.

Another time, I told him that due to membership in Overeaters Anonymous, I had been successful in not eating sugar for six years, but I was ready to break my abstinence. He tied my hands with rope, blindfolded me, and "forced" me to eat chocolate. I remember being disappointed because it tasted like low-quality chocolate![81]

Next, he invited me to a "safer sex" event called a Jack-and-Jill-Off Party. Genital penetration was prohibited, and there was a table of safe sex supplies. Still, it was not a safe thing to be doing during the AIDS epidemic. Dan advised that many people would be wearing creative costumes. I was frightened to go, but decided I would go if I could dress in disguise. Today I find it culturally offensive, but I fashioned a white veil out of an old curtain and strung it under my eyes covering my face like a niqab. But from the neck down, I was naked! I find it interesting that being naked did not feel revealing as long as my face was covered! I clung to Dan, but at one point he and another man manually stimulated me to orgasm. I was pretty amazed that I could let myself go in that environment, but perhaps it was the environment that was stimulating. Also, I had developed trust in Dan and felt safe.

I went to a few more Jack-and-Jill-Off parties by myself, mostly just observing, but on one occasion, I accepted several men pleasuring me all at once. They seemed like kind, sweet people—not at all creepy—and highly skilled. Definitely a peak experience!

Although the Jack-and-Jill-Off parties were not the stereotypical orgy with naked bodies writhing around, my experience may have indirectly inspired my painting *How Many?*

AFTER THAT, DAN suggested I explore the world of BDSM: bondage, discipline (or domination), sadism (or submission), masochism. Statistics vary but show that at least 10 percent of the population has experienced "kinky" activities, and as many as 50 percent have had BDSM fantasies. Mainstream mental health professionals currently state that BDSM practices are only pathological if the person "feels personal distress about their interest."[82]

Before setting out on this path, I made an agreement with myself that I would cease participation if I felt abused or degraded in any way. I was in it solely for the fantasy and variety of sensations, in service of heightening my sexual response and ultimately fulfilling my dream of romantic stability.

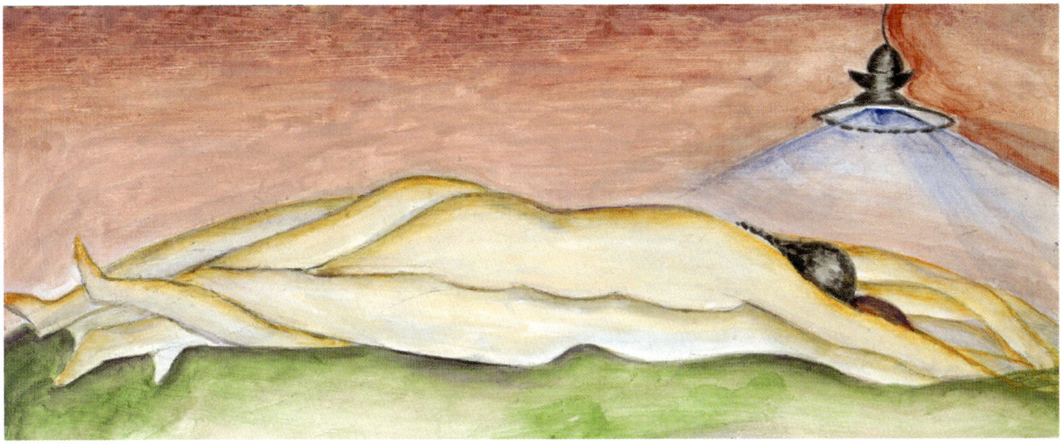

(ABOVE) Detail: *How Many?*, 2002. Acrylic on mat board, 9½ × 16 in. (24.13 × 40.64 cm)

I went to an orientation session of the Society of Janus, where I learned about the BDSM code of behavior, summed up in the phrase "safe, sane, and consensual." Of primary importance was to have a predetermined safe word which would be respected by all parties. Many people adopt the phrase "safe word" as their safe word so there is no confusion.

Soon after the orientation, I attended a Society of Janus "play party." My wardrobe did not include any leather—the classic uniform of the "power exchange" community—so I donned regular clothes and my yellow rain boots, which garnered a lot of attention. I walked around the "playroom" observing people being tied up and whipped with various implements—it did not turn me on. Then I saw a stout man, in his late forties, with nerdy glasses and a mediocre comb-over. He was tending to a woman tied to a wooden frame—not whipping her, but stroking her body in a most sensuous manner. I watched for a while and then asked if he would do the same with me. He obliged, and I found it quite a turn-on. He was amused by my yellow rubber boots and invited me to his house.

I arrived at Ernest's house, an unremarkable single-family dwelling in an outlying neighborhood of San Francisco. Having understood my proclivity, he stroked my arms, fully clothed, which was again such a turn-on. Then he led me downstairs to a full-service dungeon that took up the entire basement floor. He tried various equipment on me—a light whipping could feel good, like a massage. But as soon as he upped the ante, it was not pleasant, and I asked him to stop. I never needed to use my safe word.

In addition to his kinky candy store of whips, chains, handcuffs, and even electrical equipment (yikes!), Ernest was an aficionado of sexual technique. He easily located my

"G-spot," an area two to three inches up the front of the vaginal wall that triggers orgasm.[83] It was a revelation that I could have an orgasm that was not clitorally inspired, although I prefer a clitoral orgasm or a combination of both. I had previously tried to locate my G-spot without success. Perhaps the correct angle is not accessible with self-stimulation, or a skillful person or G-spot vibrator is needed to elicit the response.

Ernest was overweight, diabetic, and in terms of erections non-functioning. It did not matter, as what we were exploring was outside the realm of traditional sex. In spite of his sexually dominant and sadistic interests, he was a kind and considerate man. Many people in the power exchange community make a clear distinction: that this dynamic operates only on the sexual plane, not in their everyday life, although there are exceptions to this.

Perhaps the most useful thing I learned from my time in the "leather community" was to put aside what I considered attractive in a man and to appreciate other qualities, such as sensuality. This insight served me well, as seeing beyond looks opened up a larger pool of men to consider as potential lover or husband.

Similarly, in my art, I veer away from conventional standards of beauty, which can look trite, worn, or just boring. Rather, I try to capture a mood or expression based more on what the person is thinking or feeling. This is extremely challenging because, in addition to shunning typical beauty, I try to avoid caricature or the grotesque. At times, I default to pretty or classical features because, after all, I do want to create a beautiful painting, and an alluring figure or face can be a shortcut to that.

My time with Ernest did not turn into a relationship but was seminal (excuse the pun) in understanding my sexuality. Sensuality became the key to my erotic responsiveness.

The Final Straw

Although I had learned much, I felt the pieces had not all come together. A friend suggested I connect with a man named Werner. I happened to run into him at a party and we "made love"—if you can call it that. He wanted to see me again, and when I went to his house, he had bought flowers, saying he wanted me to be his girlfriend. It seemed odd to be offered girlfriend status on just the second date, but I went along with it. It turned out we both loved art and enjoyed being together. It was a simple relationship—I called it my "pleasure bond." He called me "sweet stuff" and Amos "short stuff." Whenever my flowers wilted, he brought fresh ones.

He was a strange creature, tall with long hair (which he dyed), and he sometimes wore earrings made from the rattle of a genuine rattlesnake. Because I was open sexually, Werner felt free to tell me about his "kinks." He had drilled holes in a wall of his bathroom in

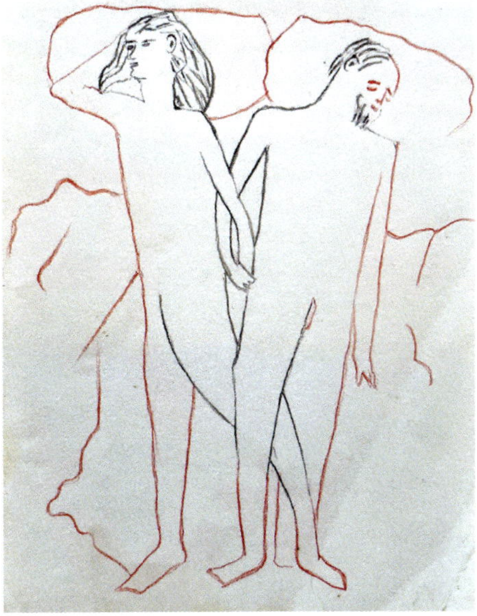

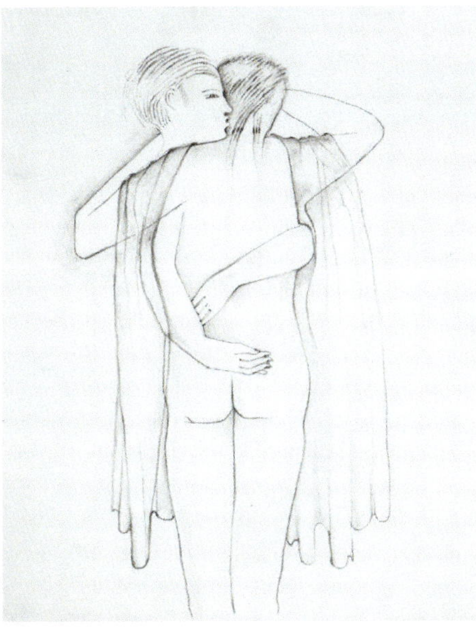

(ABOVE LEFT) *Lovers Entwined*, c. 2003. Ink on paper, 3 × 2 in. (7.6 × 5 cm)

(ABOVE RIGHT) *The Embrace*, c. 2003. Pencil on paper, 11 × 8½ in. (27.9 × 21.5 cm)

order to spy on his two unsuspecting female roommates. He also purposely had no locks on the door and would barge in while a woman was using the bathroom, feigning embarrassment and saying, "Oh, I'm so sorry!"

When I confronted him, he said it did no harm and that if the women knew he was observing them, they would like it. This creeped me out, but somehow I stayed with him. I now understand this is "unlawful surveillance," and I deeply regret that I did not break up with him and report it to the police. Another time, he told me that he exposed himself to women who walked down a path that went by his bedroom window. I told him this was horrible and illegal. He said he would never be arrested because he did it in his own home. Later, I found out that this behavior is criminal even in one's own bedroom.[84] Again, I'm ashamed that I did not report him to the police immediately.

Eventually, I did report all of his illegal activities, but the officer said there was nothing they could do at that point. But it is documented on his record, and since this is a psychological compulsion as well as criminal behavior, I'm certain it has recurred and will again.

Then came the final straw. He had a new roommate who had an exquisite vintage clothing collection, which he adored. While she was out of the house, he would go into her closet and masturbate. But the ultimate "bad little boy" fantasy would be getting caught in the act. One day, she came home and found him masturbating in her closet. She was beyond herself with rage. When I heard about it, I broke up with him immediately.

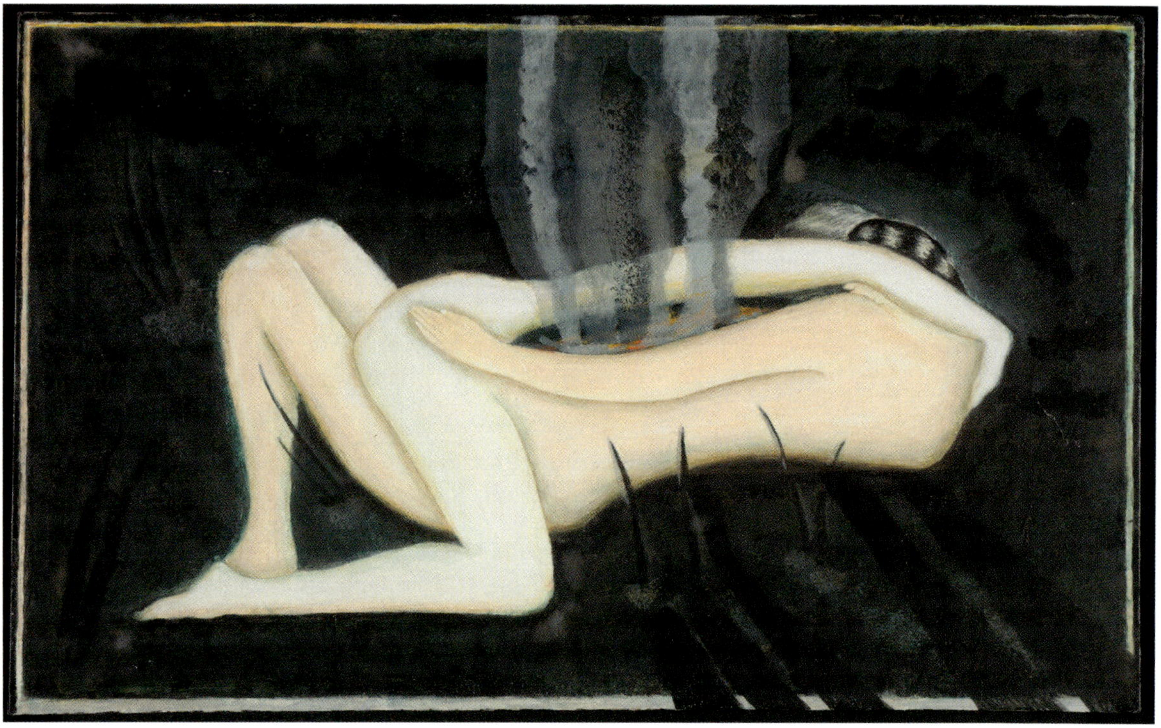

(ABOVE) *The Dying of Love: Smoke and Embers,* c. 1996. Egg tempera on gesso panel, 13 × 20 in. (33 × 50.8 cm)

(RIGHT) *Self-Portrait*, c. 2022. Pencil on paper, 7 × 5 in (17. 7 × 12.7 cm)

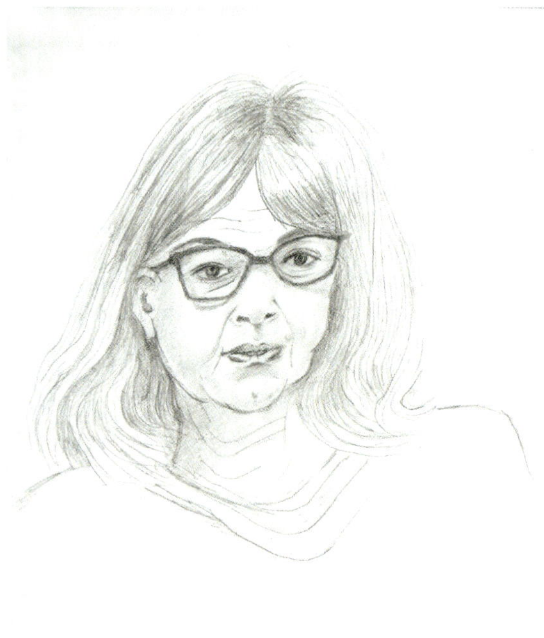

CHAPTER NINETEEN

RETREAT TO CELIBACY & MEETING MY MATE

After Werner, I knew I needed an extended period of abstinence from sex. Two ten-year periods of celibacy followed, as I purposely stopped exploration in order to find a man who would become my life partner.

I had experienced a wide variety of sexual practices, from the mild to the criminal. What started out seeming creative and fascinating had come to seem rote and boring—limiting as the only path to fulfilling sex. I made a conscious decision to turn away from it, for the most part, and I eventually learned to tune into a deep sense of intimacy that I found more satisfying and bonding.

The idea for *The Dying of Love* came to me while painting *The Blossoming of Love.* I certainly had experienced many more failed relationships than flourishing ones. In *The Dying of Love,* a few embers remain but not enough to revive the passion. This waning phase of a relationship is a universal experience but rarely portrayed in visual art. Interestingly, some viewers have interpreted the image as a smoldering passion.

While I was not successful in creating a nurturing relationship, I did find ways to care for myself during the long stretches of celibacy.

I don't recall indulging in many massages, but the concept for *Total Relaxation* must have been conceived in an experience of squashed body parts. A now-standard feature of massage tables is an opening for the face when the person is lying prone. With whimsical intent, I created additional

THE DYING OF LOVE

background black
smoke rising
nakedness
reminiscent
of a passion past
resignation
removed life
embraced
death of love

—ILSE LEHNERT

openings for the breasts and belly. Of course, in reality, massage therapists use pillows to cushion any body parts that need extra accommodation. *Total Relaxation* won first place in the Anatriptic Arts Expo in 1992.

THE TITLE OF the painting *Fish Without Bicycle* comes from the feminist saying "A woman needs a man like a fish needs a bicycle." The slogan was popularized by feminist Gloria Steinem but was actually coined by Irina Dunn, an Australian writer, social activist, and filmmaker.[85]

The concept that a woman does not need a man to experience pleasure was promoted by Betty Dodson, a sex educator who pioneered the sex-positive feminist movement. Dodson was still conducting workshops at the age of ninety-one, teaching women how to achieve orgasm. She passed away in 2020.

Traditionally, her workshops featured the Hitachi Magic Wand, the vibrator pictured in the painting. As a nod to Dodson, and for stylistic reasons, I painted the older model with

TOTAL RELAXATION

let go
of shaping
devices
restraints
fabrics
let go
of yourself
into
hands

—ILSE LEHNERT

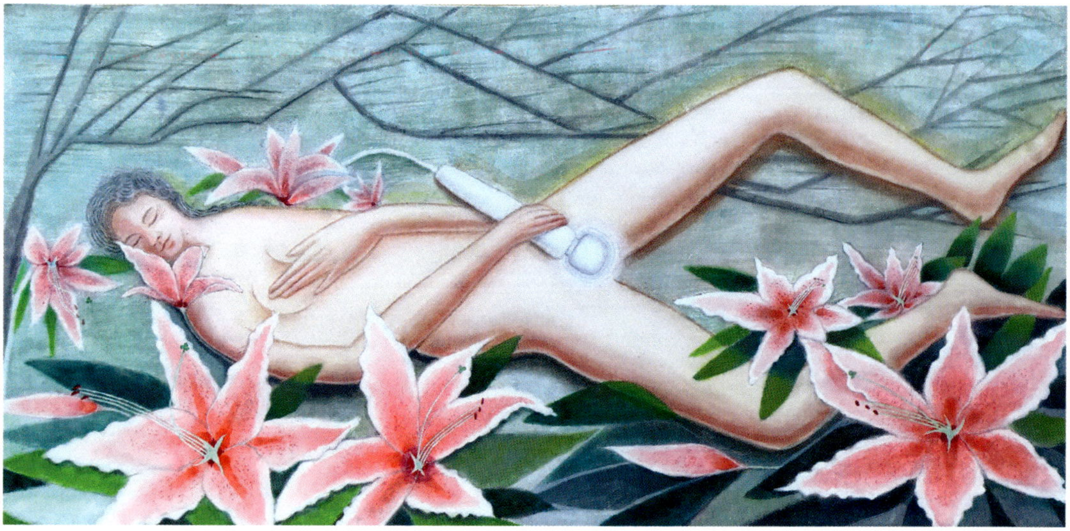

(ABOVE) Preparatory study for *Fish Without Bicycle*, c. 2022. Egg tempera on gesso panel, 12 × 24 in. (30.4 × 60.9 cm)

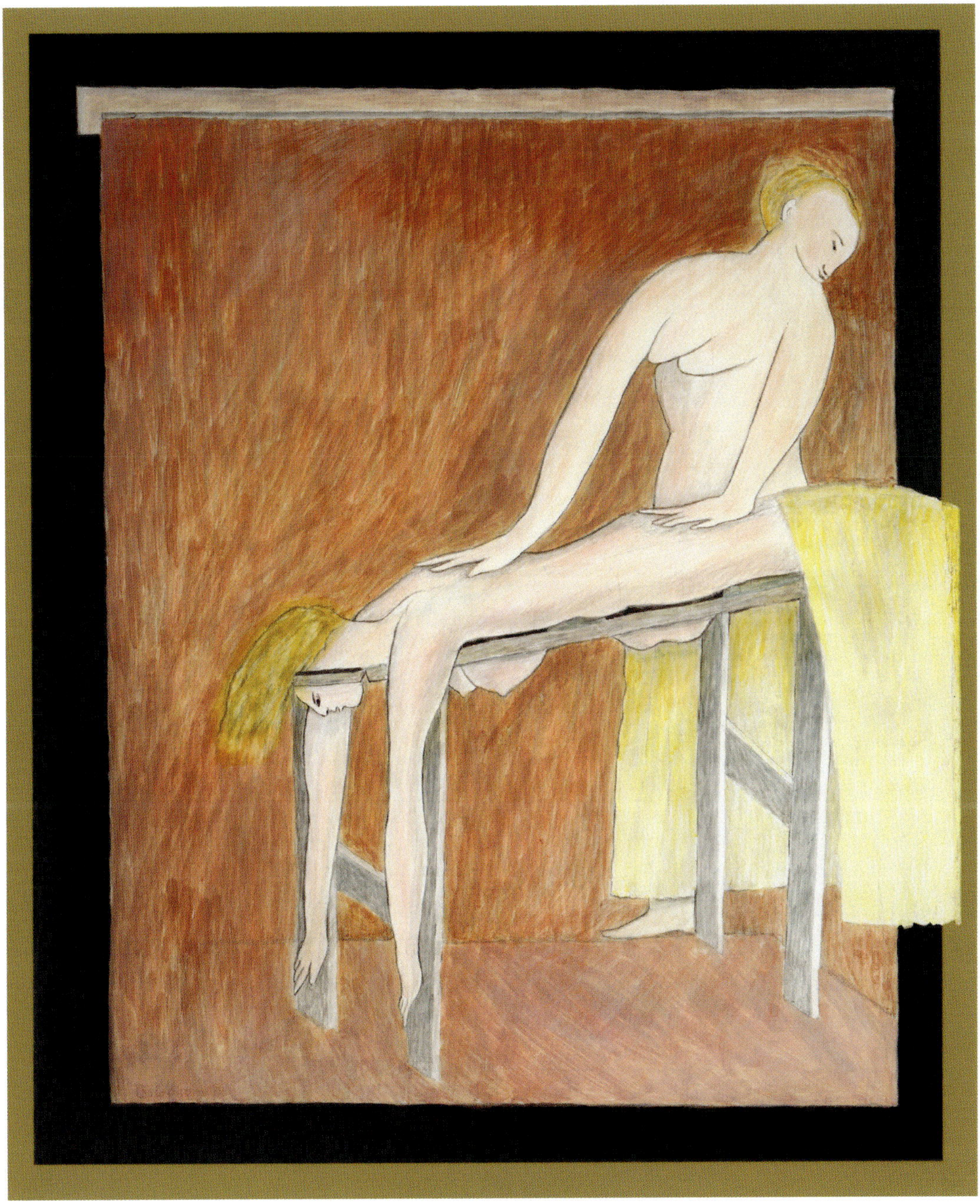

(ABOVE) ***Total Relaxation,*** c. 1990. Egg tempera on gesso panel, 15 × 12 in. (38.1 × 30.4 cm)

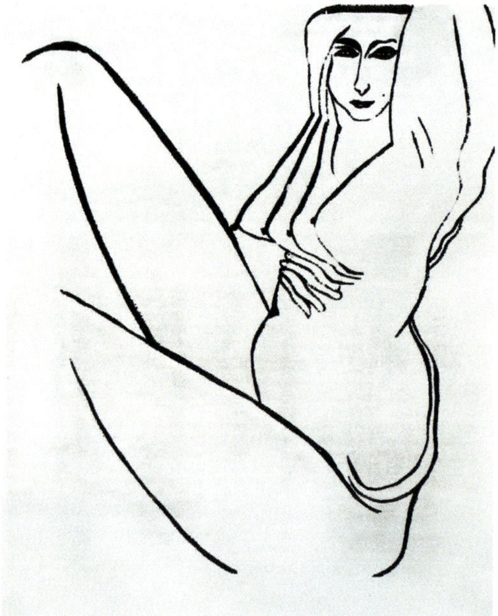

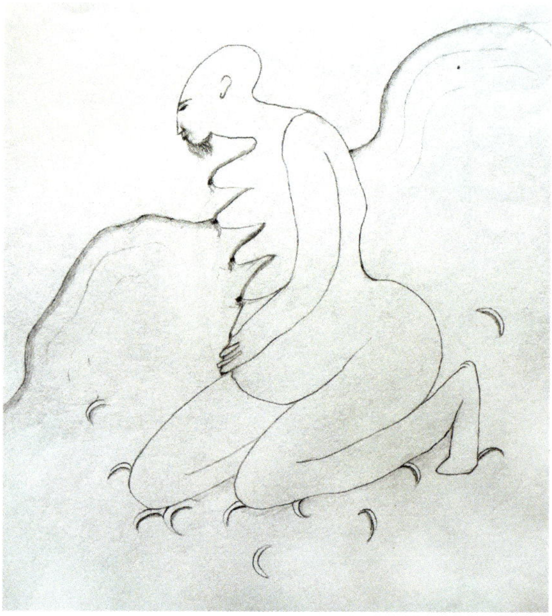

(ABOVE LEFT) *Four-Breasted Woman*, c. 2010. Pencil on paper, 11 × 8½ in. (27.9 × 21.5 cm)
(ABOVE RIGHT) *Four-Breasted Woman with Beard*, c. 2010. Pencil on paper, 11 × 8½ in. (27.9 × 21.5 cm)

electric cord. The composition is a celebration of sensuality, with fragrant lilies in a lush environment. The woman's gray hair and the leafless branches are references to sexuality in older women. This is a preparatory study for a four-by-eight-foot painting in which the figure will be larger than life-size. As I write in 2025, the painting is well underway.

This period in my life bred fanciful drawings that came from my subconscious, bypassing the censor. Four breasts? A woman with a tail, or is it a long strand of hair? Another four-breasted woman, this one with a hermaphroditic beard? Ambiguity serves as a hedge against cliché.

Love Addiction

The first ten years of celibacy ended when I connected with an honorable man, but the relationship collapsed. In hindsight, I had chosen a person who was not capable of loving me fully. It was disappointing because he was a kind person, but after six months, he never said

"I love you." After a year and a half, I gave him an ultimatum—either we go to therapy or we break up. He chose the latter, but instead of licking my wounds and moving on, I tried hard to get him back for the next five years. Finally, I admitted to myself that my behavior was dysfunctional and making me miserable.

I heard about Sex and Love Addicts Anonymous (SLAA) from my membership in other 12-step fellowships. Although I knew I wasn't a sex addict, the term "love addict" leaped out, supplying a name for a state of mind that had imprisoned me for years.

The SLAA meetings were held evenings in a church basement. I walked through a poorly lit college campus, down a flight of stairs to a dingy room with worn furniture. The sex addicts, mostly men, outnumbered the love addicts about 2:1. I did not see the wisdom of lumping sex addicts together with love addicts, except that we were both seeking healthy relationships. As people told their lurid stories, I was dubious that any of us could change. But as the months passed, I heard inspiring stories of recovery. I read Pia Mellody's *Facing Love Addiction* (2003) and found an SLAA sponsor.

In the 12-step world, a sponsor is a coach, an advocate, and a fellow sufferer. My homework assignment was to write an autobiography of my love life.

I had created paintings related to my love life and poured my suffering heart out in sporadic journal entries but never explored in detail the chronology of dysfunction and pain.

Next, I was directed to answer two questions. Number one: "Were you ever abused?" I was never verbally or physically abused, with one exception. I had a boyfriend who called me the B-word. I told him he had three chances before I would leave him. Then one day, he threw a cast iron frying pan next to my head. I don't believe he intended to target my head, but we broke up soon after.

The second question was: "Have you ever been neglected?" Bells went off, triggering a memory of my mother saying, "You were such a good baby, we could just leave you in your carriage." I was born a mere fourteen months after my sister—she was still a baby herself and needed attention. I connected the dots between my childhood and how I accepted less-than-adequate attention from the men in my life. When I did start a relationship in which I was showered with love, I would turn my back on it, chasing after somebody who was either rejecting, not emotionally generous, or inappropriate.

Although I continued to seek a romantic relationship, another ten-plus years of celibacy ensued until I found a man with whom I could share both a vibrant sensuality and a mutual expression of love.

Meeting Jake

I met Jake in 2016 on the dating app OkCupid. Both of us had been on dozens of dates before taking a chance on each other.

I believe he said "I love you" on our fifth date. I thought it was rather early; how can he love me when he doesn't even know me? But I found it endearing and healing.

I had done my homework and was now in a psychological place to accept love and attention. I am thankful I had the courage to plumb the depths of my sexuality and was ready to integrate this knowledge into the context of a long-term relationship. We've been together ever since, building a bond of affection, shared values, sensuality, and laughter.

But I'm learning that sharing one's life with another requires effort, and, like skill in egg tempera painting, relationship skills must be learned and practiced—with heavy doses of patience, acceptance, and forgiveness.

At times, the closeness triggers irritation—even hostility. Instead of reacting impulsively—or, equally damaging, repressing our emotions—we are learning to express feelings and needs with the help of techniques such as Nonviolent Communication (NVC).[86] NVC is not always effective but it has helped to prevent ugly conflicts and maintain an atmosphere of harmony.

We did not meet until we were in our late sixties, so I'm amazed that we've been able to maintain a sensual connection for many years. It's a lifelong process of learning and adjusting, especially as our bodies age.

Good communication has helped; we often debrief after lovemaking to better understand each other's responses and preferences. In my profession of nursing, I'm required to take thirty hours of continuing education every two years. I've become aware that in a relationship it's likewise a good idea to keep abreast of new developments in human sexuality.

These two books were eye-openers for me: *Becoming Cliterate* by Dr. Laurie Mintz (2017) and *She Comes First* by Ian Kerner (2004). In her 2004 book *Reclaiming Your Sexual Self*, Kathryn Hall puts into words what I've experienced and still need to practice: "Sexual desire is not a given, it needs to be elicited."

Hall makes the point that many women (including myself) are not necessarily horny but rather must have certain conditions met in order to be receptive or interested in sex. Some examples might be "I need verbal affection before any touch," "I need lots of sensual touch before you reach for my erogenous zones," and "I prefer sex in the morning when I'm not tired." I find this to be crucial, especially now that I am at an age when sexual drive may naturally decline. But, I retain a gentle interest because I have cultivated my "sexual self" and have chosen a partner who values sensual touch and emotional connection.

I don't mean to imply that a lifestyle that does not include sex, partner sex, or sensuality is in any way inferior. I believe it's about having choices and the ability to change course throughout our lives. After years of loneliness, I find solace and joy in having a mate. But art is my primary focus—the relationship only works when I honor painting as my first priority.

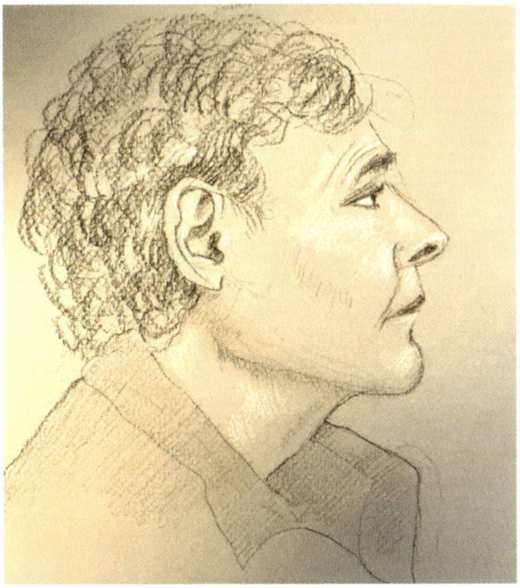

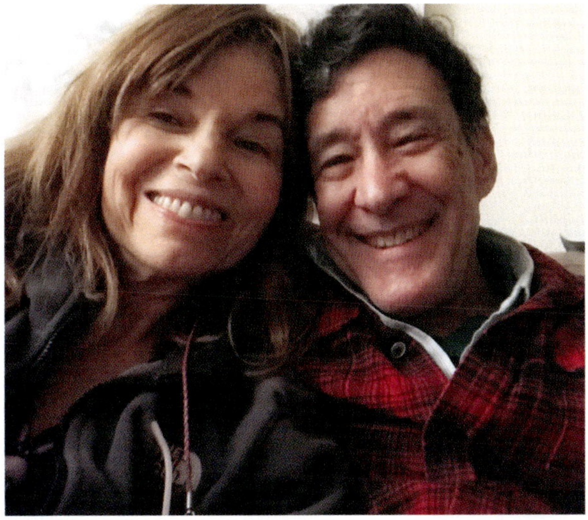

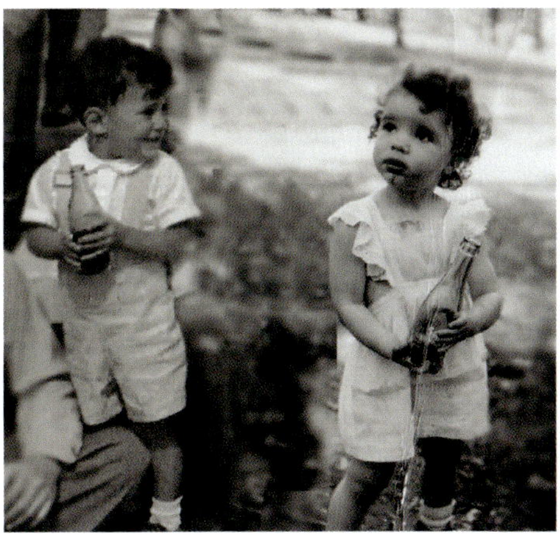

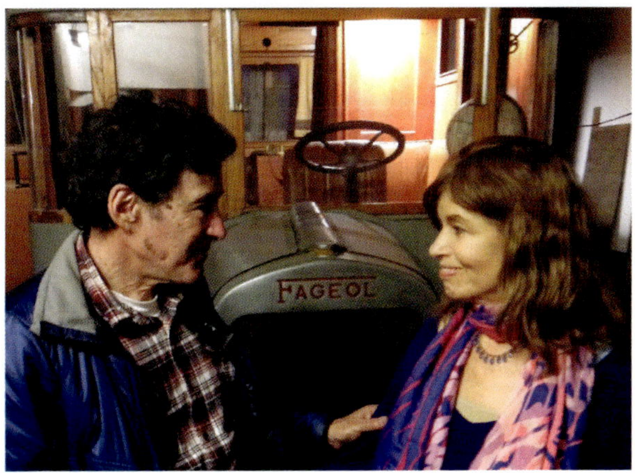

(ABOVE LEFT) *Portrait of Jake,* 2019. Charcoal pencil on colored paper, 14 × 12 in. (35.5 × 30.4 cm).

(ABOVE RIGHT) Me and Jake, c. 2018. Photo by E & E Andrade.

(BELOW LEFT) Jake combined two surprisingly similar photos of each of us as toddlers to make this composite, even though we met when we were both in our sixties.

(BELOW RIGHT) With Jake, c. 2019, vintage Fageol RV in background. Photo by E & E Andrade.

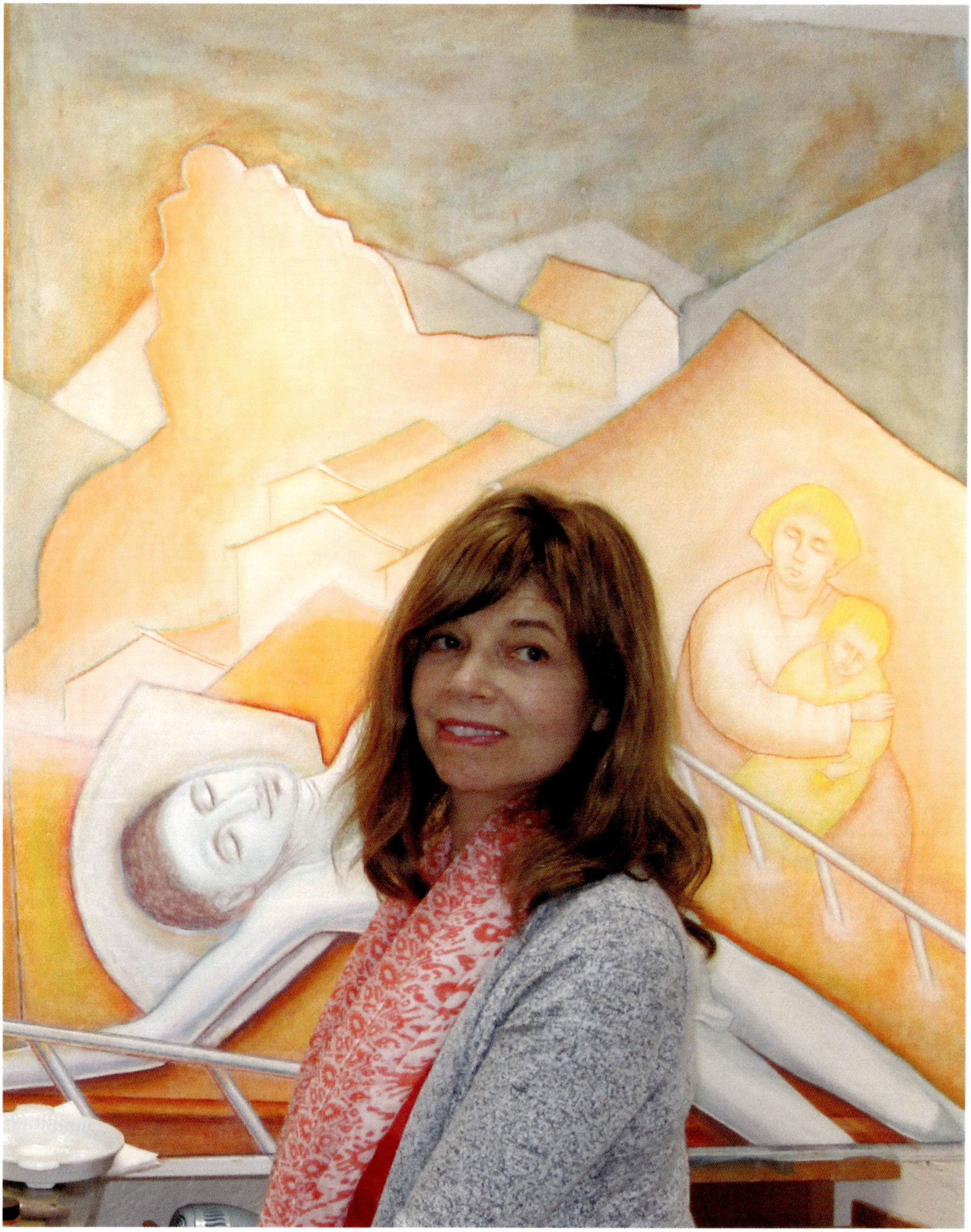

(ABOVE) With *No More Pollution; No More Somalia: The Death of Peter Ryan*, 2016. This painting took seven years to complete; I was not working on any other painting during that time.

CHAPTER TWENTY

SURRENDER TO SLOW

Having observed, with chagrin, that it took sixteen years to complete just the four paintings of the *Ways of Dying* series, I had to ask myself, "Why am I such a slow painter?" The first painting, *Don't Go My Friend*, only took one year to complete, but *Bon Voyage* took six years, *No More Pollution; No More Somalia* took seven years, and *Birds of Pray* 🙏 took two years.

True, while painting, I was also working as a nurse and during some of those years raising my son, but that did not fully account for my slow-as-molasses MO. So, I challenged myself to understand why it takes me so long to complete a painting.

The Slow Movements, starting with Slow Food, emanate a spiritual aroma, but I cannot use this to rationalize my lagging productivity. My slow art has more to do with the nature of the egg tempera medium, my painting process, and especially my own mindset, which has at times bordered on pathological.

The Slow Movement

The Slow Movement began with Carlo Petrini's protest against the opening of a McDonald's restaurant in Piazza di Spagna, Rome, in 1986. This triggered the first of the Slows, the Slow Food Movement.

Other slow movements emerged, including Slow Medicine, Slow Fashion, and Slow Cities, to name a few. The idea was to slow down life's pace, with implications for mental health, environmental preservation, beauty, and many other tentacles.

And then there is Slow Art. Slow Art Day (slowartday.com) is a global movement that was launched by Phyl Terry in 2009. Researchers found that the average time that adults spend looking at one work of art in a museum is 27.2 seconds.[87] On Slow Art Day, people are encouraged to spend at least ten minutes savoring each of five works of art in a museum, after which the participants gather to discuss their experience.

The Nature of Egg Tempera

Egg tempera technique tends to be slow by its very nature.

Building Up Layers

Although egg tempera paint dries in seconds, it still takes time to build up the many layers needed to achieve the jewel-like effect that tempera is known for. There are shortcuts, such as starting with a thicker base coat and applying glazes and veils over that, but it is still slow. The best one can do is "make haste slowly."[88]

Making Corrections in Tempera

When I'm writing on a computer, I can easily return to an earlier draft or rearrange text. However, making corrections in tempera can be daunting. If I want to change something or make a correction, first I need to remove the layers of paint I had carefully built up. This is easy to do with a razor blade, damp cloth, or brush. But it can be a major undertaking to build the layers back up again to match and harmonize with the surrounding areas.

Panel Preparation

Even before the application of paint, the preparation of a panel is a time-consuming process, involving carpentry, gesso-making, and sanding. This is especially true when working in a large format.

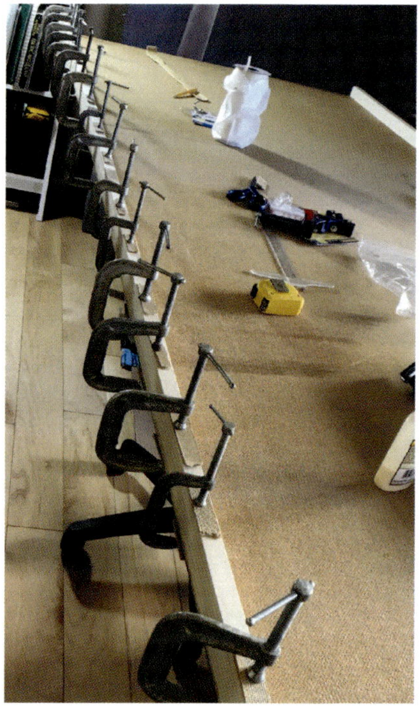

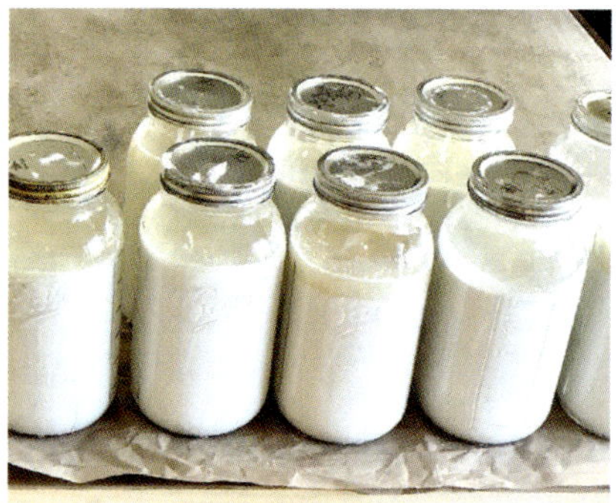

(ABOVE) My extensive collection of C-clamps, used to glue oak bracing strips to the back of the panel

(BELOW) Jars of gesso

Large Format

Most egg tempera artists work very small—sometimes their paintings are just a few inches. There's a good reason for this: countless hours are spent using tiny brushstrokes and/or sponges to build the layers of paint. Prior to starting the *Ways of Dying* series, most of my paintings were relatively small, most measuring 20 × 16 inches.

In the *Ways of Dying* paintings, I started using a larger format. Each successive painting grew larger, with the final painting, *Birds of Pray* 🙏, measuring eight feet by four feet, a full sheet of hardboard. This painting took up a good part of my living/dining room space as it lay flat on a large table during the two years that I worked on it.

Choosing the size of a painting is mysterious; a directive seems to come from the unborn artwork telling me the size it wants to be. Although creating a large painting takes more time, I came to appreciate a sense of power and grandeur due to sheer scale. And because of the complexity, each painting took many months … even years … to complete. But the adage "small painting: small brushes, large painting: large brushes" is applicable, and I was able to adapt the egg tempera technique to a large format.

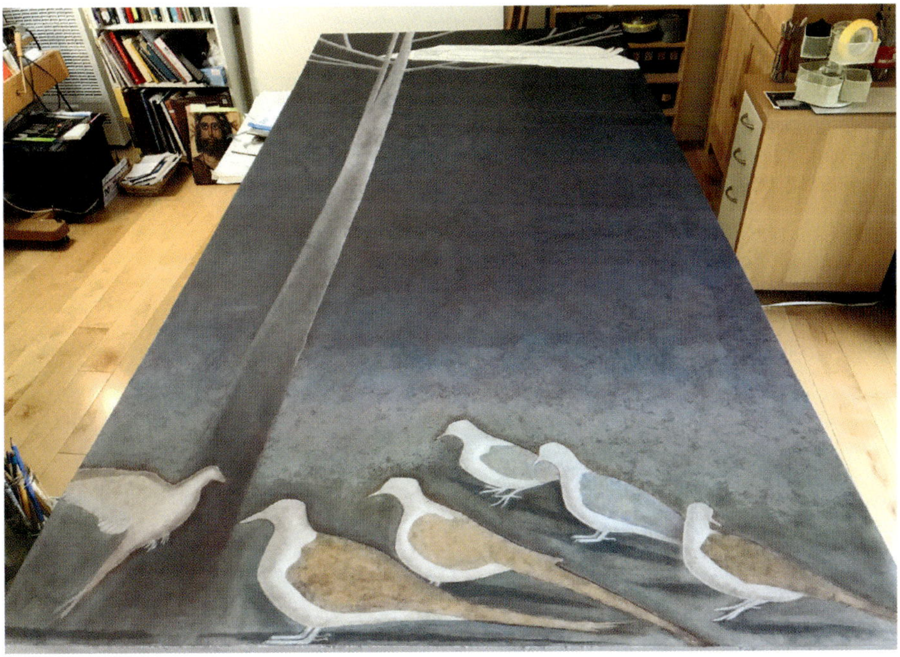

(BELOW) ***Birds of Pray*** 🙏, in progress, lying flat on a table

My Egg Tempera Process

In addition to the innate slowness of the medium and the large format I currently favor, I have adopted other practices that further slow my painting process.

"Dress Rehearsals"

I struggle with the design of every figure and object in a painting, so I try out my ideas by making preparatory studies. I call these "dress rehearsals." I used to practice using watercolor on paper but found it did not translate well to the final egg tempera painting. So, with the exception of initial sketches, I do my prep work in egg tempera on a traditional gesso ground.[89] Working in tempera takes more time, but it gives me a better idea of how it will look in the final painting.

Work from Imagination

For the most part, I choose not to make a literal rendering of my ideas. I prefer to work from my imagination in order to produce an image that has an otherworldly feeling to it.

To accomplish this, I page through my art books to adapt a figure, face, or hand from the work of a sublime artist of the Proto-Renaissance, such as Giotto or Piero della Francesca.[90]

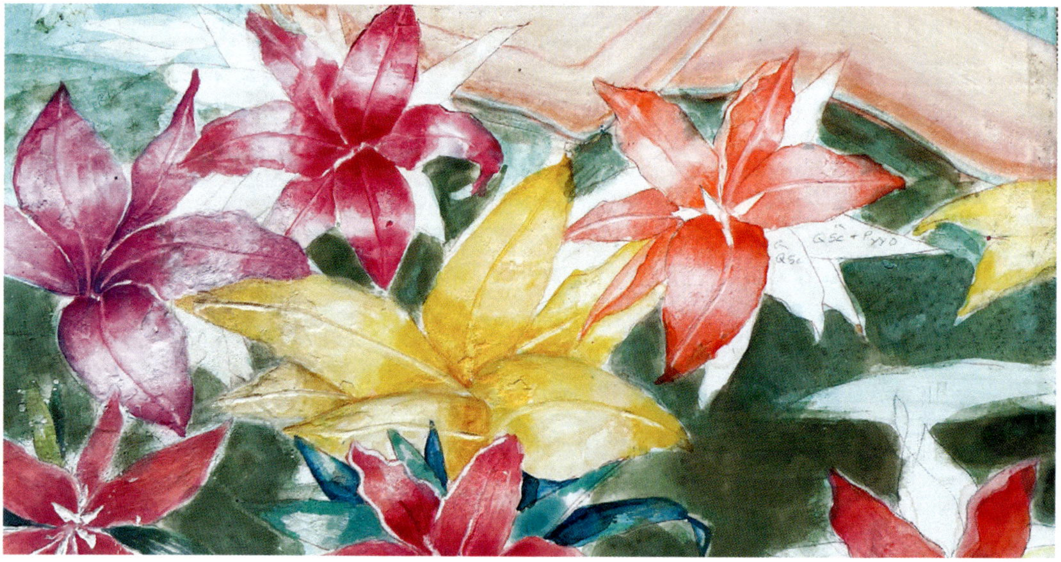

(ABOVE) **Detail: Preparatory study for *Fish Without Bicycle*, c. 2023**

Because this art features a more simplified, flat, and static style, my paintings have been labeled "primitive," which has the connotation "amateur." This hurts, but I prefer to speak a consistent visual language that is recognizable but not realistic. And besides, I love primitive art!

Polishing the Painting

Once the painting is finished, it is best to wait three to six months for polymerization or curing to complete; otherwise, the paint surface can be easily scratched. After curing, the painting can be polished or varnished. Polishing an egg tempera painting is a magical process, but this also takes time, depending upon the size of the painting and whether a matte or semigloss finish is desired.[91]

The Psychology of Slow

Although the above reasons are legitimate explanations of why I paint slowly, to be honest, half or more of the reason is simply garden-variety procrastination.[92]

Art Avoidance

The spirit-killing effect of procrastination has prodded me to delve into its causes and remedies.

At one point, I attended meetings of Arts Anonymous, a 12-step program in which "avoidance" is considered the drug of choice, as opposed to alcohol or other substances. Avoidance provides a short-term respite from the angst of making art. We indulge in avoiding what we most love, because it is an "easier, softer way."[93] I've also learned that our brains favor easier tasks and that is why so many of us succumb to distraction.

I've applied several strategies to combat the scourge of procrastination. Getting started is an antidote to avoidance. The key is to break the task down into tiny pieces, taking it *Bird by Bird*, as the title of Anne Lamott's book advises. If I don't know what my next step is, I either write in my journal or meditate in order to access guidance from my intuition. Resistance often comes if the next step is not broken down sufficiently.

An example of a next step might be as simple and easy as getting up from my chair. Getting up also provides another advantage: as we know from Newton's first law, often paraphrased as "a body in motion stays in motion," physical movement can break through a bout of stuckness.

Once in motion, the injunction to create what Anne Lamott calls a "a shitty first draft" is crucial to avoid succumbing to perfectionism.[94] If I reach resistance, I ask myself, "Is this laziness or fear?" It's usually one or both. "Laziness" is a loaded word—"low energy" feels less judgmental. Often laziness is born of fear, perpetuated by negative self-talk: "I'm not talented, I'll never produce anything great, so why even begin?" Using a tool from cognitive behavioral therapy, I replace the toxic thought with something kinder, such as "I've made great paintings before, and I'm capable of making more."

"Advanced pencil sharpening" is a sneaky variety of procrastination. Instead of tackling a difficult painting dilemma, I find myself Googling something art-related—for example, researching the best electric pencil eraser. Hours go by, and I'm left with that empty, gnawing feeling that art avoidance perpetuates.

At times, my procrastination takes the form of reading blogs or books about procrastination and productivity. No painting gets done, but at least I'm absorbing some strategies that have proven helpful. Three favorites are *Fearless Creating* by Eric Maisel (2000), *Essentialism* by Greg McKeown (2020), and *The One Thing* by Gary Keller & Jay Papasan (2013).

Surrender to Slow

I would much prefer *not* to be a slow painter—being prolific would be so much better! If I made more art, I might be able to share it more widely. For example, I might engage a gallery, whereas now I don't produce enough to satisfy their commercial needs. Most of all, I feel sad that many ideas for future paintings will never come to fruition because of my constipated process. And I am solemnly aware that being a slow artist is limiting in terms of legacy. True, Vermeer and Leonardo produced very few paintings in their lifetimes, but I am not in their league.[95]

The Angst and Exhilaration

People say, "How wonderful that you paint. It must be so relaxing ... like meditation!" Quite the opposite; it is more often a source of angst. So why do I do it? Because the flashes of exhilaration are so powerful, they fuel the patience I need to withstand the daily frustration.

I know a few artists who paint without difficulty, feeling only joy and loving the results. I have an inkling, though, that for me the struggle provides the traction that gives rise to intensity or mystery in my work.

I would like to produce more paintings, but not at the expense of deep exploration of a subject. It's not unusual for an author to spend years writing just one novel. So perhaps I am *not* a slow painter—this is just how long painting takes for me. The times when I adopt this mindset, I can surrender to the slow pace.

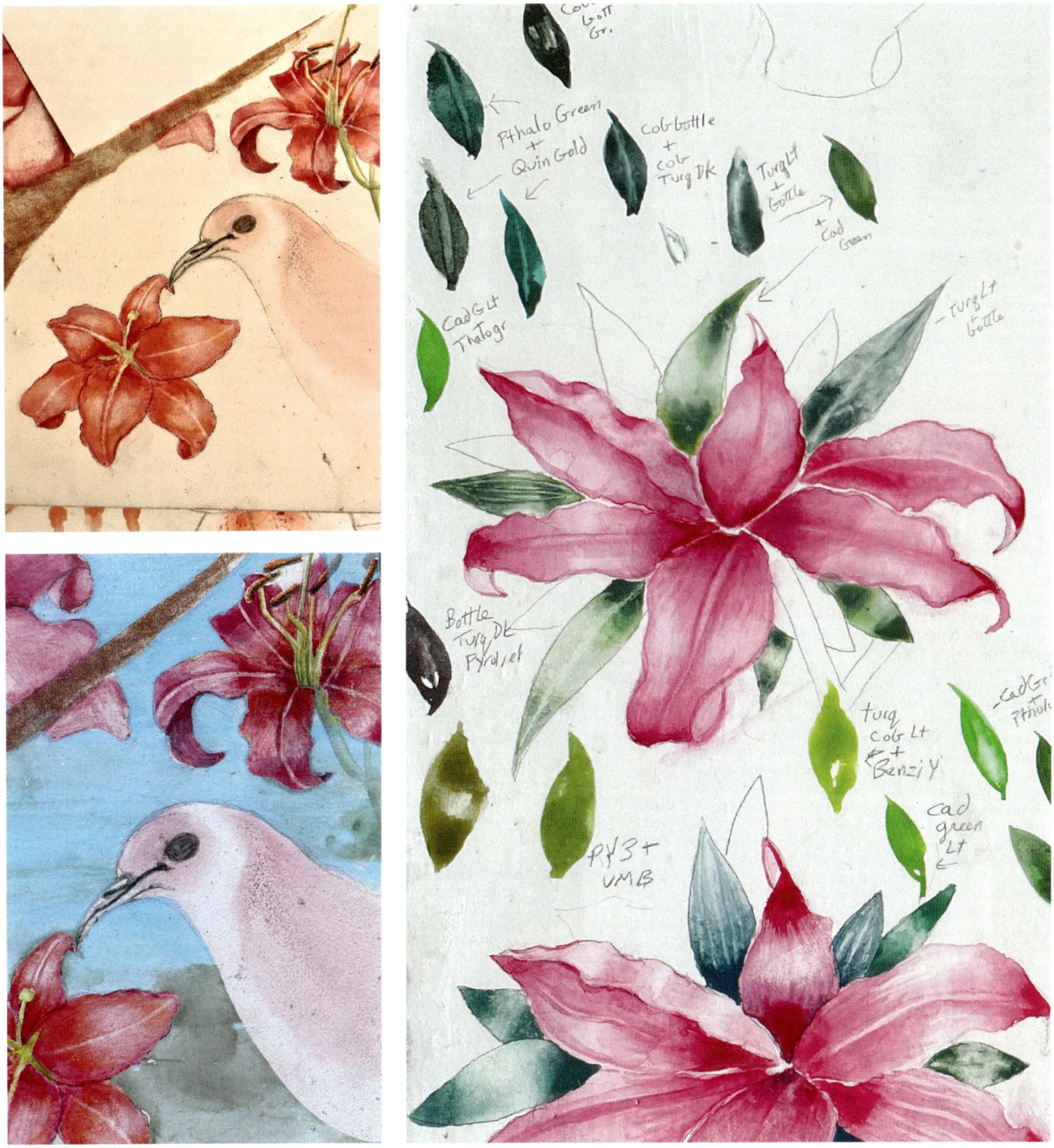

(ABOVE) Details: Preparatory studies for *Fish Without Bicycle*, featuring a watercolor wash technique. The leaves are notated with the names of pigments I'm experimenting with.

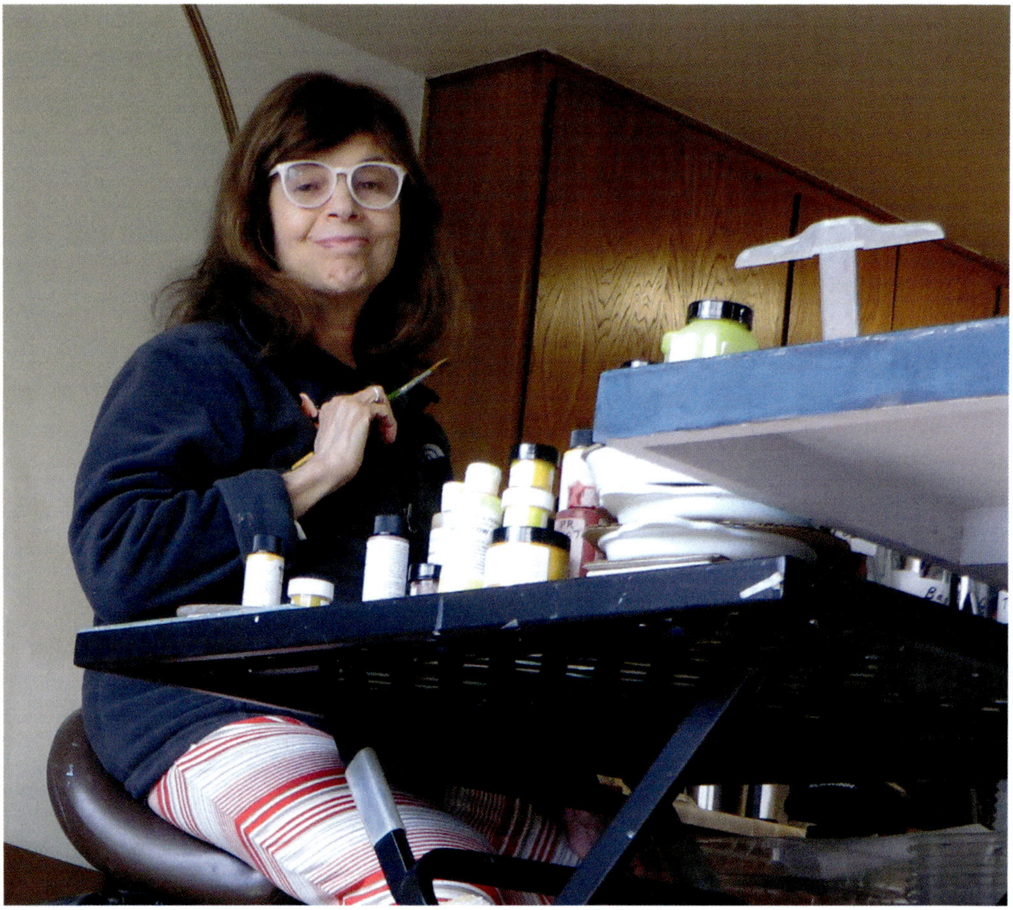

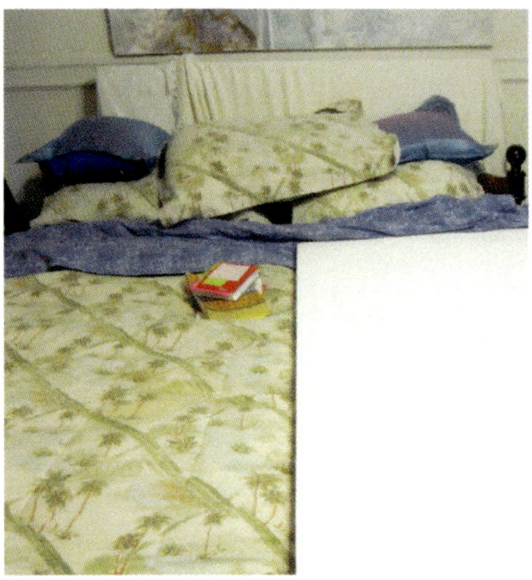

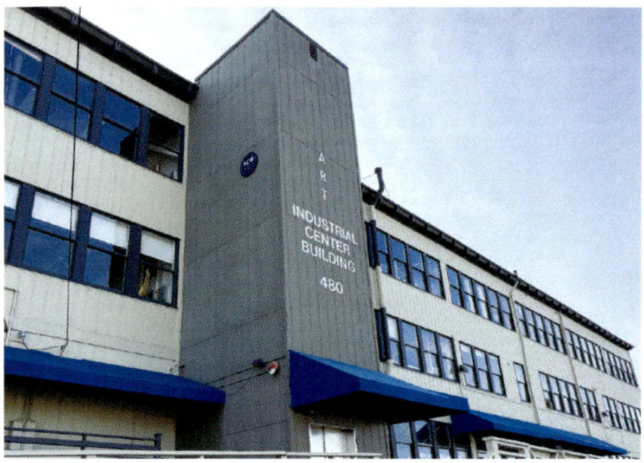

(ABOVE) In my home studio, 2021. Photo by Jake.

(BELOW LEFT) Sharing my double bed with my painting, 2011

(BELOW RIGHT) The ICB Building in Sausalito, 2025

CHAPTER TWENTY-ONE

ART PARADISE

Many Are Called?

Despite the many abortive relationships and sexual adventures elaborated in this book, most of my years have been spent as a single person. The Christian roots of icon painting led me to read works by Christian monk Thomas Merton, and the books *The Cloud of Unknowing* and *The Little Flowers of St. Francis* (both 14th century). I never understood the meaning of the biblical saying "many are called, but few are chosen," but the phrase kept permeating my consciousness with a message about my art.[96]

I knew I was "called" to make art, but I longed to be "chosen," which would mean having the fortitude to bring to life paintings that were painfully urgent in their dormant or seedling state. The pain of my failed love life was transmuted into a spiritual equanimity. Reading about how nuns take Christ as their husband (some even wearing a wedding ring and gown when they take their vows), I envisioned myself as married to my art. At one point, the metaphor became real when I shared my double bed with a large painting. There was space to work on the painting vertically on my easel, but for certain messy techniques, I needed to lay the panel flat, and there was insufficient surface space even on the floor. The celibate striving (not starving) artist trope appealed to my sense of devotion and melodrama.

A Wider Audience

I always wanted to be part of an artist community with the opportunity to share my work with a wider audience. In the past, mostly friends and acquaintances would come to open studios held in my home.

Then, in 2010, my ninety-seven-year-old father moved to The Redwoods, a hip retirement community in Marin County. I was making the trip from San Francisco several times a week to supervise his care. It was becoming stressful, so I often slept on the floor in his room to avoid the commute. But I found my painting time was suffering, so I decided to look for an art studio nearby. I was thrilled to find a vacancy in the ICB Building in Sausalito.[97]

My Studio

The space was a 400-square-foot cube with white walls and no windows. Each individual studio had no ceiling, but light flooded in from huge skylights in the roof. Although it was way over my budget, I fell in love and settled in. It was cold in the winter, and I was distracted by noises coming from neighboring studios, but the artists and staff were supportive, and I loved having a large dedicated painting space. Despite the downsides, one day I said to myself, "This is art paradise."

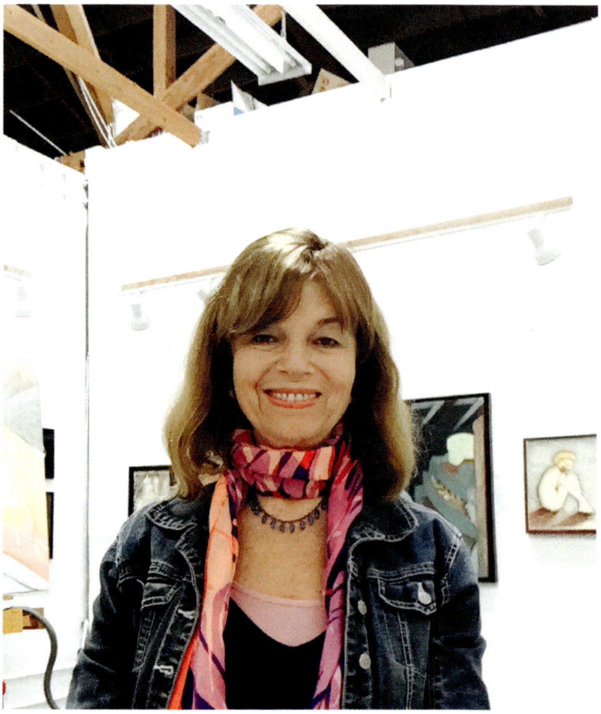

(ABOVE) In my ICB studio, c. 2015

It was thrilling to be in the ICB building when open studios were held. Hundreds of people visited the three floors of studios, and I received a concentrated dose of feedback. Like a child who has grown up and left home, a painting is set free in the world to meet diverse people.

Although it's nice to hear "very interesting" or "your work is beautiful," that can sound flat and generic. It was soul-penetrating to hear words that flew to the heart of my creative intentions.

This feedback resulted in a solid feeling that I was on the path of fulfilling my vision. Here is a sampling of viewer comments I heard, then jotted down in a notebook.

"You tread where no one else goes."

I'm not sure this is true. However, I do feel that I have a unique vision that erupts once I settle on a story that must be told.

"Your paintings are devoid of cliché."

This is my most treasured compliment. Yet when I look back at my work, I do smell cliché—especially in art that did not make the cut for this book.

"You have no fear."

In general, I am a fearful person—I have a fear of planes, cars, and boats, and I am perhaps overly cautious about crime. Yet I find a release in painting, where I can let caution dissolve and plumb the depths of my experience. Later, when I share the work in an exhibition, or in the pages of this book, I do feel trepidation and worry that I may be cast out of the village or even harmed.

"Your work resonates with so much integrity that it gives me goose bumps."

I enjoy when someone has a visceral reaction to my work. People have wept when viewing the *Ways of Dying* paintings.

"There is pain, but there is hope."

This person must be a poet! It does capture the essence of what I am trying to bring forth.

A fellow artist, George Brooks-Hutton, wrote this comment after visiting my website:

"I am heartened to see that you continue with egg tempera, and that you continue your unapologetic images trying to tell true stories about unspeakable moments, of the extremes you and those around you have stumbled through, of the mystery of it all. And always there's the text you've given us with each painting: as though you use your words to soften an image that perhaps you worry is too hard or painful, and sometimes use them to harden and deepen a painting you think has come out too soft otherwise."

Home Studio in San Francisco

Although I loved the exquisite natural surroundings and less stressful lifestyle of Marin County, my friends, job, and other activities were in San Francisco. So, in 2017, a year after my dad passed, I moved back to the city. I felt sad giving up my dedicated painting space, but it was a necessity given the expense and commute, plus after three years the audience at open studios started to feel homogeneous. I was ready to return to painting in my home.

As I was setting up my home studio, I remembered visiting my teacher Dianne Mitchell in 2005 in her new home in Cambria, California. As she showed me around her cottage, I noticed a large drafting table in the middle of her tiny living room. When she showed me a good-sized empty room in the back of the house, I asked her, "Why don't you use this space for your studio?" I remember her words: "It's important that art be central in my living space as it is in my life." This made an impression on me, and I now paint in my large living/dining area. A decorator would not approve, but I love being confronted with my painting first thing every morning.

Parting Words

The challenge of mastering egg tempera while confronting demons of self-doubt paradoxically provided the dread I needed to forge through obstacles—at times creating moments of artistic miracle. I feel myself moving toward a belief in my artistic power and vision. Thank you for sharing this journey.

—LORA ARBRADOR
SAN FRANCISCO, 2025

Please Stay in Touch

Subscribe to my newsletter at:

artblotterplus.substack.com

Visit my website:

arbrador.com

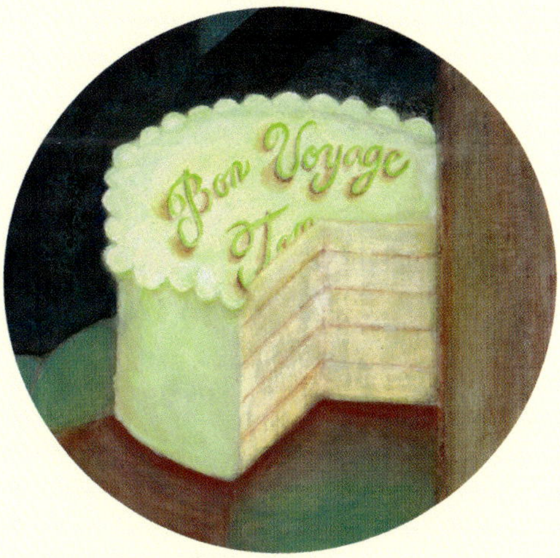

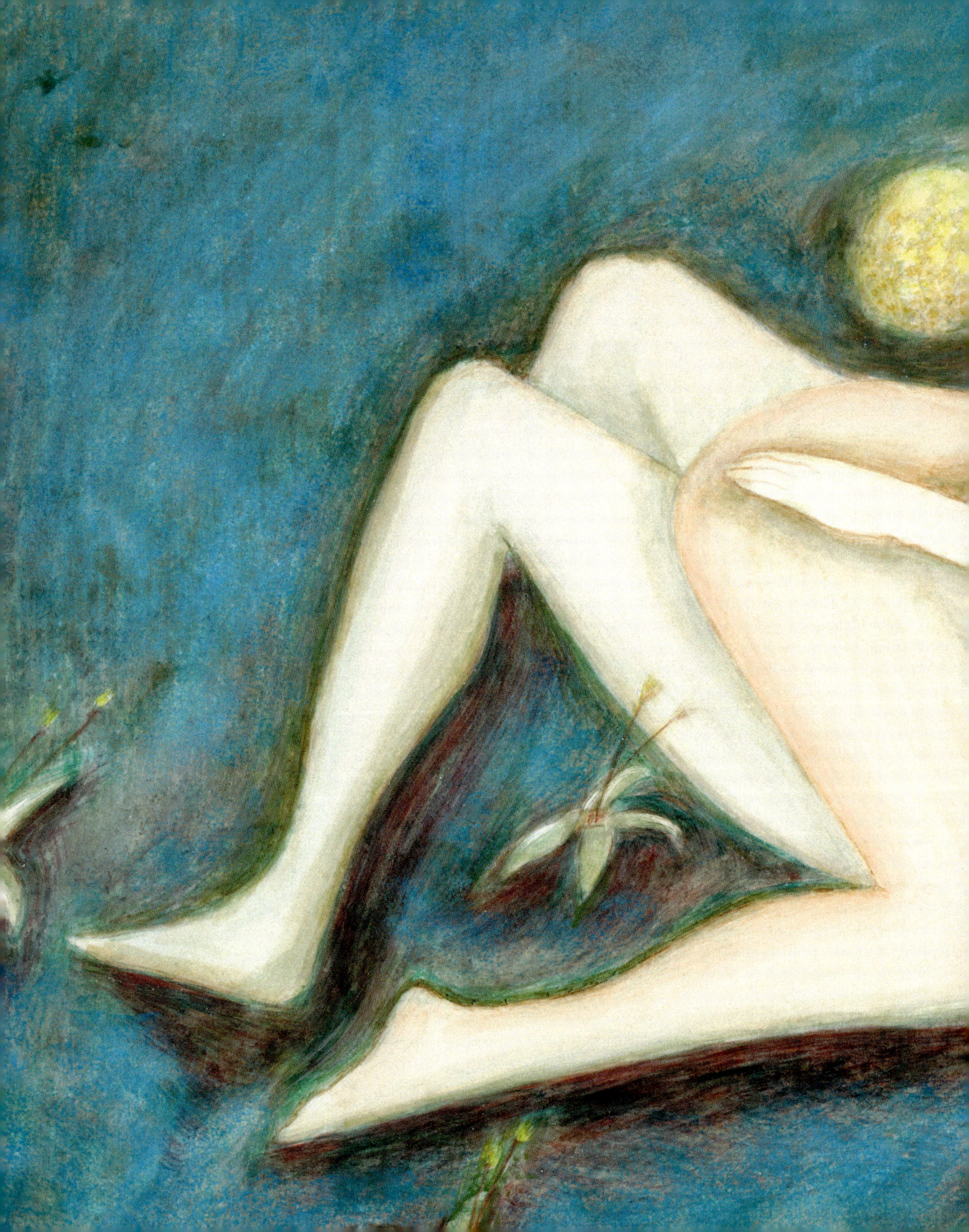

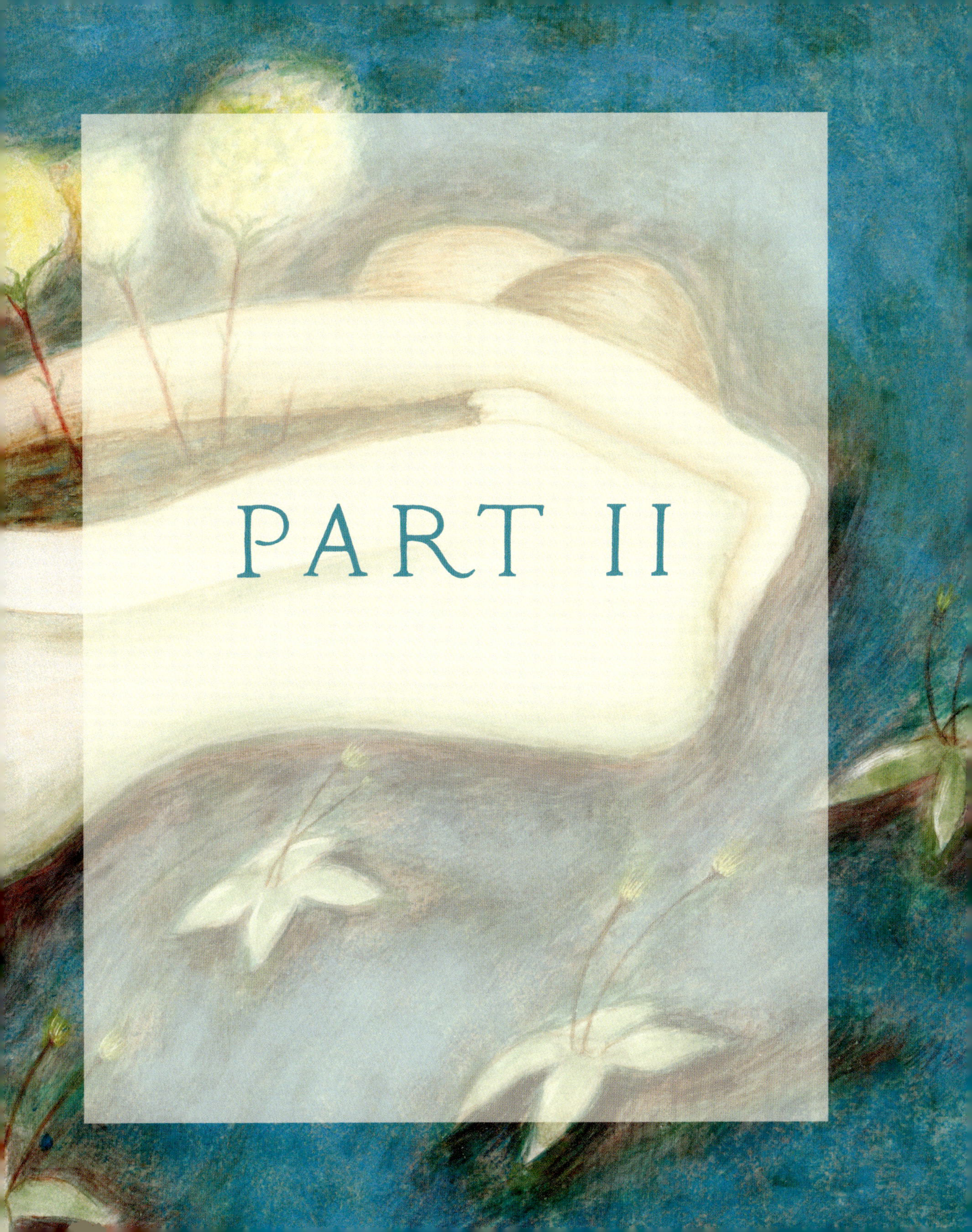

PART II

WHICH CAME FIRST? A TASTE OF EGG TEMPERA HISTORY

Introduction

I am not a historian, conservator, or curator, so my approach to egg tempera history draws mainly from my passion for the technique and my hands-on experience. Plus, as a former research nurse, I have some skill in digging into academic literature.

Since this was originally meant to be a full-length book and is now compressed into an essay, I've allowed myself to cherry-pick my favorite episodes in egg tempera history. These may seem trivial or obscure but hopefully will be eye-opening or entertaining. Where facts or answers are hard to come by, I leave the reader, and myself, with questions to ponder.

What Is Paint?

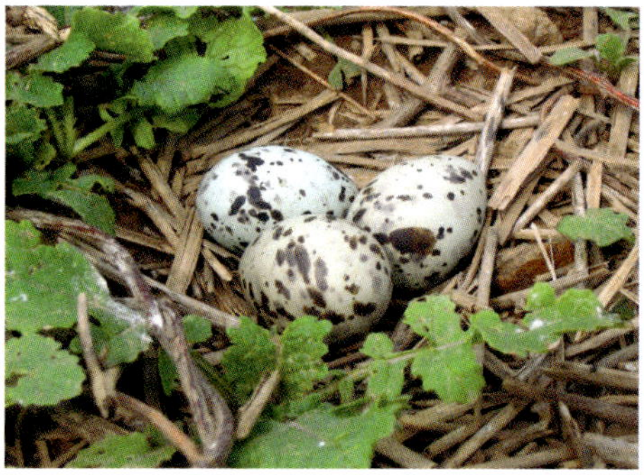

(ABOVE) Common tern nest with three eggs. Photo by Michelle Kinsey Bruns, 2009.

To understand egg tempera, we need to learn the elements of any paint. Paint is made up of three ingredients: the colored matter, called **pigment**; the **binder**, which is the substance that holds the pigment particles together and attaches them to a surface; and water or other **liquid** to thin the mixture. Each paint medium is defined by its binder: watercolor is bound with gum arabic (a tree gum); oil paint is bound with oil (linseed, walnut, or poppy seed oil); encaustic uses wax; and acrylic paint uses a plastic polymer. The binder for egg tempera is egg yolk.

Through the ages, a wide variety of paint binders were used, including egg, milk, plant oils, blood serum, urine, wax, glue made from animal skins, fish egg, animal marrow, and gum from trees.

Neolithic Era

We tend to think of egg tempera as an esoteric medium, but egg was in the human diet by pilfering eggs from nests even before the domestication of birds in India in 3200 BC. So, it is not surprising that egg has been found in some early wall paintings.

Here is just one example of many: The Domus de Janas (House of the Fairies) are tombs cut into rocks located in Sardinia, Italy, which date back to the late Neolithic Age (3400–2700 BC). An analysis performed in 2007, using advanced techniques, detected egg, a binder, in samples from several sites.[98]

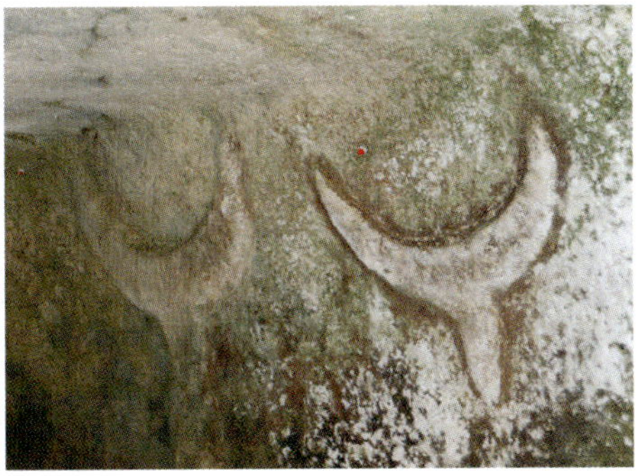

(ABOVE) Bull's Horns, necropolis of Su Crucifissu Mannu, Porto Torres, Sardinia, c. 3200-3800 BC. Photo by Gianni Careddu, 2012.

Bronze Age Mycenaean Culture

Moving from the Neolithic to the Bronze Age, egg yolk has been identified in wall paintings of the Mycenaeans from about 1300 BC. The Mycenean culture flourished mostly on the Peloponnese, the southern peninsula of mainland Greece, and was heavily influenced by the Minoans, who resided on the island of Crete. The Mycenaeans conquered the Minoans in about 1400 BC.[99]

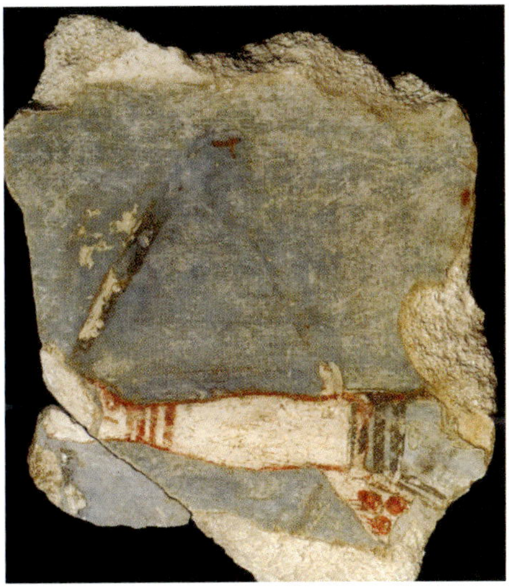

(ABOVE) An archer from the Palace of Nestor, near Pylos, Greece. Fresco secco. Archaeological Museum of Chora, Messenia, Greece, c. 13th century BC. Photo by J. Stephens.

The exquisite wall paintings of the Minoans were executed in "buon fresco," or true fresco, but the technique the Mycenaeans used is called "fresco secco," or dry fresco. Buon fresco is a technique in which the artist brushes pigments, previously ground in water, directly onto wet "fresh" lime plaster. A chemical reaction takes place that permanently fixes the image without the need for a binder, such as egg or gum. But the artist has only a window of about eight hours in which to paint before the plaster is too dry to bind the pigments.

In contrast with the buon fresco technique used by the Minoans, in the fresco secco technique used by the Mycenaeans, the paint is applied to dry plaster. The great advantage is that there is no restricted window of time for painting. But to compensate for the loss of adhesive strength, lime water or a binder is needed. Egg yolk has been identified in fragments of Mycenaean wall paintings in the Palace of Nestor.[100]

The Mycenaean civilization may have been the seed culture from which Greek panel paintings evolved. This evolution continued from Greek panels to Byzantine icons, which were in turn a direct influence on Early Renaissance panels, which directly preceded the High Renaissance.[101]

Egg Tempera and Panel Painting

We're not sure when egg tempera painted on wooden panels (as opposed to wall painting) began, but there is conjecture that it was practiced in Classical Greek times or even earlier. The Pitsa panels found in Corinthia, Greece, are the earliest surviving panel paintings (dated to c. 540–530 BC), but due to their fragility, they have not yet been analyzed for paint binder. In 2024, I exchanged emails with archaeologist Hariclia Brecoulaki. She stated that she hopes to have the Pitsa panels analyzed for binder ingredients in the near future and will let me know the results.

Egypt

I've frequently read on websites featuring rehashed content that egg tempera was the medium of ancient Egyptian wall paintings. This is not correct—the Egyptians mostly used gum arabic derived from acacia trees to bind the pigments found on their wall paintings.[102]

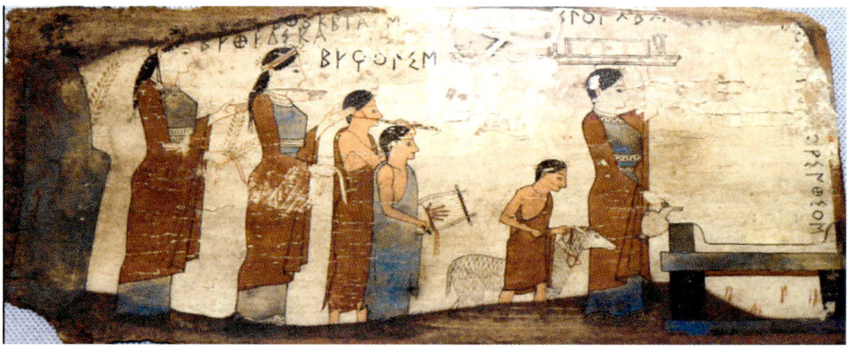

(ABOVE) Pitsa Panel, 549–530 BC, found in Pitsa, Corinthia, Greece. National Archaeological Museum, Athens

But egg as paint binder *has* been found in architectural fragments from the Palace of Apries in Memphis, Egypt, dated 589–568 BC. I also found references to egg white used in combination with beeswax and tree resin as a kind of varnish for wall paintings in the tomb of Nefertari (1255 BC).[103]

Greco-Roman Tradition in Egypt

There *is* evidence of egg tempera on panel painting in Egypt, but it traces back to the Greek and Roman conquests of Egypt, not indigenous Egyptian tradition. King Philip II of Macedonia was a great admirer of Greek culture and hired Aristotle to be the tutor of his young son Alexander. After his father died, Alexander the Great went on to conquer Greece in 335 BC. Like his father, Alexander revered Greek culture, and after conquering Egypt in 332 BC, he brought Greek artists to Alexandria, the city he founded on the northwest coast of Egypt.

After Alexander died in 323 BC, one of his generals, Ptolemy I Soter, became the first pharaoh of the Ptolemaic dynasty. He was a patron of the arts and brought some of the best Greek artists to Egypt. Cleopatra VII was the last Ptolemaic queen of Egypt before the Greeks were overtaken by the Romans in 31 BC.

The Romans ruled Egypt from 30 BC to the Islamic Conquest in 641 AD. The Greeks living in Roman Egypt adopted some of the funeral customs of the Egyptians, such as mummification, but instead of mummy masks, a portrait of the deceased was painted in the tradition and style of Roman portraiture on a thin wooden panel. Due to preservation in the dry sands of Egypt, more than 1,000 of these mummy portraits dated from the first to the third centuries AD have been excavated from the Fayum region.

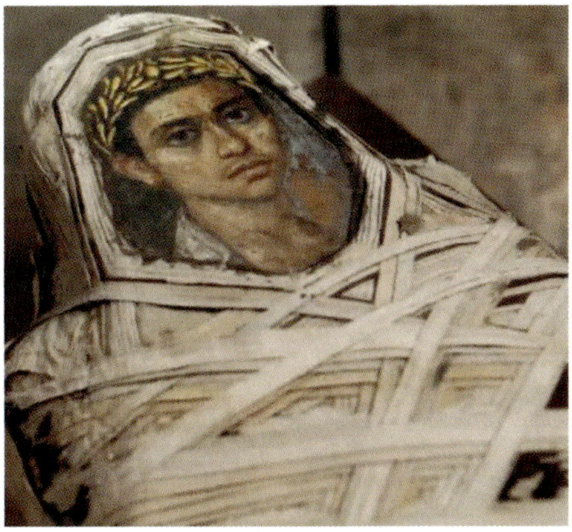

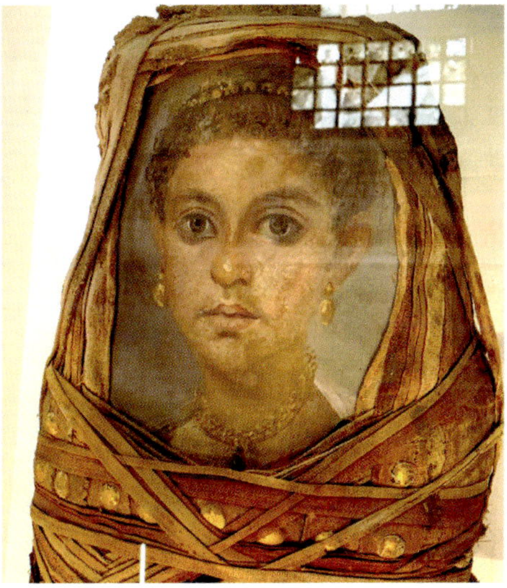

(ABOVE) Mummy portrait, Fayum district, Egypt, Greco-Roman era. Current location unknown.

(BELOW) Mummy portrait of a child, Hawara-Fayum region, Egypt, 2nd century CE. Egyptian Museum, Cairo

The portraits follow the Classical Greek painting formula, posing the subject in a three-quarter view with a single light source casting realistic shadows and highlights on the face. Since no panel paintings from the Greek world have been preserved (other than the Pitsa panels mentioned above), these mummy portraits are some of the only examples of an art derived from the Classical Greek tradition. Although the art technique matches what is thought to be that of classical Greek times (4th c. BC), the hairstyles, jewelry, and clothing reflect Roman fashion contemporary to the period they were painted in (2nd c. AD).

Most of the portraits were executed in encaustic (wax painting), but based on visual inspection, several were assumed to be egg tempera. Art books and websites still reference egg tempera as the medium of some Fayum mummy portraits, but with advanced laboratory analysis, we now know that most of the ones assumed to be tempera were painted with an animal glue binder.[104] Egg was found on some but was determined to be a coating over the glue painting.[105]

Egg Tempera in Tebtunis

In a residence in the town of Tebtunis, also in the Fayum district, paintings were confirmed to have been painted with egg binder, however this could change as more sophisticated tools for analysis are used.[106] An example is a painting of the god Heron, probably used for domestic worship. This and others like it are remarkably similar to early Christian icon paintings, bolstering the hypotheses that icon paintings were deeply rooted in their Greco-Roman predecessors.

The Roman Empire, which conquered Greece and then adopted and spread Greek culture, was itself eventually destroyed in the sack of Rome in 455 AD. Egypt

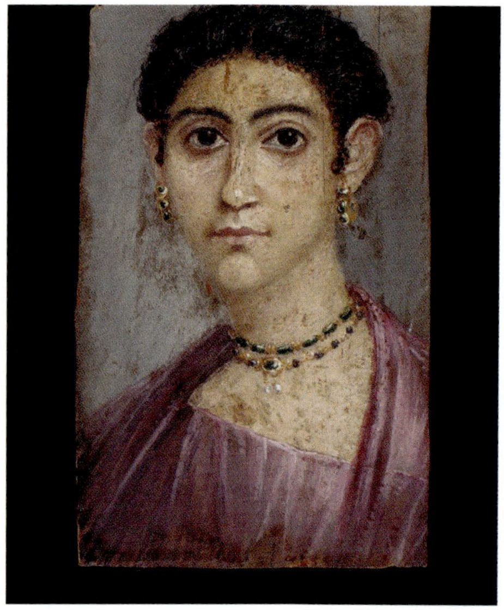

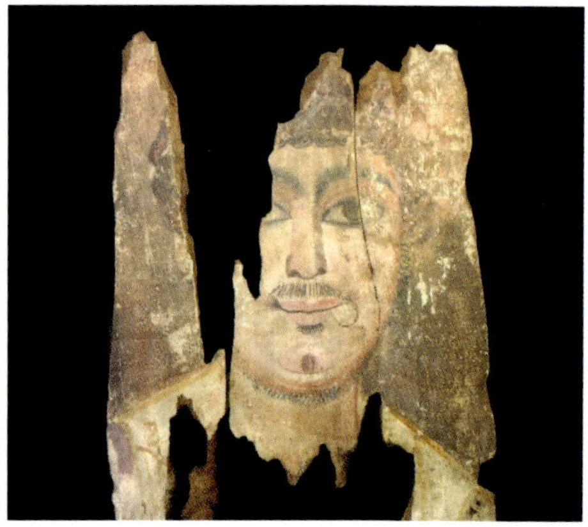

(ABOVE) Mummy portrait of a woman, Hawara-Fayum district, Egypt, 100–120 AD. Encaustic on lime wood, 15 1/16 × 8 1/16 in. (38.2 × 20.5 cm). British Museum, London

(BELOW) Mummy portrait, Romano-Egyptian, Kafr Ammar, Egypt, 160–180 AD. Animal glue paint binder on wood panel, 12 1/4 × 7 1/8 in. (31.1 × 18 cm). Petrie Museum of Egyptian Archaeology, University College, London. Originally analyzed as egg tempera but reanalyzed as animal glue.

and later the Byzantine Empire, especially the city of Constantinople, became the invaluable repository and protector of Greek art and learning. It is from this tradition that the roots of the Renaissance can be traced.

The Byzantine Empire

The Byzantine Empire looms large in the history of egg tempera. In 324 BC, the Emperor Constantine moved the capital of the Roman Empire to a town strategically located on the Bosphorus Strait that had been a Greek colony called Byzantium. The city was officially given the name Constantinople in 330 AD. Today, Constantinople is the city of Istanbul in modern Turkey. Although Constantine only converted to Christianity on his deathbed in 337, he was a believer and constructed Constantinople as a Christian city, commissioning art and architecture with Christian imagery.

There is evidence that egg tempera was practiced, but encaustic (wax painting) was the predominant medium of icon painting in the early Byzantine Empire. The infamous periods of Iconoclasm, when images were banned and many destroyed, were a setback for Byzantine art. However, when icons were permanently restored in 843 AD by Empress Theodora, egg tempera superseded encaustic as the preferred panel painting technique because it was easier to use.

In the centuries that followed, especially from the ninth to fifteenth centuries, egg tempera was brought to new levels of aesthetic and technical achievement.

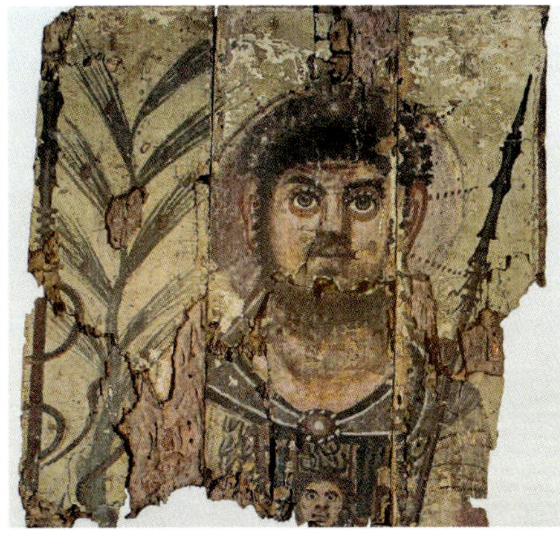

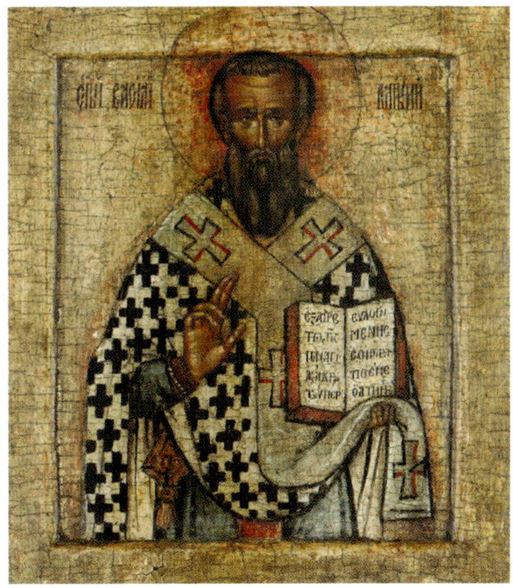

(ABOVE) Detail: *Heron and Lykourgos*, mid-2nd century AD. Egg tempera on wood panel. 15 × 8 in. (38 × 20 cm), discovered in Tebtunis, Egypt. Berlin Staatliche Museen, Ägyptisches Museum

(BELOW) *St. Basil the Great*, late 1500s to 1600s. Egg tempera and gold leaf on gesso panel, 12¼ × 10¾ × 1⅜ in. (30.9 × 27.4 × 3.5 cm). Icon Museum and Study Center, Clinton, Massachusetts

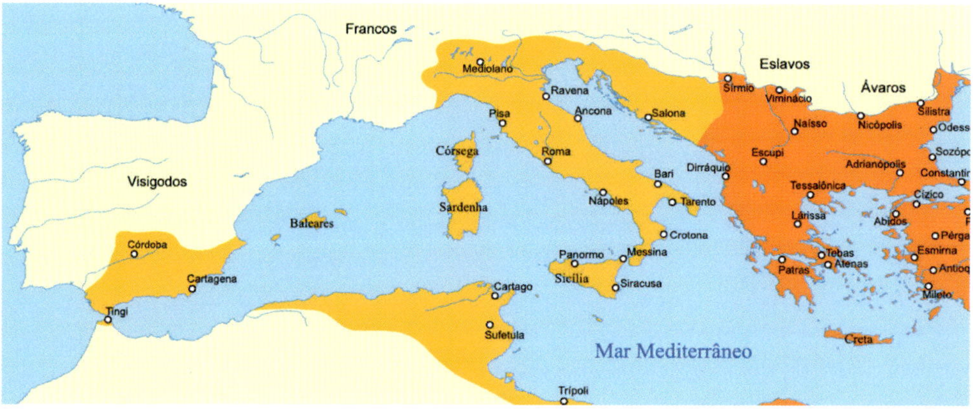

(ABOVE) The Byzantine empire at the rise of Justinian I to the throne in 527 AD (in brown), and at his death in 565 AD (orange and brown combined). Source: *Historical World Atlas,* by George Duby, 2002

Although territories were lost and gained, at its height, under Justinian I, the Byzantine Empire ruled across the Middle East, Balkan regions, and parts of Italy, Crete, and Cyprus. Byzantine art was adopted in these conquered territories, and so the technique of egg tempera was practiced in Italy long before the fall of the Byzantine Empire in 1453.

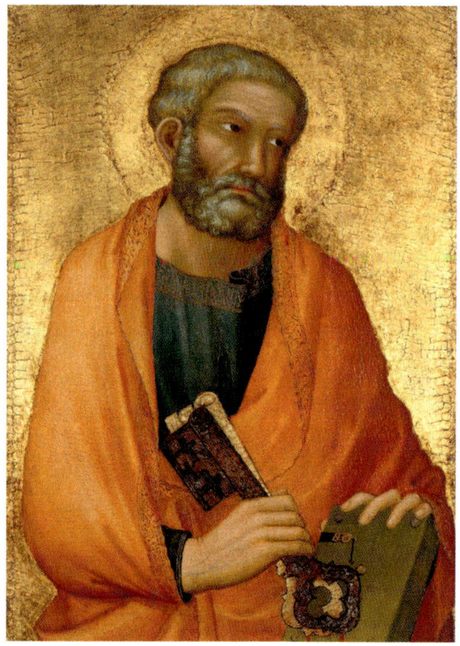

(ABOVE) Simone Martini, *Saint Peter,* 1325–1328. Tempera and gold on panel, 22⅞ × 15³⁄₁₆ in. (58 × 38.5 cm). Thyssen-Bornemisza Museo Nacional, Madrid. Martini was a key artist in the Proto-Renaissance.

Proto-Renaissance and Disdain for Icons

Proto-Renaissance (c. 1280–1400 AD) is the term now used for the period of transition in Italy between the flat, symbolic Byzantine style and the highly developed realism of the High Renaissance. Egg tempera was brought to rapturous heights during this era.

But with the emergence of the exquisite works of realism created in the High Renaissance, icon painting, with its flat imagery and gold backgrounds, became disrespected by art historians and the public.

Giorgio Vasari, considered the first (but not always reliable) art historian, disdainfully dubbed work painted in the Byzantine style the *maniera greca* (the Greek manner). But as abstract art became accepted and embraced in the twentieth century, icon painting found an admiring audience and is now considered by many equal in beauty to the art of the Renaissance and beyond.

The Rise of Oil Painting

It's a myth that oil painting was invented by Jan van Eyck in the fifteenth century. The twelfth-century German monk, artist, and writer Theophilus (Roger of Helmarshausen) describes oil-based decorative painting in his treatise *On Divers Arts*, written in 1125. Artists in the Middle Ages, and even before, sometimes painted with oil, though often in a crude form that darkened the pigments. In the 1400s, Northern European artists, including Van Eyck, learned how to improve the working properties of oils so that they would dry more quickly and be lighter in tone.

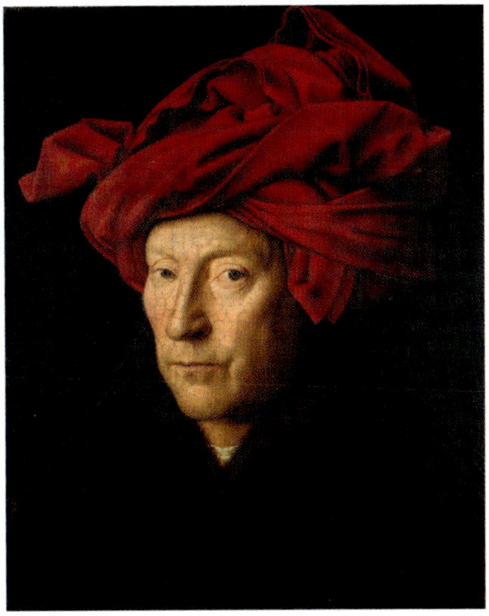

(ABOVE) Jan van Eyck, *Portrait of a Man (Self-Portrait?)*, 1433. Oil on oak, 10¼ × 7½ in. (26 × 19 cm). National Gallery, London

The slow-drying nature of oil makes the blending of colors more easily achieved, allowing for naturalistic effects that were desirable as a more humanistic, rather than religious, philosophy emerged. The oil also saturates the colors, imbuing them with a deeper, richer tone. And because oil paint can be built up to a buttery texture called "impasto," highlights can be created that "pop." All this contributes to a more realistic rendering that was so valued in the pre-photography era.

In addition, being able to work on stretched canvas rather than wood made the art lighter and more portable. Since textile manufacturing was a booming industry in Italy, this saved artisans the time and expense of constructing panels. Purportedly, some artists gave up egg tempera reluctantly and only for convenience and the economic advantages of oils, but I have not been able to verify this.

There was a long transition in which both tempera and oil painting were practiced—often egg tempera served as an underpainting for oil glazes—but by the sixteenth century, almost all artists had switched to oil painting. However, the icon painters of the Eastern Orthodox Church maintain a continuous tradition of egg tempera painting to this day.

First Egg Tempera Revival

In the early 1800s, some artists were looking for a purer painting technique, as they were not happy with how their oil paintings were aging. A reaction against the industrial revolution brought these seekers to Italy, where they sought older techniques. Unlike egg tempera paintings, which tend to retain their original color, oil paintings often darken and turn yellow with age. This depends upon several factors: the oil used (poppy seed and stand oil are less yellowing than linseed oil), exposure to light (oil paintings stored in the dark will temporarily yellow), and selection of pigments (lead, cobalt, and copper-based pigments tend to yellow).[107] In addition, most historical varnishes yellow with age, and so both oil and egg tempera paintings may darken if varnished.

The French painter Jean-Auguste-Dominique Ingres was among the first to arrive in Italy, in 1806, after winning the Rome Prize (Prix de Rome). He became enamored with egg tempera but only painted one painting in the technique, *Romulus' Victory over Acron* (1812). However, his biographer, Henri Delaborde, found the following in Ingres's notes: "I should do all my large paintings in tempera and then varnish them with oil." Another Ingres-tempera connection is that one of his students, Victor Mottez, produced the first French translation of *Il Libro dell'Arte* by Cennino Cennini.

The Nazarenes and Pre-Raphaelite Brotherhood

In 1809, a group of German artists were searching for a more pure, spiritual painting technique. They were not monks but were called the Nazarenes due to their biblical way of dressing. They traveled to Italy and lived together in an abandoned monastery in Rome, where they learned painting techniques of the Early Renaissance, such as mosaic and fresco. They also learned egg tempera but used it mostly to touch up their fresco paintings, not for panel painting.

Inspired by the Nazarenes, the Pre-Raphaelite Brotherhood (PRB), founded in 1848, was also seeking a more craft-based art form. They rejected all art beginning with Raphael, although I've since learned that the PRB did revere Raphael. Most of the PRB artists painted in a very refined oil painting technique, but some explored egg tempera—specifically, Holman Hunt. A "second-wave" Pre-Raphaelite, John Roddam Spencer Stanhope started to paint in egg tempera in the late 1870s, contributing to its revival. However, his famous "egg tempera" painting *Death and the Maiden* has recently been analyzed and found to have been executed in oil paint.

Another artist inspired by the Pre-Raphaelite movement was Marianne Stokes. Stokes started to paint in tempera from about 1895.

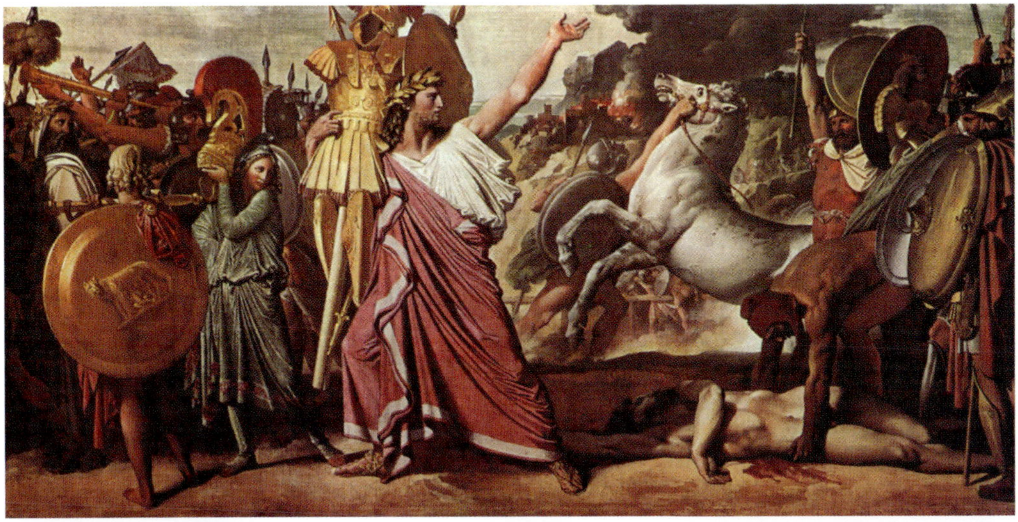

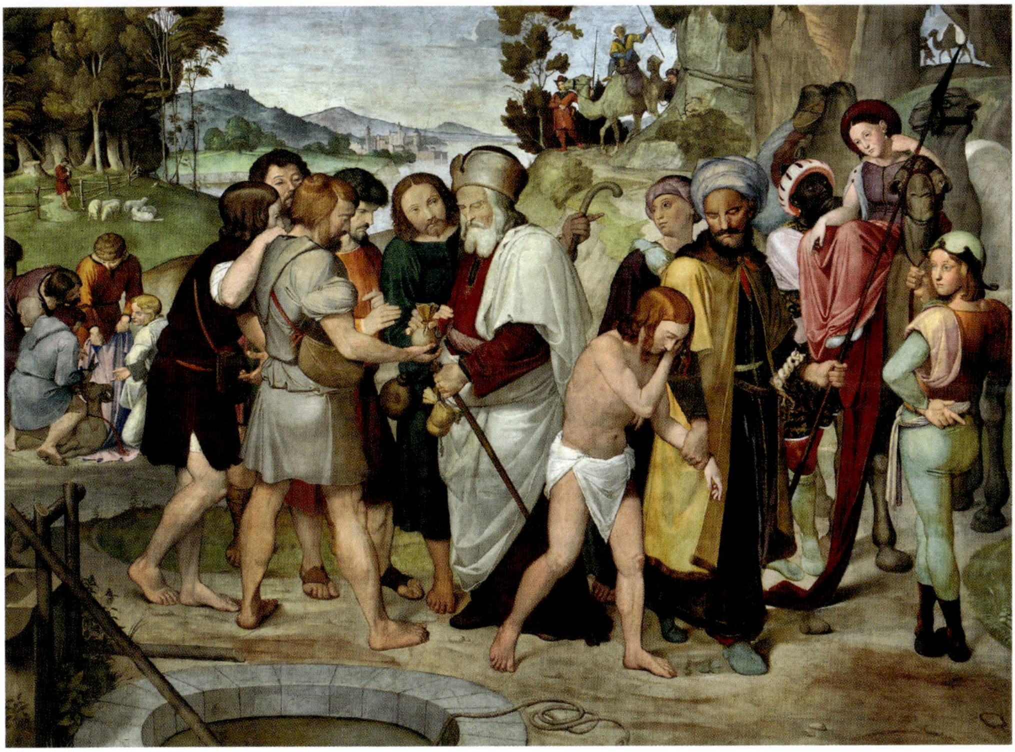

(ABOVE) Jean-Auguste-Dominique Ingres, *Romulus' Victory over Acron*, 1812. Egg tempera on canvas, 108½ × 82⅛ in. (275.8 × 529.8 cm), Louvre, Paris

(BELOW) Johann Friedrich Overbeck, *Joseph Sold into Slavery by His Brothers*, 1816–17. Fresco with some tempera, 95⅔ × 119⅔ in. (243 × 304 cm). Formerly in the Casa Bartholdy in Rome; now in the Alte Nationalgalerie, Berlin. Overbeck was a founding member of the Nazarenes.

She progressively abandoned oils, becoming a member of the Society of Painters in Tempera in 1905. Her *Madonna and Child* from 1905 is an example of her highly skilled, exquisite tempera technique.

Neglect & Rediscovery of Botticelli

The rediscovery of Botticelli was the spark that ignited the first revival of egg tempera painting.[108] It's hard to believe that the magnificent paintings of Sandro Botticelli were largely forgotten between his 1510 death and the 1860s due to being overshadowed by masters of the High Renaissance, such as Michelangelo and Leonardo. Another factor was Botticelli's fervent devotion to Girolamo Savonarola, a Dominican monk who preached against corruption in the Catholic Church, exploitation of the poor, and the immorality of secular art and culture. Starting in February 1495, Savonarola presided over regular bonfires in which paintings were burned along with other "vanities." Some sources say that Botticelli brought some of his paintings to be burned in the "bonfire of the vanities" but these have not been substantiated.

John Ruskin, English author and art critic, claimed to have rediscovered Botticelli: "It was me, and to me alone, first to discern, and then to teach the excel and supremacy of five great painters, despised until I spoke of them; of the five were Turner, Tintoret, Luini, Botticelli, and Carpaccio."[109] But actually, it was painter and poet Dante Gabriel Rossetti, a cofounder of the PRB, who first sparked interest in long-forgotten Botticelli amongst nineteenth-century art lovers. Rossetti visited Paris in 1849 and, according to an account by his brother William Michael Rossetti, was particularly struck with one or two Botticellis, which he talked about on his return to England.[110] William claimed that his brother was largely "responsible for the modern vogue of Botticelli."[111]

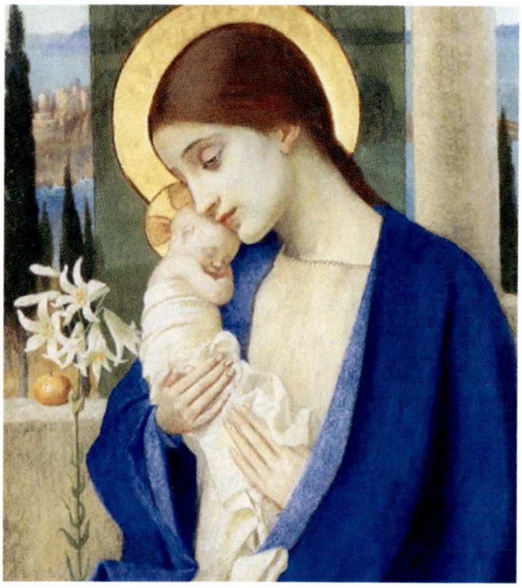

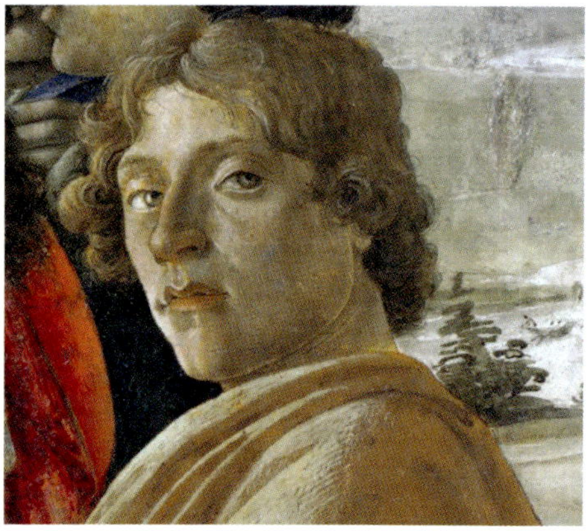

(ABOVE) Marianne Stokes, *Madonna and Child with Symbols*, c. 1905. Egg tempera and gold on panel, 14½ × 12½ in. (36.8 × 31.7 cm). Private collection.

(BELOW) Detail: Sandro Botticelli, *Self-Portrait*, from *Adoration of the Magi*, 1470–75. Tempera grassa, 43 7/10 × 52 ¾ in. (111 × 134 cm). Uffizi Gallery, Florence

Botticelli worked in tempera, tempera/oil combination, and later 100% oil paint. (See more paintings by Botticelli in Chapter 16.)

Edward Burne-Jones, another "second- wave" Pre-Raphaelite, was the artist most influenced by Botticelli's style at that time. He, too, was turned on to Botticelli by Rossetti, who became his mentor and then collaborator.

Il Libro dell'Arte by Cennino Cennini

The rediscovery of Botticelli spurred interest in tempera, which was boosted by the translation into English of *Il Libro dell'Arte*. Written by Cennino Cennini, probably around 1400, it describes painting techniques practiced in the thirteenth and fourteenth centuries, including egg tempera.

Cennini's authority stems from his lineage, which traces back to the great Giotto di Bondone. Cennini was a pupil of Agnolo Gaddi, who trained under his father, Taddeo Gaddi. Taddeo Gaddi was said to be the favorite pupil of Giotto and remained in his workshop from 1313 until the master's death in 1337.

Lara Broecke—historical linguist, conservator, and superb egg tempera artist—refutes the commonly held understanding that *Il Libro dell'Arte* was written as a practical studio guide. Broecke writes in the introduction to her translation, published in 2015, that the treatise was written not as a practical manual, guild book, or presentation book, but rather "The *Libro dell'Arte* seems to be intended as a spectacular display of the summit of Cennini's knowledge

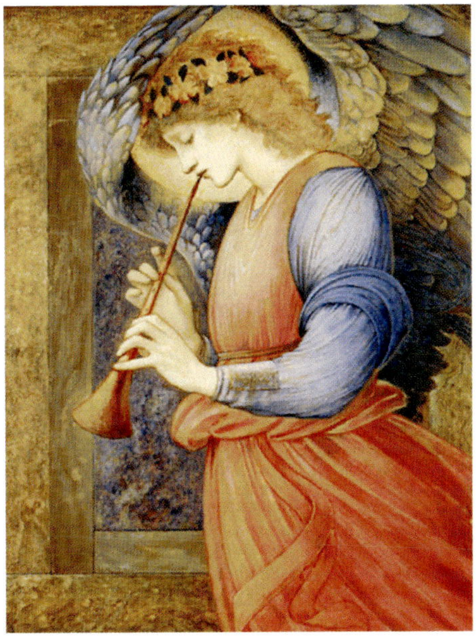

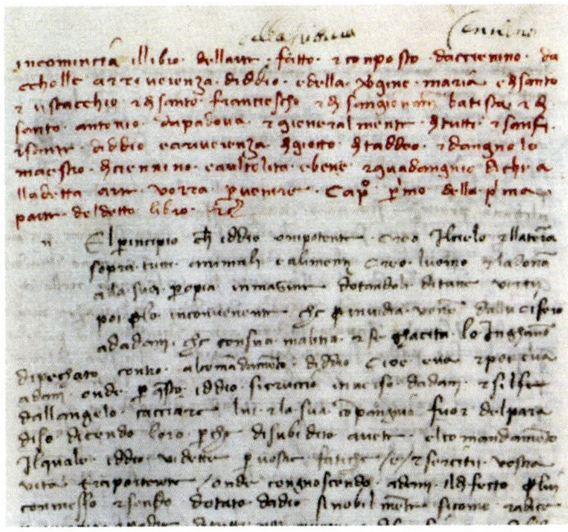

(ABOVE) Edward Burne-Jones, *An Angel Playing a Flageolet*, 1878. Oil and tempera, 29⅓ × 24 in. (74.4 × 60.9 cm). Sudley House, Liverpool, England

(BELOW) Detail: Handwritten transcription of Cennino Cennini's *Il Libro dell'Arte*, c. 1400. Biblioteca Medicea Laurenziana, Florence. The original manuscript has never been found.

and abilities, formed into a satisfying literary whole designed to impress the cutting-edge intellectuals of the Carrara court."

The Great Fire of 1834

The first English translation of *Il Libro dell'Arte,* published in 1844, had everything to do with the Great Fire of 1834 that destroyed most of the Palace of Westminster, home to both Houses of Parliament. A royal commission was established in 1835 to plan for the rebuilding of the parliament, and in 1841, a Fine Arts Commission was set up to envision the artwork that would complement the architecture. Surprisingly, fresco was the medium that captured the attention of the commission. Painting with pigments brushed onto wet plaster was unheard of in England, and some thought it unsuitable in the northern climate.

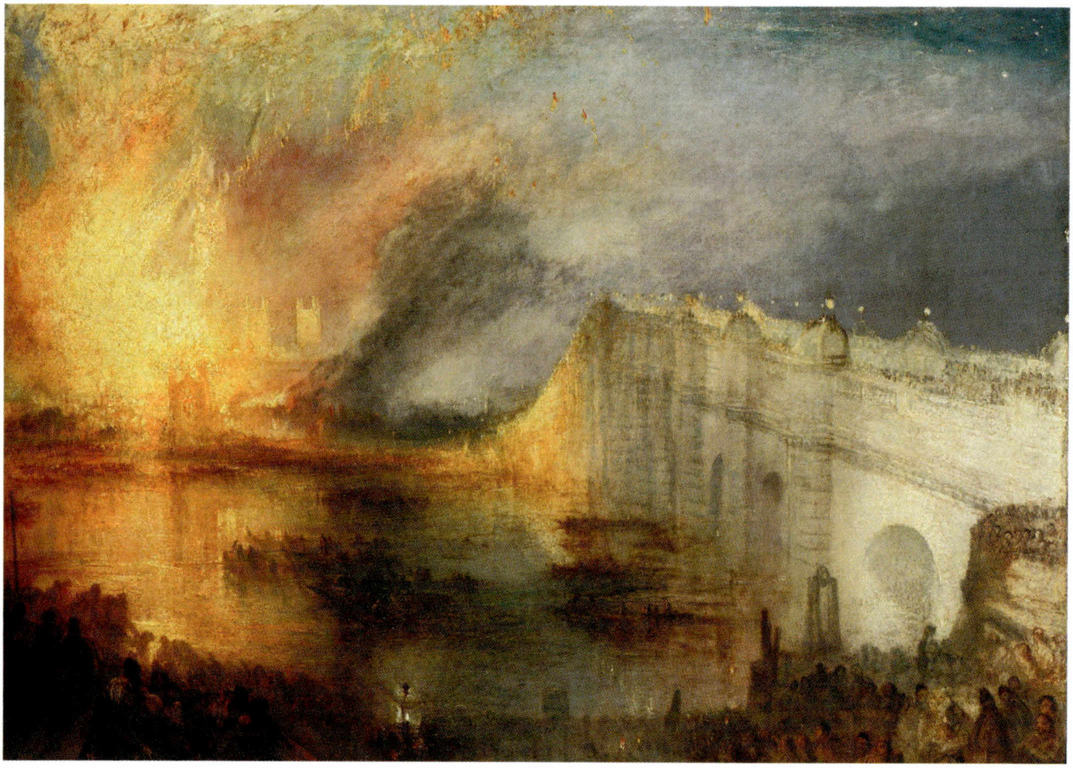

(ABOVE) Joseph Mallord William Turner, *The Burning of the Houses of Lords and Commons, October 16, 1834,* 1835. Oil on canvas, 36¼ × 48½ in. (92 × 123 cm). Philadelphia Museum of Art. Turner and other artists were eyewitnesses of the fire. A large crowd, held back by soldiers, watched firemen fight the blaze.

Fresco Fever

When visiting Rome after the end of the Napoleonic Wars (1803–1815), English painters were attracted to the frescoes painted by the Nazarenes. And fresco was all the rage in Germany. Prince Ludwig (later King Ludwig I) visited Rome in 1817 and invited Nazarene artist Peter von Cornelius to come to Munich to paint frescoes on the walls of the Glyptothek, a new museum built to house a collection of classical sculpture. Travelers returning to England from Germany spoke admiringly about public art in Munich, especially the frescoes. The British art press wrote about Ludwig's patronage of the arts, particularly fresco painting, and reported on how Ludwig I had transformed Munich into an aesthetic showplace. Rather than spending money on his army and weapons, Ludwig had been investing his personal funds as well as those of the Kingdom of Bavaria on art and architecture.

The commissioners decided that fresco painting would restore the character of British art, which they believed had become degraded. This decision spawned a "fresco fever" that triggered research on Italian and German painting methods. In November 1841, Prime Minister Peel appointed Charles Lock Eastlake secretary of the Fine Arts Commission. Eastlake was a highly respected artist and researcher who studied original sources of artists' techniques, many of which had been lost or forgotten.

Enter Mrs. Merrifield

In a letter published in the *Art Union* in October 1841, it was advised that translations be made of eight historic treatises named by art historian Luigi Lanzi. One of them was *Il Libro dell'Arte* by Cennino Cennini. Eastlake understood the usefulness of Cennini's treatise and encouraged Mary Philadelphia Merrifield to undertake its translation. Merrifield was a wife, mother of five, linguist, artist, and writer. At that time, women were not taken seriously as scholars but were accepted as translators. Merrifield wrote in her introduction that she was "making an English version of the work of Cennini in consequence of the estimation in which it appears to have been held by the Commissioners on the Fine Arts."

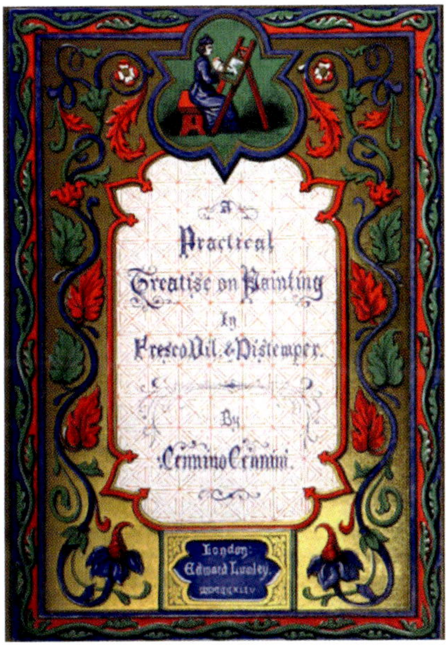

(ABOVE) Cover of the first English translation of Cennino Cennini's treatise, *A Practical Treatise on Painting in Fresco, Oil, and Distemper by Cennino Cennini*, translation by M. P. Merrifield, 1844

Merrifield's Switch to Seaweed

By the middle of the 1860s, Merrifield had turned away from her art studies and had become a leading authority in coastal algae. She published in the *Annals of Botany* and the *Journal of the Linnean Society* and even has a seaweed named after her: *Rytiphlaea merrifieldiae.* I can't resist mentioning here that in the 1980s, I developed a keen interest in seaweed identification, collecting, and cooking. I also built a simple flower press and pressed some seaweeds.

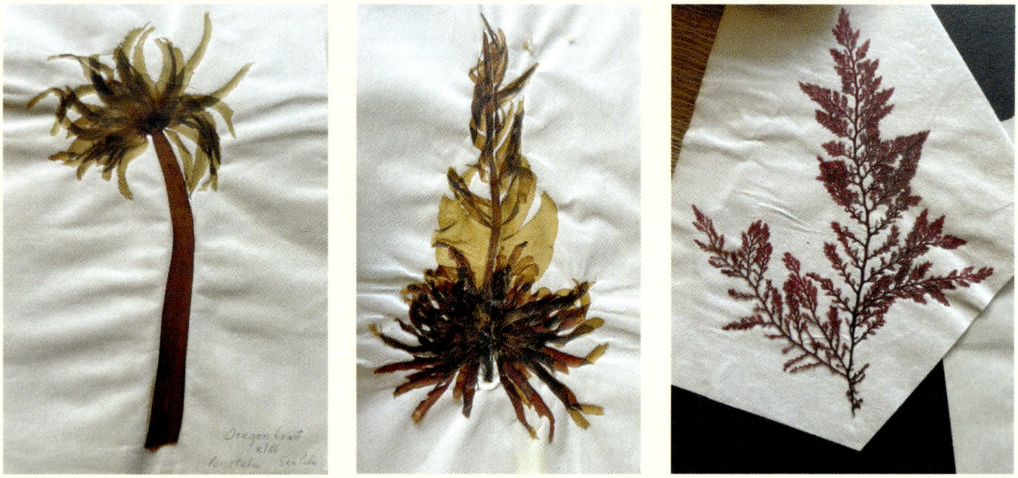

(ABOVE) Pressed seaweed from my collecting excursions. Left to right: Sea palm (*Postelsia palmaeformis*), badderlocks (*Alaria esculenta*), possibly Irish moss (*Chondrus crispus*)

In Merrifield's translation, the focus was on Cennini's instruction in fresco technique in order to prepare for the decoration of the newly rebuilt parliament. Egg tempera was described but not elaborated on.

On the merit of her Cennini translation, published in 1844, the commission endorsed Merrifield's travel to France and Italy to identify and transcribe manuscripts on Italian methods of fresco painting.[112] Next, the Fine Arts Commission underwrote expenses for her extended travel to research manuscripts that described oil painting in several Italian cities and in France and Brussels.[113]

Informed by her training in art, passion for natural science, and advanced linguistic skills, Merrifield's work is now considered a pillar of the foundation of the profession of scientific art history.

A Tale of Two Translations

For many years, I subscribed to the opinion that Merrifield's 1844 translation of *Il Libro dell'Arte* was not helpful to aspiring egg tempera artists and that it wasn't until the 1899 publication of Christiana Herringham's English translation that egg tempera artists found a useful guide. There is some truth to this, but I recently learned that Herringham herself and Joseph Edward Southall, leader of the Birmingham egg tempera revival, both relied on Merrifield's translation to learn the basics of egg tempera painting. (See a Southall painting in Chapter 10.)

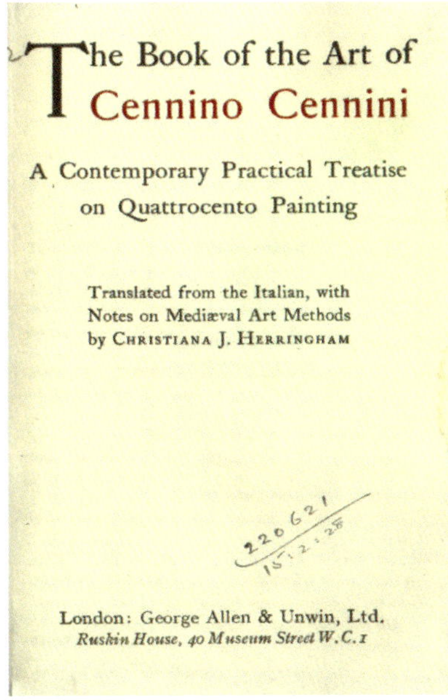
The Book of the Art of Cennino Cennini

A Contemporary Practical Treatise on Quattrocento Painting

Translated from the Italian, with Notes on Mediæval Art Methods by CHRISTIANA J. HERRINGHAM

London: George Allen & Unwin, Ltd. *Ruskin House, 40 Museum Street W.C. 1*

(ABOVE) Title page, *The Book of the Art of Cennino Cennini*, translated by Christiana Herringham, 1899

An issue with Merrifield's translation was that it was based on Giuseppe Tambroni's edition of *Il Libro dell'Arte,* published in Italian in 1821. Tambroni had used the 1737 copy of the Laurentian manuscript, not the actual Laurentian manuscript dated 1437, which is considered much more authentic. Cennini's original "autograph copy" has never been found. Since their release, both Merrifield and Tambroni's work have been criticized for many errors and seventeen missing chapters. (I checked, and of the missing chapters, tempera is only mentioned in one, and only peripherally.)

Herringham's translation, titled *The Book of the Art of Cennino Cennini: A Contemporary Practical Treatise on Quattrocento Painting,* was directed toward the would-be tempera painter and includes a section that provides detailed instructions based on her own extensive experience with the medium. Plus, she annotates Cennini's text with footnotes that relate to her hands-on experience as an egg tempera painter. She found Merrifield's text, based on Tambroni's, to be frequently incorrect, "owing perhaps to a want of practical knowledge." Herringham's translation became for a time the standard English text.

Egg Tempera Revival in the United States

Soon after graduating from Harvard in 1895, Edward Waldo Forbes took an interest in collecting Italian art. In 1898, he arrived in Europe to study and collect "Italian Primitive" art. Seeing many paintings in disrepair, sometimes made worse by ignorant restorations, opened his eyes to the importance of conservation. Forbes was referred to English painter and art historian Charles Fairfax Murray, who had intensely studied and copied the works of the Italian masters.

Murray advised Forbes to contact Signor Desideri in Venice, an expert in tempera painting. Forbes located the humble Desideri at his day job at a post office. This apprenticeship became the basis of Forbes's course at Harvard, Methods and Processes of Italian Painting, known to students as the "Egg and Plaster" course, which he began teaching upon returning to the US in 1904.

Enter D. V. Thompson

Daniel Varney Thompson took the "Egg and Plaster" course at Harvard and later taught egg tempera and art history at Yale, from 1926 to 1933. Thompson's classic egg tempera instruction manual, *The Practice of Tempera Painting*, came out in 1936. It was my bible for many years as I struggled to learn the technique without a teacher.

Yale was an important center of the egg tempera revival that took place in the US from 1930 to 1950. Thompson was succeeded at Yale by Louis York, who taught egg tempera technique in the 1930s.

Among York's students was Robert Vickrey, whose "anything goes" approach made egg tempera more accessible to less traditional artists. In 1973, Vickrey published his book *New Techniques in Egg Tempera,* which served to liberate the technique from the more rigid prescription of Thompson's *The Practice of Tempera Painting.*

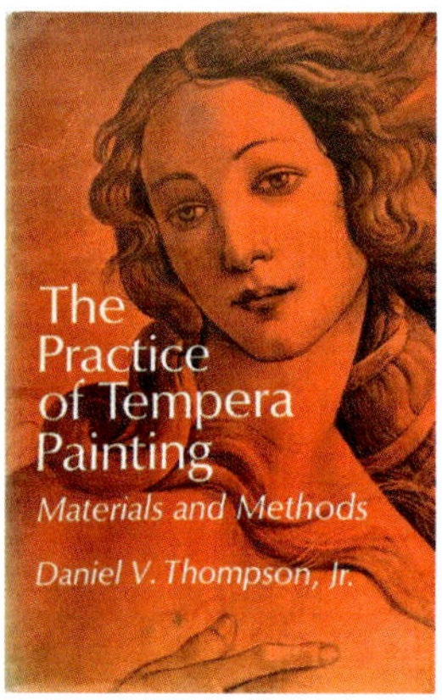

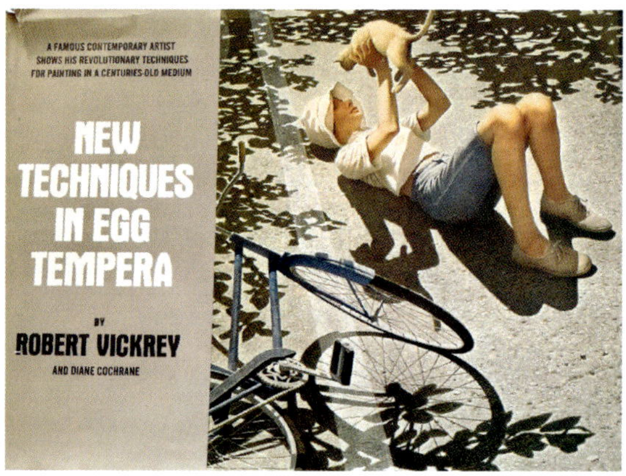

(ABOVE LEFT) *The Practice of Tempera Painting* by Daniel V. Thompson, Jr., originally published by Yale University Press in 1936, now published by Dover Publications

(ABOVE RIGHT) *New Techniques in Egg Tempera* by Robert Vickrey, 1973

Two More English Translations

Thompson was an art historian, conservator, and chemical engineer whose focus was the techniques of medieval and Renaissance painting. Although Thompson stated that he found great merit in Herringham's translation of *Il Libro dell'Arte,* he cited numerous errors, which he set out to correct in his translation, the third English one, published in 1933.

The most recent translation of *Il Libro dell'Arte* was penned by Lara Broecke in 2015. Broecke's aim was to be more precise and scientific. To that end, she includes Cennini's original Italian text close by her English translation so that readers and scholars can come up with their own interpretation of a difficult or ambiguous word or turn of phrase. Broecke corrected 400 errors she identified in Thompson's translation.

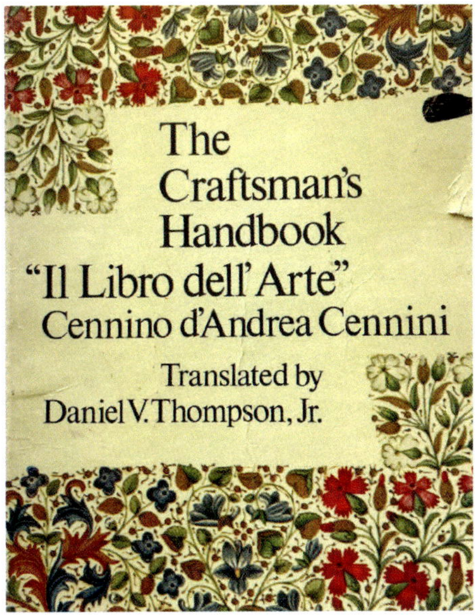

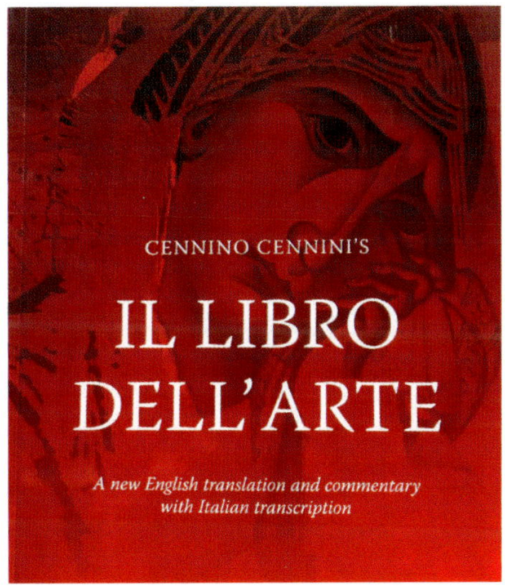

(ABOVE) Daniel V. Thompson, Jr., *The Craftsman's Handbook: "Il Libro dell'Arte" by Cennino d'Andrea Cennini,* 1933

(BELOW) Lara Broecke, *Cennino Cennini's Il Libro dell'Arte,* 2015

Works Progress Administration

The Works Progress Administration (WPA) was an employment program created by President Franklin D. Roosevelt in 1935, during the worst years of the Great Depression.[114] Best known for its public works and infrastructure projects, the agency also employed tens of thousands of creatives, including artists working in the egg tempera medium: Ben Shahn, O. Louis Guglielmi, Mitchell Siporin, Paul Cadmus, Jacob Lawrence, Jared French, and many others.

The Mother's Building was built in 1925 near the Pacific Ocean in San Francisco as part of a huge recreation complex that no longer exists. It sat next to a children's zoo and served as a sanctuary for mothers and young children. The Mother's Building survived, and the San Francisco Zoo exhibits were constructed around it.

In 1934, the WPA commissioned Helen Forbes and Dorothy Puccinelli to paint a 1,200-square-foot mural, which is probably the largest egg tempera work of art in the western US. While sketching animals in the zoo, Forbes and Puccinelli found inspiration for the four panels that comprise *Noah and his Ark—The Waters Subsiding and Renewal.* As the building deteriorated due to its proximity to sand and ocean air, it was declared seismically unsafe and was closed to the public in 2002. It will cost $15 million to restore the building and murals.[115]

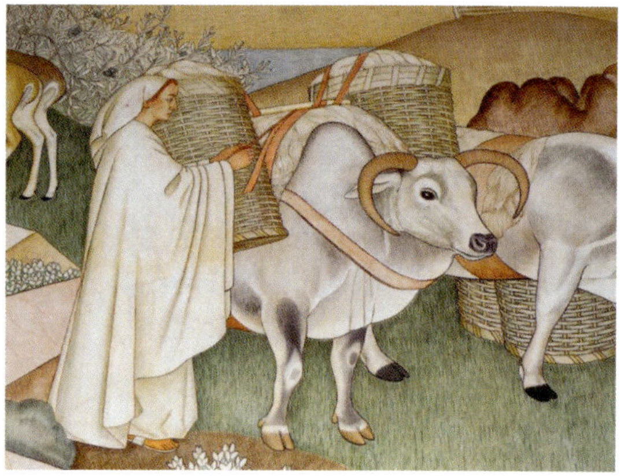

(ABOVE) Detail: Helen Forbes and Dorothy Puccinelli, *Noah and his Ark—The Waters Subsiding and Renewal*, 1938. Four panels totaling approximately 1,200 square feet. The Mother's Building, San Francisco Zoo. Photo by Richard Rothman.

Egg Tempera at the Art Students League

With no entrance exam or degree program, the Art Students League (ASL), founded in 1875 in New York City, was and still is a go-to institution for aspiring artists. I can conjure up the pungent smell of turpentine that permeated the halls and studios during my short-lived stints there.

The classes of Kenneth Hayes Miller were hugely influential in the revival of egg tempera painting. His four-decade association with the ASL began in 1922. Thomas Hart Benton was another artist who taught classes, including egg tempera, at the ASL, from 1926 to 1935.[116]

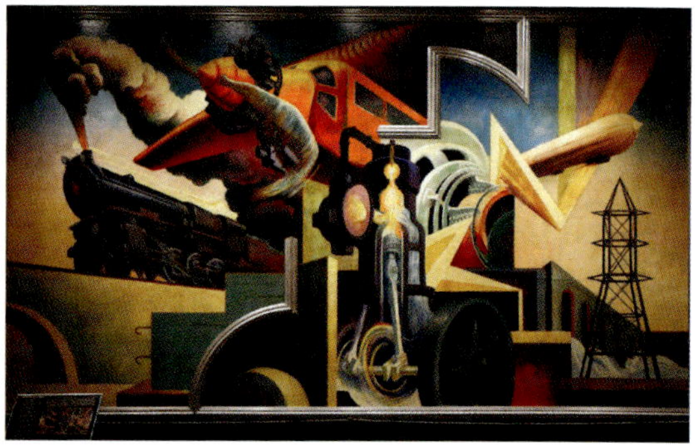

(ABOVE) Detail: Thomas Hart Benton, *America Today*, 1931. Egg tempera with oil glazes on gesso ground over 10 linen-covered wood panels, each approximately 8 × 9 feet. The mural was created for the New School in 1931 and is now in the Metropolitan Museum of Art, New York City.

Miller and Benton both promoted egg tempera for creating large-scale work. I find this interesting—in the twenty-first century, many egg tempera artists paint in a small or very small format.

When he worked as a scene painter in theater, Benton learned the distemper technique, which uses animal glue as a paint binder. In the 1940s, he adapted the technique using egg yolk instead of glue. Apparently, he learned the egg tempera technique not from a living instructor but from *Il Libro dell'Arte* by Cennini.[117]

Reginald Marsh, famous for his depictions of crowded New York City scenes, such as Coney Island, learned egg tempera from Benton. In 1929, Marsh recorded in a notebook, "Met Tom Benton. He has boils on his neck and isn't painting. Comes up to my studio and shows me how to paint with eggs—fortunate event." Marsh was a student at the ASL in the 1920s and taught there from 1934 to 1954. After twelve years of painting in egg tempera, his love affair with the technique ended, and he returned to oil painting.

The Fire Island School of Painting: French, Cadmus, and Tooker

Jared French, Paul Cadmus, and George Tooker met at the ASL and became a tight-knit group who encouraged each other to pursue painting in pure egg tempera. The style of their work has come to be categorized as "magic realism."[118] The egg tempera technique complements this otherworldly yet realistic imagery.

Both French and Cadmus learned tempera at the ASL—French from Benton, and Cadmus probably from Miller. French and Cadmus met in 1928 in an etching class there and became lovers. French encouraged Cadmus to abandon commercial illustration and pursue a career as a fine artist.

Recently discharged from the Marines, George Tooker met Cadmus in 1944 when Tooker was a monitor in Marsh's drawing class. Tooker had likely already learned egg tempera in Marsh and Miller's classes.

Cadmus was sixteen years older and already well established in the art world. He had gained notoriety in 1934 when his painting *The Fleet's In!* triggered an outcry even before its planned debut in the Corcoran Gallery. It depicts inebriated

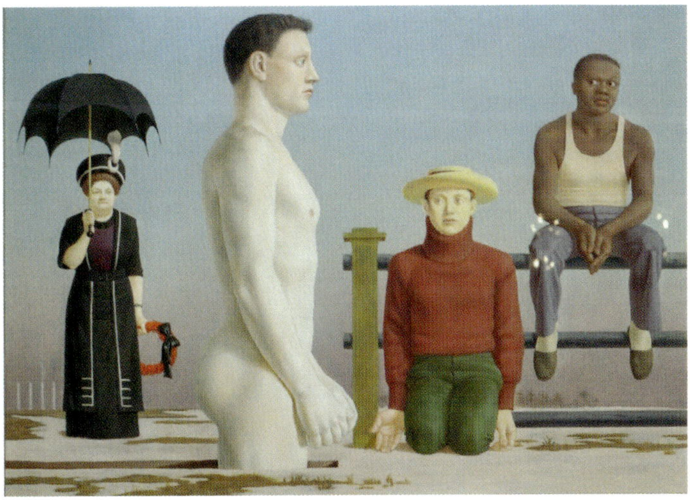

(ABOVE) Jared French, *The Double*, 1997. Egg tempera on board, 21½ × 31 in. (54.6 × 78.7 cm). Private collection.

sailors on shore leave interacting with civilian women—possibly prostitutes. All the figures sport tight, sexualized clothing and create an unflattering picture of military men. There are also coded references to homosexuality. For example, the red tie worn by the blond man, in the gay parlance of the 1930s, signals his availability. The painting was created under the auspices of the WPA, but due to the controversy, the Navy assumed custody of the painting, and it was removed from the gallery before the opening of the show.

Cadmus stated, "I owe the start of my career really to the admiral who tried to suppress it." The painting is now in the collection of the Naval History and Heritage Command and is often on loan to domestic and international museums.

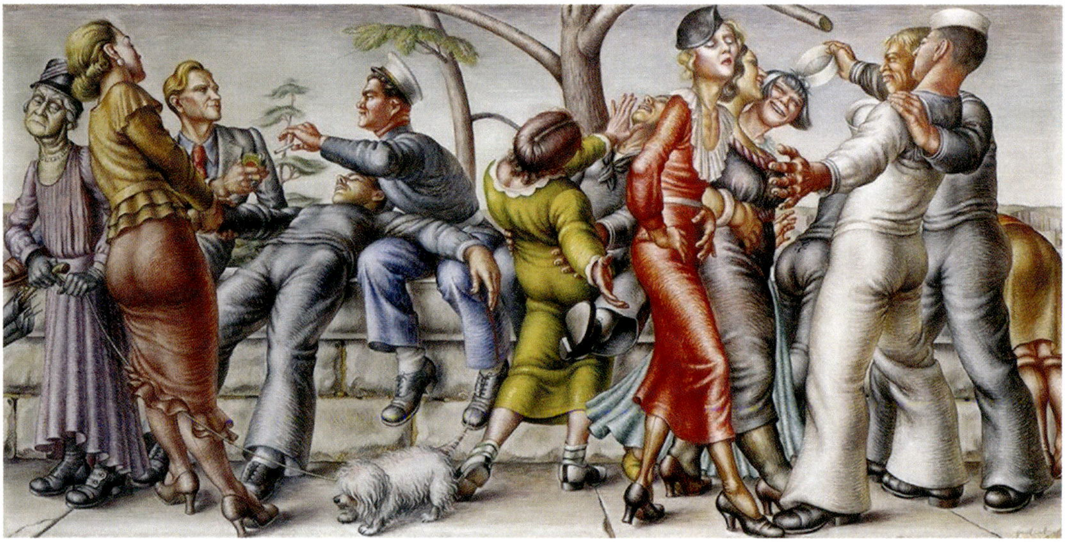

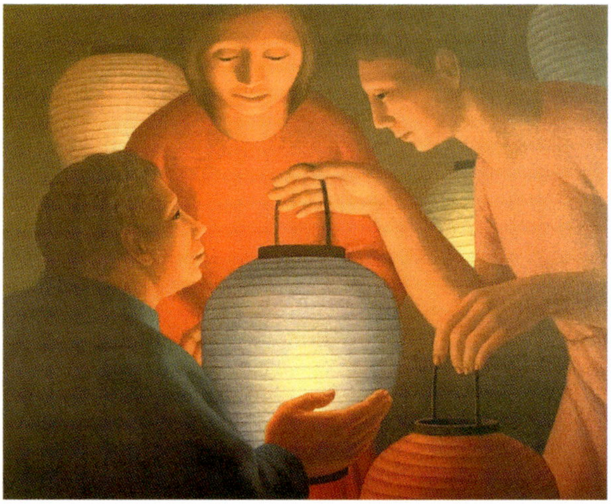

(ABOVE) Paul Cadmus, *The Fleet's In!* Oil and tempera on canvas, 37 × 67 in. (93.9 × 170.1 cm), 1934. Naval History and Heritage Command

(RIGHT) George Tooker, *Lanterns*, 1986. Egg tempera on gesso panel, 22 × 26 in. (55.8 × 66 cm). Private collection.

The 1940s brought several changes to Cadmus's work. Much of his prior work had been executed in a combination of egg tempera and oil called "tempera grassa" (fat tempera), but at the urging of French, Cadmus switched to painting in pure egg tempera. The medium appealed to Cadmus, as it had been used by the Renaissance masters: "When I found that medium, I loved it so much I didn't really want to use anything else," he said.

Cadmus took Tooker under his wing and introduced him to his painter friends Jared and Margaret Hoening French (Jared's wife).[119] Although Tooker had begun to experiment with egg tempera through Marsh, Cadmus and French taught him their method of using tempera and encouraged him to adopt it as his primary medium. Cadmus, Tooker, and the Frenches summered together on Fire Island for many years. Recognizing the common painterly affinity between them, art historian and curator A. Hyatt Mayor referred to their work as "the Fire Island School of Painting."[120]

As of 2025, Doug Safranek, who was mentored by Cadmus, is continuing the long tradition of egg tempera teaching at the Art Students League. Safranek paints in the style of magic realism as well as other genres.

Cadmus also mentored Michael Bergt, virtuoso egg tempera figurative artist, active today, in 2025, and cofounder of the Society of Tempera Painters.

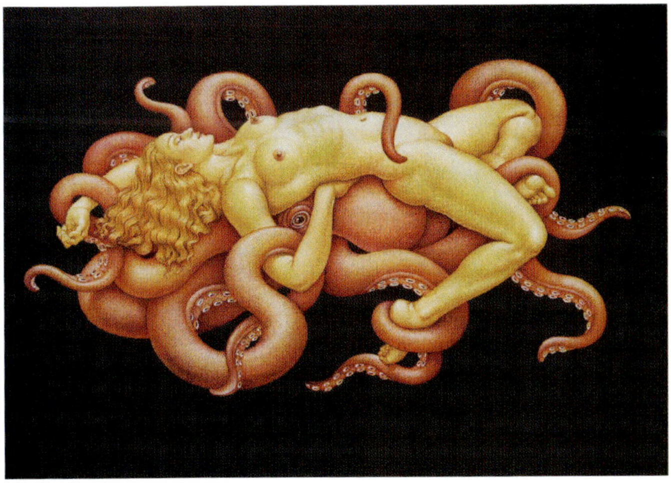

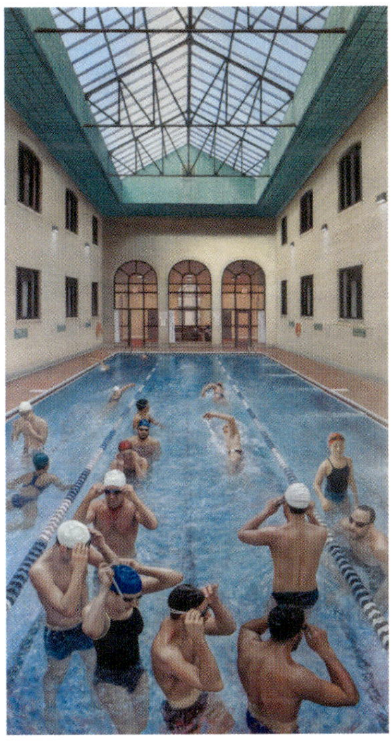

(ABOVE) Michael Bergt, *Succumb*, 2021. Egg tempera on panel. 18 × 24 in. (45.7 × 60.9 cm)

(RIGHT) Doug Safranek, *Circle Pool (Metropolitan Pool, Williamsburg, Brooklyn)*, 2022. Egg tempera on panel, 61 × 32 in. (154.9 × 81.2 cm)

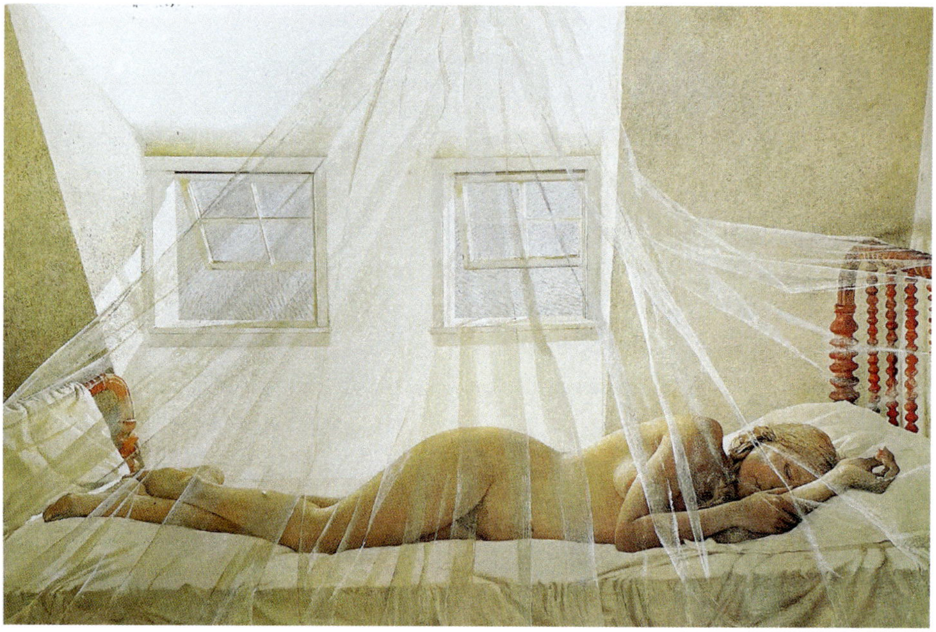

(ABOVE) Andrew Wyeth, *Day Dream*, 1980. Egg tempera, 18½ × 26½ in. (46.9 × 67.3 cm). Private Collection.

The Wyeth Connection

Andrew Wyeth is, without argument, the most well-known egg tempera artist of the twentieth century. In 1902, N. C. Wyeth, famed illustrator and father of Andrew, moved from Massachusetts to Chadds Ford, Pennsylvania, to study with the great illustrator Howard Pyle. N. C. eventually took on a few students of his own, one of whom, Peter Hurd, married his daughter, the artist Henriette Wyeth Hurd. Peter Hurd taught N. C. and Andrew the egg tempera technique.[121] N. C. soon abandoned tempera, but Andrew took to it and created many of his major works in tempera, including his masterpiece *Christina's World* and several of the Helga Pictures.

Abstract Expressionism

Following the widespread destruction in Europe after World War II, the center of the art world moved to New York City, and abstract expressionism overshadowed representational art. The political climate was ripe for art that was neutral, plus there was the McCarthy-era censorship, so having a veiled message or no message at all was the safer artistic expression.

Even though they were ignored by art critics and were no longer in the public view, the magic realists continued their figurative painting in egg tempera.

Another Revival?

I find it ironic that egg tempera was largely replaced by oil painting by the sixteenth century primarily because oil paint could convey a more realistic portrayal. Yet today, realism seems to be a dominant feature in twenty-first-century tempera painting, and some egg tempera artists call themselves "magic realists."

However, there are many egg tempera painters working with abstraction or representational art that is not strictly realistic.

Dean Entwistle is part of the informal group New Egg Tempera, who describe their mission in their Instagram bio as "new forms of the egg tempera painting medium, explored by a small group of artists, who collaborate and cooperate with each other."

Lara Broecke is an expert practitioner of historic tempera painting. In addition to traditional subject matter, she uses "a decorative and sometimes symbolic style to pick out the grace in natural forms and imbue them with spirituality."[122]

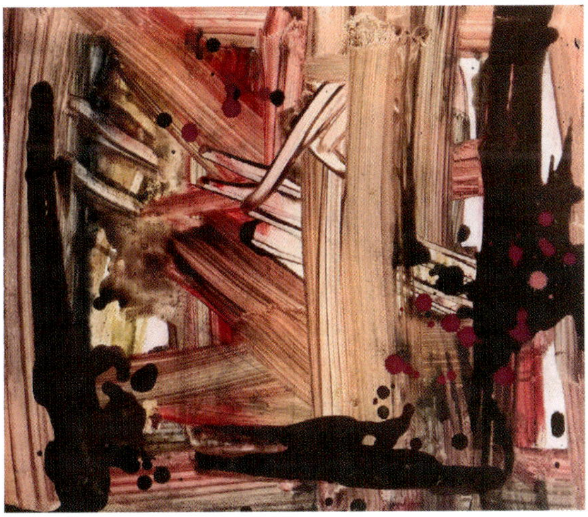

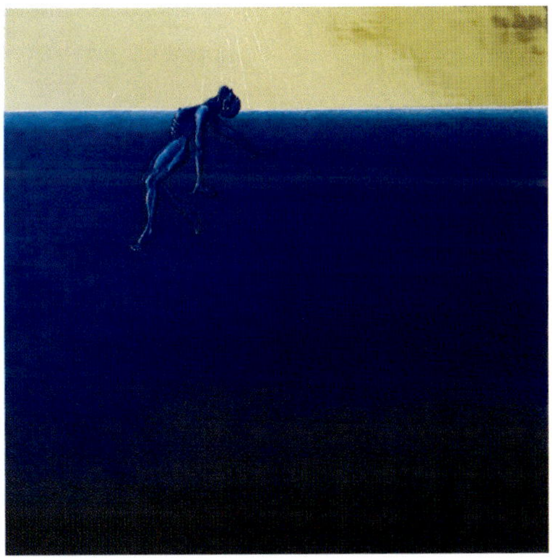

(ABOVE LEFT) Dean Entwistle, *Study in Red and Green*, 2022. Egg tempera with proprietary ingredients, 24 × 24 in. (60.9 × 60.9 cm)

(ABOVE RIGHT) Lara Broecke, *Floating*, 2021. Egg tempera and gold leaf on panel, 9⅞ × 9⅞ in. (25 cm × 25 cm)

Contemporary Society of Tempera Painters

Inspired by the Society of Painters in Tempera that thrived in the early twentieth century in England, Michael Bergt and I founded the non-profit organization Society of Tempera Painters in 1997. I'm not sure if this represented a revival or perhaps just a reflection of increased interest in the medium. The Society of Tempera Painters is currently dormant, but I'm hoping for its revival sometime in the future.

The Future of Egg Tempera

The practice of egg tempera painting has slowly grown in the twenty-first century, but due to the obstacles and limitations of the medium, such as panel preparation and the sometimes slow and finicky handling of the paint, I doubt it will ever be as widely practiced as watercolor, oil, or acrylic. Today, in 2025, one need only search "egg tempera artist" on the internet or visit the Facebook group Artists and Patrons of Egg Tempera to experience a smorgasbord of contemporary works executed in egg tempera.

Koo Schadler has reached an extremely high level of expertise in the technique and has documented her methods in her book, *Egg Tempera Painting: A Comprehensive Guide.* The 2021 edition is almost 300 pages of priceless information. It is encouraging that there are now many instructors teaching egg tempera technique to help people avoid the common pitfalls that discourage artists from persevering with the medium.

(RIGHT) Koo Schadler, *Three Peaches, Sur Sum Corda*, 2022. Egg tempera on true gesso panel, black casein background, gold point & aluminum point lettering, 7¼ × 8¾ in. (18.4 × 22.2 cm)

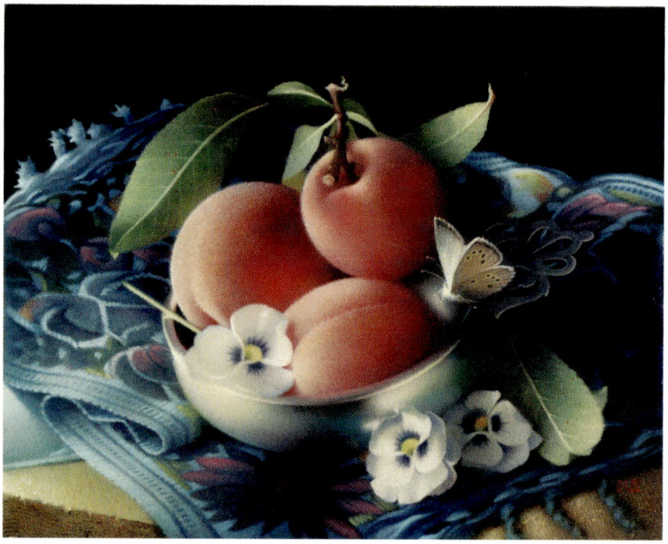

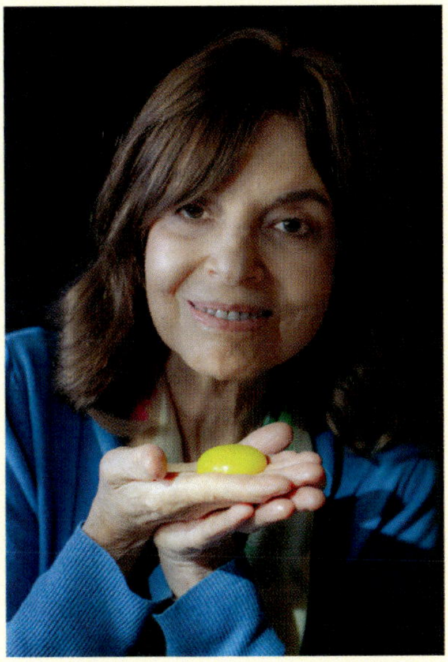

Thank you for joining me on this journey through egg tempera history. Please let me know if you have any corrections, additions, or other feedback.

—LORA ARBRADOR

SAN FRANCISCO, 2025

I invite you to join my newsletter list at:
artblotterplus.substack.com

Visit my website:
arbrador.com

OBITUARIES FROM THE *WAYS OF DYING* SERIES

Courtesy of the *Bay Area Reporter.*

John Walsh: published October 22, 1992

Greg Dubs: published July 2, 1998

Peter Ryan: published June 10, 1993

John J. Walsh, M.D.

John died on August 21 of AIDS. He was 50. The Haight Ashbury Free

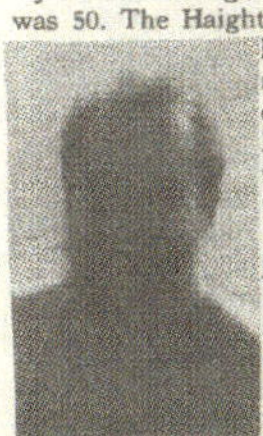

Medical Clinic recently dedicated their new Early Intervention AIDS Clinic to Dr. Walsh.

Dr. Walsh, or Jacquot, as he was lovingly known by friends, enjoyed an eclectic career that is legend among his associates. Dr. Walsh was born in Baltimore, Md., and came to San Francisco in 1966. In 1968, he joined the Sutter Street commune, which published *Kaliflower*, a free weekly magazine. Dr. Walsh started a free midwife service in 1970 and ultimately delivered several hundred babies in home births from 1970-73.

He earned his Bachelor of Science and Physician Assistant degrees at George Washington University in 1975. Returning to San Francisco in 1976, he was the main clinician at the Haight Ashbury Free Medical Clinic until 1981. During the years 1981-83, Dr. Walsh worked in the Bo'o Refugee Camp on the Ethiopia/Somali border. His experiences in this camp of 40,000 refugees strengthened his resolve and would always be close to his heart.

Fulfilling his lifelong dream, Dr. Walsh began medical school at St. George's University School of Medicine in Grenada, West Indies. He graduated in 1989, and began a residency in pediatrics at St. Vincent's Hospital in New York City. In 1990, Dr. Walsh was diagnosed with AIDS. Last year, he returned home to San Francisco. His lifelong inspiration was selfless service.

Survivors include his father, John J. Walsh, Sr.; Jeanie Walsh; and brother Tom Walsh, all of the Washington, D.C. area; and many adoring friends. A gathering is planned for October 25. Please call 821-2543 for details. Donations may be made to the John J. Walsh Early Intervention AIDS Clinic, c/o Haight Ashbury Free Medical Clinic, 558 Clayton St., SF, CA 94117, or to Doctors Without Borders, 30 Rockefeller Pl., Ste. #5425, NY, NY 10112 for their work among Somali refugees. ▼

Greg Dubs, Ph.D.

Nov. 8, 1952 — June 11, 1998

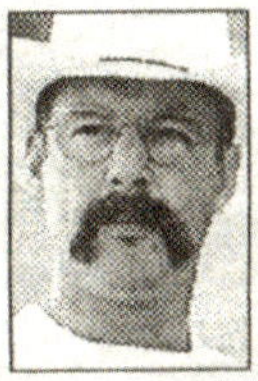

Born in Tonawanda, N.Y., Greg moved to San Francisco in 1978 after falling in love with the Bay Area's natural beauty and personal freedom. He had earned his undergraduate degree at Johns Hopkins University in Baltimore, and later finished his graduate degrees in developmental psychology at the University of Michigan in Ann Arbor.

Greg's professional career included work as a psychotherapist at the Haight-Ashbury Free Clinic; administrator of AIDS research protocols at Stanford University Genetics Department and the Foundation for Integrated Research in New York; educator and administrator at JFK University; professor at Cal State Hayward and Sonoma State University; and director of research at AIDS Community Research Consortium in Redwood City.

Greg died from HIV-related, non-Hodgkin's lymphoma and subsequent liver failure on June 11 at 4:12 p.m., surrounded by his parents, partner and several close friends. He is survived by his parents, Marne and Carla of New Canaan, Conn.; his brother and sister-in-law, Michael and Melanie of Chapel Hill, N.C.; his sister and brother-in-law, Andrea and Robert of Deerfield, Mass.; his partner, Michael; and his good friends, Cheryl, Duke, Lewis, Frances and Michael, Sharon, Helen, Zoe, Barbara, Terry, Jean, Wayne and many, many others.

A memorial gathering will take place on July 18 at 6 p.m. on Mount Tam. Donations in Greg's memory may be made to the Nature Conservancy, Predator Project, and American Indian College Fund. Please call Mike at 415-566-2414 for details.

Peter Ryan (a.k.a. Marion Leonard Ryan III)

May 11, 1961–April 21, 1993

After living with HIV in good health

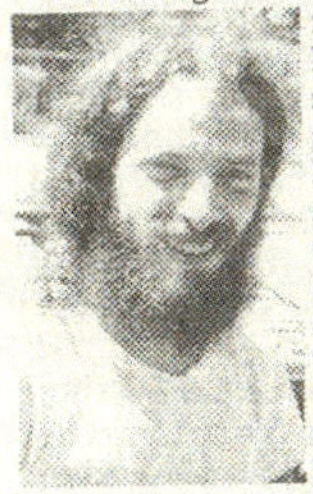

for 10 years, Peter Ryan surrendered to a peaceful death, less than three months after his first ever hospitalization after acquiring the virus.

Peter had the intellect of a Leonardo Da Vinci, and the soul of Buddha. A self-taught high school "dropout" Peter could teach MD's about retrovirology and PhD engineers about electronic design and computer programming. In his last six years, he worked at Dr. Mike McGrath's AIDS Immunobiology Research Laboratory at UCSF, attempting to bring nearer the day when the Plague is conquered. There his mechanical and intellectual genius became an invaluable asset to the everyday operation of the lab. In years past he at times worked at Co-op Radio in Vancouver, and at times lived in the Kaliflower commune in San Francisco. He is also known as the author of Graphicom, Wefax, and RTTY software for the Radio Shack color computer.

Peter and I stood together on the highest point in Baja in 1984. We reached the summit of Boundary Peak (highest point in Nevada) two years ago, when Peter's T-cell count was zero. Together we walked many a trail, and hunted down and soaked in many a wilderness hot spring. May you find more hot springs, Peter, wherever you may be. I'm sorry we couldn't make that one last trip.

Mourning Peter's death are Susan Pete, his lover of the last six years; Elizabeth Pete, to whom he was "daddy;" Mike K., his companion for many years; and the many others of us whose lives he touched with his gentleness and wisdom.

There will be a memorial gathering for Peter in Point Reyes on Sunday, June 13. Call Laura Goldman (415) 824-7668 for details and directions. ▼

ENDNOTES

1. University of California, Berkeley, December 2, 1964.

2. "Turn on, tune in, drop out" is a counterculture-era phrase popularized by Timothy Leary. In a 1988 interview with Neil Strauss, Leary said that the slogan was "given to him" by Marshall McLuhan.

3. According to the Wikipedia article "Opium of the people," Marx saw religion as functioning similarly to opium (which was legal at the time): it relieved pain and gave people "pleasant illusions which gave them the strength to carry on," but it also obscured reality in ways that prevented people from seeing their circumstances clearly and thus from rising up. Marx had no use for religion but no scorn for those who trusted in it.

4. People's Park is a struggle that started in 1969. UC Berkeley originally bought the 2.8 acres of land in June 1967 to construct dorms, but after bulldozing several buildings, the university left the lot vacant. In April 1969, people created a park with gardens and a playground. On May 15, 1969, the university erected a fence around the park in advance of building a soccer field. A protest erupted, with six thousand people participating at its height. It turned violent, resulting in the fatal shooting of James Rector and dozens of injuries to protesters and police. In 1984, the city of Berkeley named People's Park a cultural and historical landmark. Other attempts have been made by the university to take back the land but protests always derailed the plans. As of 2025, the land has been graded in preparation for building student housing and supportive housing, however protests continue.

5. There are several companies that sell reliable pigments, and it's also fun to buy them when traveling. Many of us egg tempera artists have visited the historic Zecchi company in Florence, where I purchased my cherished green earth (terre verte) pigment that I still use.

6. Another example is Indian yellow. Indian yellow is actually moderately lightfast but is no longer manufactured due to the animal exploitation involved in its manufacture. Cows were fed exclusively on mango leaves, their urine collected, evaporated, and formed into balls. It's a beautiful shade of golden yellow now successfully duplicated by various reliable pigments without animal exploitation.

7. Although the quinacridones were originally rated as lightfast, there is now some question of their suitability for permanent artistic use.

8. Natural Pigments also makes an aluminum composite panel called Artefex Tempanel which is primed with a product that is similar to Tempera Ground.

9. However, in both acrylic and traditional gesso the substance that provides the white surface are types of calcium carbonate (whiting, chalk, marble dust, or other). Some egg tempera artists add a small amount of titanium dioxide (an opaque white pigment) to their gesso, while acrylic gesso contains a much larger proportion of titanium dioxide. For detailed instructions for making traditional gesso, see *Koo Schadler, Egg Tempera: A Comprehensive Guide* (Keene, NH: Independently published, 2021).

10. Schadler, *Egg Tempera: A Comprehensive Guide.*

11. I had hoped to stay at UC Santa Cruz, but because I was now in my senior year, I was required to return to UC Berkeley, where I completed my BA in Fine Art in 1971.

12. The cause/effect relationship between mental illness and enhanced creativity remains unresolved in the scientific literature.

13. Quoted in Nancy Rudner and Patricia Kelly, "Year of the Nurse," Pace University Alumni website, August 2019, www.alumni.pace.edu.

14. Present-day pulmonary rehabilitation classes sometimes include singing.

15. Initially, Carol brought Peppie home to live with her, with the aid of her two roommates plus two caregivers from a New York City program. Later, Peppie moved to her own apartment.

16. Visit www.akivathebeliever.com to learn more about Peter, who now goes by Akiva the Believer.

17. Studio For was a wonderful place for experimental art in Oakland, California, which featured a monthly "showcase" of art, theater, music, and dance. It was the creation of Eponine Cuervo Moll and ran from about 1994 to 2004. The street address of the warehouse was the number 4, hence the play on the word "For."

18. The concept of the "teach-in" started as a response to the Vietnam War. It was (and still is) used to raise awareness about a political or social issue and is generally informal, participatory, and oriented toward action.

19. The tree in the painting is actually a London planetree (*Platanus acerifolia*), a hybrid between American sycamore (*P. occidentalis*) and the Oriental planetree (*P. orientalis*).

20. According to the Foundation for Intentional Community, an intentional community is a "group of people who have chosen to live together or share resources on the basis of common values."

21. In March 2024, a devastating fire burned the entire industrial complex of Twin Oaks, sparing only the residences. Rebuilding will cost at least one million dollars as the structures were not insured. Donations can be made at www.twinoaks.org.

22. The legal definition of pedophilia is complex, but in general the child is usually under the age of twelve or fourteen and the perpetrator at least sixteen years or older. The specifics are beyond the scope of this book but readily available online.

23. Anna Sterling, "The Feministing Five: Ina May Gaskin," 2012, www.feministing.com.

24. The "changeover" happened in 1984 when each person, or family, was required to support themselves financially. Many people left, but as of 2025 about 200 residents remain, preserving many of the founding spiritual and humanistic values.

25. HealthRight360 is the umbrella organization of statewide health clinics and social service providers that now includes the Haight Ashbury Free Clinic. HAFMC no longer operates out of 558 Clayton Street but still serves clients at 1563 Mission Street. 558 Clayton Street is currently the site of the Homeless Youth Alliance.

26. Dr. Smith has said he was inspired by the San Francisco Diggers to adopt the phrase "health care is a right, not a privilege" as the HAFMC motto. The phrase has been documented as early as 1959 in a *Salt Lake Tribune* report on the annual luncheon of the Intermountain Hospital Service (the Utah Blue Cross plan). James E. Stuart, executive vice president of the Blue Cross Association, is quoted as saying in his speech, "It is now recognized that health care is a right, not a privilege."

27. According to Johns Hopkins Medicine, AIDS dementia complex, also called HIV-associated dementia, "is typically seen in advanced stages of the disease." Johns Hopkins Medicine, "HIV and Dementia," www.hopkinsmedicine.org.

28.K. G. Boon, *Rembrandt: The Complete Etchings*, trans. Elizabeth Willems-Treeman (Secaucus, NJ: Wellfleet Press, 1962).

29. Obituary of Peter Ryan, *Bay Area Reporter*, June 10, 1993.

30. Their relationship was not romantic but rather one of mentor/mentee and friends.

31. "A council flat is an apartment that is owned by the local council and rented to people at a low rent." *CambridgeDictionary*, "council flat," www.dictionary.cambridge.org/dictionary/english/council-flat. As years go by, some of these tenants earn more but are not required to move to make way for poorer people.

32. According to Special Collections at the University of Reading: "Why don't we use white cotton gloves? Gloves reduce your dexterity. Gloves get dirty. Gloves stop you from learning about an item. So, what do we recommend instead? Handle our manuscripts and rare books with clean, dry hands." "To Glove or Not to Glove," September 12, 2013, Special Collections, https://collections.reading.ac.uk/special-collections

33. It seems almost uncanny that any French pastry in Paris would be made with margarine, but I recently discovered that the first margarine was created by the French chemist Hippolyte Mège-Mouriès in 1869. As of 2025 most cafes in Paris offer mostly "croissant au buerre" but many supermarkets offer croissants made with butter or margarine ("croissant ordinaire").

34. Günter Busch and Liselotte von Reinken, eds., *Paula Modersohn-Becker: The Letters and Journals*, (Evanston, IL: Northwestern University Press, 1990), 79.

35. Rilke stayed in Worpswede in 1900 where he met Clara Westoff. In 1908, a year after Modersohn-Becker's death, he wrote "Requiem for a Friend." Although it does not reference Modersohn-Becker specifically, this famous poem is clearly a tribute to her.

36. The Colarossi was an alternative to the official École des Beaux-Arts. It admitted women and allowed them to draw from nude male models.

37. Modersohn-Becker, *The Letters and Journals*, 395.

38. Modersohn-Becker, *The Letters and Journals*, 324.

39. According to the website of the United States Holocaust Memorial Museum, "The exhibition's organizers arranged more than 600 artworks in intentionally unflattering ways. Slogans painted on the walls mocked artworks as 'crazy at any price' and 'how sick minds viewed nature.' The walls also displayed quotes from Hitler and Goebbels. Their words provided the public with the official Nazi Party views on the purpose of art. Organizers went to great lengths to discourage appreciation of the artworks. Despite this, public attendance exceeded all expectations. It is estimated that more than 2 million people passed through the cramped space in 1937." United States Holocaust Memorial Museum, Holocaust Encyclopedia, "'Degenerate' Art," www.encyclopedia.ushmm.org/content/en/article/degenerate-art-1

40. She had complained of pain in her leg, so may have been advised to stay in bed longer than had she not had leg pain.

41. "She combed her hair, adorned it with red roses received as presents, and slowly walked to the living room, where her daughter was in her crib. Paula took Mathilde in her arms and said, 'Now it's almost as beautiful as Christmas,' then suddenly fell to the floor. 'What a pity' were her last words." Marina Bohlmann-Modersohn, *Paula Modersohn-Becker: eine Biographie mit Briefen* (Munich: Btb Bei Goldmann, 1995).

42. In particular, art historian Diane Radycki has championed her work. See *Paula Modersohn-Becker: The First Modern Woman Artist* (New Haven, CT: Yale University Press, 2013).

43. Giorgio Vasari, *The Lives of the Most Excellent Painters, Sculptors, and Architects*, 1568.

44. William Michael Rossetti, *Encyclopædia Britannica*, (11th ed., 1911), "Angelico, Fra."

45. Perhaps my interest in indigenous cultures began with immersion in the hippie counterculture (which borrowed from Native American traditions), then living in a Sioux-style tipi, and later working at the Native American Health Center in San Francisco.

46. I hypothesize that reducing the load on my heel due to a twenty-pound weight loss (thanks to dysentery), plus two weeks of bedrest, accounted for the resolution of the plantar fasciitis.

47. "During the occupation, the French established brothels around Morocco and abducted Amazigh women from rural regions to work as prostitutes. Since many of the Amazigh women had tattoos, a relationship grew between prostitution and facial tattoos. Slowly, Moroccan society began to judge women with facial tattoos, associating them with prostitution." Carolina McCabe, "The Disappearing Tradition of Amazigh Facial and Body Tattoos," *Morocco World News*, April 7, 2019.

48. It is still possible to buy a human skeleton in most states in the US. The prices are high, starting at about $6,000, as of 2025, because they are sold on the secondary market. It is illegal to purchase the skeleton of a Native American.

49. Email correspondence with Gary Faigin, January 21, 2024.

50. In the May 6, 1971, issue of *Kaliflower*, the commune revealed the source of much of the inspiration for their communal practices—the Oneida Community (1848–1879), led by John Humphrey Noyes.

51. This began in the twelfth century and escalated between 1450 and 1640.

52. John Humphrey Noyes, *A Treatise on the Second Coming of Christ*, 1840.

53. Ernest R. Sandeen, "John Humphrey Noyes as the New Adam," *Church History*, vol. 40 (1971): 83.

54. Sandeen, "John Humphrey Noyes," 83.

55. I'm not ethically opposed to polyamory or other transparent forms of open relationships; I just was not interested in it for myself at that time.

56. To his credit, Irving discouraged anonymous and indiscriminate sex and may have saved some lives in the era of AIDS before effective treatment was available.

57. This quote is a composite of writings from the following issues of *Kaliflower*: "The Meddle Way," vol. 3, no. 13, July 29, 1971, p. 1; "Complex Marriage Relocated,"vol. 3, no. 2, May 13, 1971 , p. 5; "The Meddle Way," vol. 3, no. 13, July 29, 1971, p. 1; "Ritual Magic," vol. 3, no. 3, May 20, 1971, p. 1. Accessed through The Digger Archives, www.diggers.org.

58. Lawrence Foster, "Free Love and Feminism: John Humphrey Noyes and the Oneida Community," *Journal of the Early Republic*, vol. 1, no. 3 (Summer 1981).

59. Noyes wrote that "labor, no longer excessive, will become naturally attractive ... labor will become sport." *Bible Communism: A Compilation from the Annual Reports and Other Publications of the Oneida Association and its Branches* (Brooklyn, NY: Office of the Circular, 1853), p. 22.

60. In Matthew 18:15 (New International Version), Jesus recommends that "if your brother or sister sins, go and point out their fault, just between the two of you." If he or she does not listen, bring a few others so that "every matter may be established by the testimony of two or three witnesses." If that fails, the matter should be brought before the whole church.

61. Stalin wrote in 1928, "I think, comrades, that self-criticism is as necessary to us as air or water. I think that without it, without self-criticism, our Party could not make any headway, could not disclose our ulcers, could not eliminate our shortcomings. And shortcomings we have in plenty. That must be admitted frankly and honestly." Joseph Stalin, "The Work of the April Joint Plenum of the Central Committee and Central Control Commission: A Report Delivered at a Meeting of the Active of the Moscow Organisation of the C.P.S.U.(B.)," April 13, 1928. *Works, vol. 11: January 1928 to March 1929* (Moscow: Foreign Languages Publishing House, 1954), p. 133.

62. William M. Kephart, *Extraordinary Groups: The Sociology of Unconventional Life-Styles* (New York: St. Martin's Press, 1976), 69.

63. The San Francisco Mime Troupe, founded by R. G. Davis, broke with convention in 1962 by staging their performances for free in city parks, as they still do today, in 2025.

64. Jay Babcock, "A Guiding Vision: A Conversation with Peter Berg of the San Francisco Diggers," *Diggers-Docs*, September 16, 2020, www.diggersdocs.org/2020/09/16/peter-berg-of-the-san-francisco-diggers.
65. Peter Coyote, email message to Eric Noble, April 2, 2025.
66. The San Francisco Diggers mounted their final grand spectacle at the Summer Solstice in 1968, after which many participants joined the broader back-to-the-land movement. A number of those who had taken part in the Free City project traveled among rural communes over the next year. The Digger ethos continued to ripple outward, influencing a wide swath of the counterculture. Thanks to archivist and historian Eric Noble for assisting with this endnote and the paragraph it references. Many of the words are his, used with his generous permission.
67. Miehle (with an h) is a totally different company than Miele, the appliance company.
68. Many of the characteristics listed are adapted from Margaret Singer's book *Cults in Our Midst*, (San Francisco: Jossey-Bass, 2003).
69. See Chapter 8 for my adventure in making lapis lazuli pigment.
70. This poem was written on a Remington Rand manual typewriter.
71. We lived together during my third year at New Moon House, then we rented our own apartment.
72. As of 2025, David has retired from teaching, and the Underpainting Collective: School of Drawing and Painting, has inherited David's mission of preserving classical realism art techniques.
73. "The black mirror's chief value is that it gives me a new vision of both picture and sitter and therefore enables me to discover any faults there may be in drawing, or in the relations of tones. It acts like the fresh eye, which can often perceive defects that the painter, having got accustomed to them, has failed to detect.... the mirror is an honest critic." Philip de László and Alfred Lys Baldry, *Painting a Portrait* (New York: The Studio Publications, 1934), 40. In David Hardy's class, we made our own black mirrors by inserting a piece of black paper behind the glass of a picture frame.
74. Tempera grassa or "fat tempera" is a type of tempera painting where oil is added to the egg yolk mixture. This creates a medium that is still water soluble (unless an amount of oil is added that will require turpentine or other solvent). The paint is more flowing, like oil paint, but the painting yellows less with time. Another mixed method is executing an underpainting in egg tempera, then glazing over it with oil paint.
75. Dianne Mitchell Ball, "One Egg, Over Medium: The Struggle to Master Egg Tempera Painting," *American Artist*, 50, issue 527 (1986): 58–63.
76. Christina Olson was a neighbor of Andrew Wyeth's in Cushing, Maine, where he spent summers. Olson was initially thought to have contracted polio as a young girl, but medical art detectives now agree that her condition was caused by a neurodegenerative disease called Charcot-Marie-Tooth. Olson did not use a wheelchair—she preferred to crawl. Wyeth's wife, Betsy, posed for the painting and also came up with the title *Christina's World*.

77. I'm not opposed to erotic art or even some pornography, if it is not exploitive or violent. I think it would be challenging to create paintings with the goal of arousing the viewer while maintaining high ethical and artistic standards. I'm not interested in taking that on, and there are other artists working effectively in that genre.

78. David J. Handelsman, Angelica L Hirschberg, and Stephane Bermon, "Circulating Testosterone as the Hormonal Basis of Sex Differences in Athletic Performance," *Endocrine Review 39,* no. 5 (2018): 803–29.

79. In contrast, my maternal grandmother, Hannah, was also in an arranged marriage but had a very loving relationship with my other grandfather, Moishe.

80. Happy to receive feedback at www.arbrador.com.

81. Later, I got back on the wagon, and as of this writing, in 2025, I have not eaten a dessert in twenty-five years. My struggle with binge eating disorder is a topic for other writing (subscribe to my newsletter/blog at www.artblotterplus.com). Eventually, I joined an effective 12-step program for food addicts (www.kaysheppard.com).

82. American Psychiatric Association, "paraphilic disorder," *Diagnostic and Statistical Manual of Mental Disorders* [DSM–5-TR], 2013.

83. "The G-spot, also called the Gräfenberg spot (for German gynecologist Ernst Gräfenberg) is characterized as an erogenous area of the vagina (usually located two to three inches up the front of the vaginal wall) that, when stimulated, may lead to strong sexual arousal, powerful orgasms, and potential female ejaculation." (Wikipedia, "G-spot.") There is still debate in the medical community (since the 1940s!) as to whether the G-spot is a distinct structure.Some researchers maintain that the G-spot is part of the "clitoral complex," which includes an extensive internal expanse of the clitoris as well as the visible parts, such as the glans and hood, and others hypothesize that it is the "female prostate."

84. Chapter 8 of California Penal Code: "Indecent Exposure, Obscene Exhibitions, and Bawdy and Other Disorderly Houses [314–318.6]. Every person who willfully and lewdly exposes his person, or the private parts thereof, in any public place, or in any place where there are present other persons to be offended or annoyed thereby."

85. Irina Dunn email from January 28, 2002, recipient unknown. There is no mention of Irina Dunn specifically mentioning Charles S. Harris in her email from January 28, 2002. However, it is known that the original phrase "A man without faith is like a fish without a bicycle" was coined by Charles S. Harris and published in the *Swarthmore Phoenix* in 1958.

86. www.cupofempathy.com features introductory videos and courses in Nonviolent Communication. An excellent NVC book is *What We Say Matters* by Judith Hanson Lasater and Ike K. Lasater (Boulder, CO: Shambhala Publications, 2022).

87. Jeffrey K. Smith and Lisa Smith, "Spending Time on Art," *Empirical Studies of the Arts* 19, no. 2 (2001): 229–36.

88. I first read "make haste slowly" (unattributed) in *The Practice of Tempera Painting* by Daniel V. Thompson (New York: Dover Art Instruction, 1962). But it is actually an ancient motto, "festina lente," adopted by the emperors Augustus and Titus as admonishments for their generals in battle. "Festina lente" is the classical Latin translation from the original classical Greek.

89. Julio Reyes and Candice Bohannon recommend "stone paper" as a good surface for preliminary studies and they are experimenting with it for more permanent work.

90. When I'm stuck, I do resort to using myself, my son, or my boyfriend as a model, and even images from the internet. I've even tried AI; so far I've hated the results but will continue to try new AI tools as they improve.

91. Scientific research on polymerization in egg tempera painting is lacking, but useful guidelines may be found in Schadler, *Egg Tempera Painting: A Comprehensive Guide.*

92. Just about everyone claims to suffer from procrastination, but for some people it may involve serious mental illness that needs treatment. Examples are clinical depression, obsessive compulsive disorder (OCD), inattentive-type attention-deficit disorder (ADD), and others.

93. Bill W., *Alcoholics Anonymous: The Story of How More Than One Hundred Men Have Recovered from Alcoholism*, 4th ed. (New York: Alcoholics Anonymous, 2001), 58.

94. Anne Lamott, *Bird by Bird* (New York: Pantheon Books, 1994), 21–27.

95. Thirty-four existing Vermeer paintings have been accepted by experts as being painted by his hand. According to Jonathan Janson, "John Michael Montias, who has analyzed every shred of historic evidence regarding Vermeer's art and life, has speculated that the total number of paintings executed between his first dated work, *The Procuress* (1656) and 1675, range approximately between forty and sixty." "Vermeer's Methodology: Why did Vermeer Paint so Few Works?," Essential Vermeer, www.essentialvermeer.com. Twenty-four paintings by Leonardo are either universally accepted (only eight), generally accepted, traditionally accepted, or widely accepted as either by his own hand or done in collaboration, according to Wikipedia. Of course, Leonardo has his voluminous notebooks to explain how he spent his time when not painting; over 1,000 drawings are attributed to Leonardo.

96. Matthew 22:14.

97. According to marinarts.org, "The landmark ICB (Industrial Center Building) was built in 1942 as part of a large shipyard complex during WWII."

98. Laura Rampazzi, et al., "Prehistoric Wall Paintings: The Case of the Domus De Janas Necropolis (Sardinia, Italy)," *Archaeometry* 49, no. 3 (2007): 559–69.

99. Around 1600 BC, a huge volcanic eruption destroyed the Minoan settlement in Akrotiri, a village on the island of Santorini. A massive tsunami followed that devastated the coast of Crete and led to an economic downfall that made the island vulnerable to conquest by the Mycenaeans.

100. Hariclia Brecoulaki, et al., "An Archer from the Palace of Nestor: A New Wall-Painting Fragment in the Chora Museum," *Hesperia: The Journal of the American School of Classical Studies at Athens* 77, no. 3 (2008): 363–97.

101. This theory comes from Thomas F. Mathews in *The Dawn of Christian Art in Panel Paintings and Icons* (Los Angeles: Getty Publications, 2017).

102. Ehab Awad Al-Emam et al., "The Paint Layers of Mural Paintings at Abydos Temples-Egypt: A Closer Look at the Materials Used," *Mediterranean Archaeology And Archaeometry* 15, no. 3, 113–21.

103. Rickerby, Stephen, "Original Painting Techniques and Materials Used in the Tomb of Nefertari," in *Art and Eternity: The Nefertari Wall Paintings Conservation Project 1986–1992* (Los Angeles: Getty Conservation Institute, 1993), 43–55. Nefertari is a different Egyptian queen than the more well-known Nefertiti.

104. Joy Mazurek, "Characterization of Binding Media in Romano-Egyptian Funerary Portraits," in *Mummy Portraits of Roman Egypt: Emerging Research from the APPEAR Project* (Los Angeles: Getty Publications, 2020), 142–47.

105. Joy Mazurek, et al., "GC/MS Characterization of Beeswax, Protein, Gum, Resin, and Oil in Romano-Egyptian Paintings," *Heritage* 2, no. 3 (2019): 1960–85.

106. This painting was analyzed by gas chromatography/mass spectrometry, (protocol of the Getty Conservation Institute). Mathews, *The Dawn of Christian Art in Panel Paintings and Icons*, Appendix B, 239. However, as more advanced techniques are developed, future analysis may reveal that a binder other than egg was used.

107. Stand oil is an oil, usually linseed, that is thickened by heating to 600°F. Its advantages are that it creates a tough paint film without as much yellowing and has a flowing quality that minimizes visible brushstrokes.

108. The rediscovery of Botticelli is a multifaceted field of study that I have simplified for the purpose of my focus on egg tempera history.

109. John Ruskin, Letter 76, April 1877, *Fors Clavigera: Letters to the Workmen and Labourers of Great Britain*. *Fors Clavigera* is a series of pamphlets.

110. Henrietta Ward, "The Rising Genius: Simeon Solomon's unexplored interpretation of Sandro Botticelli," *British Art Journal* 12, no. 3 (2011): 60.

111. Turned on to Botticelli by D. G. Rossetti, in 1868 the poet Charles Swinburne was the first to write about Botticelli after a visit to the Uffizi Gallery in 1864 (*Notes on Designs of the Old Masters at Florence*, 1868.) Then, in 1870, art critic Walter Pater wrote the first in-depth assessment of Botticelli's work, "A Fragment on Sandro Botticelli." A year later, Ruskin was the first to mention Botticelli in a lecture, which he presented to a class of undergraduates at Oxford (*Lectures on Landscape*, 1871).

112. In 1846, she published *The Art of Fresco Painting as Practised by the Old Italian and Spanish Masters, with a Preliminary Inquiry Into the Nature of the Colours Used in Fresco Painting, with Observation and Notes.*
113. In 1849, Merrifield published *Original Treatises Dating from the XIIth to XVIIIth Centuries on the Arts of Painting, in Oil, Miniature, Mosaic, and on Glass; of Gilding, Dyeing, and the Preparation of Colours and Artificial Gems*, volumes 1 and 2.
114. The Works Progress Administration was renamed the Work Projects Administration in 1939.
115. As of 2025, Richard Rothman continues to bring awareness and hope to the project with his Friends of the Mother's Building at the San Francisco Zoo Facebook page.
116. Benton left New York in 1935 to teach at the Kansas City Art Institute, where he passed on his knowledge of painting, including egg tempera, until 1941. He became known as a regionalist painter but said, "The name Regionalism suggested too narrow a range of inspiration to be quite applicable. I was after a picture of America in its entirety.... I ranged from north and south, and from New York to Hollywood and back and forth in legend and history." "American Regionalism: A Personal History of the Movement," *University of Kansas City Review* 18 (Autumn 1951): 42.
117. "During the winter of 1925 and 1926 ... having come across Cennini's famous treatise on Renaissance techniques, I started working with the tricky problems of egg-tempera painting." Source unknown, quoted in the *Papers of the 27th Annual Meeting of The American Institute for Conservation of Historic and Artistic Works,* St. Louis, MO, 1999. Many of his murals were executed on linen-covered wallboard (also called drywall or sheetrock) coated with traditional gesso.
118. The term "magic realism" was popularized by the exhibition *American Realists and Magic Realists* at the Museum of Modern Art in New York in 1943. One definition is "a shifting away to lesser or greater degrees from the straightforward depiction of reality, while maintaining the depiction of recognizable objects.... It is imaginative not imaginary." Jeffrey Wechsler, "Magic Realism: Defining the Indefinite," *Art Journal* 45, no. 4 (Winter 1985): 293–98.
119. Margaret Hoening French married Jared French in 1937. She was mainly an oil painter but produced some egg tempera paintings and is best known for her work with the photography collective PaJaMa (for "Paul, Jared, Margaret"). Margaret was accepting of the ongoing intimacy of Jared and Paul Cadmus.
120. Fire Island is the largest of the barrier islands off of Long Island in the state of New York.
121. What remains a mystery to me is how Peter Hurd learned the egg tempera technique. It is known that he studied Cennini's manual, but other possibilities remain. I have not been able to confirm any of the other theories. Please contact me if you have any knowledge or clues.
122. Lara Broecke's website, www.broecke.com. This is the same Lara Broecke who authored the most recent translation of *Il Libro dell'Arte*.

SELECTED BIBLIOGRAPHY

BOOKS AND ARTICLES ABOUT EGG TEMPERA

Boyle, Richard J., Hilton Brown, and Richard Newman. *Milk and Eggs: The American Revival of Tempera Painting 1930–1950*. Chadds Ford, PA: Brandywine River Museum, 2002.

Broecke, Lara. *Cennino Cennini's Il Libro Dell'Arte: A New English Translation and Commentary with Italian Transcription*. London: Archetype Publications, 2015.

DeGhetaldi, Kristin. "From Egg to Oil: The Early Development of Oil Painting During the Quattrocento." PhD diss., University of Delaware, 2016.

Dietemann, Patrick, Wibke Neugebauer, Eva Ortner, Heike Stege, Eva Reinkowski-Häfner, and Renate Poggendorf. *Tempera Painting 1800–1950: Experiment and Innovation from the Nazarene Movement to Abstract Art*. London: Archetype Publications, 2019.

Dunkerton, Jill. *Giotto to Durer: Early Renaissance Painting in the National Gallery*. New Haven and London: Yale University Press, 1991.

Evans, Magdalen. *Utmost Fidelity: The Painting Lives of Marianne and Adrian Stokes*. Bristol, England: Sansom & Company, 2009.

Garver, Thomas H. *George Tooker*. New York: Chameleon Books, 1992.

Hart, Aidan. *Techniques of Icon and Wall Painting: Egg Tempera, Fresco, Secco*. Herefordshire, England: Gracewing Publishers, 2011.

Mathews, Thomas F., and Norman E. Muller. *The Dawn of Christian Art in Panel Paintings and Icons*. Los Angeles: Getty Publications, 2017.

Schadler, Koo. *Egg Tempera Painting: A Comprehensive Guide*. Keene, NH: Independently published, 2021.

Sultan, Altoon. *Luminous Brush: Painting with Egg Tempera*. New York: Watson-Guptill, 1999.

Thompson, Daniel Varney Jr.. *The Practice of Tempera Painting: Materials and Methods*. New York: Dover Art Instruction, 1962. Rev. ed.

Valdes, Ed. *Fundamentals of Egg Tempera Painting: An Exploration of Traditional Painting Techniques Using Egg Tempera*. Tampa, FL: Independently published, 2023.

Vickrey, Robert, and Diane Cochrane. *New Techniques in Egg Tempera*. New York: Watson-Guptill Publications, 1973.

GENERAL ART BOOKS

Bischoff, Ulrich. *Munch 1863–1944*. Los Angeles: Taschen, 2011.

Boon, K. G. *Rembrandt: The Complete Etchings*. Translated by Elizabeth Willems-Treeman. Secaucus, NJ: Wellfleet Press, 1962.

Busch, Günter, and Liselotte von Reinken, eds. *Paula Modersohn-Becker: The Letters and Journals*. Evanston, IL: Northwestern University Press, 1990.

Busch, Günter, and Liselotte von Reinken, eds. *Paula Modersohn-Becker: The Letters and Journals*. Evanston, IL: Northwestern University Press, 1990.

Doxiadis, Euphrosyne. *The Mysterious Fayum Portraits: Faces from Ancient Egypt*. New York: Harry N. Abrams, 1995.

Faigin, Gary. *The Artist's Complete Guide to Facial Expression*. New York: Watson-Guptill Publications, 1990.

Marx, Ina Brosseau, Alan Marx, and Robert Marx. *Professional Painted Finishes: A Guide to the Art and Business of Decorative Painting*. New York: Watson-Guptill Publications, 1991.

Melius, Jeremy Norman. "Art History and the Invention of Botticelli." PhD diss., University of California, Berkeley, 2010.

Radycki, Diane. *Paula Modersohn-Becker: The First Modern Woman Artist*. New Haven and London: Yale University Press, 2013.

Royal Academy of Arts. *Leonardo Da Vinci Anatomical Drawing from the Royal Collection*. London: Royal Academy of Arts, 1977.

Todd, Ellen Wiley, *The "New Woman" Revised: Painting and Gender Politics on Fourteenth Street*. Berkeley, Los Angeles, Oxford: University of California Press, 1993.

Venturi, Lionello, and Rosabianca Skira-Venturi. *Italian Painting: The Creators of the Renaissance*. Translated by Stuart Gilbert. Milan, , Skira, 1950.

Wolff, Justin P. *Thomas Hart Benton: A Life*. New York: Farrar, Straus and Giroux, 2012.

BOOKS ABOUT PROCRASTINATION AND PRODUCTIVITY

Keller, Gary and Jay Papasan. *The One Thing*. Portland, OR: Bard Press, 2013.

King, Patrick. *The Science of Overcoming Procrastination*. CreateSpace Independent Publishing Platform, 2018.

Lamott, Anne. *Bird By Bird: Some Instructions on Writing and Life*. New York: Pantheon Books, 1994.

Maisel, Eric. *Fearless Creating: A Step-By-step Guide to Starting and Completing Your Work of Art*. New York: Tarcher/Putnam, 2000.

McKeown, Greg. *Essentialism*. New York City: Currency, 2020.

BOOKS ABOUT RELATIONSHIPS AND SEX

Chapman, Gary. *The 5 Love Languages*. Chicago: Moody Publishers, 2014.

Gottman, John and Nan Silver. *The Seven Principles for Making Marriage Work: A Practical Guide from the Country's Foremost Relationship Expert*. New York: Harmony Books, 2015.

Hall, Kathryn. *Reclaiming Your Sexual Self*. Hoboken, NJ: Wiley, 2004.

Kerner, Ian. *She Comes First*. New York: HarperCollins, 2004.

Lasater, Judith Hanson, and Ike K. Lasater. *What We Say Matters: Practicing Nonviolent Communication*. Boulder, CO: Shambhala Publications, 2022.

Mellody, Pia, Andrea Wells Miller, and J. Keith Miller. *Facing Love Addiction*. San Francisco: HarperOne, 1992.

Mintz, Laurie. *Becoming Cliterate*. New York: HarperCollins, 2017.
Snyder, Stephen. *Love Worth Making*. New York: St. Martin's Press, 2019.

BOOKS AND ARCHIVES ABOUT COMMUNITIES, AND MISCELLANEOUS

Anonymous. *Deep Tried Frees*. San Francisco: Free Print Shop, 1978.
Anonymous. *Kaliflower Vol V.* San Francisco: Free Print Shop, 1980.
Carlson, Evan Edwin. "Outrageous Pamphleteers: A History of The Communication Company, 1966–1967." Masters thesis, San Jose State, 2012.
Coyote, Peter. *Sleeping Where I Fall: A Chronicle*. Berkeley, CA: Counterpoint Press, 1998.
Gaskin, Ina May. *Spiritual Midwifery*. Summertown, TN: Book Publishing Company, 2010.
Grogan, Emmett. *Ringolevio*. New York: New York Review of Books, 2008.
Gurney, John. *Gerrard Winstanley: The Digger's Life and Legacy*. London: Pluto Press, 2012.
Hawley, Victor, and Robert Fogarty. *Special Love/Special Sex: An Oneida Community Diary*. Syracuse, NY: Syracuse University Press, 1994.
Herrick, Tirzah Miller, and Robert S. Fogarty. *Desire & Duty At Oneida*. Bloomington, IN: Indiana University Press, 2000.
Noble, Eric. The Digger Archives (www.diggers.org)
Noble, Eric. "Apostles of Free: A History of the Kaliflower Experiment. "Master's thesis, San Francisco State University, 2024. www.bit.ly/Apostles-of-Free_History-of-Kaliflower
Singer, Margaret Thaler. *Cults in Our Midst*. San Francisco: Jossey-Bass, 2003.
Tent, Pam. *Midnight at the Palace: My Life as A Fabulous Cockette*. New York City: Alyson Books, 2004.
Wayland-Smith, Ellen. *Oneida: From Free Love Utopia to the Well-Set Table*. New York City: Macmillan, 2016.

PERMISSIONS & CREDITS

- Photographs in this book that are not listed below are in the author's collection, taken by Lora or unknown photographers, and assumed to be in the public domain or used in accordance with fair use.
- Photographers of people and places, when known, are given credit in image captions. Institutions, when known, are identified in captions; when formal licensing was required, permission was obtained and noted below.
- When a copyright notice was provided, permission is cited as "© [year] [name]" When no explicit © was provided, work is cited as "courtesy of [name/institution]"; authorship implies copyright

CHAPTER 1: NOT A PRODIGY: EARLY YEARS

Ruth Brody: photo courtesy of Maddie & Wally Banzhoff.

Frenzy **by Ruth Brody:** photo courtesy of Maddie & Wally Banzhoff.

CHAPTER 2: FLOWER CHILD OF THE SIXTIES

Janis Joplin, 1970, Hollywood, California: photo used by permission of Barry Feinstein Photography and the estate of Janis Joplin via Jampol Artist Management.

Timothy Leary speaking at press conference at New Haven College, 1968: Colorado State University Archives; Everett Collection / Alamy Stock Photo.

Maharishi Mahesh Yogi, founder of transcendental meditation, c. 1970s: Everett Collection Inc. / Alamy Stock Photo.

1948 Ford F-1 panel truck: Internet Movie Cars Database; in the public domain.

Bliss Apocalypse, **(performed by The Floating Lotus Magic Opera Company):** courtesy of UC Berkeley, Bancroft Library. Photographer unknown

"I-Feel-Like-I'm-Fixin'-to-Die Rag": words and music by Joe McDonald, © 1965, renewed 1993 Alkatraz Corner Music Co., BMI. Used by permission of Alkatraz Publishing.

CHAPTER 3: DISCOVERING EGG TEMPERA

Jasper Rose: Courtesy of Special Collections, University Library, University of California Santa Cruz. © Regents of the University of California.

Hardy Hanson teaching, 1981: Photo by Andrew Neuhart. Courtesy of Jody Hanson.

CHAPTER 4: ADVENTURES IN NURSING SCHOOL

Starry Night **by Vincent van Gogh:** Museum of Modern Art; painting in the public domain; image courtesy of Wikimedia Commons (faithful reproduction of Google Arts & Culture/MoMA high resolution scan).

Florence Nightingale: Perry Pictures / Library of Congress, Washington, D.C. (LC-USZ62-5877). Photographer unknown

Aerial photograph of Roosevelt Island in the East River, New York City: Photo by Cameron Davidson; Westend61 GmbH / Alamy Stock Photo.

Miss Elizabeth M. Plummer: photo courtesy University Archives, Pace University. Photographer unknown.

CHAPTER 6: THE BLOOD MYSTERIES

***Our Bodies, Ourselves*:** photo courtesy of Our Bodies, Ourselves.

***Vision of St. Bernard with Nun*:** Museum Schnütgen, Cologne; permission and photo courtesy of Museum Schnütgen/Rheinisches Bildarchiv Köln.

CHAPTER 7: COMMUNES & CALIFORNIA

In the hammock shop at Twin Oaks: Photo courtesy of twinoaks.org.

Shal Loeser and Valerie Renwick working in the hammock shop at Twin Oaks: photo courtesy of David Holtzman (from a 12/29/17 article in the *Central Virginian*, "Twin Oaks celebrates 50 years in Louisa County.")

3 x 5 Board: photo courtesy of Twin Oaks Community.

The Farm caravan: photo courtesy of Gerald Wheeler.

The Farm store: photo © Douglas Stevenson.

CHAPTER 8: WAYS OF DYING: A CHRONICLE OF THE AIDS EPIDEMIC

Lapis Lazuli in its raw form: photo by Hannes Grobe; license: CC-BY-SA-2.5.

Jan Cornelis Sylvius, Preacher **by Rembrandt van Rijn:** Metropolitan Museum of Art. Painting and photo in public domain; Metropolitan Museum of Art Open Access policy (CC0 1.0).

Deposition of Christ from the Cross **by Pietro Lorenzetti:** painting in public domain; photo in public domain via Web Gallery of Art; license: PD-Art.

The Sick Child **by Edvard Munch:** Painting and photo used by permission of Tate Images.

The Sick Girl **by Christian Krohg:** National Museum of Art, Oslo, Norway; photo by Jacques Lathion; license: CC-BY.

North American Indian Burial Customs **(cover art based on drawing by Dr. Washington Mathews):** photo by Lora Arbrador.

Sermon to the Birds **by Giotto di Bondone:** painting in public domain via Wikimedia Commons; photo by Web Gallery of Art; license: PD-Art.

CHAPTER 9: ART & LOVE COME TOGETHER

Kaliflower Compound: Photo courtesy of Joseph Johnston.

CHAPTER 10: TRAVELS IN EUROPE AND NORTH AFRICA

British Museum Reading Room: photo in public domain via Wikimedia Commons; License CC BY 2.5.

Papers of the Society of Painters in Tempera, First Volume, 1907-1924: book in the public domain; photo by Lora Arbrador.

***Belgium Supported by Hope* by Joseph Edward Southall:** photo and painting used by permission of Tate Images.

***Otto Modersohn Sleeping* by Paula Modersohn-Becker:** Owned by the Paula Modersohn-Becker Foundation and housed at the Paula Modersohn-Becker Museum, Bremen; painting in the public domain via Wikipedia Commons; photo license CC0.

***Old Peasant Woman* by Paula Modersohn-Becker:** Detroit Institute of Arts; painting in the public domain via Wikipedia Commons; photo license CC BY-SA 2.0.

***Woman in Profile, Turned Right* by Paula Modersohn-Becker:** Art Institute of Chicago; drawing in the public domain; photo license CC0.

***Portrait of Rainer Maria Rilke* by Paula Modersohn-Becker:** Louisiana Museum of Modern Art, Humlebæk, Denmark; painting in the public domain; photo The Yorck Project; license GNU Free Documentation.

Photo of Paula Modersohn-Becker: Paula Modersohn-Becker Foundation, Bremen; photo in the public domain. Photographer unknown.

***Self-Portrait at Sixth Wedding Anniversary* by Paula Modersohn-Becker:** Paula Modersohn-Becker Museum, Bremen, Germany; painting in the public domain via Wikipedia Commons; photo in the public domain via Google Arts & Culture.

Paula Modersohn-Becker with daughter Mathilde: photo by Hugo Erfurth; Paula Modersohn-Becker Foundation; license Creative Commons Attribution 2.0 Generic.

***Deposition from the Cross* (detail) by Fra Angelico:** National Museum of San Marco, Florence, Italy; painting in the public domain; photo courtesy of Rufus46; license CC BY-SA 3.0.

Sagrada Familia (exterior with cranes): designed by Antoni Gaudi; photo by Greg Balfour Evans / Alamy Stock Photos.

Sagrada Familia (exterior): designed by Antoni Gaudi; photo courtesy of Neil Steinberg.

Sagrada Familia (interior vaulted ceilings): designed by Antoni Gaudi; photo © Domini Dragoone, 2019.

Sagrada Familia (interior stained glass): designed by Antoni Gaudi; photo © Domini Dragoone, 2019.

Berber Woman with Tattoos: Photo by Skye Hohmann/ Alamy Stock Photos.

***Studies of Fetus in the Womb* by Leonardo da Vinci:** Print Room of the Royal Library, Windsor Castle, Windsor, England; drawing in the public domain; photo in the public domain via Wikimedia Commons.

CHAPTER 11: LIFE IN THE KALIFLOWER COMMUNE

***Gerrard Winstanley*:** courtesy of the artist Clifford Harper.

***Beginning to Plant and Manure the Waste land upon George-aHill, in the parish of Walton, in the County of Surrey*:** artist and date unknown; photo accessed from wigandiggersfestival.org; in the public domain.

***John Humphrey Noyes in Profile*:** Courtesy of Oneida Community Collection, Special Collections Research Center, Syracuse University Libraries. Photographer unknown.

Tirzah Miller in her room: digital recreation by Emmanuel Bazin, using an archival photo of Tirzah Miller and a photo of her former room in the Oneida Community Mansion House in Oneida, New York; used by permission of Emmanuel Bazin.

***Mansion House Quadrangle c. 1870*:** Courtesy of Oneida Community Collection, Special Collections Research Center, Syracuse University Libraries.

CHAPTER 12: THE CONCEPT OF FREE

***Diggers giving out food in Golden Gate Park*:** used with permission of © Jim Marshall Photography LLC.

***Death of Money Parade*:** Photo by Gene Anthony; used with permission of Bill Graham Archives, LLC

Chief 15 offset printing press: photo by Miriam Bobkoff; courtesy of The Digger Archives (www.diggers.org).

***Free City News*, February, 24, 1968 by the Free City Collective:** courtesy of The Digger Archives (www.diggers.org).

"Against the Tars": Kaliflower Vol. 3, No. 8 (June 24,1971): courtesy of The Digger Archives (www.diggers.org).

"Body and Soul": Kaliflower Vol. 3, No. 15, (August 12, 1971): courtesy of The Digger Archives (www.diggers.org).

CHAPTER 13: MOTHERHOOD CALLING

***Gantry House / Opera Crane* by Amos Goldbaum:** The Box Shop, San Francisco, California; painting and photo courtesy of Amos Goldbaum.

***Drawing Machine* by Amos Goldbaum:** painting and photo courtesy of Amos Goldbaum.

CHAPTER 14: NEW MOON HOUSE

***Legend of St. Joachim and St Anne Meeting at the Golden Gate* by Giotto di Bondone:** Scrovegni Chapel, Padua, Italy; painting in the public domain; photo in the public domain via Web Gallery of Art.

***Saint Basil the Great*, Russian icon late 1500s-1600s:** painting and photograph used with permission of The Icon Museum and Study Center, Clinton, MA.

***St. Nicholas the Wonderworker* by Maria Miteva:** Painting © 2023 Maria Miteva; photo courtesy of Maria Miteva.

Malachite mineral with markings: photo courtesy of Dakota Matrix Minerals.

CHAPTER 15: REALER THAN REALITY – STUDY OF CLASSICAL REALISM

***A Special Time* by David Hardy:** © David Hardy, date unknown; courtesy of David Hardy.

CHAPTER 16: DIVING INTO EGG TEMPERA HISTORY

Sandro Botticelli, *Primavera* (detail showing The Three Graces): Painting in the public domain; photo in the public domain from The Yorck Project.

***Portrait of a Young Man* by Sandro Botticelli:** painting in the public domain; photo in the public domain from The Yorck Project.

***The Birth of Venus* by Sandro Botticelli:** painting in public domain; photo in the public domain via Google Arts & Culture.

CHAPTER 17: AT LAST! THREE EGG TEMPERA TEACHERS

***Green XC* by Christopher Castle:** Courtesy of Christopher Castle.

Dianne Mitchell: Photo courtesy of Dianne Mitchell.

***Christina's World* by Andrew Wyeth:** © 2024 Wyeth Foundation for American Art / Artists Rights Society (ARS), New York; Digital Image / The Museum of Modern Art / Licensed by SCALA / Art Resource, NY.

***Virgil* by Dianne Mitchell:** © 1984 Dianne Mitchell; photo courtesy of Dianne Mitchell.

***Madonna and Child* (Rucellai Madonna) by Duccio di Buoninsegna:** painting in the public domain; photo in the public domain via Google Arts & Culture.

***Illuminated Self-Portrait II* by Koo Schadler:** © 2007 Koo Schadler; photo courtesy of Koo Schadler.

***Ama Nesciri with Apples* by Koo Schadler:** © 2020 Koo Schadler; photo courtesy of Koo Schadler.

Egg Tempera Painting: A Comprehensive Guide by Koo Schadler: Photo by Lora Arbrador.

CHAPTER 19: RETREAT TO CELIBACY & MEETING JAKE

Me and Jake: photo courtesy of E & E Andrade.

Lora and Jake as Toddlers: Two archival photos, combined digitally by Jake; courtesy of Jake.

With Jake: photo courtesy of E & E Andrade.

***Reclaiming Your Sexual Self* by Kathryn Hall:** quote used by permission of the author.

CHAPTER 20: SURRENDER TO SLOW

In my home studio: photo courtesy of Jake.

WHICH CAME FIRST? A TASTE OF EGG TEMPERA HISTORY

***Common Tern Nest*:** photo by Michelle Kinsey Bruns; license Creative Commons Attribution 2.0 Generic.

***Bull's Horns*:** necropolis of Su Crucifissu Manny, Porto Torres, Sardinia, Italy: Photo courtesy of Gianni Careddu via Wikimedia Commons; license CC BY-SA 3.0.

***Archer*:** Photo from article in Hesperia (2008): "An Archer from the Palace of Nestor: A New Wall-Painting Fragment in the Chora Museum" by Hariclia Brecoulaki et. al. Painting in public domain; photo by J. Stephens.

Pitsa Panel: National Archaeological Museum, Athens, Greece: painting and photo in the public domain; license CC BY-SA 4.0.

Mummy Portrait, Fayum district, Egypt: painting in the public domain; photo by Brad 7753; license CC BY-SA 4.0.

Fayum Mummy Child Portrait, Egyptian Museum, Cairo: Painting in public domain; photo by Brad7753; license CC BY-SA 4.0 DEED.

Fayum Mummy Portrait of a Woman: painting in the public domain; photo © The Trustees of the British Museum; used by permission.

Mummy portrait, Petrie Museum of Egyptian Archaeology, University College, London: UC 14768; image and photo in the public domain; license CC BY-NC-SA 4.0 DEED.

Heron (detail of *Heron and Lykourgos*), Agyptisches Museum of Staatliche Museen zu Berlin: painting in the public domain; photo by Lora Arbrador from the book *The Dawn of Christian Art in Panel Paintings and Icons* by Thomas F. Mathews.

***Saint Basil the Great*:** Russian icon late 1500s-1600s: image and photo permission of the Icon Museum and Study Center, Clinton, MA.

The Byzantine empire at the advent of Justinian I to the throne (527 CE) and at his death (565 CE): Source; Historical World Atlas, by George Duby; photo License CC BY-SA 2.5.

***Saint Peter* by Simone Martini, Thyssen-Bornemisza Museo Nacional, Madrid, Spain:** Painting in the public domain; photo; Heritage Image Partnership Ltd /Alamy Stock Photo.

***Portrait of a Man* by Jan van Eyck, National Gallery, London:** painting in the public domain; photo: Realy Easy Star / Alamy Stock Photo.

***Romulus' Victory Over Acron* by Jean-Auguste-Dominique Ingres:** Louvre; painting is in the public domain; photo is in the public domain via The Yorck Project.

***Joseph Sold into Slavery by His Brother*s by Johann Friedrich Overbeck:** Alte Nationalgalerie, Berlin; photo by Peter Horree / Alamy Stock Photo.

***Madonna and Child* by Marianne Stokes, Private collection:** painting and photo in the public domain via Wikimedia Commons.

***Adoration of the Magi* by Sandro Botticelli, Uffizi Gallery, Florence:** painting in the public domain; photo in the public domain via The Yorck Project.

***An Angel Playing a Flageolet* by Edward Burne-Jones, Sudley House, Liverpool, UK:** Painting in the public domain; photo by Wm M. Martin in the public domain via masterpieceart.net.

***The Burning of the Houses of Lords and Commons*, October 16, 1834 by Joseph Mallord William Turner:** Philadelphia Museum of Art; painting in the public domain. Photo in the public domain via The Yorck Project.

***A Practical Treatise on Painting in Fresco, Oil & Distemper* by Cennino Cennini, translated by M.F. Merrifield:** book is in the public domain; photograph is in the public domain via Google Books.

***The Book of the Art of Cennino Cennini*, translated by Christiana Herringham:** book is in the public domain; photograph by Lora Arbrador.

***The Practice of Tempera Painting* by Daniel V. Thompson:** book is in the public domain; photo by Lora Arbrador.

***New Techniques in Egg Tempera* by Robert Vickrey:** Photo by Lora Arbrador.

***The Craftsman's Handbook "Ill Libro dell'Arte" Cennino d'Andrea Cennini*, translated by Daniel V. Thompson, Jr.:** Photograph by Lora Arbrador.

Cennino Cennini's Il Libro dell'Arte: a new English language translation and commentary and Italian transcription by Lara Broecke, 2015: image © Hamilton Kerr Institute, University of Cambridge, photography by Chris Titmus; used by permission.

***Noah and his Ark—The Waters Subsiding and Renewal* by Helen Forbes and Dorothy Puccinelli:** mural is in the public domain; photo courtesy of Richard Rothman.

***America Today* by Thomas Hart Benton:** Metropolitan Museum of Art, New York City. Photo by Joe Quinn / Alamy Stock Photos.

***The Double* by Jared French:** Sipa USA / Alamy Stock Photos.

***The Fleet's In* by Paul Cadmus:** Painting is in the public domain; photo courtesy of Navy Art Collection, Naval History and Heritage Command.

***Lanterns* by George Tooker:** photo by Lora Arbrador from the book, George Tooker by Thomas H. Garver © Estate of George Tooker; courtesy of DC Moore Gallery, New York.

***Circle Pool* by Doug Safranek:** © 2022 Doug Safranek; permission to use image of painting and photo courtesy of Doug Safranek.

***Succumb* by Michael Bergt:** © 2021 Michael Bergt; permission to use image of painting and photo courtesy of Michael Bergt.

***Day Dream* by Andrew Wyeth, 1980:** © 2022 Christie's Images Limited; used by permission.

***Study in Red and Green* by Dean Entwistle:** © 2022 Dean Entwistle; permission to use image of painting and photo courtesy of Dean Entwistle.

***Floating* by Lara Broecke:** © 2021 Lara Broecke; permission to use image of painting and photograph courtesy of Lara Broecke.

***Three Peaches*, Sur Sum Corda by Koo Schadler:** © 2007 Koo Schadler; permission to use image of painting and photograph courtesy of Koo Schadler.

Note: Every effort has been made to supply complete and correct credits. Please contact the author If errors or omissions are noted, so corrections can be made in future editions.

INDEX

A

abstract expressionism, 230–231
acrylic gesso/paint, 23, 29, 208
Afterglow, c.1990, 176, 178
A History of Roman Calligraphy (Arbrador), 32
AIDS epidemic chronicle, 65–85
Alexander the Great, 211
Alpert, Richard (Ram Dass), 16
Ama Nesciri with Apples, 2020 (Schadler), 167
Amazigh (Berber) people, 102, 103
American Social Realism, 5
America Today, 1931 (Benton), 226
Amos, Age Fourteen, 1999, 139
An Angel Playing a Flageolet, 1878 (Burne-Jones), 219
anatomy study, 104, 105
ancient cave art, 209
Angelico, Fra, 56, 100, 143
Arkes, Pete, 148–149
Art & Healing exhibit, 67
artistic expression
  of anatomical features, 105
  in author's childhood, 5
  beyond conventional beauty, 182
  joy and angst in, 198, 203
  and McCarthy politics, 230–231
  and mental illness, 35
  and passion, 155
  prioritizing, 191
  psychedelics and, 12–13
  of sensual/emotional relations, 175–184
  skill vs. portrayal in, 73
Artists and Patrons of Egg Tempera, 159, 232
Arts and Crafts (A&C) movement, 31–32
Art Students League (ASL), 226–227
art training
  Atelier School of Classical Realism, 149, 151–154
  City College of San Francisco, 90
  and mentorship, 90
  by Ruth Brody, 5
  three tempera teachers, 161–167
  at UC Berkeley, 8, 21
  at UC Santa Cruz, 31–32
Artwest Gallery, Jackson, 67
A Small Free Inn, 126
A Special Time (Hardy), 151, 153
Atelier School of Classical Realism, 149, 151–154
avoidance/procrastination, 197–198
Azira, Felipe, 132, 133, 140

B

Baby between Breasts, c. 1994, 136
beat literature, 89
beauty, beyond conventional, 182
Becoming Cliterate (Mintz), 190
Beginning to Plant and Manure the Waste land upon George-Hill, in the parish of Walton, in the County of Surrey (artist unknown), 108
Belgium Supported by Hope (Southall), 94
Bellini, Giovanni, 143
Benton, Thomas Hart, 226
Berg, Peter, 121
Bergt, Michael, 158–159, 229, 232
Biblical references, 56, 57, 76–78
Birds of Pray 🙏: The Death of Greg Dubs, 2021, 65, 80–85, 193, 195
The Birth of Venus (Botticelli), 156, 157
Bleeding on a Pine Tree, c. 1984, 56, 126
Bleeding on a Sycamore Tree, c. 1980, 54, 55
Bliss Apocalypse, 18
Blue Meanies, 18
Bon Voyage: The Death of Tom Mabie, c 2002, 65, 70–73, 74, 193

The Book of Dau (Freitag), 126
Botticelli, Sandro, 156, 157, 218–219
Briegleb, Christina, 138
British Museum Library, 93, 158
Brody, Ruth, 4, 5
Broecke, Lara, 219, 225, 231
Bronze Age Mycenaean culture, 209–210
Brooks-Hutton, George, 203
buon fresco technique, 209–210
burial customs, 80, 83
Byzantine works, 141, 143, 145, 210, 213–214

C

cadmium, 25, 26
Cadmus, Paul, 225, 227, 228, 229
calligraphy, 32
Camp Fire, 164
Castle, Christopher, 160, 161
celibacy, 185–188, 201
Cennini, Cennino, 68, 216, 219–223
cerulean blue, 168
chalk dust (whiting), 30, 31
Chicago Review, 89
childbirth, 61–62, 98
Childbirth, c. 1985, 135
Christian Perfectionism, 109
Christina's World, 1948 (Wyeth), 162, 230
Circle Pool (Metropolitan Pool, Williamsburg, Brooklyn), 2022 (Safranek), 229
Civic Center Residence, 131, 133
Classical Realism, 149, 157
cliché, absense of, 188, 202
cobalts, 25, 26, 27
Cohen, Dr. Alan Y., 16
color
  color temperature theory, 155
  death and, 74
  pigments for, 24
  of the Southwest, 168
  underpainting a complementary, 168, 172
  value changes, 153–155
communal living
  and cults, 127, 148
  and finances, 110
  Kaliflower Compound, 87, 90, 107–119, 148
  and marriage/relationships, 110–111
  and mutual criticism, 116
  New Moon House, 74, 141, 143, 148
  Twin Oaks and The Farm, 59–62
communism, 6
Compassion: Scene from Surgery II, c. 1987, 145, 146
completion, stress of, 100
Compound Q, 74
counterculture movements
  in the 17th century, 108
  beat literature, 89
  in Berkeley, 1, 11
  collapse of, 36
  college life during, 13–15
  and communal living, 59–62
  Free Speech Movement, 11
  at Kaliflower Compound, 114
  Kaliflower newsletter in, 123
  music of, 12, 18
  police/protester clashes in, 18
  "question authority" spirit of, 38
  San Francisco Diggers, 116, 121–122
  scholastic research in, 16
Coyote, Peter, 122
creativity, 35, 118, 175
Crimean War, 37
Crown of Branches, c. 1976, 47
Cruickshank, Carol, 38, 41, 131
Curie, Madame Marie, 6
curing/polymerization, 197

D

da Vinci, Leonardo, 104, 105
Day Dream, 1980 (Wyeth), 230
death, 65–85
Deposition of Christ (Angelico), 100
Deposition of Christ from the Cross (Lorenzetti), 76
depression, 95
di Bondone, Giotto, 82
Diggers, the
  English Diggers, 107, 108
  of San Francisco, 116, 120–122
Dodson, Betty, 186
dominant/submissive roleplay, 179–182
Don't Go My Friend: The Death of John Walsh, MD, c. 1993, 64, 65–67, 193
Drawing Machine, 2019 (Amos Goldbaum), 139
Dubs, PhD, Greg, 80
Dunn, Irina, 186
The Dying of Love: Smoke and Embers, c. 1996, 185

E

Eagle Pose (Garudasana), c. 2008, 168, 170, 171
earth pigments, 25
Eastlake, Charles Lock, 221
education
  on anatomy, 104–105
  Atelier School of Classical Realism, 149, 151–154
  Betty Dodson sex education, 186–188
  City College of San Francisco, 90
  nursing school, 34, 35–41
  three tempera teachers, 161–167
  at UC Berkeley, 8, 21
  at UC Santa Cruz, 31–32
egg tempera
  author's process in, 1, 21, 196–199, 204
  corrections in, 194
  future of, 232
  gesso use, 29–31
  history of. *see* history of egg tempera
  layering in, 162, 194
  making of, 22
  pigments for. *see* pigments
  Proto-Renaissance, 141–143
  reasons for using, 21–23
  slow pace of, 194
  societies of painters in, 158–159
  tempera grassa (fat tempera), 97, 98, 229
  term defined, 22
  as water resistant, 136
Egg Tempera Painting: A Comprehensive Guide (Schadler), 23, 166, 167, 232
Egyptian tempera history, 210–213
emotions, arousal and, 175, 176
employment/work
  communal labor, 59, 110
  at Kaliflower Compound, 110, 113–116, 124
  making money from art, 172
  and pregnancy, 131
  to support art, 16, 116
  . *See also* nursing career
English Diggers, 107, 108
Engorgement, c. 1986, 136
Entwistle, Dean, 231
erotic/sensual subjects, 175–184
Essentialism (McKeown), 198
European travels, 93–101

F

Facing Love Addiction (Mellody), 189
Faigin, Gary, 104
The Farm, 61–62, 63
Fearless Creating (Maisel), 198
feedback on artworks, 202–203
feminism
  in author's life, 1
  Oneida Community and, 113
  sex-positive, 186–188
  women's health movement, 53

Fertile Flesh, c. 1990, 47, 49
The Fillmore, 11, 12
Fire Island, 229
Fish Without Bicycle, c. 2022, 186, 196, 199
Floating, 2021 (Broecke), 231
Floating Lotus Magic Opera Company, 16, 18
Forbes, Edward Waldo, 223
Forbes, Helen, 226
Formal Flexibility series, 168–172
Four-Breasted Woman, c. 2010, 188
Four-Breasted Woman with Beard, c. 2010, 188
Free City Collective, 122
Free Frame of Reference, 121–122
Free Print Shop, 122–123
Free Speech Movement, 11
French, Jared, 225, 227, 229
fresco techniques, 209–210, 220, 221
Friend Reading a Book, 1979, 90, 91
Friends of Perfection, 109

G

Gantry House/Opera Crane, 2020 (Amos Goldbaum), 139
Gaskin, Ina May, 61
Gaskin, Steve, 61
Gaudí, Antoni, 100
German art, 99
gesso
  how to make, 29–31
  panel preparation, 194
  traditional, 29, 151–153
The Ghost, c. 1967, 11
Giotto di Bondone, 83, 143, 219
glue, collagen hide, 29
Goines, David Lance, 90
Goldbaum, Abraham Albert ("Al"), 6, 7, 19
Goldbaum, Amos Felipe, 133–134, 138–140, 149
Goldbaum, Etta Stock, 6, 7, 19
Goldbaum, Reizel, 95, 176
Goldbaum, Ruthie, 10, 19, 168
Goodman, Marty, 74
Goren, Aunt Clara, 38
Grateful Dead, 12
Great Fire of 1834, 220
Greco-Roman tempera traditions, 211–212
Greek classical painting, 210, 212, 214
Green (Castle), 160

H

Haight Ashbury Free Medical Clinic (HAFMC), 62, 63, 87, 121
hands, rendering, 72
Hand to Foot Pose (Padahastasana), c.1992, 168, 169, 172
Hanson, Professor Hardy, 32
hardboard, 28
Hardy, David, 151, 153
hatch marks, 162–165
Hendrix, Jimi, 11, 12
herbal medicine, 35
Heron and Lykourgos, 2nd century, 213
Herringham, Christiana, 93, 158, 216, 223
history of egg tempera
  Art Students League, 226–227
  Botticelli's works, 156, 157, 218–219
  Bronze Age Mycenaean culture, 209–210
  Byzantine works, 141, 143, 145, 210, 213–214
  egg tempera societies, 158
  in Egypt, 210–213
  European masters, 93–94, 96–99, 100, 156–157, 163, 216–219
  European revival, 216–219
  Greek panel paintings, 210
  Neolithic era paintings, 209
  Proto-Renaissance, 141–143, 214
  rise of oil painting in, 215
  U.S. revival, 162, 223–225
  Works Progress Administration, 225–226
hitchhiking Europe, 99

How Many?, 2002, 180, 181
Human Be-In, Golden Gate Park, 12

I

ICB art studio, Sausalito, 200, 201–202
Iconoclasm, 145
Il Libro dell'Arte (Cennini), 68, 216, 219–223, 225, 227
Illuminated Self Portrait II, 2007 (Schadler), 167
illumination, 153–155
immigrant experience, 6
Ingres, Jean-Auguste-Dominique, 216
inorganic natural pigments, 26
inorganic synthetic pigments, 26
intentional communities, 127
Islam, 103
Italian Painting: The Creators of the Renaissance (Venturi and Skira-Venturi), 141

J

Jan Cornelius Sylvius, Preacher, 1646 (Rembrandt), 72
Japanese Eggplant, c. 2000, 154
Jefferson Airplane, 11
Joplin, Janis, 11, 12
Joseph Sold into Slavery by His Brothers, 1816–17 (Overbeck), 217
Juniper, Meryl, 149, 164

K

Kaliflower Compound, 87–90, 107–127
Kaliflower newsletter, 123–126
Kassoy, Merry, 19, 127
Kassoy family, 19
Kerner, Ian, 190
kink, sexuality and, 179–182
Krishna consciousness movement, 18
Krohg, Christian, 77

L

Lamott, Ann, 197
Lanterns, 1986 (Tooker), 228
lapis lazuli pigment, 68–69
large format works, 195, 226
La Sagrada Família, 100, 101
laziness and negative self-talk, 197–198
lead pigments, 25
Leary, Timothy, 15, 16
Lehnert, Ilse
    "The Dying of Love", 185
    "Limb to Limb", 50
    "Love on a Black Sheep Farm", 176
    "Madonna of the Menses", 56
    "Scene from Surgery I", 148
Leight, Bernie, 38
Lesh, Stephanie, 73
levigation, 147
lightfast pigments, 24
"Limb to Limb" (Lehnert), 50
Limb to Limb, c. 1989, 48
Loeser, Shal, 58
Lorenzetti, Pietro, 76
love addiction, 1, 188–189
"Love on a Black Sheep Farm" (Lehnert), 176
Love on a Black Sheep Farm, c. 1989, 176, 177
Lovers Entwined, c. 2003, 183
Lovers with Colostomy, c. 1992, 50, 51
luminosity, 21

M

Mabie, Tom, 70, 73
Madonna and Child (Duccio di Buoninsegna), 163
Madonna and Child with Symbols, c. 1905 (Stokes), 218
"Madonna of the Menses" (Lehnert), 56
Madonna of the Menses, c. 1981, 56, 57
Magic & Ceremony course, 179
magic realism, 227, 230–231
Maharishi Mahesh Yogi, 15

Maine living, 42, 50
malachite pigments, 147
Man Nursing a Baby, c. 1985, 135
Markings, c. 1980, 54, 55
marriage to art, 201
Marsh, Reginald, 227, 229
Martini, Simone, 214
Marx, Karl, 15
materials
  egg tempera. *see* egg tempera
  gesso, 29–31, 151–153, 154
  hardboard, 28
  paint ingredients, 208
  paint type comparison, 21–23
  pencil vs. paint, 151, 155
  pigments. *see* pigments
McCarthy era, 1, 6, 230
McKernan, Ron "Pigpen", 12
Meeting at the Golden Gate, 1305 (Giotto), 142
menstruation themes, 52–57
Merrifield, Mary Philadelphia, 221–223
Meryl & Elena, c. 1998, 128
Midwifery Center at The Farm, 61
Milk Flowing into an Urn, c. 1985, 134, 137
Milking Cycle, c. 1985, 135
Milk Mystery series, 134–137
Milk Rollups, c. 1985, 135
Miller, Kenneth Hayes, 226, 227
Miller, Tirzah, 112
Mintz, Dr. Laurie, 190
Mission District, 87–88
Mitchell, Dianne, 158, 161–165, 168, 204
Modernism, 96
Modersohn-Becker, Paula, 96–99
Moroccan Woman, c. 1981, 102, 103
Morocco, travels in, 102–103
motherhood, 129–133
Mother's Building, 225–226
mourning doves, 83
Mt. Amiata burnt sienna, 26, 27
mummy portraits, 211, 212
Munch, Edvard, 77
Mycenean culture, 209–210
My Father Sleeping at Age Eighty, 1992, 7
My Mother, Last Year of Life, 2009, 7

N

Napa State Hospital, 35
Native American culture, 43, 80, 168
Native American Health Center, 90
natural pigments, 26
nature, living in, 43–46
Nature's Call, c. 1988, 45, 46, 47, 145
Nazarenes, 216, 221
Neolithic era paintings, 209
New Egg Tempera, 231
Newman, Jake, 190–191, 200
New Moon House, 74, 141, 143, 148
New Techniques in Egg Tempera (Vickrey), 224
New York City, 6, 19, 36, 227, 230
Nightingale, Florence, 37
Noah and his Ark—The Waters Subsiding and Renewal, 1938 (Forbes and Puccinelli), 226
No More Pollution; No More Somalia: The Death of Peter Ryan, c. 2015, 65, 74–79, 192
North American Indian Burial Customs (Yarrow), 82
Norwegian "pillow painters", 77
Noyes, John Humphrey, 109, 110, 112, 113, 116
nursing career
  Haight Ashbury Free Medical Clinic, 62
  nursing school, 34–41
  origins of interest in, 6
  painting supported by, 32, 172
  and pregnancy, 131
  in rural Maine, 50
  subject matter inspired by, 1

O

oil paint, 21–23, 23, 155, 208, 215, 216, 229
O'Keefe, Georgia, 168
Old Peasant Woman (Modersohn-Becker), 97
Oneida Community, 107, 109, 111, 112, 114
organic natural pigments, 26
organic synthetic pigments, 26
orgasm and sexuality, 179, 180, 181, 186
Otto Modersohn Sleeping (Modersohn-Becker), 97
Our Bodies, Our Selves, 53
ownership and privatization, 108

P

Pace University, 36
paint. *See* egg tempera; materials; oil paint
passion for painting, 155
Pastoral Romantic series, 176–178
patient-centered nursing care, 37, 38
pattern transfers, 172
Paula Modersohn-Becker Museum, 99
People's Park, Berkeley, 18
performance art, 16, 121
Pete, c. 1988, 149
Pete, Susan, 74, 79
petit lac (little lake) technique, 160, 161
Petrini, Carlo, 193
Picasso, Pablo, 1
Pied Piper, 126
pigments
  archival, 24
  cerulean blue, 168
  characteristics of, 24
  in gesso, 31
  lapis lazuli, 68–69
  malachite, 147
  as paint component, 208
  preparation of, 23
  toxicity of, 25
  types of, 26–27
Pitsa panels, 210
Plaster Cast with Bottle, c. 1988, 153
Plummer, Miss Elizabeth E., 38, 39
police encounters, 18, 19
politics, 6, 121, 230–231
polymerization/curing, 197
pornography, emotion and, 175, 176
Portrait of a Man (Self-Portrait?), 1433 (van Eyck), 215
Portrait of Aunt Clara Goren, 1971, 39
Portrait of a Young Man (Botticelli), 156
Portrait of Carol Cruickshank, c. 1978, 41
Portrait of Jake, 2019, 191
Portrait of Rainer Maria Rilke (Modersohn-Becker), 97
portraits vs. landscape, 96
The Practice of Tempera Painting: Materials and Methods (Thompson, Jr.), 21, 224
pregnancy/childbirth
  author's experience of, 129–133
  at The Farm, 61–62
  Milk Mystery series, 134–137
Pre-Raphaelite Brotherhood, 216, 218
Primavera (Botticelli), 156, 219
primitive art, 197, 223
privatization of land, 108
Process of Elimination series, 45–47
procrastination/art avoidance, 197–198
profane, sanctification of the, 45, 175
protests, Vietnam War, 18
Proto-Renaissance art, 141–143, 214
psychedelic experimentation, 12–13
public artworks, 225
Puccinelli, Dorothy, 226

Q

quinacridone magenta pigment, 26, 27

R

Rainbow, Anne, 1
Ram Dass (Richard Alpert), 16
Raphael House, 131, 132
realism
  magic realism, 227, 230–231
  in modern egg tempera painting, 231
  pencil vs. paint, 155
  value changes for, 153–155
Reclaiming Your Sexual Self (Hall), 190
relationship skills, 190
religion and spirituality, 15–16
Rembrandt van Rijn, 72, 93, 143
Renwick, Valerie, 58, 60
resource allocation, 122
romantic/sensual subjects, 175–184
Romulus' Victory over Acron, 1812 (Ingres), 216, 217
Roosevelt Island, 38, 39
Rose, Professor Jasper, 31–32
Rosenthal, Irving, 89, 113, 116–119, 122, 125, 129–130
Ryan, Peter, 74

S

Safranek, Doug, 229
Saint Basil the Great, 142
Saint Peter (Martini), 214
Sam, c. 1983, 88
Sam, relationship with, 87–90, 107, 110–111, 125, 127, 129–130
San Francisco
  Diggers of, 107, 116, 120–122
  Haight Ashbury Free Medical Clinic, 62
  hippie movement in, 12
  Kaliflower Compound, 87–90, 107–119, 122
  Steve Gaskin's Monday Night Class, 61
  underground sex scene, 179–182
San Francisco Mime Troupe, 121
Savio, Mario, 11
"Scene from Surgery I" (Lehnert), 148
Scene from Surgery I, c. 1986, 142, 143, 144, 147
Schadler, Koo, 23, 29, 166–167, 232
science interest, 6
seaweed, botany of, 222
self-doubt, 1, 5, 31, 155, 198, 204
Self-Portrait, 1983, 106
Self-Portrait, Age Fifteen, c. 1964, 8
Self-Portrait, c. 1965, 9
Self-Portrait, c. 1968, 14
Self-Portrait, c. 1969, 17
Self-Portrait, c. 1971, 20
Self-Portrait, c. 1978, 85
Self-Portrait, c. 1981, 104
Self-Portrait, c. 1982, 58
Self-Portrait, c. 1984, 115
Self-Portrait, c. 2001, 150, 152
Self-Portrait, c. 2022, 184
Self-Portrait, from Adoration of the Magi, 1470–75 (Botticelli), 218
Self-Portrait at 6th Wedding Anniversary (Modersohn-Becker), 98, 99
Self-Portrait in Europe, c. 1981, 95
Self-Portrait on Orange Paper, c. 1970, 33
Sex and Love Addicts Anonymous, 189
sexuality
  abstinence from, 185–188
  as artistic subject, 1, 175–184
  BDSM and kink, 179–182
  and communal living, 61, 110–111
  homosexuality, 61, 228
  and lack of consent, 182–183
  1960s sexual revolution, 1, 12
  for older women, 190
  in Oneida Community, 112
  San Francisco underground scene, 179–182
  women's health movement, 53
She Comes First (Kerner), 190
Sheeper (Rosenthal), 89
The Sick Child (Munch), 77

The Sick Girl (Krohg), 77
skill, technical
  hatching vs. stippling, 162–165
  passion/training combined in, 155
  pattern transfers, 172
  portrayal and, 73
  sponging vs. brushwork, 166
  stylistic mentors, 143
Slow Art movement, 193
Smith, David, 62
Society of Janus, 180–181
Society of Painters in Tempera, 92, 158, 218, 232
Southall, Joseph Edward, 93, 223
Soyer, Raphael, 5
spiritual equanimity, 201
Spiritual Midwifery (Gaskin), 62
sponging technique, 110, 166
The Starry Night, 1889 (van Gogh), 34, 35
St. Basil the Great, late 1500s, 213
Steinem, Gloria, 186
St. Francis Preaching to the Birds (Giotto di Bondone), 82, 83
stippling vs. hatching, 162–165
St. Nicholas the Wonderworker, 2023 (Miteva), 142
Stokes, Marianne, 216, 218
STP (Society of Tempera Painters), 159, 166, 229, 232
Studio For, 50
Study in Red and Green, 2022 (Entwistle), 231
subject matter
  AIDS epidemic/death, 65–85
  Biblical references, 56, 57, 76–78
  emotions as, 143
  menstruation, 52–57
  Milk Mystery series, 134–137
  nature/body as nature, 45–52
  nursing as inspiration for, 41
  physical/sensual, 1, 175–184
  yoga poses as, 168–172
Succumb, 2021 (Bergt), 229
Summer of Love, 62
Sun Dance, 80
Surgical Surrealism series, 143–146
Sweet Feeling, c. 1992, 176, 177
synthetic pigments, 26

T

tattoo tradition, Berber, 103
temperature, color and, 155
terre verte (earth pigments), 25, 26
Terry, Phyl, 193
The Blossoming of Love, c. 1995, 174, 175, 176
The Burning of the Houses of Lords and Commons, October 16, 1834, 1835 (Turner), 220
The Double, 1997 (French), 227
"The Dying of Love" (Lehnert), 185
The Dying of Love: Smoke and Embers, c. 1996, 184
The Embrace, c. 2003, 183
The Fleet's In!, 1934 (Cadmus), 227, 228
The One Thing (Keller and Papasan), 198
Thompson, Jr., Daniel V., 21, 224, 225
Three Peaches, Sur Sum Corda, 2022 (Schadler), 232
tipi life in rural Maine, 42, 43–46
Tooker, George, 227, 228, 229
Total Relaxation, c. 1990, 185, 186, 187
toxicity, pigment, 25
traditional gesso, 29, 151–153
Transcendental Meditation, 15
tree burial/sky burial, 80, 83
Tree Pose (Vrksasana), c. 2004, 172, 173
Triangle Pose (Trikonasana), c. 2006, 168, 170
Turner, Joseph Mallord William, 220
Tuttle, David, 66
Twin Oaks community, 58, 59–60, 127

U

UC Berkeley, 8, 11, 13–15
UC Santa Cruz, 31–32

ultramarine ash, 68
underpainting, 168, 172
Untitled, c. 1965, 4, 5
Untitled, c. 1980, 54, 55

V

Vafiadis, Despina "Peppie", 39–41
value changes, 153–155
van Eyck, Jan, 215
van Gogh, Vincent, 34, 35
Vasari, Giorgio, 215
Vietnam War, 18
Virgil, 1984 (Mitchell), 162
The Vision of St. Bernard (artist unknown), 52

W

Walsh, MD., John "Jacquot", 64, 65–67
watercolor, 21–23, 208
Ways of Dying: A Chronicle of the AIDS Epidemic, 65–85, 193, 195, 203
Wharton, Peter, 42, 43
white privilege, 19
Winstanley, Gerrard, 108
Wiping with a Leaf, c. 1976, 47
Woman Bleeding on Rocks, c. 1981, 52
Woman in Profile, Turned Right (Modersohn-Becker), 97
Woman with Koala, c. 1980, 55
women
  Amazigh (Berber) women, 103
  dangers of childbirth, 98
  female orgasm, 182, 186
  in the hippie movement, 19
  in medicine, 143
  in nursing, 37
  in Oneida Community, 112–113
  sexuality for older, 190
  sexual self-sufficiency of, 186–188
  women's health movement, 53
  See also feminism
work. *See* employment/work; nursing career
Works Progress Administration (WPA), 225–226, 228
Worpswede artist colony, 96
Wyeth, Andrew, 162, 230
Wyeth, N. C., 230

Y

Yale University School of Art, 162, 224
Yarrow, H.C., 82
yoga paintings, 168–172

Z

Zallinger, Rudolph "Rudy", 162

ACKNOWLEDGMENTS

I find it difficult to craft words—I prefer the fluidity and sensuality of paint, so I have relied on friends and professionals to help me express myself in writing.

First, I am indebted to my writer friends, my "alpha" readers, who read the very rough draft I wrote in 2017: the late Betsy Bannerman, Irene Moore, and Elaine Drew. Thank you for your guidance and giving me the confidence to continue developing the book.

Since then, the manuscript has evolved and benefited from other support: Thank you to my editor. By chance, I connected with Anne Rainbow, English novelist, playwright, Scrivener guru, truthteller, and author of *Editing the RedPen Way: 10 Steps to Successful Self-Editing.* After I followed all ten steps described in her book, Anne agreed to read my manuscript and offered such insightful suggestions that I was honored when she agreed to be my editor. She also came up with the seeds for a title, which is now the subtitle of this book.

My original intention was to highlight the paintings with elaborated captions. I had not intended to reveal myself quite so much—although the paintings are plenty revealing. I took a leap of faith in submitting to her guidance—to add more text in order to "let the passion come through" and "let the reader know who you are." Anne was incredibly accessible. If I wrote at night, I would have answers in the morning, and if I sent email to England in the morning, by evening, there was Anne. Her ideas were spot-on—from punctuation to flow and organization of the text, she did it all. And made tons of extra work for me that resulted in polishing the text as vigorously as I polish my egg tempera paintings. Just when I thought I had submitted my final draft, Anne came back with a sharp scalpel and dissected the manuscript from stem to stern. She assuaged my tears by saying, "There is pain with any birth."

Thank you to my beta readers. I had way too many, but each of you contributed in ways big and small and nothing is too small! I wish to especially thank Christina Briegleb, my first beta reader. She paved the way for the next sixteen beta readers, who found even more issues, keeping me in revision mode for months: Daniel Ambrose, Judy Beck, Lisa Bullwinkel, Eponine Cuervo Moll, Hilary Diamond, Claire Fergusson, Barbara Friedman, Rebecca Moss Guyver, Eileen Kennedy, Julie Kiser, Sheila Krstevski, Ilse Lehnert, Irene Moore, Jake, Megan Players, Ed Valdes, and Rick Winston.

Thank you also to my "gamma readers," who did a final read before passing the manuscript on to the copy editors: the late Betsy Bannerman, Cathryn Domrose, Amos Goldbaum, Laurie Rosencranz, Margot Schaal, and David Shortell.

Deciding on a title for the book was daunting. Anne Rainbow came up with the original title, *My Life Illuminated,* and Lisa Bullwinkel came up with the subtitle *Art & Love.* Margot Schaal had the brilliant idea to flip the title and subtitle, which created the title, *Art & Love: My Life Illuminated in Egg Tempera.*

Thank you to participants in the Burrow's Beez Sunday Zoom gatherings, for going with me down memory lane to help make sense of my time associated with the Kaliflower commune.

Thank you to Eric Noble, archivist and historian of The Digger Archives (www.diggers.org), for consultation on all Kaliflower and Digger-related text. Eric is a true gift to the historical record, bringing alive the individuals and organizations of the period with love, accuracy, and attention to detail. Any remaining errors are mine.

Thank you to my mentors, Koo Schadler, Dianne Mitchell, David Hardy, and Ruth Brody, to whom I dedicate this book.

I acknowledge Ilse Lehnert for her continual support of my artistic efforts and our twin journeys—hers as writer and mine as painter. She wrote poems to accompany my paintings for a show at Studio For in 1998, several of which appear in this book with her permission.

Elaine Drew has been my artistic soulmate for many years. We started out as egg tempera buddies and now are both producing books, finding our way in the self-publishing universe. Her intelligence, biting humor, and aesthetic perfect pitch have guided and inspired me.

Thanks to Bob Ressler for showing penetrating interest in my work and sharing the angst of the creative process and his skill in creativity coaching.

And to Claire Fergusson for acknowledging my devotion to painting with a grant from the Claire and Jan Binney Lang Foundation, and for always signing off, "Carry on Bravely!"

And to Meryl Juniper for being the 100 percent all-in artist, poet, singer, dancer—oozing art from every pore.

Thank you to these other artists, writers, and appreciator friends and relatives who buoyed me on this art and writing journey: Felipe Ariza, Edison Andrade, Elena Andrade, Carol Cruickshank, Hilary Diamond, Kathy Friedman, Neal Friedman, Stephani Lesh, Giorgia Neidorf, Maria Nieri, Gabriele Hoff, L&K, and Sheila Yoshpe.

Special love to my darling sister Ruthie. Even though we live on separate coasts, I am so grateful that we travel through life together.

Family love from the grave—you sacrificed so much so that our generation could feel free to be artists: Parents: Etta Goldbaum, Al Goldbaum. Grandparents: Hannah and Moishe Stock, Reizel and Wolf Goldbaum. Aunts and uncles: Herman & Mildred Stock, Clara Goren, Amalia Stock, Pauline Goldbaum, and Etta and Seymour Friedman.

Dearly departed friends and relatives who encouraged my art: Betsy Bannerman, Ladd Bower, Chandler Downs, Mark Friedman, and Merry Kassoy.

Book designer: Thank you to Domini Dragoone, who had the patience of an angel waiting in the wings for almost a year until the manuscript was finalized, then attacking the complexity of formatting over 300 images into text with creative flair and accuracy. Although she preferred I select one of her more contemporary design options for the cover, I'm so happy with her eye-popping yet classic, elegant design that graces this book.

Copy editors: I was blessed with two copy editors: Jacqueline Parkison and Jennifer Duardo. Jackie focused micro attention to hundreds of tiny issues plus coming up with alternative sentences that sounded much better but still matched my writer's voice. Jen combed through the manuscript with her professional experience in art book publishing, drilling down to precise editorial conventions and extensive fact-checking that greatly benefited the manuscript. She also added humor and flair to the chapter titles.

I am grateful to my proofreader, Eli Diner. With his eagle eye, intellect, hard work and thoughtfulness, he corrected dozens of esoteric errors and deviations from professional editorial standards, elevating the manuscript to a higher plane.

Digital Grange: Bill Kane spent hours expertly retouching photos for the book. He made people disappear and (don't tell anyone) enhanced the art with his Photoshop magic. Joe McDonald lent his camera expertise and successfully photographed a severely warped humongous painting. Digital Grange has been my guiding light in advising, photographing and creating archival reproductions of my artwork for decades.

Instagram guru and cheerleader Dayana Dancheva from Sofia, Bulgaria, taught me how to grow my Instagram organically, resulting in wonderful relationships with artists around the world.

To my son, Amos: I am eternally grateful for your presence in my life and in the world. I wanted a baby and received a miracle. I bask in your sweet personality and the fun of being artists together. And I could not imagine a more wonderful daughter-in-law than Christina Briegleb, so authentic, insightful, intelligent, beautiful, and kind.

To Jake: "You make me feel like a natural woman." When I'm you with you, everything is fun and funny, refreshing for a serious person like me. "You take me as I am." I can be myself around you. You applaud when I sing to you, and in your magic hands, a five-minute back rub feels like an hour massage. I'm in awe of your technical skill and how you rescue abandoned or orphaned objects and give them new life. And who knew? You've gone over this manuscript sentence by sentence with a talent for no-bullshit prose that I didn't know I needed.

My apologies and thank you to anyone I left out of these acknowledgments.

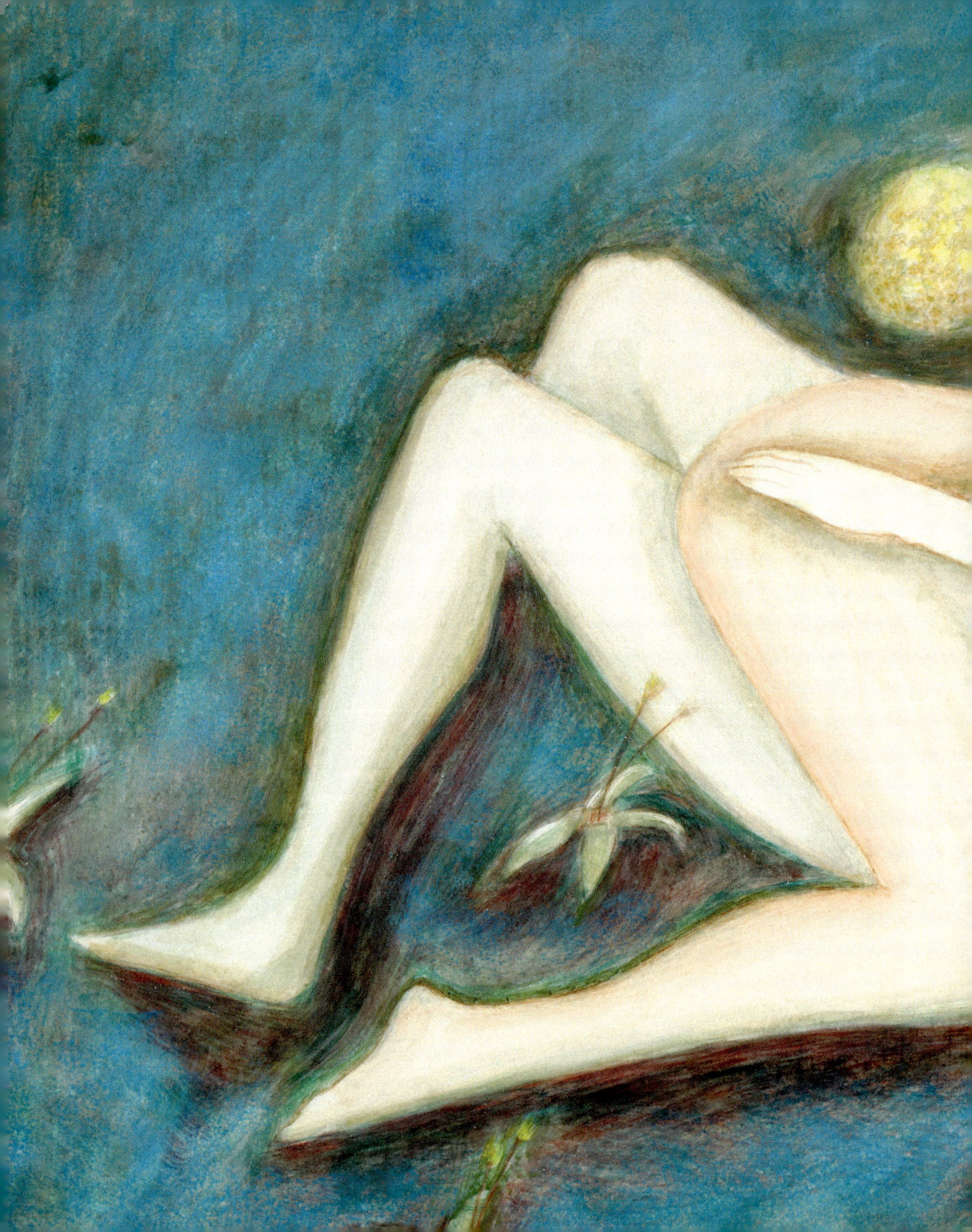

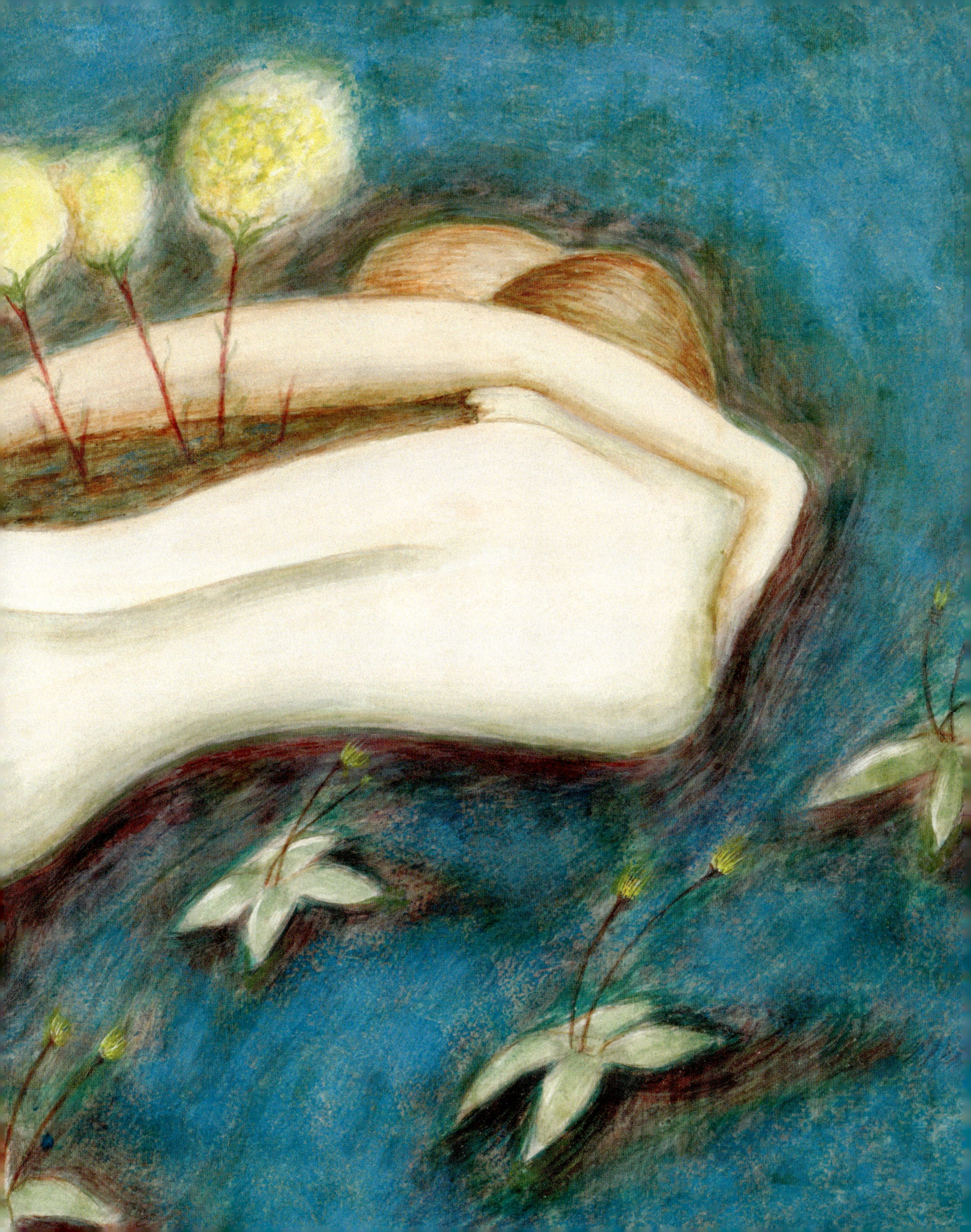

ABOUT THE AUTHOR

At age nineteen, Lora Arbrador was given a one-page recipe for making egg tempera paint by a professor who had no knowledge of the technique. Like a musician with a strong affinity for a particular instrument, Arbrador found her creative home in egg tempera.

To support her art practice, Arbrador became a registered nurse. Nursing has been the inspiration for many of her paintings, including *Don't Go My Friend*, which won first place at the *Art & Healing* exhibit at Artwest Gallery in 1997.

In addition to acquiring skill in egg tempera, Arbrador immersed herself in the fascinating history of the medium and in 1995 was invited to speak at the Johnson Museum of Art at Cornell University. That lecture evolved into the presentations "What is Egg Tempera?" and "Which Came First? A Taste of Egg Tempera History," which is a bonus chapter in this book. In 1997, Arbrador cofounded the Society of Tempera Painters which was modeled after the 1901 Society of Painters in Tempera in England.

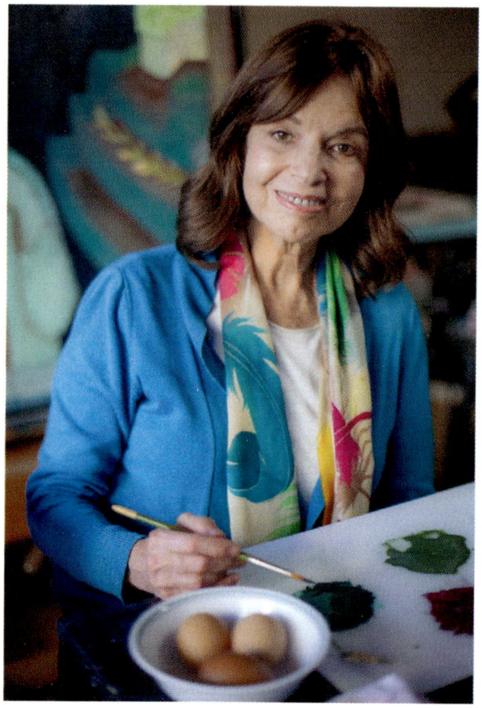

LORA ARBRADOR, 2024
PHOTO BY THE ARTIST HINES

Arbrador has exhibited in galleries and museums throughout the US, including South Bend Regional Museum of Art, Wenatchee Valley College Art Gallery, and the Bade Museum of the Pacific School of Religion. Her first book, *A History of Roman Calligraphy,* is housed in the Marjorie G. and Carl W. Stern Book Arts & Special Collections Center of the San Francisco Public Library.

Arbrador shares her love of egg tempera with young children, professional artists, and other curious people. When not painting, writing, or practicing nursing, Arbrador discovers new plants for her shade garden, plays banjo, and immerses herself in the timeless melodies of the Great American Songbook. Her home studio is in San Francisco, California.

To contact the author or sign up for her newsletter, please go to: www.arbrador.com.